MACMILLAN
TEACHER'S EDITION • GRADE K

Senior Authors: Barbara Staton, Merrill Staton   **Authors:** Marilyn Copeland Davidson, Susan Snyder

MUSIC and YOU

Innovative, sequenced instruction for you, the teacher

Macmillan Publishing Company
866 Third Avenue, New York, NY 10022
Collier Macmillan Canada, Inc.
Collier Macmillan Publishers, London

Printed in the United States of America

ISBN: 0-02-295008-7
9 8 7 6 5 4 3 2 1

TABLE OF CONTENTS

INTRODUCTION TO
MUSIC AND YOU   iii

UNIT 1   GETTING STARTED
UNIT OVERVIEW   1A
Lessons 1–10   1C
Fast and Slow • Steady Beat • Part
and Whole • Fast and Slow • Loud
and Soft • Loud and Soft • Part
and Whole • Loud and Soft • Style
• Fast and Slow
Review and Evaluation   36

UNIT 2   FALL FESTIVAL
UNIT OVERVIEW   38A
Lessons 1–6   38
Long and Short • Melody • Long
and Short • High and Low
• Melody Alone or with Accom-
paniment • High and Low
Review and Evaluation   54

UNIT 3   MUSICAL FRIENDS
UNIT OVERVIEW   56A
Lessons 1–6   56
Tone Color and Dynamics
• Rhythm • Pitch • Tempo • Tone
Color and Rhythm • Rhythm
Review and Evaluation   78

UNIT 4   HOLIDAY FUN
UNIT OVERVIEW   80A
Lessons 1–6   80
Classroom Instruments • High
and Low • Steady Beat • Steady
Beat • Classroom Instruments
• Comparing Musical Elements
Review and Evaluation   98

RELATED ARTS: A Story Told
with Music: *Hansel and Gretel*   100

UNIT 5   WINTER DAYS
UNIT OVERVIEW   104A
Lessons 1–10   104
Rhythm • Tone Color • Rhythm
• Pitch • Rhythm • Rhythm
• Rhythm and Tempo • Pitch
• Tone Color and Rhythm
• Rhythm
Review and Evaluation   140

UNIT 6   SAME AND DIFFERENT
UNIT OVERVIEW   142A
Lessons 1–6   142
Tone Color • Higher and Lower
• Higher and Lower • Rhythm
• Same and Different • Rhythm
Review and Evaluation   164

UNIT 7   MOVE INTO SPRING
UNIT OVERVIEW   166A
Lessons 1–10   166
Tone Color • Same and Different
• Same and Different • Tone
Color • Rhythm and Movement
• Upward and Downward • Same
and Different • Upward and
Downward • Beat and Strong Beat
• Two Sounds to a Beat
Review and Evaluation   196

UNIT 8   SOUNDS ALL AROUND
UNIT OVERVIEW   198A
Lessons 1–10   198
Tone Color • Beat and Strong
Beat • Tempo • Strong Beat
• Rhythm • Pitch • Pitch • Style
• Tempo and Tone Color • Musical
Elements
Review and Evaluation   226

MUSICAL: *Raggedy Ann and Raggedy
Andy™ Visit Amazing Amazo*   228

MUSICAL: *Hats*   236

SONGBOOK   244

**TEACHER'S GLOSSARY OF
TERMS**   290

RESOURCE GUIDE TO
MUSIC AND YOU   293

BIBLIOGRAPHY   301

CLASSIFIED INDEX   302

**RHYTHMIC AND MELODIC
ANALYSIS OF SONGS**   313

ACKNOWLEDGMENTS   318

COMPONENTS

Grade	K	1	2	3	4	5	6
Pupil's Editions		✓	✓	✓	✓	✓	✓
Big Books	✓	✓	✓				
Teacher's Editions	✓	✓	✓	✓	✓	✓	✓
Piano Accom-paniment Books	✓	✓	✓	✓	✓	✓	✓
Teacher's Resource Package	✓	✓	✓	✓	✓	✓	✓
Music Reading Charts		✓	✓				
Records/ Compact Discs	✓	✓	✓	✓	✓	✓	✓

BARBARA STATON

Barbara Staton has taught music at all levels, kindergarten through college, and for eight years was music television teacher for the State of Georgia. She is author of a four-volume series of books and records designed to teach music concepts through movement. She holds a B.S. degree in Music Education and an M.A. in Dance and Related Arts. Mrs. Staton has written numerous songs for television and recordings and is a composer member of ASCAP.

DR. MERRILL STATON

Dr. Merrill Staton earned his M.A. and Ed.D. degrees from Teachers College, Columbia University, and is nationally known as a music educator, choral conductor, singer, ASCAP composer, and record producer. He has been music director of and has conducted the Merrill Staton Voices on many network TV series and recordings. Dr. Staton has been a leader in the field of music education for over thirty years, and pioneered the use of children's voices on recordings for education.

MARILYN COPELAND DAVIDSON

Marilyn Copeland Davidson has taught music for over thirty years at all levels and is presently teaching elementary general music in Pequannock, New Jersey. She also teaches graduate music education courses. She holds a B.S. degree from Ball State University in Muncie, Indiana, a diploma from the Juilliard School of Music, and has completed the Master Class level of Orff-Schulwerk. She has served as national vice-president and national president of the American Orff-Schulwerk Association.

DR. SUSAN SNYDER

Dr. Susan Snyder has taught general music for over twenty years. She holds a Ph.D. in Curriculum and Instruction and an Orff Master Teacher's Certificate. She has worked with preschool and handicapped children and has done extensive study in aesthetics, early childhood, and the Kodály approach. Currently, Dr. Snyder is teaching in the Greenwich, Connecticut, public schools. She is an adjunct faculty member of Teachers College, Columbia Unviersity, and Director of the Ridgewood Summer Courses, Ridgewood, New Jersey.

RECORDINGS

Dr. Merrill Staton – *Conductor and Executive Producer of Recordings*

KINDERGARTEN CURRICULUM

Lynda Sime Huff – *Consultant*
Pequannock Township Public Schools, Pequannock, New Jersey

TEACHER ADVISORY BOARD

James Corley, Jr. – *Classroom Teacher*
Shinnston Elementary, Shinnston, West Virginia

Rose Johnson – *Classroom Teacher*
Zach White Elementary, El Paso, Texas

James Kenward – *Classroom Teacher*
Howe Avenue Elementary, Sacramento, California

Jeannie Miller – *Classroom Teacher*
Daniel Webster Elementary, New Rochelle, New York

Sister Catherine Therese – *Classroom Teacher*
Incarnate Word Academy, Cleveland, Ohio

Russ Abraham – *Music Specialist*
Dewey Fundamental Elementary, Fairoaks, California

Nancy Cox – *Choral Director*
West Junior High, Altus, Oklahoma

Karen Goh – *Music Specialist*
Bakersfield, California

Clayton Miller – *Music Specialist*
Albert Leonard Junior High, New Rochelle, New York

Juan Ortiz – *Mariachi Program Director*
San Antonio Independent Schools, San Antonio, Texas

Carolyn Roberts – *Music Consultant*
Los Angeles, California

Belle San Miguel-Ortiz – *Music Supervisor*
San Antonio Independent Schools, San Antonio, Texas

Cynthia Terry – *Music Specialist*
Thomasville Heights Elementary, Atlanta, Georgia

Mollie Tower – *Music Supervisor*
Austin Independent Schools, Austin, Texas

Active involvement in singing, playing, moving, listening, and creative activities gives children confidence and pride in their abilities.

PHILOSOPHY

Step-by-step sequencing of concepts and skills teaches children how the different elements fit together — and how to listen *critically* to what they hear.

Integration of current music practices of Orff, Kodály, and Dalcroze with traditional instruction engages a child's mind, body, and spirit in the richness of music.

ff

PROGRAM PHILOSOPHY

MUSIC AND YOU represents a fusion of the best current practices in the teaching of music. Important trends in music education over the past two decades have tended to split the ranks of music educators, resulting in a concentration of energies in one mode of teaching.

The authors of MUSIC AND YOU feel it is time to integrate, not isolate these approaches using their proven practices in reaching and teaching music students today. The MUSIC AND YOU series synthesizes the wealth of research derived from the Comprehensive Musicianship Project, Manhattanville Project, Kodály Institute, Dalcroze Society, Orff-Schulwerk and aesthetic education movements, and presents these materials in an easy to use sequential format.

Although the value of sequencing in the learning process has been established in most other subject areas, music educators have not had a structured and truly

sequential course of study available in a basic music series.

Working from a master Scope and Sequence for Grades K through 8, the authors have identified *measurable objectives* for each of the 8 units at each level. Each unit is long enough (either 6 or 10 lessons, depending on the natural division of the school calendar) for real learning to take place and for each step to be accomplished before the next is presented. Concepts are introduced through experiences that first emphasize learning by doing, gradually leading the student to conscious awareness of the concept, its name and symbol.

The presence of a measurable sequence for learning frees the teacher, and in turn the student, to be more creative. Teachers no longer need to spend most of their creative energies making basic lesson plans. Time is provided for extending and applying new understanding of concepts in creative ways.

The design of each lesson includes clearly stated objectives, motivators to capture the students' interest and focus them on the learning to take place, step-by-step teaching procedures, reinforcement of concepts, and appraisals that match the lesson objectives.

A Unit Review and Evaluation summarizes the unit's contents and offers both an informal checking for understanding and a recorded aural evaluation requiring a written response. These materials are designed to make assessment of growth quick and easy and yet result in a high level of confidence and satisfaction for both students and teachers.

MUSIC AND YOU is a program designed by teachers for all teachers , keeping in mind the nature and needs of all students and concerns of school administrators, educators, and parents.

A GUIDE TO USING MUSIC AND YOU

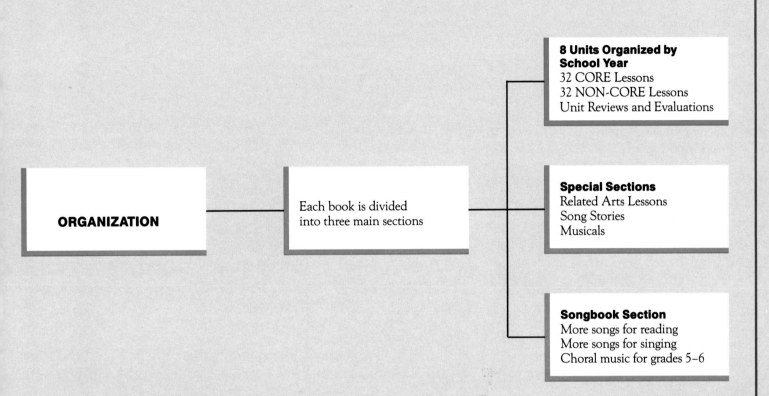

ORGANIZATION

Each book is divided into three main sections

8 Units Organized by School Year
32 CORE Lessons
32 NON-CORE Lessons
Unit Reviews and Evaluations

Special Sections
Related Arts Lessons
Song Stories
Musicals

Songbook Section
More songs for reading
More songs for singing
Choral music for grades 5–6

NEW TEACHING STRANDS

In addition to these three main sections, MUSIC AND YOU provides teachers with these strands:

VOCAL DEVELOPMENT

The songs in MUSIC AND YOU are presented in an appropriate style and singing range, and have been carefully chosen to help teachers teach singing skills in Grades K through 8. The development of part singing begins with rhythmic chants, ostinatos, partner songs and descants, and leads to 2- and 3-part songs at upper grade levels. *Vocal Development* suggestions are provided in each Teacher's Edition, with ideas for teaching correct vocal techniques.

MUSIC READING

Throughout the basic 8 units, music reading skills are taught in a sequential way following the guidelines of the Kodály approach. Each Unit Overview shows specific pitches and rhythms to be experienced, sung, labeled and practiced. In addition, songs in the first part of the SONGBOOK are correlated to these units and provide more material to develop music reading skills. Pitches and rhythms within these songs are arranged according to reading difficulty.

IMPROVISATION AND PLAYING INSTRUMENTS

The Orff process is an integral part of both the basic lesson and the *More Music Teaching Ideas* section at the bottom of the teacher's page. Beginning with simple chants and ostinatos this strand offers experiences in moving, singing, improvising, and playing instruments, culminating in the playing of special orchestrations in *Orchestrations for Orff Instruments* Grades 3–6.

TIME MANAGEMENT

Our authors suggest that teachers who have limited time to teach music start with the 32 Core Lessons which introduce grade level concepts and skills. They may also wish to use the SPECIAL SECTIONS and parts of the SONGBOOK. Teachers who have more time for music instruction could use CORE and NON-CORE lessons, SPECIAL SECTIONS, and the SONGBOOK SECTION.

NEW

The **Songbook** section in the back of each book contains an alternate selection of song material cross-referenced to unit lessons. Easy access to more song choices for teaching concepts and skills saves valuable preparation time.

MUSIC and YOU

MUSIC AND YOU features an innovative Teaching Plan that *integrates* current music practices such as Orff, Kodály and Dalcroze, rather than *isolating* them.

FOCUS
The main concept or skill to be developed in the lesson

Objectives
Specific goals to be accomplished

Materials
Materials and equipment needed

Vocabulary*
Important terms introduced or used in the lesson

1 **SETTING THE STAGE**
A creative "lesson starter" related to the Focus

2 **TEACHING THE LESSON**
A basic instructional statement (in bold print), followed by step-by-step student behaviors

* Does not appear in every lesson.

EXTENSION
This section may include More Music Teaching Ideas as well as Biographies, Curriculum Connections, alternate Songbook selections, Cooperative Learning, Vocal Development, and Suggestions for Special Learners.

Teaching Suggestions are easily organized for all teachers by color coding and placement on the teacher's page.

☐ Lesson preparation information

☐ Basic teaching plan

☐ Extended activities for in-depth study

Additional background materials are provided in the *Extension* section at the bottom of most pages.

Record Information

C O R E

LESSON 6

Focus: Upward and Downward

Objectives
To see, hear, and move to upward and downward melodic patterns
To identify and play upward and downward patterns

Materials
Recordings: "Butterfly"
　　　　　　Recorded Lesson—
　　　　　　"Upward and
　　　　　　Downward"
　　　　　　"Rig-a-Jig-Jig"
Chart 48
Pitched classroom instruments
Copying Masters 7-11, 7-12 (optional)

1 **SETTING THE STAGE**
Have the children review finding their own space. Review the rules for moving around the room. Have the children walk around the room, considering the other children's spaces as they move. Then have them each choose one spot in the room and walk to that spot, crouching lower and lower as they walk. Then have them return to their original space, stretching taller and taller. Identify this movement as moving downward and upward.

2 **TEACHING THE LESSON**
1. Introduce "Butterfly" to reinforce upward and downward. Have the children:
• Look at Chart 48 and identify the direction of each group of flowers on each line.
• Listen to "Butterfly," moving their hands to show the melodic direction as you point to the chart. (Each flower and butterfly is one pitch of the song.)
• Discover that measures 1–4 and 9–12 have the same melodic pattern. (You may wish to use Copying Master 7–11 at this time.)

E X T E N S I O N

MORE MUSIC TEACHING IDEAS
Have the children review "Spring Is Here" on page 169 to reinforce high and low. Have them sing the song and stand to show the high pitch and bend their knees to show the low pitch.

CHART 48 *LISTENING MAP: "BUTTERFLY"*

182 UNIT 7

More Music Teaching Ideas
A section in which higher level skills are presented in sequence

Key: D   Starting Pitch: D   Scale Tones: *do re mi fa so la do'*

Butterfly

Piano Accompaniment on page PA 77

*Words and music by
Lynn Freeman Olson*

But - ter - fly,   but - ter - fly,   where do   you   roam?

Whose luck - y   gar - den   do   you   call   your   home?

But - ter - fly,   but - ter - fly,   why   won't   you   stay?

Why   are   you   al - ways   flut - ter - ing   a - way?

• Move like butterflies, using hands or bodies to show upward downward patterns.

2. Show phrases in "Butterfly." Have the children:
• Sit with partners you assign them.
• Listen to the song while looking at Chart 48. (You may wish to use Copying Master 7–11 at this time.)
• Decide who will move during lines 1 and 3 and during lines 2 and 4.
• Sit facing their partners and listen to "Butterfly" again. Group 1 moves one hand like a butterfly during lines 1 and 3, group 2 moves during lines 2 and 4.
• Listen again, moving through the room. Group 1 moves through the room during lines 1 and 3, landing on the last word of each line. Group 2 moves during lines 2 and 4, landing next to their partners on the last word of each line.

3. Play upward and downward questions and answers. Have the children:
• Listen and watch as you play five-note stepwise upward or downward patterns. Identify the direction of each pattern.
• Take turns playing an answer to your question by playing the pitches you played in reverse order.

Reinforcing the Lesson
Review "Rig-a-Jig-Jig" on page 181. Have the children listen to the words *down the street* each time they occur in the song and identify the melodic direction as downward. Play the game.

3 APPRAISAL
The children should be able to:
1. Identify upward and downward patterns in "Butterfly" by sight and sound, and show them by moving.
2. Play upward and downward patterns as answers to musical questions.

MORE MUSIC TEACHING IDEAS
After the children have played upward and downward questions and answers with you, have them work in pairs. Give one pitched instrument to each pair and have them play upward and downward questions and answers to each other. After a short period of time have several pairs who are good at this activity play their questions and answers for the rest of the class. (You may wish to use Copying Master 7-12 at this time.)

SPECIAL LEARNERS
Help the children in each pair focus on the chart lines to which they are to respond by labeling them. Use two red squares (from Stick-On Sheet 6) to label lines 1 and 3 and two yellow circles (from Stick-On Sheet 7) to label lines 2 and 4. Assign one shape to each member of the pair.

SONGBOOK
"Ah! Les Jolis Papillons," page 263 (upward and downward; butterflies)

RECORDED TEACHING LESSONS
A FIRST FOR MUSIC BOOKS!
Two-to-four minute model lessons for direct teaching taught by master teachers, to demonstrate the most current strategies in teaching pitch, rhythm, and listening. The red bracket and logo designate the part of the lesson that is recorded.

Reinforcing the Lesson
Appears in most lessons to support and reinforce the objectives

3 APPRAISAL
A tool for assessing student progress that is directly related to the Objectives

COPYING MASTER
An accompanying blackline master found in the Teacher's Resource Package (*Does not appear in all lessons.*)

MUSIC and YOU

General Information for all Teachers is indicated by headings with a white background.

Songbook
References to *alternate* songs in the Songbook section that can be used to teach the concepts or reading skills in this lesson

MUSIC AND YOU FOCUSES ON THE CHILD

Songs, listening selections, poetry, games, and dances in MUSIC AND YOU were chosen from children's favorites around the country. They have been carefully woven into a comprehensive learning sequence.

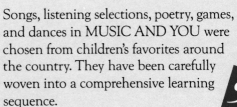

NEW

The first series with songs organized by the school calendar year, integrating the musical content of seasonal and holiday songs into daily lesson plans

Development of concepts and skills

continues as students observe special days and prepare for programs through strategically placed holiday, seasonal, and patriotic songs. If other songs are preferred, alternate selections are provided in the Songbook section in the back of each pupil book.

FAVORITE SONGS

Included in Grade K
Brush Your Teeth
Down at the Station
Happy Birthday
Hush, Little Baby
Little Ducky Duddle
Little Red Caboose
London Bridge
Mail Myself to You
My Thumbs Are Starting
   to Wiggle
Peanut Butter
Put Your Finger in the Air
The Farmer in the Dell
This Little Light of Mine
Where is Thumbkin?
Willoughby Wallaby Woo

Total of 122 Songs in Grade K

LISTENING MAP "E.T.'s HALLOWEEN"

POETRY AND CHANTS

Eight Balloons
Jack Be Nimble
One Potato, Two Potato
The Giant's Shoes

GAMES AND DANCES

Charlie Over the Ocean
Comanche Hand Game Song
Hokey Pokey
Looby Loo
My Head and My Shoulders
Uncle Jessie

FAVORITE LISTENING SELECTIONS

Included in Grade K
A variety of listening selections integrated into lessons will delight children, and help develop their listening skills.

"E.T.'s Halloween" from *E.T. The Extra-terrestrial* by John Williams

Children's Symphony (first movement) by Harl McDonald

"The Wild Horseman" from *Album for the Young* by Robert Schumann

viii

NEW

The first series with a sequential learning program that saves preparation time

Sequenced Lessons help children develop concepts, skills, and creativity through active involvement in making music.

ff

1 2 3 4

STRONG BEAT **53**

HANSEL AND GRETEL ACT III **29**

Musicals, Related Arts Lessons, and Song Stories with music, dramatization, movement, and dialogue are included for children to perform.

MUSIC and YOU

ix

Correlated copying masters in the *Teacher's Copying Masters* book can be used with the Big Book. Included are:

- activity sheets
- sequencing activities
- picture maps for listening
- puppet ideas
- creative evaluation

MASTER SONG INDEX

A thorough index provides easy access to all the music from Grades K–8 MUSIC AND YOU. Alphabetical and classified indexes help locate songs, poems, chants, and listening materials quickly.

MUSICAL INSTRUMENTS FOR BULLETIN BOARDS AND COPYING MASTERS

Copying masters of instruments provide illustrations for students as they are introduced to instruments. The visuals are also useful for bulletin board display and for kindergarten students to color.

Name

ABA Form

USE WITH PAGE 174.
MACMILLAN PUBLISHING COMPANY   GK

Name

LISTENING MAP: Acadian Songs

USE WITH PAGE 149.
MACMILLAN PUBLISHING COMPANY   GK

Name

"One, Two, Tie My Shoe"

COPYING MASTER
3-7

USE WITH PAGE 71.
MACMILLAN PUBLISHING COMPANY   GK

79

A COLORFUL BIG BOOK TO FOCUS GROUP LEARNING

The Kindergarten Big Book invites attention as students sing and learn together. The Big Book provides visual cues as students explore basic music concepts through shared activities.

The Kindergarten Big Book:

- opens conveniently like a book
- contains 60 large charts of colorful photographs and illustrations of the program
- helps children to understand their world, sharing, sounds and silences, high and low, long and short, beat, rhythm, melody, form, colors, numbers, body parts
- includes new peel and stick art designs called "Stick-Ons" which adhere to the chart pages and provide additional visual reinforcement

Listen for the Macmillan excellence in recorded songs, poems, chants, visits with famous musicians, and listening selections.

BRAVO! FOR MERRILL STATON

Our Executive Record Producer and Conductor

Merrill Staton pioneered the recorded sound of children's voices with music series, and has long been considered the foremost expert in the field of educational song recordings. He was the first to introduce the technique of divided tracks, and has recorded over 3000 songs with children. He has skillfully featured young voices as the best of vocal models for the songs in MUSIC AND YOU.

RECORDINGS OF THE HIGHEST TECHNICAL QUALITY

Songs, chants, poems, and other listening selections in MUSIC AND YOU were recorded with divided tracks, locked bands, and stereophonic sound for years of enjoyment and classroom use.

OUR NEW RECORDINGS FEATURE:

• The natural sound of children's and teenagers' voices as vocal models.

• Divided parts highlight vocal parts on separate tracks so students can hear one part at a time while learning to harmonize.

• Divided tracks highlight instrumental accompaniments and vocal performances on separate tracks.

HEAR FAMOUS MUSICIANS DESCRIBE THEIR MUSIC

Aaron Copland, Charles Strouse, Robert Shaw, Alice Parker and other professional musicians talk about their work and feelings about music in FOCUS ON recordings for Grades 4–6.

Our thanks to the students and adults around the country who recorded for MUSIC AND YOU.

A FIRST IN MUSIC EDUCATION!

These two- to four-minute model recorded lessons demonstrate the portions of a lesson that teach rhythm, pitch, foreign language pronunciations, movement, playing instruments, listening to music, and practicing vocal warm-ups.

For the Classroom Teacher:
These lessons provide a recorded demonstration to help you teach music concepts and skills.

For the Music Specialist:
These lessons provide you with an alternate way to teach a portion of the lesson.

---

1. Review "Jim Along, Josie" for pitch. Have the children:
• Sing the song, using their books.
• Identify the pitches used in the first line.

Line 1   so la so mi   re do re mi so
          5 6 5 3   2 1 2 3 5

• Find the line of the song that is the same as the first line (line 3).
• Sing these lines with syllables or numbers, using words for the rest of the song.

Grade 2   Page 111

Play an accompaniment with "The Alpine Song." Have the children:
• Sing the song, pretending to strum on the first beat of each measure.
• Take turns playing the pattern. Press the F button with the left-hand index (pointing) finger. Press the C7 button with the middle finger. Strum each chord once, making the strum last three beats. (You may wish to use Copying Master 2-6 at this time.)
• Take turns playing the accompaniment for one verse. Add an introduction to the song and an *interlude* (short sections of music that connect parts of a longer composition) consisting of the chord pattern played one time through between each verse.
• Tell that when the strum lasts three beats it can be shown by a *dotted half note*.

Grade 3   Page 35

---

3. Introduce *The Moldau* **by Bedrich Smetana.** Have the students:
• Look at the text about *The Moldau* on page 64 and identify the song as nationalistic in style.
• Listen to the melody of the main theme as they follow the music on page 64.
• Compare it with the melody to "Sing It All Together" by describing the movement of the melody in terms of steps and skips. (Both melodies begin by moving by steps in an upward motion. However, the main theme of *The Moldau* has repeated tones, while "Sing It All Together" does not.)
• Identify whether they are in major or minor. (Both are in minor, although the main theme of *The Moldau* is also heard in major.)
• Compare the meters. (The meters are different. The theme from *The Moldau* is in $\frac{6}{8}$, while "Sing It All Together" is in $\frac{4}{4}$. Both have many repeated rhythm patterns.)

Grade 6   Page 64

RHYTHM OF TRAINS

🔊 1A, 1B
💿 1

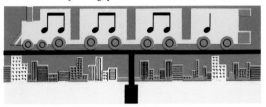

• As you sing, point to a car for each beat.

• Look at the notes on the train.
  Which beat has only one sound?   *the last beat*
• Find this pattern in "Engine, Engine Number Nine."   *lines 1, 2, 3, and 4*

9

EXTENSION

MORE MUSIC TEACHING IDEAS
Have the children:
1. Read the rhythm of "Engine, Engine Number Nine," saying *ta* for ♩ and *ti-ti* for ♫.

2. Practice the rhythm of the *bordun pattern* (a repeated pattern using only the first and fifth scale steps) below by patting it on their legs as they sing "Engine, Engine Number Nine." Then play it on a bass or alto xylophone or other pitched instrument.

3. Add an ostinato to accompany "Engine, Engine Number Nine." Recorders play on any pitch, simulating a train whistle.

recorders   sand blocks

train train   en - gine en - gine

(Start with an introduction, beginning softly and getting louder. At the end of the song, continue playing the pattern four more times, gradually getting softer. The children can also say the chant before and after the song.) Play softly to accompany the song.

4. Practice drawing ♩ and ♫.

C O R E
LESSON 6

Focus: Rhythm

Objectives
To distinguish between steady beat and rhythm
To identify ♩ and ♫
To follow visual cues while listening attentively to an orchestral composition

Materials
Recordings: Recorded Lesson—"City Echo Rhythms"
"Engine, Engine Number Nine"
Recorded Lesson—"Engine, Engine Rhythms"
Recorded Lesson—Themes in "The Little Train of the Caipira"
Listening—"The Little Train of the Caipira"
Copying Master 1-2 (optional)

Vocabulary
rhythm

1 SETTING THE STAGE
Have the children say the "City Echo Rhythms" on page 2 while patting the beat, and identify the patting as the beat. Then have them echo the sentences again, clapping once for each syllable. Tell them they are clapping the rhythm of the words. (For clapping, have the children hold the non-dominant hand still and tap with the dominant hand. If a child has difficulty clapping in this way, adapt the activity to tapping a desk with the dominant hand.)

2 TEACHING THE LESSON
1. Teach the children to read the rhythm of "Engine, Engine Number Nine." Have the children:
• Look at the notes on the drawing of the train. (Each car represents a beat.) Sing the song, pointing from left to right to the engine on the first beat and to a car on each of the other beats. Do the line four times.
• Figure out the number of sounds to a beat by counting the note heads in each train car.
• Look at the notes of the song on page 8 and find this rhythm pattern. Discover that the rhythm is the same in every line of the song.
• Look at the rhythm of the song, saying "train" for ♩ and "engine" for ♫. (It is not necessary for the children to learn the names of these notes at this time.)
• Sing the song again. While the class sings, have a few children form a train and move around the room, sliding their feet twice per beat.
• Listen to the beat and rhythm of "Engine, Engine Number Nine" played on two different instruments and identify which instrument is playing the steady beat and which is playing the rhythm of the words.

UNIT 1 **9**

The red bracket and logo 🔴 indicate the portion of a lesson that is recorded.

MUSIC and YOU

A consistent Teaching Plan focuses on concepts and skills that are first experienced, then identified and labeled, creatively reinforced, and finally evaluated.

• **Basic concepts and skills** shown here with a white background are taught in the main parts of **Core** and **Non-Core** lessons in each unit.

Boldface type indicates a *basic concept or skill* is measured.

• **Higher level concepts and skills** shown here in blue tint are taught in the **More Music Teaching Ideas** sections of lessons.

Concepts and skills are measured informally at the end of each unit.

Written Unit Evaluations are provided in *Teacher's Copying Masters*.

ELEMENTS OF MUSIC	UNIT 1 GETTING STARTED Objectives	UNIT 2 FALL FESTIVAL Objectives	UNIT 3 MUSICAL FRIENDS Objectives
Dynamics	Sing, hear, use varying dynamic levels Use term, hear, sing *echo* **Identify loud/soft**	Use terms *loud* and *soft* in singing and moving	Choose appropriate levels of dynamics Explore dynamic possibilities of some classroom instruments
Tone Color	Hear good examples of speaking, singing voices Use singing, calling voices Hear orchestra	Use singing and speaking voices Explore environmental and classroom instruments' capacity to make long/short, high/low sounds	Use four voices Hear solo instruments **Identify the triangle, rhythm sticks, drum, and tambourine by sight and sound**
Tempo	Use various tempos **Identify fast/slow**	Use various tempos	Recognize faster/slower
Duration/ Rhythm	Hear music with strong feeling of beat Keep beat with body percussion, moving in place (imitating teacher)	**Identify long/short sounds and symbols** Speak, play combinations of long and short sounds Keep beat with body percussion	Say, pat, play rhythm of names, short word patterns Compare beat with no beat Walk individually to drum matched to their own natural tempos Sing, hear music with silent beat **Recognize and use the term *beat***
Pitch	Hear, use high and low sounds Hear, sing, recognize echoes	Associate high with small, low with large Identify melody as the tune Use terms *high/low* Learn songs from charts that show high/low	Identify pitches as higher or lower than one another Continue to associate high with small, low with large
Texture	Hear, sing melody with accompaniment	Begin to recognize melody alone or with accompaniment	Continue to use and recognize melody alone and with accompaniment
Form	Recognize difference between whole and part Show understanding of section of song (verse, refrain)	Hear whole/part Begin to recognize same/different (melody, rhythm, words of song) Begin responding to phrase length	Continue to recognize same/different Imitating teacher, find and count phrases in a short song Identify introduction of songs Wait for introductions, interludes
Style	Sing folk and composed songs Notice effect caused by dynamic change Show understanding of differing styles (march vs. lullaby) Hear 19th- and 20th-century orchestral styles	Notice ways that elements of music affect style Listen to contemporary composition	Hear, sing American Indian song, Thanksgiving songs, folk songs, composed songs Hear 20th-century orchestral music

UNIT 4	UNIT 5	UNIT 6	UNIT 7	UNIT 8
HOLIDAY FUN Objectives	**WINTER DAYS** Objectives	**SAME AND DIFFERENT** Objectives	**MOVE INTO SPRING** Objectives	**SOUNDS ALL AROUND** Objectives
Respond to different dynamics when echoing, singing, and speaking	Hear and use loud and soft	Use loud/soft appropriately	Use, hear, different dynamic levels	Recognize and use soft/ loud, softer/louder
Identify voices of men, women, children Explore instruments for high and low **Name and play jingle bells, wood block, xylophone, glockenspiel, bells, and drum**	**Recognize the difference between an instrument of definite pitch and one of indefinite pitch** Hear, see orchestral instruments Continue learning names of classroom instruments	Continue to learn names of classroom instruments **Identify four types of voices (whispering, singing, speaking, calling)** Hear trumpet, tuba, piano, band Hear symphony orchestra	Vary tone color using body percussion and classroom instruments **Identify flute, piccolo, violin**	**Identify trumpet, timpani, flute, and violin** Use various vocal and instrumental tone qualities Practice the four voices Listen to children, men
Recognize, use faster/ slower	Identify slow, fast, and changes in tempo	Experience and use appropriate tempos	Practice locomotor movements at different tempos	Hear, use different tempos
Pat beat with familiar songs and rhymes Echo clap/say short phrases See representation of beats in picture form Sing and hear music containing silent beat Play trotting rhythm pattern (♫) Practice identifying long sounds	Review beat, no beat See pictorial representation of beat, silent beat **Recognize notation for a sound one beat long and for a silent beat (♩,𝄽)** Sing songs with ♩ ♫ 𝄽	Aural/oral experiences with ♩, ♫, 𝄽 (echoing, singing songs, using ostinatos, find words that fit basic combinations) Hear, sing, use strong beat Practice basic locomotor movements	Recognize rhythm of locomotor movements Devise pictures of one and two equal sounds to a beat Do four-beat patterns Sing, use $\frac{2}{4}$ and $\frac{2}{4}$ meters	Learn songs in $\frac{2}{4}$ $\frac{2}{4}$. and $\frac{4}{4}$ Hear song in $\frac{3}{4}$ Practice patting rhythm or beat of songs, poems **Show identification of strong beat in music with two beats per measure** **Recognize two equal sounds to a beat**
Sing songs using high/low **Identify high/low**	Sing songs containing mi so or mi so la Sing, hear higher/lower See and devise ways to show higher/lower	See mi so in pictorial notation (sing with words, point to representation of sounds) for known songs **Recognize higher/lower** Sing and hear clear examples of upward/downward Sing known songs showing mi so with higher/lower arm movements (imitating teacher at first)	Practice using two-note patterns (mi so) Hear, sing, play three-note patterns (mi so la) **Identify upward/downward** Create, play upward/downward question/answer patterns	Sing song with three pitches (mi so la) Practice identifying upward/downward
Add accompaniments to songs	Play accompaniment Sing with an ostinato	Perform melody with rhythm and/or speech ostinato Recognize a melody with accompaniment	Perform melody with rhythm and/or speech ostinato Hear melody with accompaniment	Continue identifying melody alone or with accompaniment Sing songs with rhythm or speech ostinatos
Find and name same/ different sections Follow map showing introduction/interlude/coda Say poem and sing songs in AB form	Find, label same/different Follow visual representation of same/ different Identify, use interlude	**Identify same/different in songs and listening selections** Create short melodic or rhythmic compositions by combining short patterns created by individual children	Identify same/different phrases and sections **Create question/answer patterns**	Discover same/different phrases and sections Label short ABA forms
Discover how changes in music elements can change style of music Hear music from operetta Sing spiritual, American and Spanish folk songs, composed songs	Listen to orchestral compositions	Hear and review comparing lullaby and march styles Hear music of 18th, 19th, and 20th centuries	Move to show style and elements of music	Identify several musical elements that affect style Sing African song Hear Japanese song Hear music in Asian style

UNIT 1 • OVERVIEW

ELEMENTS OF MUSIC	UNIT 1 OBJECTIVES	Lesson 1 CORE Focus: Fast and Slow	Lesson 2 CORE Focus: Steady Beat	Lesson 3 Focus: Part and Whole	Lesson 4 Focus: Fast and Slow
Dynamics	Sing, hear, use varying dynamic levels Use term, hear, sing *echo* **Identify loud/soft**	Hear, sing echo	Experience varying dynamic levels	Experience varying dynamic levels	Experience varying dynamic levels
Tone Color	Hear good examples of speaking, singing voices Use singing, calling voices Hear orchestra	Hear good examples of speaking, singing voices Hear orchestra	Hear good examples of singing voices Use singing voices Use student names in a song	Hear good examples of singing voices Use singing voices	Hear good examples of singing voices Use singing voices
Tempo	Use various tempos **Identify fast/slow**	Sing, hear, move to, identify fast/slow Use pinwheels to explore tempo	Practicing identifying fast, medium, slow Move to show tempo	Experience various tempos	Practice identifying and using fast/slow
Duration/ Rhythm	Hear music with strong feeling of beat Keep beat with body percussion, moving in place (imitating teacher)	Hear music with strong feeling of beat Pat beat, imitating teacher	Hear music with strong feeling of beat Pat beat, imitating teacher	Hear music with strong feeling of beat	Hear music with strong feeling of beat
Pitch	Hear, use high and low sounds Hear, sing, recognize echoes	Hear, sing echoed phrases Experience high and low sounds	Hear, sing echoed phrases Experience high and low sounds	Sing song using each student's name, having them respond by saying how they are today	
Texture	Hear, sing melody with accompaniment	Hear, sing melody with accompaniment	Hear, sing melody with accompaniment	Hear, sing melody with accompaniment	Hear, sing melody with accompaniment
Form	Recognize difference between whole and part Show understanding of section of song (verse, refrain)		Identify the beginning and ending of a song	Recognize the difference between whole and part Recognize that the first verse is part of a two-verse song	Recognize part/whole Move in a different way to recognize verses Develop dramatization of a song
Style	Sing folk and composed songs Notice effect caused by dynamic change Show understanding of differing styles (march vs. lullaby) Hear 19th- and 20th-century orchestral styles	Sing folk and composed songs Hear 19th-century orchestral style	Sing folk and composed songs	Sing folk and composed songs	Hear lullaby Sing folk and composed songs

PURPOSE Unit 1: Getting Started

This unit introduces music for the school year. Selections in this unit include folk songs, composed songs, poems, and listening selections carefully chosen for the kindergarten child's beginning musical experiences. The main purpose of this unit is to help develop a secure musical environment and to promote positive attitudes toward music through successful and happy singing, moving, and listening experiences. The basic music concepts emphasized in this unit include distinguishing between slow and fast and between loud and soft.

SUGGESTED TIME FRAME

September			October		

FOCUS

Core Lessons 1, 2, 5, 6, 9
• Fast and Slow
• Steady Beat
• Loud and Soft
• Loud and Soft
• Style

Lessons 3, 4, 7, 8, 10
• Part and Whole
• Fast and Slow
• Part and Whole
• Loud and Soft
• Fast and Slow

BULLETIN BOARD

Draw or cut out pictures that represent songs in the core lessons and place them on the bulletin board. These pictures should be large enough so that the entire class can see them. Before the class begins the Review story, direct their attention to the pictures on the bulletin board. The pictures serve as a helpful visual clue to the songs in the Review and to the order in which they will be sung.
Representative pictures for songs in the Unit 1 core lessons might be:
"Sing a Little Song"—a sun
"Brush Your Teeth"—a toothbrush and a toothy smile
"Walk to School"—a child walking

Lesson 5 CORE Focus: Loud and Soft	Lesson 6 CORE Focus: Loud and Soft	Lesson 7 Focus: Part and Whole	Lesson 8 Focus: Loud and Soft	Lesson 9 CORE Focus: Style	Lesson 10 Focus: Fast and Slow
Identify loud/soft Sing echoes more softly Use term *echo* Explore sound sources for loud/soft	Identify loud/soft		Identify loud/soft	Identify loud/soft	
Hear and use speaking, singing voices Develop awareness of environmental sounds Hear orchestra	Hear good examples of speaking, singing voices Use singing, calling voices Hear orchestra	Hear good examples of speaking, singing voices Use singing voices Use student names in a song	Hear good examples of speaking, singing voices Use singing voices Use loud and soft sounds on instruments with a poem	Hear good examples of speaking, singing voices Use singing voices Hear orchestra Respond to tone color of triangle and drum	Hear good examples of speaking, singing voices Use singing voices
Use various tempos		Use fast/slow	Use various tempos	Identify fast/slow	Identify fast/slow
Hear and move to music with strong feeling of steady beat Notice silences in a melody line	Hear and move to music with strong feeling of steady beat	Hear music with strong feeling of beat Keep beat with body percussion, moving in place	Hear music with strong feeling of beat Keep beat with body percussion, moving in place (imitating teacher)	Hear music with strong feeling of beat	Hear music with strong feeling of beat
Recognize, sing echo		Experience high and low sounds	Experience high and low sounds	Experience high and low	Experience high and low
Hear, sing melody with accompaniment	Hear, sing melody with accompaniment	Hear, sing melody with accompaniment	Hear, sing melody with accompaniment	Hear, sing melody with accompaniment	Hear, sing melody with accompaniment
Recognize the difference between whole and part Sing the refrain of a song	Recognize the difference between whole and part Show understanding of a refrain of a song by singing only the refrain (use term *refrain*)	Recognize the difference between whole and part			
Sing composed songs Hear 19th-century orchestral style	Sing folk and composed songs Hear 19th-century orchestral style	Sing folk and composed songs	Sing folk and composed songs Identify changes in effect caused by different levels of loud and soft	Sing folk and composed songs Show understanding of differing styles (march vs. lullaby) Hear 20th-century orchestral style Share known lullabies	Sing folk and composed songs

"Where Is Thumbkin?"—a closed fist with the thumb up
"Music of the World a-Turnin'"—a picture of the earth with notes around it.

LESSON 1

1A

CD 1

Focus: Fast and Slow

Related Subject
Going to school

Objective
To hear, sing, move to, and identify fast and slow tempos

Materials
Recordings: "Singing-Time"
"Sing a Little Song"
"Sing a Little Song" (slow version; optional)
"Walk to School"
Listening—"The Top" from *Children's Games*, by Georges Bizet

Charts 1, 2, and 3
X and O stick-ons
Star stick-on
Copying Masters 1-1, 1-2 (optional)

Vocabulary
slow, slowly, medium, fast

1 SETTING THE STAGE

As you pat a steady beat, have the children pat their knees, starting and stopping with you as they are able. Ask the children to try to start and stop patting with you at these different speeds: very slow, medium fast, moderately fast (do not identify the tempos to the class). Have the children look at Chart 1. Ask the class if some of the people in the chart appear to be moving faster than others, and have them identify which ones (the boy and girl running). Then have them identify other things in the chart that appear to be moving faster (the dog, the airplane).

FAST AND SLOW

CHART 1

E X T E N S I O N

VOCAL DEVELOPMENT

Children entering Kindergarten may be unable to match the pitches of the songs you sing in class. Some children will be using their lower or "chest" voices and will be "speaking" the song more than singing it. They will need to learn to use their higher or "head" voices for singing.

Throughout this book, you will be given suggestions for helping the children develop their singing voices. To begin, encourage them to sing softly. This promotes the use of a higher, lighter singing voice and allows them to hear the correct pitches of the songs as you sing with them.

Singing-Time

I wake in the morning early
And always, the very first thing,
I poke out my head and I sit up in bed
And I sing and I sing and I sing.

—*Rose Fyleman*

2 TEACHING THE LESSON

1. Introduce "Singing-Time" to motivate singing. Have the children:
• Listen to "Singing-Time." Briefly discuss how singing can be a pleasant way to start the day.
• Name songs that they like to sing. (Tell the children that they are going to learn a song that can be fun to sing in the morning.)

EXTRA HELP
Many kindergarten teachers like to begin each school day with a "circle time," with everyone standing or sitting in a circle as they share songs and poems. This can be an effective way to focus the attention of the class toward the daily objectives and also helps create a class spirit.

C O R E
LESSON 1

2. Introduce "Sing a Little Song" to practice singing with a steady beat. Have the children:
• Listen to "Sing a Little Song," trying to pat a steady beat with you. (You may wish to use the slow version on the recording as a learning tempo.)
• Listen to the song again, this time singing the words *sing a little song* each time they are echoed.

Sing a Little Song

Piano Accompaniment on page PA 2

Words and music by
Henry Dennis, Jr.

Sing a lit-tle song of sun-ny skies, Sing a lit-tle song (Sing a lit-tle song.) Run and catch the sun-light in your eyes, sing a lit-tle song. (Sing a lit-tle song.) And we all will smile for noth - ing can go wrong when we Sing a lit - tle song. (Sing a lit-tle song.) Sing a lit-tle song.

CHART

2 *WORD SEQUENCING*

C O R E

LESSON 1

• Look at Chart 2. Identify the pictures as representing words in "Sing a Little Song."
• Say the words represented by each picture after you. Then point to each picture in order as they listen to the song. (You may wish to use Copying Master 1-1 at this time.)
• Listen to the song again, singing along as they are able.
• Sing the song, patting the steady beat. (You may wish to have half the class pat, imitating you, while the other half sings the song. Then switch parts. Finally, have the whole class sing and pat the beat at the same time.)
• Try to pat each line of the song on a different part of the body, for example, knees, shoulders, head, and so on.

C O R E
LESSON 1

3. Introduce "Walk to School" to identify and use different tempos. Have the children:
• Pat a medium fast tempo with you as they listen to the first part of "Walk to School."
• Change tempo as the tempo of the music changes first to slow, and then to very fast. (Describe the slow tempo as how they would walk if they were very tired. Describe the fast tempo as how they would walk if they were late for school.)
• Look at Chart 3 and identify the speed at which each child seems to be walking (slow, medium fast, fast). Have a child put an X on the picture showing slow, a star on the picture showing medium, and an O on the picture showing fast.
• Watch as several children take turns walking at a slow, medium fast, or fast speed. (Each child chooses his or her own speed.) Identify the speed at which each child walks.
• Listen to "Walk to School" again, singing along as they are able.

4. Introduce "The Top" from *Children's Games* by Georges Bizet to practice identifying tempo. Have the children:
• Discuss ways they can move their hands and arms to suggest a spinning top.
• Listen to the music, moving their arms to show whether they think the top is moving slowly, medium fast, or fast (fast).
• Discuss ways they can move their whole bodies to suggest a spinning top.
• Listen to the music again as several children move to show how they think the top is spinning.

Walk to School

Piano Accompaniment on page PA 4

American Folk Song
Words by Mary Jaye

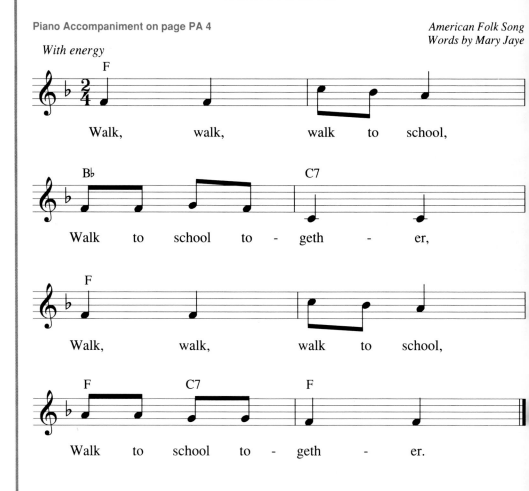

Walk, walk, walk to school,
Walk to school to - geth - er,
Walk, walk, walk to school,
Walk to school to - geth - er.

E X T E N S I O N

THE COMPOSER

Georges Bizet (zhorzh bē-zā') (1838–1875) —French composer, was born in Paris. He showed musical talent at an early age, entering the Paris Conservatory when he was nine. At nineteen he had won prizes for playing the piano and organ, and for composition. Bizet was a brilliant pianist, but his main interest was composing, especially opera. The opera *Carmen* is his best-known work. *Children's Games* was originally written as a piano duet. Parts of this work were later orchestrated by Bizet and others.

KEYBOARD

Many children have access to small electronic keyboards, which may be used to explore musical concepts. To reinforce the concept of slow, medium, and fast tempos on an electronic keyboard, use either the preset melody or record a series of pitches (a melody) into the keyboard memory. Have the children listen to the melody several times, adjusting the tempo before each repeat by using the tempo control button. They may also wish to adjust the tempo as the piece is playing, to hear an example of getting faster and getting slower.

SLOW, MEDIUM, FAST

CHART 3

Reinforcing the Lesson

Review "Sing a Little Song" on page 2, or "Walk to School" on page 4. (If time permits, you may wish to review both songs.) Have the children pat the beat to show the speed of the music as they sing.

3 APPRAISAL

The children should be able to identify fast and slow music with appropriate hand movements.

MORE MUSIC TEACHING IDEAS

Have the children make pinwheels. Then have them blow on their pinwheels to make the wheels spin at slow, medium, and fast speeds. You may wish to take the class outside and hold their pinwheels in the wind to determine if the wind is blowing at a slow, medium, or fast speed. (You may wish to use Copying Master 1-2 at this time.)

CLASSROOM MANAGEMENT

Some children have difficulty moving around without touching other children. Establish a rule that each child should respect the other children's spaces and that they should not move into any other space, whether the child in that space is moving or standing still. As the class prepares to move to "The Top," ask a volunteer to move to the music. Comment on how much space is needed around that child. Have the child turn slowly around with arms outstretched to "feel" the space. Have one or two other children join the first child and do the same movement at the same time. Gradually add more children as they seem able to control their spaces.

SONGBOOK

"Clap Your Hands," page 267 (same tune as "Walk to School")
"Little Red Caboose," page 278 (steady tempo)

LESSON 2

Focus: Steady Beat

Related Subjects
Names, colors, safety

Objectives
To practice patting a steady beat
To identify the beginning and ending of a song
To practice identifying fast, medium, and slow

Materials
Recordings: "Sing a Little Song"
"Hello Song" (version 1)
"Hello Song" (version 2)
"Safety Song"
"Walk to School"
Charts 2, 4
Copying Master 1-3 (optional)

Vocabulary
beginning, begin, ending, end

1 SETTING THE STAGE

Have the children listen to "Sing a Little Song" and pat the steady beat with you, raising their hands when they think the song has ended. Review the words of "Sing a Little Song" on page 2 with Chart 2, and identify the first and last words of the song (*sing, song*). Remind the children that the words *sing a little song* are sung three times at the end of the song. Have them sing the song again, raising their hands when the song ends.

E X T E N S I O N

MORE MUSIC TEACHING IDEAS

Sing "Hello Song" (version 1), substituting the name of each child in the class for the second "Hello" in each line. If the class is large, sing "Hello Song" using individual names of only part of the class. Sing the song using the rest of the names on another day.

1A
CD 1

Key: E♭   Starting Pitch: G   Scale Tones: *la, ti, do re mi fa so*

Hello Song

Piano Accompaniment on page PA 5   *Traditional*

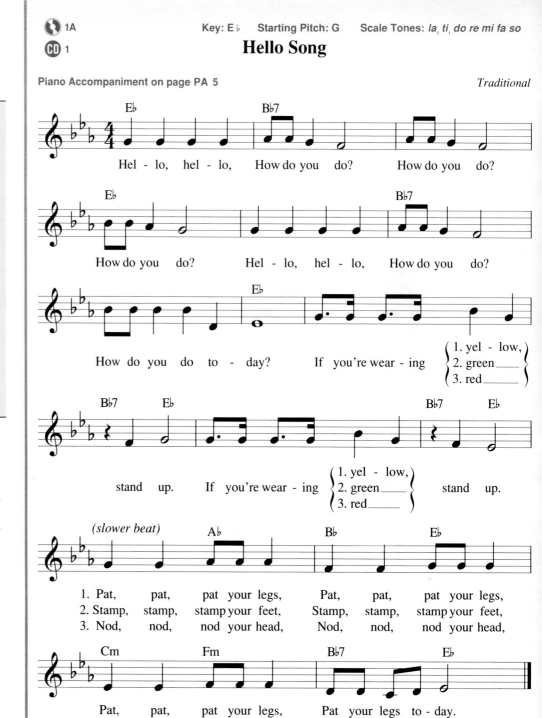

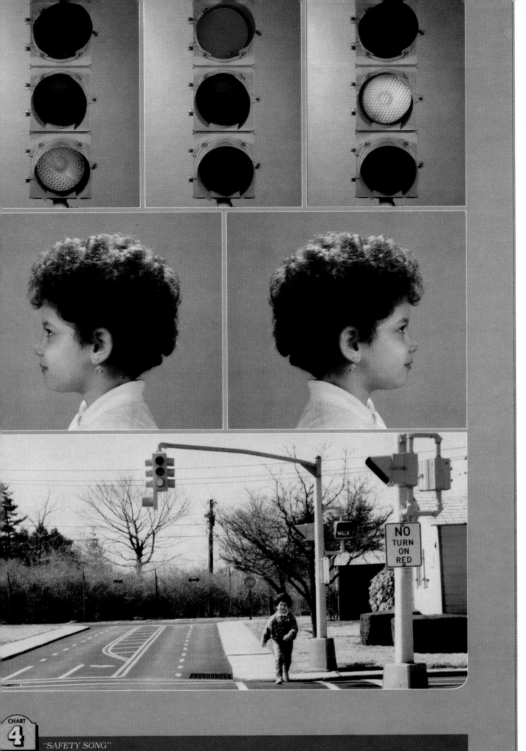

CHART 4

"SAFETY SONG"

2 TEACHING THE LESSON

1. Introduce "Hello Song" (version 1, measures 1-8) to identify first and last words. Have the children:

• Listen to "Hello Song" (version 1).

• Listen again, singing along as they are able.

• Identify the first and last words in "Hello Song" (version 1) (*hello, today*).

• Sing "Hello Song" (version 1) again.

2. Introduce the concept of steady beat. Have the children:

• Listen to "Hello Song" (version 2). Keep the steady beat by patting, stamping, and nodding.

• Sing the whole song, following the directions and keeping the beat in the way indicated by the words in each verse.

LESSON 2

3. Introduce "Safety Song" to practice identifying colors and order. Have the children:
• Listen to "Safety Song." Identify the colors and the order in which they occur in the song (green, red, yellow).
• Look at Chart 4 on page 7 and identify the colors of the lights at the top of the chart (from left to right). Notice that the colors appear in the same order as they occur in the song.
• Listen to "Safety Song" again, singing along as they are able.
• Practice the words. (Emphasize the importance of obeying these safety rules in everyday life.)
• Sing the whole song.
(You may wish to use Copying Master 1-3 at this time.)

Safety Song

Piano Accompaniment on page PA 7

Flemish Folk Tune
Words by Margaret Lowery

1. We skip on our way to school each day,
2. The green light says "Go," the red says "Stop";

We nev - er like to be late;
A yel - low light in be - tween.

When - ev - er we reach a traf - fic light,
We look to the left and to the right,

We know the sig - nal to wait.
And then we cross on the green.

MOVEMENT

Have the children review the safety rules for crossing the street by dramatizing "Safety Song." Choose one child to be the signal and hold three cards, each card showing one color on the traffic signal. The rest of the class pretends to be pedestrians. As the "signal" shows one of the colors, the pedestrians move or stand still as directed by the color they see.

MORE MUSIC TEACHING IDEAS

Have the children form two groups. Each group chooses a leader. Sing "Walk to School" with one group following their leader's movements. Then sing the song with the other group moving. You may wish to repeat this activity to give other children turns being the leader of each group.

SPECIAL LEARNERS

Color-blind children may have difficulty distinguishing red from green. However, they may be able to distinguish one color from the other by noticing subtle differences in shade and by the relative position of the colors on the chart. Before singing the song, help the children get their cues by naming each color and by clarifying which color is on top, in the middle, and on the bottom.

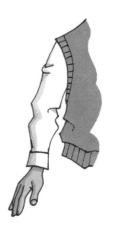

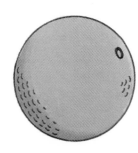

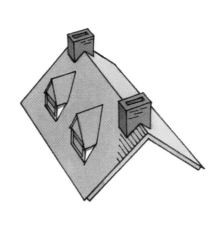

PART AND WHOLE

CHART 5

Reinforcing the Lesson

Review "Walk to School" on page 4 to practice fast, medium, and slow. Have the children sing the song and identify the speed of each part (medium, slow, fast). Sing the song again as one child moves at each of the three speeds.

3 APPRAISAL

The children should be able to:

1. Pat the steady beat with reasonable accuracy while listening to or singing a song.

2. Show that they can identify the beginning and the end of a song by raising their hands when they think the song has ended.

3. Identify fast, medium and slow music with appropriate movements.

SONGBOOK

"Little Red Caboose," page 278 (colors)
"Clap Your Hands," page 267 (steady beat)
"My Head and My Shoulders," page 281 (steady beat)

LESSON 3

Focus: Part and Whole

Related Subjects
Names, body parts

Objective
To practice distinguishing between part and whole

Materials
Recordings: "Hello Song" (versions 1 and 2)
"I Am a Person"
"My Thumbs Are Starting to Wiggle"
"Safety Song"
Charts 4 and 5
Copying Master 1-4 (optional)

1 SETTING THE STAGE

Have the children review "Hello Song" on page 6. Sing just measures 1-8 (version 1) and identify it as part of a song. Then sing the whole song (version 2).

2 TEACHING THE LESSON

1. Practice identifying part and whole.
Have the children:
• Look at Chart 5 on page 9 and identify the pictures that show part and the pictures that show whole. (The arm is part of the whole person; the orange section is part of the whole orange; the roof is part of the whole house.)
(You may wish to use Copying Master 1-4 at this time.)
2. Introduce "I Am a Person" and practice identifying part and whole. Have the children:
• Echo these words, using the movement:
  I am a person   point to self
• Listen to the first verse. Notice that they only learned part of it. Identify the first verse as part of the whole song.

I Am a Person

Piano Accompaniment on page PA 8

Words and music by
Fairfax, Virginia Public School Music Teachers

E X T E N S I O N

CURRICULUM CONNECTION: SOCIAL STUDIES

All About Me—Have the children put together "All About Me" booklets that tell all about themselves, such as what they look like, who is in their family, what pet they have, what their favorite colors, foods, stories, songs, sports, hobbies, and so on are, and what some of their dreams and wishes are. Each day, choose one child to be the Star of the Day to emphasize the fact that each child is special. The Star of the Day shares her or his booklet with the rest of the class. You may also have the Star of the Day choose a favorite song for the class to sing, or choose a favorite instrument to play with a song.

Key: D   Starting Pitch: D   Scale Tones: *do re mi fa so la*

My Thumbs Are Starting to Wiggle

Piano Accompaniment on page PA 9

Traditional

1. My thumbs are start-ing to wig - gle,
2. My hands are start-ing to wig - gle,
3. My arms are start-ing to wig - gle,

my thumbs are start-ing to wig - gle,
my hands are start-ing to wig - gle,
my arms are start-ing to wig - gle,

my thumbs are start-ing to wig - gle
my hands are start-ing to wig - gle
my arms are start-ing to wig - gle

A - round and a - round and a - round.

4. My legs are starting to wiggle . . .

5. Now, all of me is a-wiggling . . .
   I think that I'd better sit down.

• Echo these words using the following movements:

a very nice person	extend hands to sides, palms up
I am special as I can be	turn slowly in a circle
I like me	gently touch chest on each word

• Do the movements, singing along with the first verse as they are able.
• Listen to both verses of the song.

3. Introduce "My Thumbs Are Starting to Wiggle" to practice identifying parts of the body. Have the children:
• Listen and watch as you sing "My Thumbs Are Starting to Wiggle," moving with you as they are able. (Make the song more fun by acting surprised as you sing, as if what is happening is beyond your control. The children will join in. At the end of the song, feign relief and sit still for a few seconds. Then sing the song again, acting surprised as before.)
• Identify the parts of the body mentioned in the song. Recognize these as parts of the whole body, mentioned in the last verse.

Reinforcing the Lesson

Review "Safety Song" on page 8. Have the children look at Chart 4 and identify examples of part and whole (child's head, whole child; traffic signal, whole traffic light). Then have them sing the song. Have the children look at Chart 5 and identify which pictures are part of something and which pictures are whole things.

3 APPRAISAL

The children should be able to distinguish between part and whole in pictures and in songs.

MORE MUSIC TEACHING IDEAS

Sing the first part of "Hello Song" to each child, using individual names. Have each child answer with a word or phrase that describes how she or he is today. Use this word or phrase in the second part of the song, for example, "If you're feeling happy, stand up." Then all the children who stood pat their legs during the third part of the song. (As the song is repeated, use other movements such as stamp, nod.)

SONGBOOK

"My Head and My Shoulders," page 281 (steady beat; body parts; part and whole)
"Hokey Pokey," page 273 (body parts; part and whole)

LESSON 4

Focus: Fast and Slow

Related Subjects
Shapes, colors, self-concept

Objectives
To practice identifying fast and slow
To practice identifying part and whole

Materials
Recordings: "I Am a Person"
           Recorded Lesson—
             "Listening for Fast and
             Slow"
           "Hello Song"
           "Little Blue Truck"
           "Hush, Little Baby"
           "Oh, Where Has My Little
             Dog Gone?" (versions 1
             and 2)
Shapes: rectangles, squares, triangles, circles (blue)
Copying Masters 1-3, 1-5, 1-6, 1-7, 1-8 (optional)

1 SETTING THE STAGE

Have the children review the first verse of "I Am a Person" on page 10. Then sing the song at a slower tempo. Have the children tell you how the song was different the second time. Repeat the song at a fast tempo. Sing the second verse of the song and have the children echo you after each line, pointing away from themselves on the word *you*.

2 TEACHING THE LESSON

1. Review "Hello Song" on page 6 to practice shape names. Have the children:
- Sit in a circle and sing the song, doing the movements.
- Take one shape each.
- Sing "Hello Song," following your new directions. (For example, change the second part of the song to "If you have a rectangle, stand up." Place that shape on the floor in the middle of the circle. Change the last line to "Move around slowly now." Repeat the song, using the other shape names.)
(You may wish to use Copying Master 1-5 at this time.)

2. Introduce "Little Blue Truck." Have the children:
- Watch as you show them how to arrange the shapes into a picture of a truck.

(You may wish to use Copying Master 1-6 at this time.)

Little Blue Truck

Piano Accompaniment on page PA 10

Words and music by
Fairfax, Virginia Public School Music Teachers

1. Rid - ing in my lit - tle blue truck,
2. Wheels go 'round in my lit - tle blue truck,
3. One wheel broke in my lit - tle blue truck,

Rid - ing in my lit - tle blue truck,
Wheels go 'round in my lit - tle blue truck,
One wheel broke in my lit - tle blue truck,

Rid - ing in my lit - tle blue truck,
Wheels go 'round in my lit - tle blue truck,
One wheel broke in my lit - tle blue truck,

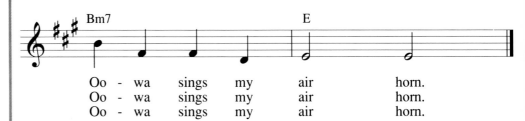

Oo - wa sings my air horn.
Oo - wa sings my air horn.
Oo - wa sings my air horn.

4. Who's gonna fix . . .

5. (Name) fixed my . . .

6. Riding in my . . .

EXTENSION

MORE MUSIC TEACHING IDEAS

Before the class sings "Little Blue Truck," designate one child to be a traffic signal (see *Movement*, page 8). Have the rest of the class sing the song with the movements, obeying the traffic signal. (You may wish to use Copying Master 1-3 at this time.)

LESSON 4

- Watch as one child places a rectangle on the floor, another child places a square beside the rectangle, a third child places a triangle above the square, and two other children place circles at the bottom of the rectangle and square to create their own truck picture, using your example as a guide. (Be sure there is one shape for each child. You should have exactly twice as many circles as rectangles, squares, or triangles. For example, for a class of thirty, you need six rectangles, six squares, six triangles, and twelve circles.)
- Repeat this activity until all of their shapes have been used to make truck pictures.
- Identify each shape as being a part of a whole truck.
- Sit and listen to the song, singing along and doing the movements with you as they are able.

Verse 1: Pretend to drive a truck
Verse 2: Move both arms around and around in a circle
Verse 3: Move one arm around in a circle as the other arm dangles awkwardly
Verse 4: Choose partners; each partner fixes the other's truck
Verse 5: Partners point to each other and sing each other's name
Verse 6: Pretend to drive a truck

- Identify the speed of the truck in the song. (Moderate at first, and quite slow when the wheel breaks.)
(You may wish to use Copying Master 1-7 at this time.)
- Discuss how to move safely around the room without bumping into other people or things.
- Take turns picking up the shapes and finding their own space to stand in the room.
- Sing "Little Blue Truck" with the movements.

CURRICULUM CONNECTION: SOCIAL STUDIES

Self-Concept—It is important in the early grades for the children to develop a sense of self-esteem and to learn respect and regard for others. After the class sings "I Am a Person," have any children who wish to do so volunteer to say something about themselves that they feel is special. You can repeat what each child says to affirm his or her thoughts, or add another positive observation of your own. If time permits, you may wish to have other children say something that they think is special about one of their classmates.

CURRICULUM CONNECTION: MATH

Shape Book—Have the children make booklets that highlight a different geometric shape on each page. The children can draw or cut out pictures from everyday life that illustrate the different shapes, for example, balloons, apples, a face for circles; a teepee, clown hat for triangles; a present, a Jack-in-the box for squares; a truck, a book for rectangles. You may wish to have each page also highlight one or two colors. (You may wish to use Copying Master 1-8 at this time.)

LESSON 4

3. Introduce "Hush, Little Baby" for more practice identifying fast and slow. Have the children:
• Sit near you and listen to the song.
• Identify the speed of the song (slow). (Reinforce good listening habits by complimenting those children who listen attentively and do not disturb the others.)

Hush, Little Baby

Piano Accompaniment on page PA 11   *Southern U. S. Folk Song*

1. Hush   lit - tle ba - by,   Don't   say   a word,
2. If   that___ mock - ing - bird   won't___ sing,
3. If   that___ dia - mond   ring   turns___ brass,
4. If   that___ look - ing   glass   gets___ broke,
5. If   that___ bil - ly   goat's   not___ smart,
6. If   that___ horse   and   cart   fall___ down,

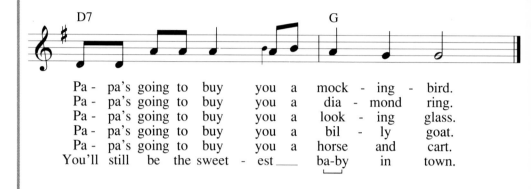

Pa - pa's going to buy   you   a   mock - ing - bird.
Pa - pa's going to buy   you   a   dia - mond   ring.
Pa - pa's going to buy   you   a   look - ing   glass.
Pa - pa's going to buy   you   a   bil - ly   goat.
Pa - pa's going to buy   you   a   horse   and   cart.
You'll still   be the sweet - est___ ba-by   in   town.

EXTENSION

SPECIAL LEARNERS

Movement is a particularly meaningful way to communicate musical concepts to all children, but it is vital to exceptional learners. Use movement to help them to feel the slow tempo of "Hush, Little Baby" in a concrete way. First ask the class to think of ways to move to music with a baby (bounce it on your knee, rock it, and so on). Then have the children decide on an appropriate way to move an imaginary baby as they listen to this song (gently rocking or bouncing). In some classes, you may have some children who respond negatively to the image of rocking a baby. To avoid this, you may wish to have them imagine they are instead rocking a pet or a favorite toy (or a favorite parent, after a long, hard day!).

MORE MUSIC TEACHING IDEAS

You may wish to have an older class prepare the following accompaniment to "Hush, Little Baby" and perform it for the children.

bass metallophone or low bells

alto or soprano metallophone or high bells

Key: F   Starting Pitch: A   Scale Tones: *so, ti, do re mi fa so la*

Oh, Where Has My Little Dog Gone?

Piano Accompaniment on page PA 12

Traditional

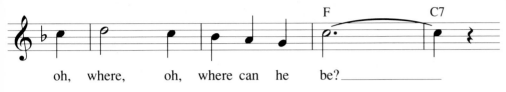

Oh, where, oh, where has my lit - tle dog gone,

oh, where, oh, where can he be? _____

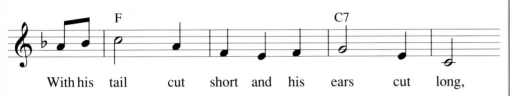

With his tail cut short and his ears cut long,

oh, where, oh, where can he be? _____

Reinforcing the Lesson

Introduce "Oh, Where Has My Little Dog Gone?" Have the children listen first to version 1 of the song and then to version 2, paying careful attention to the speed of each. Identify the speed of version 1 as slow and of version 2 as faster.

3 APPRAISAL

The children should be able to:
1. Identify the speed of different songs as fast or slow.
2. Identify part and whole with shapes.

SONGBOOK

"Marching Round the Levee," page 280 (a circle game)
"My Head and My Shoulders," page 281 (steady beat; body parts; part and whole)
"Hokey Pokey," page 273 (body parts; part and whole)

LESSON 5

Focus: Loud and Soft

Related Subject
Left, right, sizes

Objectives
To identify loud and soft
To become aware of environmental sounds
To hear and sing steady beat

Materials
Recordings: "Sing a Little Song"
    "Ears Hear"
    "Music of the World
    a-Turnin'"
    Recorded Lesson—
    "Learning 'Music of
    the World a-Turnin'' "
    Listening—"The Top" from
    Children's Games by
    Georges Bizet
Charts 2 and 6
X and 0 stick-ons
Copying Master 1-9 (optional)

1 SETTING THE STAGE

Review "Sing a Little Song" on page 2. Have the children listen for the words that repeat (*sing a little song*). Tell the children this repeat is called an echo. Then have the children listen to the song again, following the pictures on Chart 2. Notice that each time they see a child with one hand cupped to an ear there is an echo in the song. Have the children listen to the song again, singing the echoes as they occur. Encourage the children to recognize that they sang only part of the song. Then have them sing the whole song with the echoes softer than the other parts.

EXTENSION

1A, 1B
CD 1

EARS HEAR

Flies buzz,
Motors roar.
Kettles hiss,
People snore.
Dogs bark,
Birds cheep.
Autos honk: *Beep! Beep!*

Winds sigh,
Shoes squeak.
Trucks honk,
Floors creak.
Whistles toot,
Bells clang.
Doors slam: *Bang! Bang!*

Kids shout,
Clocks ding.
Babies cry,
Phones ring.
Balls bounce,
Spoons drop.
People scream: *Stop! Stop!*

—*Lucia and James L. Hymes, Jr.*

CHART
6   SOFT AND LOUD

LESSON 5

2 TEACHING THE LESSON

1. Introduce listening for loud and soft environmental sounds. Have the children:
• Discuss where they hear music in their everyday lives (radio, television, record or tape players, and so on).
• Name other interesting sounds that sometimes seem like music (birds singing, bells ringing, balls bouncing, and so on).

2. Introduce "Ears Hear." Have the children:
• Look at Chart 6. Take turns identifying each picture and the sound suggested by each picture.
• Decide which sounds are soft and which sounds are loud. Take turns identifying soft and loud sounds, either by pointing, or by placing the X on the loud sounds and the O on the soft sounds. (The fly and the bird make soft sounds. The rest of the pictures represent loud sounds.)
(You may wish to use Copying Master 1-9 at this time.)
• Practice each sound, paying attention to the level of how loud or soft each sound is.
• Listen to the first verse of "Ears Hear," joining in with the sound effects at the end of each line. Show how loud or soft each sound is by holding their hands close together for soft sounds and moving their hands apart for loud sounds.
• Listen to the rest of the poem, using hand movements to show how soft or loud each sound is, as above. (You may wish to have the children join in with the sound effects at the end of each line at this time, or repeat the whole poem and have them join in the second time.)

MORE MUSIC TEACHING IDEAS

1. Have the children experience the "noise pollution" suggested by the poem. Have each child in turn make one of the sounds, continuing until all the sounds are heard at the same time. Stop when you or one of the children say the last line of the poem. Then quietly listen for other sounds that they can still hear, for example, an airplane, the wind, people walking in the halls, children playing outside, thunder, and so on. Classify these sounds as loud or soft.
2. Take the children on a sound walk in the playground or around the neighborhood. Listen for different sounds and classify them as loud or soft. Make a list of these sounds. When you return to the classroom, have each child draw a picture of one of the sound sources. Create a bulletin board with the pictures classified under the words *Loud* and *Soft*.

LESSON 5

3. Introduce "Music of the World a-Turnin' " to practice identifying environmental sounds and loud and soft. Have the children:

• Briefly review the concept of everyday sounds that sometimes seem like music.
• Listen to "Music of the World a-Turnin'," patting the beat.
• Listen to the refrain as you lightly pat on the rests at the beginning of measures 3, 5, 7, and 11.
• Try to figure out where you patted (on silences in the melody) and the number of times you patted (four times).
• Listen again, patting with you on the rests.
• Echo-say the words in the refrain. Briefly discuss what the words mean, for example, you may wish to point out that *stop, look and listen* are three good things to do before crossing the street.
• Echo-sing each phrase of the refrain.
• Listen to entire song, singing along with the refrain and listening for the different sounds mentioned in each verse.
• Name some of the environmental sounds mentioned in the verses and classify them as loud, soft, or both.

Verse 1: laughing—both
        crying—both
        kids playing—both
Verse 2: traffic—loud
        horns blowing—loud
        heels clicking—soft
        ash cans rattling—loud
Verse 3: wind—both
        rain—usually soft
        thunder—loud

Key: G   Starting Pitch: D   Scale Tones: *so, la, do re mi so*

Music of the World a-Turnin'

Piano Accompaniment on page PA 14

Words and music by
Estelle Levitt and Don Thomas

Refrain

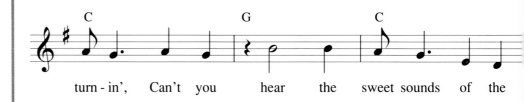

I   hear the   mu - sic of the   world   a-

turn - in', Can't you   hear   the sweet sounds of the

world   a - turn-in'?_____   Stop,   look and

E X T E N S I O N

lis - ten;   you   can   hear things a - grow-in'._____

You   can have mu - sic   wher - ev - er you   go.

1. I hear the music of the world a-turnin'.
   There are some folks laughin',
   There are some folks cryin',
   Kids playin' in the streets sound sweeter than a choir.
   All you gotta do is listen to hear.

2. I hear the symphony of the traffic in the city.
   There are horns a-blowin',
   There are heels a-clickin',
   Ash cans a-rattlin' as the sun begins to rise,
   All you gotta do is listen to hear.

3. The wind writes a special song for each and every day.
   It's got the rain a-dancin',
   And the thunder a-clappin'.
   Don't just ignore it: there's a concert all around you.
   All you gotta do is listen to hear.

LESSON 5

Reinforcing the Lesson

Review "The Top" to identify loud and soft in orchestral music. Have the children:

• Review the movements they did to show fast and slow in "The Top." (If time permits, have the children perform these movements with the music.)

• Listen to "The Top" while seated with their eyes closed. Identify the soft parts in the music by holding their hands close together, and the loud parts by holding their hands far apart.

• Discuss ways to move their whole bodies that suggest a top, and ways to show the loud parts in the music, for example, moving with their arms stretched out to each side.

• Listen to "The Top" again. Have a few volunteers move to show how they think the top moves. Repeat this activity until all the volunteers have had a turn moving with the music. (You may wish to have the children do this activity using arm movements only until the very end of the music, when at your signal they spin their bodies completely around.)

3 **APPRAISAL**

The children should be able to:

1. Identify soft music by holding their hands close together, and identify loud music by moving their hands apart as they listen to brief musical examples with their eyes closed.

2. Demonstrate awareness of environmental sounds by describing music in their everyday lives, by naming interesting sounds that seem like music, and by identifying some environmental sounds mentioned in "Music of the World a-Turnin'."

3. Pat the beat with reasonable accuracy with "Music of the World a-Turnin'."

SONGBOOK
"Hokey Pokey," page 273 (left/right)

LESSON 6

Focus: Loud and Soft

Related Subjects
Left and right, body parts, sizes

Objectives
To practice identifying loud and soft
To experience beat

Materials
Recordings: "Music of the World
a-Turnin' "
"The Giant's Shoes"
"Where Is
Thumbkin?"
"Ten Little Fingers"
(optional)
Listening—*Slavonic Dance
No. 7* by Antonín Dvořák
Chart 7
X and O stick-ons
Drum
Copying Master 1-10 (optional)

1 SETTING THE STAGE

Review "Music of the World a-Turnin' " on
page 18 to practice identifying loud and
soft. Have the children sing the refrain and
listen to the verses, as before. Then ask
them whether the part they sang, the
refrain, or the part they listened to, the
verses, was louder. (The refrain has more
people singing and is louder.)

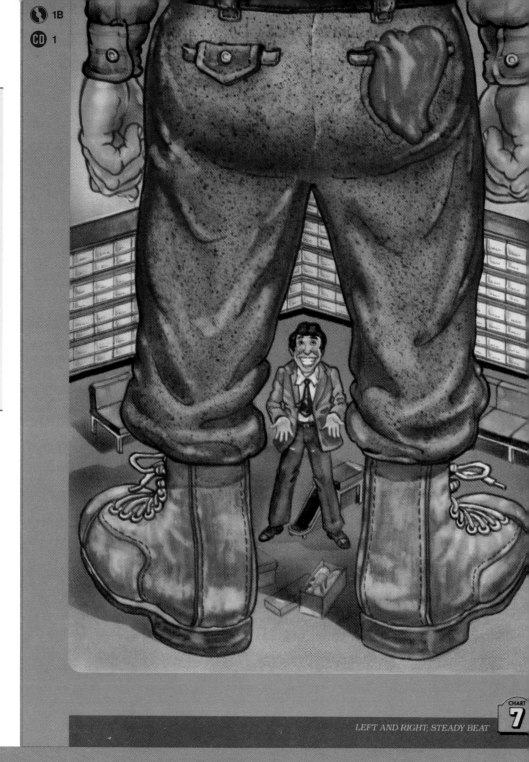

LEFT AND RIGHT: STEADY BEAT

CHART 7

E X T E N S I O N

KEYBOARD

Help the children practice identifying left
and right at the keyboard. First, have the
children hold both hands about eight
inches in front of their face, thumbs sepa-
rated from the rest of the fingers, looking
at the back of the hands. Decide which
hand forms the letter *L* (left). This device
will help them identify left and right. Give
each child the opportunity to stand at the
center of the keyboard and play several
sounds with the left hand, then several
sounds with the right hand. Encourage
them to use different fingers of each hand
to play different pitches.

THE GIANT'S SHOES

There once was a giant who needed new shoes,
  Left, right, tie them up tight.
Said he, "I'll go to the store and choose."
  Left, right, tie them up tight.
"High ones and low ones and black ones and brown."
  Left, right, tie them up tight.
"Give me the biggest you've got in the town."
  Left, right, tie them up tight.
The shoeman said, "Those are the biggest I've got."
  Left, right, tie them up tight.
"Take them and try them, Keep them or not."
  Left, right, tie them up tight.
"They fit," said the giant, "and squeak, I'll buy them."
  Left, right, tie them up tight.
He wore them all year 'cause he couldn't untie them.
  Left, right, tie them up tight.
  Left, right, *tie them up tight*!

—*Edwina Fallis*

LESSON 6

2 TEACHING THE LESSON

1. Introduce "The Giant's Shoes." Have the children:
• Look at Chart 7. Notice that the picture is of a giant buying shoes.
• Identify the giant's left foot and hand and right foot and hand. Do the same with themselves. Then watch as a volunteer points to or sticks the X on the giant's left hand.
(You may wish to use Copying Master 1-10 at this time.)
• Listen to "The Giant's Shoes," joining in on the repeated line *left, right, tie them up tight* as they are able. As they say *left, right* they pat their corresponding hand on their knees or on the floor. (Chart 7 with the X on the giant's left hand will help identify left for the children.) As they say *tie them up tight* they roll their fists around one another in front of them.
• Say the poem and do the movements again, using a louder voice when they say the giant's part and a softer voice when they say the shoe salesman's part.

MORE MUSIC TEACHING IDEAS

Have the children compare the repeated line *left, right, tie them up tight* in "The Giant's Shoes" with the refrain in "Music of the World a-Turnin'." Recognize that the repeated line is a kind of refrain, also.

CURRICULUM CONNECTION: ART

Left and Right Shoes—Have the children each make a pair of shoes for the giant. They can use crayons, stickers, fabric, and so on to decorate their shoes. Label the shoes L and R, or use different colored laces to identify left and right. Use the shoes as props as they say "The Giant's Shoes," holding up the appropriate shoe as they say *left* or *right*.

EXTRA HELP: IDENTIFYING LEFT AND RIGHT

Some children may need help identifying left and right. Put a small star, dot, or other sticker on the back of each of their left hands. As they do the movements with "The Giant's Shoes," tell them to always begin the movement with the hand which has the sticker on it.

LESSON 6

2. Introduce "Where Is Thumbkin?" to practice identifying loud and soft. Have the children:

• Listen as you sing the song, singing along and doing the finger play as soon as they are able.

Finger Play: Put both hands out of sight behind the back. As they sing each verse, bring both hands out in front, one at a time, on the words *here I am*. Only the finger mentioned in the verse is raised on each hand. On the last verse *(Where's the family?)* all the fingers are raised.

• Decide how many parts there are in the song (six). Recognize that each verse is part of the whole song.

• Sing the song again. (Choose five children to represent each of the five fingers. These children hide in different places around the room. As the class sings, each child in turn steps out of hiding and sings the responses *Here I am, here I am* and *Very well, I thank you*, and then hides again. All of the five children come out and sing together on the last verse.)

• Identify the sound of all the fingers singing together in the last verse as louder than the dynamic level of the solos in previous verses.

Key: F   Starting Pitch: F   Scale Tones: *so, do re mi fa so la*

Where Is Thumbkin?

Piano Accompaniment on page PA 16

French Folk Song

1. Where is thumb - kin? Where is thumb - kin?

Here I am, Here I am; How are you to-day, Sir?

Ver-y well, I thank you, Run a - way, run a - way.

2. pointer   5. little man

3. tall man   6. Where's the family . . .
   (Here we are, . . .)

4. ring man

CURRICULUM CONNECTION: LANGUAGE ARTS

Rhyming Words—After the children are familiar with "The Giant's Shoes" on page 21, have them listen to the poem again and identify the pairs of rhyming words (*right* and *tight, shoes* and *choose, brown* and *town, got* and *not, buy them* and *untie them*).

MORE MUSIC TEACHING IDEAS

Have the children learn "Ten Little Fingers."

Ten Little Fingers

Traditional

I have ten lit - tle fin - gers and they

all be - long to me! I can make them

do things, Would you like to see?

Key: F   Starting Pitch: C   Scale Tones: *so, la, ti, do re mi so*

LESSON 6

3. Introduce *Slavonic Dance* No. 7 by Antonín Dvořák to practice identifying loud and soft. Have the children:
• Listen with their eyes closed as you play soft and loud sounds on a drum. Identify soft sounds by holding their hands close together and loud sounds by holding their hands apart. Open their eyes and repeat the activity, making small body movements to show soft and large body movements to show loud.
• Listen to *Slavonic Dance* No. 7, responding to loud and soft in the music the same way as above. (You may wish to have the children move in small groups, with individual groups taking turns until everyone has had a chance to move.)

Reinforcing the Lesson

Play two sounds on a drum, one louder than the other. Have the children take turns identifying which of the two sounds is louder. (You may wish to have the entire class show whether the first or second sound is louder by holding up one or two fingers, as appropriate.)

3 APPRAISAL

The children should be able to:
1. Identify soft music by holding their hands close together, loud music by holding their hands apart as they listen to brief musical examples with their eyes closed, and hear two sounds and identify which one is clearly louder than the other.
2. Demonstrate beat with reasonable accuracy as they move to "The Giant's Shoes."

Ten Little Fingers from FINGER PLAY by Mary Miller and Paula Zajan. Used by permission of G. Schirmer, Inc.

THE COMPOSER

Antonín Dvořák (an' tō-nēn də-vor' zhak) (1841–1904)—Bohemian composer. Many music historians consider Dvořák to be one of the great nationalist composers. Dvořák based many of his melodies on eastern European folk music. However, his most famous work, Symphony No. 9 (*From the New World*), is influenced by American folk music. *Slavonic Dance* No. 7 is from a set of dances originally written as piano duets and later orchestrated by Dvořák.

SONGBOOK

"Hokey Pokey," page 273 (left/right)
"My Head and My Shoulders," page 281 (body parts)

LESSON 7

Focus: Part and Whole

Related Subjects
Names, colors, body parts

Objective
To practice identifying part and whole
To practice slow and fast
To experience beat

Materials
Recordings: "Hello Song"
"Willoughby Wallaby
Woo"
"My Legs and I"
"My Thumbs Are Starting
to Wiggle"
"Oh, Where Has My Little
Dog Gone?" (versions 1
and 2)

1 SETTING THE STAGE

Review "Hello Song" on page 6. Have the children pat the beat on different parts of their bodies as they sing the first verse. Sing the whole song, using different colors in different verses.

2 TEACHING THE LESSON

1. Introduce "Willoughby Wallaby Woo" to practice identifying part and whole.
Have the children:
• Listen to the song.
• Sing the song as they are able.
• Listen as you sing parts of the song, and signal whether they heard part of the song or the whole song by holding up one thumb if it was part or their whole hand if it was the whole song. Repeat the exercise two or three times.

E X T E N S I O N

MORE MUSIC TEACHING IDEAS
Have the children sing "Willoughby Wallaby Woo" using the names of children in the class.

 1A, 1B   **Key: G**   **Starting Pitch: G**   **Scale Tones:** *so, la, ti, do re mi*

 1

Willoughby Wallaby Woo

Piano Accompaniment on page PA 17

Music by Larry Miyata
Words by Dennis Lee

Wil-lough-by   wal-la-by   { wee, } { wustin, }

An   el-e-phant   sat on —   { me. } { Justin. }

Wil-lough-by   wal-la-by   { woo, } { wania, }

An   el-e-phant   sat on   { you. } { Tania. }

2. Introduce "My Legs and I" to identify fast and slow and part and whole. Have the children:
• Listen to the poem and identify the fast part (the first two stanzas) and slow part (the last two stanzas).
• Listen to the poem again, watching as a few volunteers do appropriate movements.
• Form small groups of four or five and take turns moving to the poem as the other groups watch.

3. Review "My Thumbs Are Starting to Wiggle" on page 11. Have the children:
• Sing the whole song and do the movements.
• Sing the song again, starting very slowly and gradually increasing the speed of the song and their movements until both are very fast by the end.
• Describe how the song changed (from slow to fast).

Reinforcing the Lesson

Review "Oh, Where Has My Little Dog Gone?" on page 15. Have the children listen again to each version and move in place (for example, swaying from side to side) to show that version 1 is slow and version 2 is faster.

3 APPRAISAL

The children should be able to:
1. Identify part and whole by holding up one thumb for part of a song and their entire hand for the whole song.
2. Identify slow and fast by increasing speed as they sing and move to "My Thumbs Are Starting to Wiggle."

MY LEGS AND I

I say to my legs,
"Legs," I say,
"Let's go out
To run and play."

So off we go
My legs and I
Skipping, romping,
Jumping high.

Then I say to my legs,
"Legs," I say,
"I'm much too tired
To run and play."

So legs and I
Toward home we go,
Walking and walking,
Slow, slow, slow.

— *Leland B. Jacobs*

SONGBOOK

"Hokey Pokey," page 273 (body parts; part and whole)
"My Head and My Shoulders," page 281 (body parts)

LESSON 8

Focus: Loud and Soft

Related Subjects
Animals, names

Objectives
To practice identifying and using loud and soft
To identify changes in overall effect or mood caused by changes in loud and soft

Materials
Recordings: "Willoughby Wallaby Woo"
"The Old Gray Cat"
"Bear Hunt"
"My Legs and I"
Copying Master 1-11 (optional)

1 SETTING THE STAGE

Review "Willoughby Wallaby Woo" on page 24 to practice identifying loud and soft. Have the children listen as you sing or play the recording of one verse of the song. Have them show whether they heard loud or soft by holding their hands apart for loud and holding their hands close together for soft. Then sing the song using names of different children in the class. Use different dynamic levels with each verse. (If the children join in singing with you, remind them to keep their voices at an indoor level for the louder verses.)

EXTENSION

MORE MUSIC TEACHING IDEAS

As the children sing additional verses of "Willoughby Wallaby Woo," provide an opportunity to practice planning loud and soft effects. Have each child choose beforehand whether his or her verse will be loud or soft. As each child's name is sung, have him or her indicate loud or soft with the appropriate hand sign as described in *Setting the Stage* above. Some children may wish to use a combination of loud and soft.

Key: G   Starting Pitch: D   Scale Tones: *so, la, ti, do mi*

The Old Gray Cat

Piano Accompaniment on page PA 18

Traditional American Song

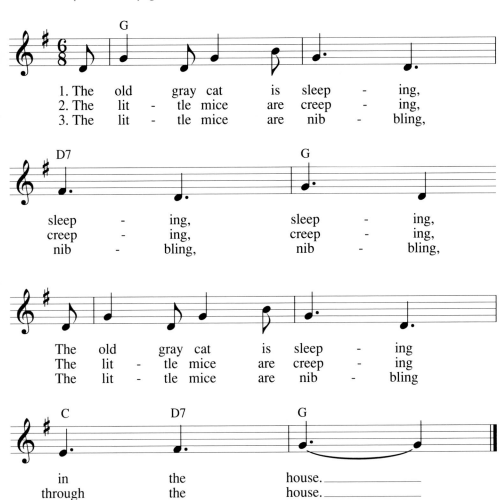

1. The old gray cat is sleep - ing,
2. The lit - tle mice are creep - ing,
3. The lit - tle mice are nib - bling,

sleep - ing,   sleep - ing,
creep - ing,   creep - ing,
nib - bling,   nib - bling,

The old gray cat is sleep - ing
The lit - tle mice are creep - ing
The lit - tle mice are nib - bling

in   the   house.
through the   house.
in   the   house.

4. The little mice are sleeping . . . in the house.

5. The old gray cat comes creeping . . . through the house.

6. The little mice all scamper . . . through the house.

---

2 TEACHING THE LESSON

1. Introduce "The Old Gray Cat" to practice loud and soft. Have the children:
• Listen to "The Old Gray Cat" to hear the story.
• Discuss the story, the sequence of events, and which verses were loud or soft. Briefly discuss how these changes in soft and loud made the song more exciting.
• Listen again, singing along as they are able. (You may wish to use Copying Master 1-11 at this time.)
• Dramatize the song. Have one child pretend to be the cat and a few other children pretend to be the mice. Repeat this activity at least once to give other children a chance to dramatize the song. (You may wish to give everyone a turn at this time, or repeat the activity using other children on another day.)

CURRICULUM CONNECTION: ART

Costumes—The children can make cat ears and mouse ears to wear as they dramatize "The Old Gray Cat." Cut out long, inch-wide strips of construction paper. Fasten them into round bands large enough to fit snugly on the head. Cut out ears—triangles for the cat and circles for the mice—and attach them to the head bands.

CURRICULUM CONNECTION: LANGUAGE ARTS

Vocabulary—Reinforce the concept of beginning and end by having the children listen carefully to the words of "The Old Gray Cat," and then identify the events at the beginning and the end of the song.

2. Introduce "Bear Hunt" to practice loud and soft. Have the children:
• Listen to you or the recording, echoing each line and doing the appropriate hand movements. (See the narration.)
• Discuss which places in the story were soft or loud. Briefly discuss how the changes in soft and loud made the story more exciting.

MORE MUSIC TEACHING IDEAS
Have the children accompany "My Legs and I" on classroom instruments. Play a few loud sounds, for example, on a tambourine, after the second stanza and a few soft sounds, for example, on a triangle, after the fourth stanza.

BEAR HUNT

Read the story one line at a time. The children echo each line, but do all the movements with the teacher at all times. Begin the story, patting the beat with alternating hands.

Going on a bear hunt! (Going on a bear hunt!)
I'm not scared! (I'm not scared!)
Got my lunch by my side... (Got my lunch by my side...)
...And my camera, too! (...And my camera, too!)
Coming to some tall grass! (Coming to some tall grass!)
Gotta get through! (Gotta get through!)
Can't go over it! (Can't go over it!)
Can't go under it! (Can't go under it!)
Gotta go through! (Gotta go through!)

(Brush palms together)

Going on a bear hunt! (Going on a bear hunt!)
I'm not scared! (I'm not scared!)
Got my lunch by my side... (Got my lunch by my side...)
...And my camera, too! (...And my camera, too!)
Coming to some thick mud! (Coming to some thick mud!)
Gotta get through! (Gotta get through!)
Can't go over it! (Can't go over it!)
Can't go under it! (Can't go under it!)
Gotta go through it! (Gotta go through it!)

(Move hands as if they were feet stepping through thick mud, making appropriate vocal sound effects. Then resume patting the beat.)

Going on a bear hunt! (Going on a bear hunt!)
I'm not scared! (I'm not scared!)
Got my lunch by my side... (Got my lunch by my side...)
...And my camera, too! (...And my camera, too!)
Coming to a big lake! (Coming to a big lake!)
Gotta get through! (Gotta get through!)
Can't go over it! (Can't go over it!)
Can't go around it! (Can't go around it!)
Gotta go through it! (Gotta go through it!)

(Move the hands as if swimming, making appropriate vocal sound effects. Then resume patting the beat.)

Going on a bear hunt! (Going on a bear hunt!)
I'm not scared! (I'm not scared!)
Got my lunch by my side . . . (Got my lunch by my side . . .)
. . . And my camera, too! (. . . And my camera, too!)
Coming to a tall tree! (Coming to a tall tree!)
Gotta get through! (Gotta get through!)
Can't go over it! (Can't go over it!)
Can't go around it! (Can't go around it!)
Gotta go up it! (Gotta go up it!)

(Move hands as if climbing up and then down a tree, making appropriate vocal sound effects. Then resume patting the beat.)

Going on a bear hunt! (Going on a bear hunt!)
I'm not scared! (I'm not scared!)
Got my lunch by my side . . . (Got my lunch by my side . . .)
. . . And my camera, too! (. . . And my camera, too!)
Coming to a dark cave! (Coming to a dark cave!)
Gotta get through! (Gotta get through!)
Can't go over it! (Can't go over it!)
Can't go around it! (Can't go around it!)
Gotta go in it! (Gotta go in it!)
It's dark in here! (It's dark in here!)

(slower)

There's something furry up ahead! (There's something
    furry up ahead!)
It has yellow eyes! (It has yellow eyes!)
And sharp teeth! (And sharp teeth!)
It's a bear!

(Move hands as if they are running feet, making appropriate vocal sound effects. Then repeat all the other movements and sound effects as fast as possible and in reverse order—climb up and down the tree, swim the lake, plod through the thick mud, wade through the tall grass. Finally, wipe brow with the back of the hand.)

WHEW!

LESSON 8

Reinforcing the Lesson

Have the children review "My Legs and I" on page 25. Show with hand signs whether they hear soft or loud. Then listen as you read the poem, saying the first two stanzas in a medium loud voice and the last two stanzas very softly. Ask the children to identify which parts of the poem were loud or soft and why. Briefly discuss the effect of loud and soft on the mood of the poem. Read the poem a few more times, with small groups of children doing appropriate movements each time.

3 APPRAISAL

The children should be able to:
1. Identify loud and soft by holding their hands close together for soft sounds and holding their hands apart for loud sounds.
2. Identify changes in effect and mood in "The Old Gray Cat," "Bear Hunt," and "My Legs and I" that were caused by changes in loud and soft.

SONGBOOK

"Jig Jog, Jig Jog," page 274 (a song about a pony)
"Little Spotted Puppy," page 276 (a song about a dog)
"Los Pollitos," page 279 (a song about baby chickens)

CORE
LESSON 9

Focus: Style

Related Subjects
Home, health

Objectives
To compare the styles of lullabies and marches
To practice identifying fast and slow
To practice identifying loud and soft

Materials
Recordings: "Hush, Little Baby"
Listening—"Berceuse" from *Dolly* Suite by Gabriel Fauré
Listening—"March" from *Summer Day* Suite by Sergei Prokofiev
"Wide Awake"
"Brush Your Teeth"
Chart 8
Triangle, hand drum
Copying Masters 1-12, 1-13 (optional)

1 SETTING THE STAGE

Have the children review "Hush, Little Baby" on page 14 and tell whether it is fast or slow (slow), and loud or soft (soft). Ask why the song is slow and soft (it is sung to help someone fall asleep). Then ask the children if they can tell what this kind of song is called (lullaby). Have them listen to the song again, singing the last word in each verse (the rhyming word), or simply singing along as they are able.

2 TEACHING THE LESSON

1. Introduce "Berceuse" from *Dolly* Suite by Gabriel Fauré and "March" from *Summer Day* Suite by Sergei Prokofiev. Have the children:
• Look at Chart 8 and briefly discuss what the child is doing in each picture (sleeping, marching).

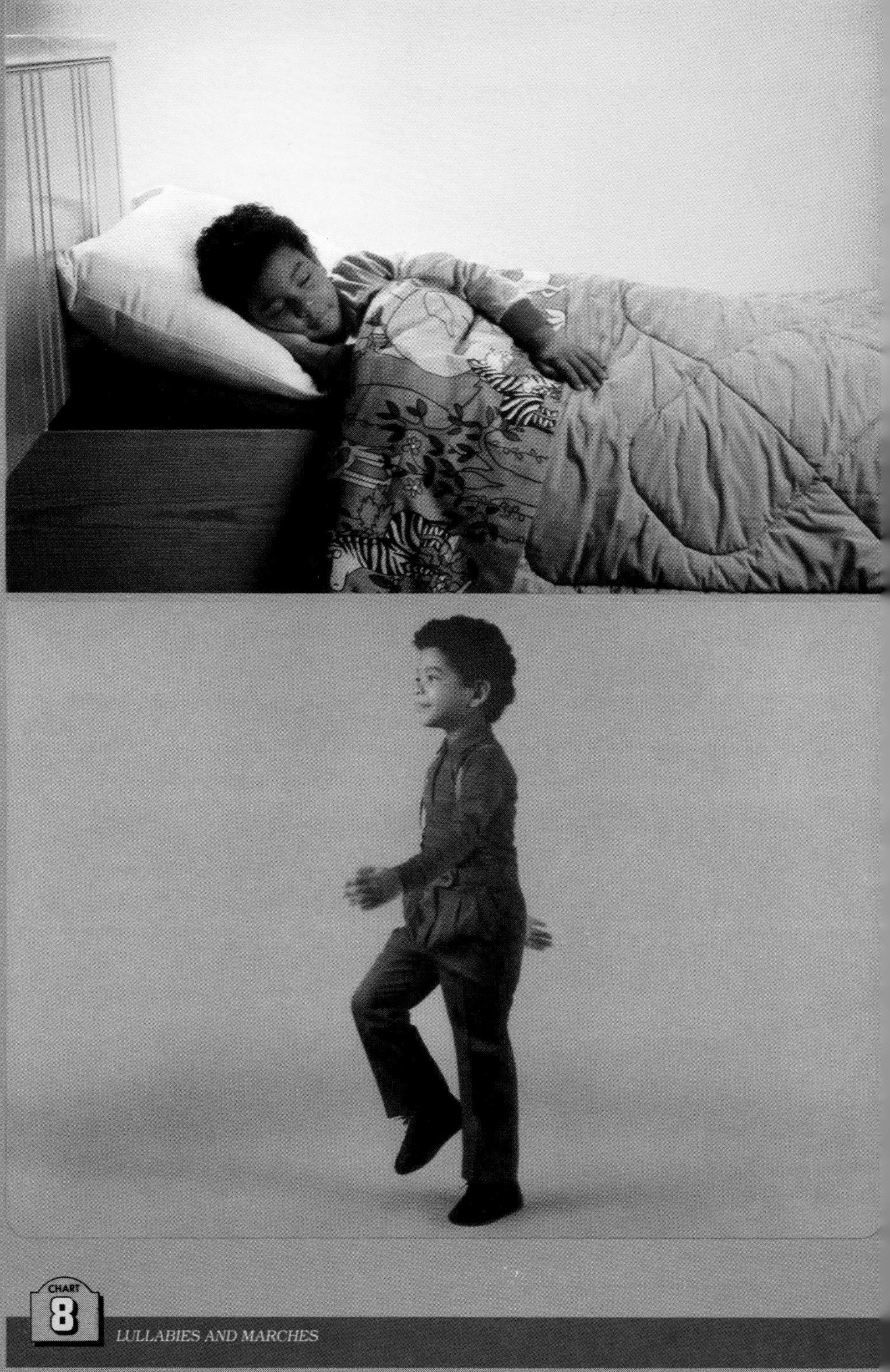

CHART
8 LULLABIES AND MARCHES

EXTENSION

THE COMPOSERS

Gabriel Fauré (gab′rē-əl fo-rā′) (1845–1924) —French composer. Fauré began his musical training at an early age. He worked mainly as an organist, and also taught. Perhaps his best-known work is his Requiem for chorus and orchestra. The *Dolly* Suite, first written as a piano duet, was later orchestrated by the French composer Rabaud.
Sergei Prokofiev (ser-gā′ prō-kof′yef) (1891–1953)—Soviet composer. Prokofiev's music shows the styles of both old and modern music. His symphonic fairy tale *Peter and the Wolf* has been called one of the best young person's guides to the orchestra, and is a children's classic. The *Summer Day* Suite is a group of seven pieces from Prokofiev's piano work *Music for Children*, which he arranged for orchestra.

MORE MUSIC TEACHING IDEAS

The children may wish to share other lullabies they know with the class.

SPECIAL LEARNERS

Reinforce the concept of different musical styles for learners who benefit from visual reinforcement of concepts. Have the children find magazine pictures or do line drawings to represent the soft, slow qualities of the lullaby "Berceuse" and the louder, faster qualities of "March." Place the Big Book on the chalkboard tray and mount the pictures on the chalkboard near the corresponding parts of Chart 8 using masking tape.

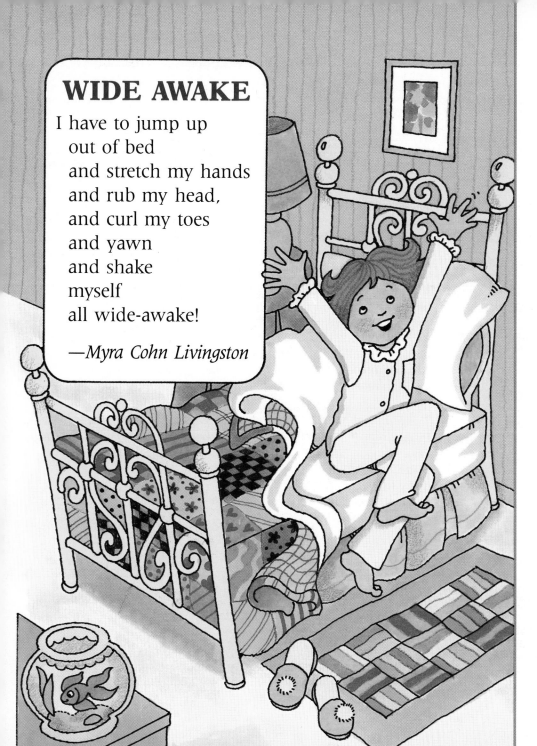

WIDE AWAKE

I have to jump up
  out of bed
  and stretch my hands
  and rub my head,
  and curl my toes
  and yawn
  and shake
  myself
  all wide-awake!

—*Myra Cohn Livingston*

• Describe in their own words what kind of music might fit each picture. (Help the children become familiar with the terms *lullaby* and *march* and encourage them to use these terms when describing each musical style.)

• Listen first to "Berceuse" and then to "March" to test their predictions. Move as each piece of music suggests.

• Discuss if the music was close to their predictions. (The predictions should be generally accurate. "Berceuse" is slow and soft, and "March" is fast. However, although "March" ends loudly, it begins softly. This is probably different from what they expected.)

2. Introduce "Wide Awake" to practice responding to directions. Have the children:

• Listen to the poem, moving as the words suggest.

MORE MUSIC TEACHING IDEAS

As the children look at Chart 8 have them decide which instrument, for example, triangle or drum, goes best with each picture. (Gentle triangle sounds go with the sleeping boy and loud drum sounds go with the marching boy.) Have the children watch as one volunteer responds by pretending to sleep or by marching as you play either the triangle or the drum. Then have the entire class do this. You may wish to make a game out of seeing who can lie quietly when they hear the triangle and march safely when they hear the drum. Have children who respond well take turns playing the instruments as the rest of the class moves.

CLASSROOM MANAGEMENT

Establish clear guidelines for listening and moving experiences to minimize inappropriate behavior. Before playing listening selections, briefly discuss the importance of listening to music without making additional sounds. Since music is "art in sound," extra sounds can cover up the musical sounds that the composer wants us to hear. Before they begin movement activities, stress the importance of each child respecting the other children's spaces. They should not move or bump into any other child's space whether that child is moving or standing still.

CORE
LESSON 9

3. Introduce "Brush Your Teeth" to hear another song in the style of a march. Have the children:
• Listen to "Brush Your Teeth," pantomiming brushing their teeth in rhythm along with the *ch ch ch ch ch* part of the song.
• Decide if the song is more like a lullaby or a march (march). Explain why (it is louder and faster than a lullaby).
• Listen to the song again, singing along as they are able. Pantomime brushing their teeth as before. (You may wish to use Copying Master 1-12 at this time.)

Brush Your Teeth

Piano Accompaniment on page PA 19

Adapted and arranged by
Louise Dain and Raffi

1. When you wake up in the morn-ing and it's
(2.) wake up in the morn-ing and it's
(3.) wake up in the morn-ing and it's
(4.) wake up in the morn-ing and it's

quar-ter to one___ And you want to have a
quar-ter to two___ And you want to find
quar-ter to three___ And your mind starts hum-ming
quar-ter to four___ And you think you hear a

lit-tle fun,
some-thing to do,
twid-dle de dee,
knock on your door,
} you brush your teeth, *ch ch ch ch ch

ch ch ch ch,___ You brush your teeth, ch ch ch ch ch

ch ch ch ch___ 2.-4. When you ch ch ch ch___ 5. When you

* "ch" is an unpitched sound

EXTENSION

CURRICULUM CONNECTION: HEALTH

Brushing Teeth—Learning good health habits is an important part of the kindergarten curriculum. The following activity can help encourage good dental care at home. Have the children make a chart that shows one calendar week. (You may wish to use Copying Master 1-13 at this time.) For a one-week period have the children check one box on their charts for each day they remember to brush their teeth. Then have them sing "Brush Your Teeth" after marking their charts. You may wish to have the children make giant toothbrushes, using the following directions, and mount the charts on their toothbrushes. Fold a 12″ x 18″ piece of construction paper in half. Cut out a 9″ x 3″ section at the open edge (see illustration a).

a.
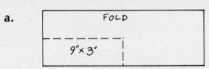

Fold a sheet of white paper toweling in half lengthwise. Cut the open edges in a jagged pattern to resemble bristles. Glue the toweling inside the wide end of the brush handle (see illustration b).

b.
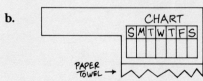

Glue the chart onto the wide end of the brush handle above the bristles.

wake up in the morn-ing and it's quar-ter to five___ And you

just can't wait to come a - live___ You brush your

teeth, ch ch ch ch ch ch ch ch ch,___ You brush your

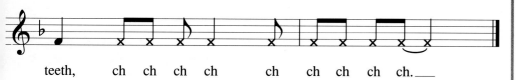

teeth, ch ch ch ch ch ch ch ch ch. ___

Reinforcing the Lesson

Have the children remember which musical pieces they heard are lullabies ("Hush, Little Baby" and "Berceuse"), and which are marches ("March" and "Brush Your Teeth"). Decide which musical pieces go with each of the pictures on Chart 8. Then have the children name and compare some musical characteristics of a lullaby (generally soft and slow) and of a march (louder and faster than a lullaby).

3 APPRAISAL

The children should be able to:
1. Compare the style of a lullaby with the style of a march.
2. Identify fast and slow in different music.
3. Identify loud and soft in different music.

SONGBOOK
"Step in Time," page 288 (march)

LESSON 10

Focus: Fast and Slow

Related Subjects
Positions, body parts, animals, health

Objective
To practice identifying fast and slow

Materials
Recordings: "Bear Hunt"
"Where Is Thumbkin?"
"Brush Your Teeth"
"The Old Gray Cat"

1 SETTING THE STAGE

Have the children pat a steady beat with you, starting slowly and getting faster. Review the terms *fast* and *slow*. Review "Bear Hunt" on page 28, with the children doing the echoes. Then have the children identify one part of the story where they moved slowly and one part where they moved fast by repeating the movement they did in that part (slow: going in the cave; fast: running from the bear).

Tell the children to think about slow and fast as they sing the songs in this lesson, deciding whether each song is slow, fast, or a combination of slow and fast.

2 TEACHING THE LESSON

1. Review "Where Is Thumbkin?" on page 22 to practice identifying slow tempo. Have the children:
• Sing the song, doing the finger play.
• Identify the speed, answering with a show of hands whether they thought the song was fast or slow (slow).
• Play the game on page 22. (You may wish to play the game more than once in order to give more children a turn doing the solos.)

EXTENSION

COOPERATIVE LEARNING

Have the children become acquainted with the concept of working in groups while reviewing the game for "Where Is Thumbkin?" Divide the children randomly into groups of five. Within each group assign the roles of thumbkin, pointer, tall man (or woman), ring man (or woman), and little man (or woman). Ask the members of each group to decide together where their hiding place will be. Then while the children remain seated, sing the questions. For each verse the appropriate child in each group sings the answer and then goes to the hiding place. On the last verse, all the groups stand together to sing "here we are." Praise the children's skill in successfully working as a group and singing together.

LESSON 10

2. Review "Brush Your Teeth" on page 32 to practice identifying fast tempo. Have the children:
• Sing the song, pretending to brush their teeth during the *ch ch ch ch ch* parts of the song.
• Identify the speed, answering with a show of hands whether they thought the song was fast or slow (fast).

Reinforcing the Lesson

Have the children review "The Old Gray Cat" on page 27. Sing the song, using appropriate hand movements to identify the slow parts (first five verses) and the fast part (last verse). Sing the song again, with a few children pretending to be the cat and the mice. Repeat this activity to give other children a chance to play the cat and the mice.

3 APPRAISAL

The children should be able to identify the tempos of different songs by moving at appropriate speeds or with a show of hands.

SONGBOOK

"Jig Jog, Jig Jog," page 274 (a song about a pony)
"Little Spotted Puppy," page 276 (a song about a dog)
"Los Pollitos," page 279 (a song about baby chickens)

REVIEW AND EVALUATION

REVIEW

Objectives
To review songs, skills, and concepts learned in Unit 1
To measure the children's ability to:
1. Identify soft and loud
2. Identify fast and slow

Materials
Recordings: "Sing a Little Song"
"Brush Your Teeth"
"Walk to School"
"Where Is Thumbkin?"
"Music of the World a-Turnin'"
Evaluation Unit 1 Copying Master

TEACHING THE LESSON

Review the songs and concepts in Unit 1 by dramatizing a story. Have the children:
• Listen as you tell the story, singing and performing the activities at the appropriate places. (As the children sing and move, observe and evaluate individuals and the class as a whole as to how their responses indicate their level of understanding.)

Going to School
You woke up one morning to see the sun shining brightly in a clear, blue sky. This made you feel very happy. You were so happy that you sang a good morning song before you even got out of bed. The song had an echo part, and you sang that, too.
• Sing "Sing a Little Song" on page 2, singing the echo parts more softly than the rest of the song. Show recognition of loud and soft by holding their hands close together when the music is soft and holding their hands apart when the music is loud.

After you sang, you hopped out of bed to get ready for school. You remembered, of course, to brush your teeth after breakfast.
• Sing "Brush Your Teeth" on page 32, pretending to brush their teeth during the *ch ch ch ch ch* parts of the song. Indicate the speed of the song (fast) with the brushing movement.

It was time to leave for school. At first you walked at your usual medium speed.
• Sing "Walk to School" on page 4, singing and walking at a medium tempo.

Soon you felt tired, and began to walk at a slow speed.
• Sing "Walk to School," singing and walking at a slow tempo.

1A, 1B, 2A
CD 1

REVIEW AND EVALUATION

Suddenly you realized that you were almost late for school, so you walked as fast as you could.
• Sing "Walk to School," singing and walking at a fast tempo.

You got to school and into your classroom as the bell was ringing, just in time to play the singing game "Where Is Thumbkin?"
• Sing "Where Is Thumbkin?" on page 22 and play the game. Then tell if the speed of the song was fast or slow (slow).

Then the class sang another song with the teacher, "Music of the World a-Turnin'." You were so glad you got to school in time to join in with the class.
• Sing "Music of the World a-Turnin' " on page 18. Name some of the environmental sounds mentioned in the verses and classify them as loud or soft (answers may vary, but accept any reasonable ones). Then sing the song again.

EVALUATION

Evaluation Unit 1 Copying Master can be found in the *Teacher's Resource Book* with full directions for providing an evaluation of the child's progress.

ELEMENTS OF MUSIC	UNIT 2 OBJECTIVES	Lesson 1 CORE Focus: Long and Short	Lesson 2 CORE Focus: Melody
Dynamics	Use terms *loud* and *soft* in singing and moving	Move to sounds until they are too soft to hear	
Tone Color	Use singing and speaking voices Explore environmental and classroom instruments' capacity to make long/short, high/low sounds	Find long and short environmental sounds Use classroom instruments to show long and short sounds	Use singing and speaking voices
Tempo	Use various tempos	Sing songs at a medium tempo	Sing and move to songs in a medium tempo Change movements when tempo of song changes
Duration/ Rhythm	**Identify long/short sounds and symbols** Speak, play combinations of long and short sounds Keep beat with body percussion	Relate long and short rectangles to long and short sounds: ☐ = long ☐ = short Move to long and short sounds Pat the steady beat	Pat the beat Pat, following signals
Pitch	Associate high with small, low with large Identify melody as the tune Use terms *high/low* Learn songs from charts that show high/low		Identify melody as the tune of a song
Texture	Begin to recognize melody alone or with accompaniment	Sing songs with accompaniments	Experience melody alone and with accompaniment
Form	Hear whole/part Begin to recognize same/ different (melody, rhythm, words of song) Begin responding to phrase length	Identify parts of a song Listen for repeated words	Identify same and different parts Identify words that are the same Move to show phrase lengths
Style	Notice ways that elements of music affect style Listen to a contemporary composition		Hear song accompanied by Orff instruments

PURPOSE Unit 2: Fall Festival

This unit is designed to be taught during the early autumn. Through songs and listening selections that focus on October activities and holidays the children will experience identifying long and short, be introduced to the term *melody*, and begin to distinguish between melody alone or with accompaniment.

SUGGESTED TIME FRAME

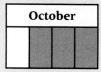

October

FOCUS

Core Lessons 1, 2, 5
• Long and Short
• Melody
• Melody Alone or with Accompaniment

Lessons 3, 4, 6
• Long and Short
• High and Low
• High and Low

Lesson 3 Focus: Long and Short	Lesson 4 Focus: High and Low	Lesson 5 CORE Focus: Melody Alone or with Accompaniment	Lesson 6 Focus: High and Low
Sing echo part more softly			
Identify classroom instruments that play long and short sounds	Use speaking and singing voices Play pitched instruments to show higher and lower sounds	Listen to synthesizer Play unpitched instruments to show long and short Play classroom instruments with a song	Speak and sing high and low Play high and low unpitched and pitched instruments
	Move to show the slow or fast tempo of the music		
Identify long and short sounds and symbols Play long and short sounds Pat, following signals Play the beat	Pat the steady beat	Practice identifying long and short	Pat and play the beat
Play A-F on bells Sing echoes individually	See relationship between lower and larger, and higher and smaller Sing, move to, and play high and low See high and low on charts Move to show upward and downward melodic direction	Practice identifying melody as the tune of a song Practice identifying high and low	Practice identifying high and low Play, move, speak, and sing high and low See, point to high and low
Play a bordun accompaniment		Distinguish between melody alone or with accompaniment Use term *melody*	Play a bordun accompaniment
		Use term *part* to focus on part of a song Identify parts of a listening selection	Identify parts of a listening selection
		Listen to contemporary composition	Listen to a contemporary composition

BULLETIN BOARD

Using seasonal objects such as pumpkins, a scarecrow, autumn leaves, and so on, divide the bulletin board into two halves. On one half of the bulletin board put pictures of classroom instruments that make long and short sounds, for example, cymbals and a wood block. Put a long or short strip of paper, yarn, or ribbon under each instrument to identify it as a long- or short-sounding instrument. On the other half of the bulletin board show two pictures of children singing; one picture by itself and the other with pictures of classroom instruments.

Fall Music Festival

Focus: Long and Short

Objective

To identify long and short shapes and sounds by observing, singing, listening, and playing

Materials

Recordings: "I'll Just Be Myself"
Recorded Lesson—"Short and Long Sounds"
"Take a Bite of Music"
Charts 9 and 10
Cymbal and wood block, or other long- and short-sound sources
Copying Master 2-1 (optional)

Vocabulary

long, short

1 SETTING THE STAGE

Have the children listen to "I'll Just Be Myself" and identify the five characters in the song (scarecrow, pumpkin, small tree, snowman, child). Identify these five characters at the top of Chart 9. Then look at the bottom of the chart. These pictures illustrate the movements for the refrain (shake head from side to side; smile and nod head; point to self with both hands; hold up both hands, palms facing out, and move them together in a circular pattern for a "cool wave"). Practice these movements and then do them with each refrain as they listen to the song again. (You may wish to use Copying Master 2-1 at this time.)

2A

CD 1

Key: G   Starting Pitch: D   Scale Tones: *so, la, do re mi fa*

I'll Just Be Myself

Piano Accompaniment on page PA 22

Casual, but moving

Words and music by
Lynn Freeman Olson

1. I   am a scare - crow,   I   want to know
2. I   am a pump - kin,   I   want to know
3. I   am a small   tree,   I   want to know

How do I look scar - y   when I scare a crow?
Who will put the light   in   when I want to glow?
What will ev - er hap - pen   when the winds do blow?

Refrain

Guess I should-n't wor - ry,   guess I'm do - in' fine,

I'll just be my-self   and I'll shine, shine, shine!

4. I am a snowman, I want to know
   Where goes mister snowman when there's no more snow?
   Refrain

5. I am a small one, I want to know
   What will ever happen, will I ever grow?
   Refrain

EXTENSION

CURRICULUM CONNECTION: ART

Character Masks—Have each child choose a character from "I'll Just Be Myself" (scarecrow, pumpkin, tree, snowman) and make a paper-plate mask of that character. (Children who choose the tree can draw leafy branches on their mask.) Attach a stick to each mask so it can be held up in front of the face. As the children sing the song have them hold up their masks during the appropriate verse. All masks remain down during the last verse.

COOPERATIVE LEARNING

To begin working together, have the children dramatize the characters in "I'll Just Be Myself" in groups. To form groups, have the class "count off" using the five character names: scarecrow, pumpkin, small tree, snowman, and small child. Repeat the sequence until every child is assigned. Then have all the "scarecrows" move to one area of the room, all the "pumpkins" move to another area, and so on. Once groups are formed, have them remember their character's problem in the song and plan simple movements to dramatize their verse as it is sung. Skills to praise are forming a group quickly, giving ideas, and listening to others.

CHART
9

"I'LL JUST BE MYSELF"

LESSON 1

2 TEACHING THE LESSON

1. Introduce long and short through sight and sound. Have the children:

• Look at Chart 10 and identify the scarecrow and the crow. Notice the long and short rectangles.

• Point toward the long rectangle when you say *long*, and toward the short rectangle when you say *short*.

• Listen to the sound of a cymbal and identify it as a sound that lasts a long time. Then listen to the cymbal again, moving one arm for as long as they hear the sound. Notice that the sound begins to get softer almost immediately. Repeat this activity, moving different parts of the body, and finally moving the whole body. Move like a scarecrow in a gentle wind.

• Listen to the sound of a wood block and move their whole bodies for as long as they hear the sound. Compare this sound to the sound of the cymbal. Move to the sound of the wood block again, making short, quick movements and freezing into a statue on every sound. Move like a crow pecking at seeds on the ground.

• Move like a scarecrow or a crow as appropriate, as you play the cymbal and wood block in random order.

• Listen to "Short and Long Sounds," making short or long movements as appropriate.

2. Introduce long and short environmental sounds. Have the children:

• Watch as one child finds a way to make a long sound on some object, for example, ripping a long piece of paper.

• Explore sounds in the classroom until everyone finds a long or short sound.

• Take turns playing their chosen sounds. Decide together whether each sound is long or short. (There is a way to play long and short sounds on any object unless the object is very smooth.)

CHART 10
LONG AND SHORT

E X T E N S I O N

CLASSROOM MANAGEMENT

Establish guidelines for exploring sounds in the classroom. For example, have the children take their time and walk around the room as they explore. Have them look for pleasant sounds. Tell the children to respect personal property. If they want to try something that belongs to another child, ask first. If the other child says no, move on and try something else. Be careful not to damage anything. If an object can be easily damaged, do not use it.

KEYBOARD

To explore long and short sounds on the keyboard, play a pitch on the piano as the children listen. Then play the pitch again, pressing down the sustaining pedal (the floor pedal farthest to the right). Help them compare the two sounds and determine that the second sound is longer. Give the children an opportunity to try the same activity. On the electronic keyboard, have them discover that some voice sounds continue as long as a key is depressed.

Key: D   Starting Pitch: D   Scale Tones: *do re ri mi fa so la do¹*

Take a Bite of Music

Piano Accompaniment on page PA 24

*Words and music by
Mary Ann Hall*

Take a bite of mu-sic,— it real-ly is a treat.

Take a bite of mu-sic,— serve it with a beat.

Take a bite of mu-sic,— there are man-y ways— to play.

Ev - 'ry-bod - y needs it— ev - er-y day.—

• Play their sound at the appropriate time as you point to the long and short rectangles on Chart 10 in random order.

Reinforcing the Lesson

Introduce "Take a Bite of Music." Have the children follow you, patting a steady beat on their knees. Then have them listen for the longer sounds at the end of each line, making long movements when they hear these sounds. Have them listen for repeated words in the song (*take a bite of music* repeats three times). Listen to the song again, singing *take a bite of music* each time they hear it. Listen for the words that end the song (*ev'rybody needs it every day*). Then practice singing that last phrase a few times. Sing the song, identifying the three remaining parts (*it really is a treat*, *serve it with a beat*, and *there are many ways to play*). Choose a different movement for each phrase to help remember it. Then sing the song, doing the movements to help remember the words. Pat the beat when they are not moving.

3 APPRAISAL

The children should be able to move to identify long and short sounds, find long- and short-sound sources, and play long or short sounds as indicated by visual cues.

SONGBOOK

"Jack-o'-Lantern," page 244 (long and short sounds)
"Epo i tai tai e," page 269 (long and short sounds)

LESSON 2

Focus: Melody

Objectives
To recognize the term *melody* as the tune
To identify words that are the same in songs

Materials
Recordings: "Take a Bite of Music"
"Pumpkin Stew"
"Let's Make a Jack-o'-
Lantern"
"Columbus Sailed with
Three Ships"
Chart 11
Copying Masters 2-2, 2-3, 2-4 (optional)

Vocabulary
melody

1 SETTING THE STAGE

Review "Take a Bite of Music" on page 41. Have the children remember the repeated words and the movements they used to help remember other words in the song. Have them step the beat on *ev'rybody needs it every day.* Then have them move about the room only during this phrase. At the end of the phrase find a partner standing nearby. Sing the song, facing their partner and doing the movements together. On the last phrase, wave goodbye to their partner and walk again until they find a new partner. Do this several times. Identify melody as the tune of the song. Notice that when they sing the song without any accompaniment they are singing melody alone.

2 TEACHING THE LESSON

1. Introduce "Pumpkin Stew" to practice identifying melody. Have the children:
• Pat the beat as they listen to the song. Identify words that they hear more than once *(pumpkin stew).*
• Sing the song, patting the beat on *pumpkin stew,* and shrugging their shoulders on *what shall we put in the.*
• Look at Chart 11 as they sing the song. Identify the same and different parts of the melody. (Remind the children that they are singing the melody or tune.) (You may wish to use Copying Master 2-2 at this time.)

MELODY ALONE

CHART 11

E X T E N S I O N

Key: G minor   Starting Pitch: D   Scale Tones: *mi so la ti do'*

Pumpkin Stew

Music by R. DeLelles
Words by S. S.

Pump-kin stew,   Pump-kin stew,   What shall we put in the pump-kin stew?

MORE MUSIC TEACHING IDEAS

As the children learn about melody and accompaniment, you may wish to have an older class prepare an accompaniment to "Pumpkin Stew." The younger children can sing the song while the older children play the accompaniment. Older children enjoy this song and the stew-making activities as much as younger children.

Key: F   Starting Pitch: C   Scale Tones: *so, la, ti, do re mi fa so la*

Let's Make a Jack-o'-Lantern

Piano Accompaniment on page PA 26

Words and music by
Daniel Hooley

1. Let's make a   jack,   jack,   jack - o' - lan - tern,
2. In - side we'll   put,   put,   put   a   can - dle,

I'll show you   how,   how,   how,   it's   done;
To make   a   shine,   shine,   shin - ing   light;

You   sim - ply   scoop   out   a   lit - tle   yel - low   pump - kin,
We'll make a   fine   jack - o' - lan - tern   for our   win - dow

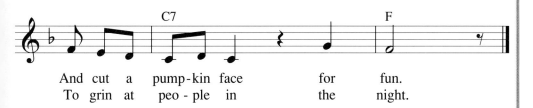

And   cut   a   pump-kin   face   for   fun.
To   grin   at   peo - ple   in   the   night.

Voice

Pump-kin stew, pump-kin stew, What shall we put in the pump-kin stew?

AG

Tri.

TB

BX

LESSON 2

2. Create a make-believe stew. Have the children:
• Think of ingredients that might go into pumpkin stew. Indicate that they have an idea by putting their hands on their head.
• When everyone has an idea, sing the song twice. Then have four children put ingredients into a make-believe stew pot placed in the center or front of the room. (You can use the classroom wastebasket as a make-believe pot. The children can put in imaginary stew ingredients or silly ingredients.)
(You may wish to use Copying Master 2-3 at this time.)
• Sing the song twice after each group of four children puts their ingredients in the stew. Pat the beat or pretend to stir stew as they sing. (Evaluate their understanding of fast and slow by changing the tempo and checking to see if they change their stirring and patting movements.)
• After everyone has had a turn putting ingredients in the stew, have one child set the stew aside to simmer.

3. Introduce "Let's Make a Jack-o'-Lantern." Have the children:
• Follow your example, tapping three times when you touch your head three times, twice when you touch your chin twice, and once when you touch your nose once.
• Listen to the song and follow your motions. (Touch your head when words repeat three times; your chin after *done, fun, light,* and *night;* and your nose after *lantern, pumpkin* [measure 6], *face, candle, window,* and *in.*)
• Identify the singing as the melody.
(You may wish to use Copying Master 2-4 at this time.)

Reinforcing the Lesson

Preview "Columbus Sailed with Three Ships" on page 44. Have the children echo-say, then echo-sing, the names of the three ships in the order they occur in the last part of the song. Have them listen to the recording and sing the echoes. Have them identify the singing as the melody.

3 APPRAISAL

The children should be able to:
1. Sing "Take a Bite of Music" and "Pumpkin Stew" and identify the tune of each song as the melody.
2. Identify the repeated words in "Take a Bite of Music" and "Pumpkin Stew."

SONGBOOK

"Little Spotted Puppy," page 276 (repeated word patterns)
"The Bus," page 266 (repeated word patterns)
"Jig Jog, Jig Jog," page 274 (repeated word patterns)

LESSON 3

Focus: Long and Short

Objective
To identify long and short by moving and playing instruments

Materials
Recordings: "Columbus Sailed with Three Ships"
"Let's Make a Jack-o'-Lantern"
"Black and Gold"
Chart 10
Cymbal and wood block, or other long- and short-sounding unpitched instruments, hand drum
Copying Masters 2-5, 2-6 (optional)

1 SETTING THE STAGE

Have the children review long and short sounds. Have them look at Chart 10 on page 40 and remember an instrument that makes a long sound (cymbal) and one that makes a short sound (wood block). Then have them play long and short sounds as one child conducts by randomly pointing to the long and short symbols on the chart.

2 TEACHING THE LESSON

1. Review "Columbus Sailed with Three Ships." Have the children:
• Echo-say, then echo-sing, the names of the three ships in the order they occur in the last part of the song.
• Show how a ship moves on the waves using long, rolling movements as they listen to the first part of the song. Then sing the echo in the second part softly.

Columbus Sailed with Three Ships

Piano Accompaniment on page PA 28

Words and music by
Margaret Dugard

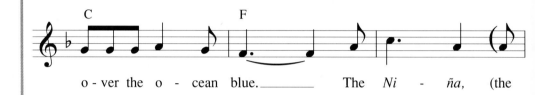

Co - lum - bus sailed with three   ships,   three   ships,

three   ships,   Co - lum - bus sailed with three   ships

o - ver the o - cean blue._____ The *Ni - ña,* (the

EXTENSION

CURRICULUM CONNECTION: ART

Long and Short Collages—Have the children glue long and short lengths of yarn onto strips of paper to create their own long and short collages. Then do the following activity. Form groups of three. Each group chooses a conductor, and the other two children in the group select between a long- and a short-sounding instrument. The conductor moves a pointer along her or his collage from left to right. The child with the long-sounding instrument plays when the pointer comes to a long piece of yarn, and the child with the short-sounding instrument plays when the pointer comes to a short piece. Switch parts so each child has a turn conducting her or his collage and playing long and short sounds.

COOPERATIVE LEARNING

To do the Curriculum Connection at left as a cooperative learning experience, form the groups of three randomly. Divide the number of children in the class by three, then count off by that number. All the children with the same number form a group. An alternative is to have the children draw prepared cards from a container. Each card will have pictured a long line, a short line, or a conductor's baton. For a class of 21, for example, make seven of each symbol using seven different colors. To form groups the children find others whose slips have the same color. Each group will have one long line, one short line, and one conductor.

MORE MUSIC TEACHING IDEAS

1. Have the children watch as you use long, rolling movements to "sail" each one of three paper boats or cutouts labeled *Niña, Pinta,* and *Santa María,* respectively to three different children. Then sing the song. During the second part, the child holding the appropriate ship sings each echo. Sing the song again, with the three children using the same long, rolling movements to sail the ships to three other children. Continue the game until every child has had at least one chance to sing a solo echo. (You may wish to use Copying Master 2-5 at this time.)
2. Have the children play the following accompaniment with "Columbus Sailed with Three Ships." Play a simple F C chord bordun on the beat. Alternate playing A

Ni - ña), the Pin - ta (the Pin - ta), the

San - ta Ma - rí - a (the San - ta Ma -

rí - a), sailed the o - cean blue._____

and F on the words *three ships* using a high-pitched instrument such as a glockenspiel.

Paper Ships—Have the children make origami sailboats and label them *Niña, Pinta,* or *Santa María.* They can use their sailboats as they sing "Columbus Sailed with Three Ships," singing the echo for their ship in the second part of the song.

LESSON 3

2. Add an accompaniment to "Let's Make a Jack-o'-Lantern" on page 43 to practice long and short. Have the children:

• Review the song, tapping softly as they follow your signals (three taps on the head, two on the chin, and one on the nose).

• Decide which of your signals is best for the cymbal (the one sound on the nose signal can sustain a ring). Then decide which signal is the best for the wood block (the three taps on the head signal must be short to be heard clearly). Choose a third unpitched instrument, such as a hand drum, for the chin signal. (You may wish to use Copying Master 2-6 at this time.)

• Sing the song while as many children as you have available instruments play on the appropriate signal. Do this activity several times if necessary to give all the children a turn playing instruments.

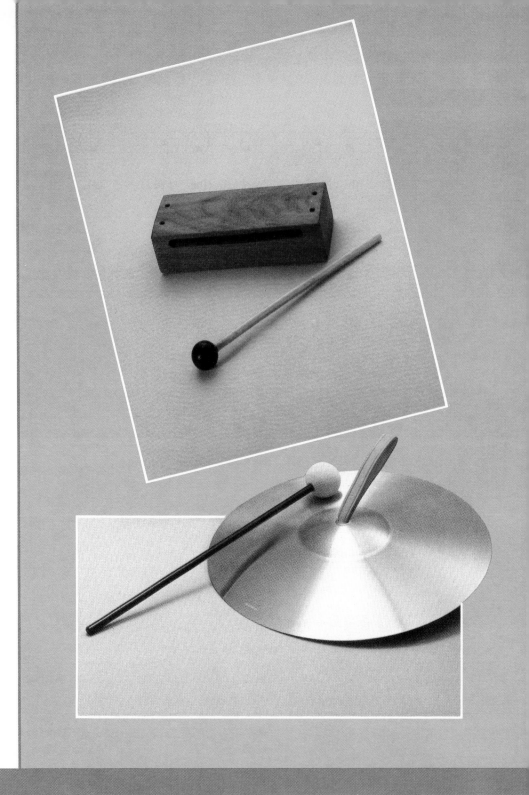

E X T E N S I O N

EXTRA HELP

Clear organization and extra practice will ensure success when adding instruments to "Let's Make a Jack-o'-Lantern." Group those with like instruments together: wood blocks on your right, cymbals in front of you, and drums on your left. Before having the children perform with the song, have them practice responding to your signals using the instruments (three taps on wood blocks when you touch your head three times, one sound on cymbals when you touch your nose once, and two sounds on drums when you touch your chin twice). Then have them sing the song with only one type of instrument responding to your cues. Do this for each group. Then repeat the song, each time adding an instrument until all groups are playing.

Key: D minor   **Starting Pitch: D**   **Scale Tones:** *la, ti, do re mi fa*

Black and Gold

Piano Accompaniment on page PA 30

Music by Carroll A. Rinehart
Words by Nancy Byrd Turner

Mysteriously

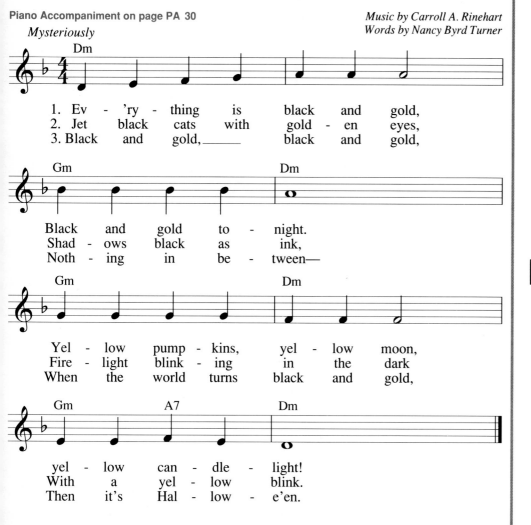

1. Ev - 'ry - thing is black and gold,
2. Jet black cats with gold - en eyes,
3. Black and gold,_____ black and gold,

Black and gold to - night.
Shad - ows black as ink,
Noth - ing in be - tween—

Yel - low pump - kins, yel - low moon,
Fire - light blink - ing in the dark
When the world turns black and gold,

yel - low can - dle - light!
With a yel - low blink.
Then it's Hal - low - e'en.

3. Introduce "Black and Gold" for more practice identifying long sounds. Have the children:
• Listen for long sounds at the end of each phrase in the song.
• Listen again. Recognize that the longest sounds are on the rhyming syllables.
• Sing the song with a few children playing the cymbals on the longest sounds.

Reinforcing the Lesson
Have the children listen to "Columbus Sailed with Three Ships" again, and identify the longest sounds in the song (both times they hear *blue*).

3 APPRAISAL
The children should be able to play long and short sounds with "Let's Make a Jack-o'-Lantern" and "Black and Gold" and make long, flowing movements with "Columbus Sailed with Three Ships."

SONGBOOK
"Jack-o'-Lantern," page 244 (long and short sounds)
"Epo i tai tai e," page 269 (long and short sounds)

LESSON 4

Focus: High and Low

Objectives
To sing, move to, and play high and low sounds
To see the relationship between lower and larger, and higher and smaller

Materials
Recordings: "Columbus Sailed with Three Ships"
"Pumpkin Stew"
Recorded Lesson—"Moving Upward and Downward"
"The Scarecrow Has a Patch"
Charts 11 and 12
Barred instruments
Instrument stick-ons
Patch stick-ons
Copying Masters 2-7, 2-8 (optional)

1 SETTING THE STAGE

Have the children review "Columbus Sailed with Three Ships" on page 44. Use arm movements that show the high-low direction of the melody as they echo the names of the three ships. Play the game to encourage solo singing.

2 TEACHING THE LESSON

1. Review "Pumpkin Stew" on page 42 and identify same and different parts in the melody. Have the children:
• Sing the song, following Chart 11.
• Choose instrument stick-ons, three similar and one different, and put them above the pictures on the chart. (For example, a drum above each of the pots, and a triangle above the question mark.)
• Sing the song with several children following the chart and playing their instrument at the appropriate time.
2. Add pitched instruments to "Pumpkin Stew" to show the direction of the melody. Have the children:
• Sing only the words *pumpkin stew.*
• Watch as you play these pitches on a pitched instrument, such as a xylophone. (Hold the instrument with the smaller bars toward the ceiling and the larger bars toward the floor. Although this is not how the instrument is played, it is a strong visual reinforcement of the relationship between lower and larger, and higher and smaller.)
• Watch as you replace the indefinite pitched instruments above the pots on the chart with barred instrument stick-ons.
• Take turns playing the pitches D F G on the words *pumpkin stew* as everyone sings the song.

CHART 12 HIGH AND LOW

EXTENSION

CURRICULUM CONNECTION: LANGUAGE ARTS

Creative Writing—Have the children create a story together about how to make pumpkin stew. Each child takes a turn making up a part of the story. You can write down each part or use a tape recorder. When the story is finished, read or play back the entire story to the class.

THE SCARECROW HAS A PATCH

(Refrain)
The scarecrow has a patch.
The scarecrow has a patch.
    Where, oh, where does
    the scarecrow have a patch?

(Verse 1)
Solo: On his big, red hat.
All: (On his big, red hat.)

(Verse 2)
Solo: On his worn-out shoe.
All: (On his worn-out shoe.)
    (Repeat Verse 1)

3. Introduce "Moving Upward and Downward" for more practice with high and low. Have the children:
• Hide behind their chairs. (Tell the children to pretend that they are little ghosts who are very shy and do not like people to see them.)
(You may wish to use Copying Master 2-7 at this time.)
• Move to the direction of the music. If it begins low and goes upward, cautiously move in an upward direction. If it starts high and goes downward, duck down and hide again.
• Use long, flowing movements to move like floating ghosts during the middle section of the music.
• Move to show the slow or fast tempo of the music.

Reinforcing the Lesson

Introduce "The Scarecrow Has a Patch." Have the children pat the steady beat with you as they listen to the poem. Then echo-chant the poem. After saying the chant twice, have each child imagine where the scarecrow might have a patch. Say the chant twice while keeping the beat. Have four children tell their ideas one at a time using a high or low voice, and then put a patch on the corresponding part of the scarecrow on Chart 12. The class echoes each child using high or low voices, and repeats all previous ideas in reverse order. Start the game over after each eight children. Continue until everyone has had a chance to tell an idea. (You may wish to use Copying Master 2-8 at this time.)

3 APPRAISAL

The children should be able to:
1. Identify high and low with singing, movement, and instrument playing.
2. Play a low-to-high pattern on a barred instrument and recognize the relationship between lower and larger, and higher and smaller.

CURRICULUM CONNECTION: ART

Scarecrow Mascot—Have the children make a scarecrow together. Stuff an old pillowcase with newspaper for the head. Draw or paste shapes on the head to make a face. Then stuff an old shirt, pants, socks, and mittens with newspaper and assemble all the parts. Fringe yellow construction paper for straw and attach the straw to the head, limbs, and body of the scarecrow. Put a red hat on the head and a pair of old shoes on the feet. Have the children take turns putting different colored shapes on the scarecrow as they chant "The Scarecrow Has a Patch."

SONGBOOK

"Jack-o'-Lantern," page 244 (high and low sounds)
"The Bus," page 266 (high and low sounds)
"Down at the Station," page 268 (high and low sounds)

LESSON 5

Focus: Melody Alone or with Accompaniment

Objectives
To distinguish between melody alone or with accompaniment
To review long and short, and high and low

Materials
Recordings: "I'll Just Be Myself"
"Let's Make a Jack-o'-Lantern"
Listening—"E.T.'s Halloween" from *E.T., The Extraterrestrial* by John Williams
Recorded Lesson—"Melody Alone or with Accompaniment"
Charts 9, 13, and 14
Indefinite pitched instruments
Instrument stick-ons

Vocabulary
melody, accompaniment

1 SETTING THE STAGE

Have the children review "I'll Just Be Myself" on page 38. Look at Chart 9 and remember the movements for the second part of the song. Discuss the problems each character has in the song. Make up new verses with different characters and possible problems these characters might have. Sing these new verses without any accompaniment. (Tell the class that when they sing the song without adding any other sounds, they are singing the tune or melody alone.)

2 TEACHING THE LESSON

1. Review "Let's Make a Jack-o'-Lantern" on page 43 and add an indefinite pitched accompaniment. Have the children:
• Sing the song, tapping appropriately as they follow your signals.
• Look at the pictures on Chart 13 and decide which instrument to play with each signal. Remember that instruments that make short sounds are better for quick, repeated sounds, and instruments that make long sounds are better for places where they have time to ring. (You may wish to put instrument stick-ons at the beginning of each row on the chart.)
• Sing the song, adding the instrument accompaniment.
• Identify the part they sang as the melody or tune, and that instruments played another part with the melody. (It is not necessary that the children learn the term *accompaniment* at this time.)

2A, 2B
CD 1, 2

MELODY ALONE AND ACCOMPANIED

CHART 13

E X T E N S I O N

MORE MUSIC TEACHING IDEAS

If there is time you may wish to have the children review "Pumpkin Stew" on page 42, using either unpitched or pitched instruments to play an accompaniment.

LESSON 5

2. Introduce "E.T.'s Halloween" from _E.T., The Extraterrestrial_ by John Williams. Have the children:

• Look at Chart 14 and listen to the story. (Some children meet a friendly creature named E.T. who comes from another planet. E.T. wants to go home, and has to get to the spaceship. But the police do not want E.T. to get away. It is Halloween, so the children disguise E.T. in a costume. They put E.T. into a bicycle basket and go off to meet the spaceship. As the police close in on the children, E.T. helps them escape by making the bicycle fly. Finally, E.T. gets to the spaceship and thanks the children for their help before he goes home.)

• Listen to the music. Determine that it has three parts. (Part 1 has mostly short sounds; Part 2 has quick, connected sounds; Part 3 has long, smooth sounds.)

• Dramatize the story, walking during Part 1, pretending to pedal a bicycle during Part 2, and pretending to fly during Part 3. (As the bicycle starts to fly, the music moves from low to high.)

Reinforcing the Lesson

Have the children listen to "Melody Alone or with Accompaniment" and hold up one hand if they hear a melody by itself, and both hands if they hear melody with accompaniment.

3 APPRAISAL

The children should be able to:

1. Distinguish between melody alone and melody with accompaniment by holding up one hand for melody alone and both hands for melody with accompaniment.

2. Move as appropriate to the long and short sounds in "E.T.'s Halloween," and identify the low to high sounds as the bicycle starts to fly.

CHART 14

LISTENING MAP: "E.T.'s HALLOWEEN"

THE COMPOSER

John Williams—was born in New York City in 1932. He later moved to Los Angeles, where he studied music with composers of movie scores. Williams has been music director and composer for many movies, including the _Star Wars_ films, _Superman, Raiders of the Lost Ark_, and _E.T., The Extraterrestrial_. He has won many awards for his music. Williams has also composed concert works, as well as the official music for the 1984 Summer Olympics. In 1980 he became conductor of the Boston Pops Orchestra, one of the most popular orchestras in the world.

SONGBOOK

"Jack-o'-Lantern," page 244 (high and low sounds; sing unaccompanied for melody alone)

"The Bus," page 266 (high and low sounds)

"Down at the Station," page 268 (high and low sounds)

LESSON 6

Focus: High and Low

Objective
To speak, sing, play, and move to high and low

Materials
Recordings: "I'll Just Be Myself"
"The Scarecrow Has a Patch"
"Pumpkin Stew"
Listening—"E.T.'s Halloween" from *E.T., The Extraterrestrial* by John Williams
Charts 11 and 14
High and low indefinite pitched instruments, resonator bells
Instrument stick-ons
Copying Master 2-2 (optional)

1 SETTING THE STAGE

Review "I'll Just Be Myself" on page 38, patting the beat during the first part of the song. Add high and low indefinite pitched instruments on the beat during the refrain as follows:

guess I shouldn't worry	four beats on a low drum
guess I'm doin' fine	four beats on a triangle
I'll just be myself and I'll	four beats on a low drum
shine, shine, shine	three beats on a triangle

HIGH

E X T E N S I O N

VOCAL DEVELOPMENT

Provide the children with opportunities to practice singing high and low sounds. This type of vocal exploration allows children to explore the outer reaches of their vocal range.

To encourage the children to use their voices to make high and low sounds, have them sit in a circle and sing the following:

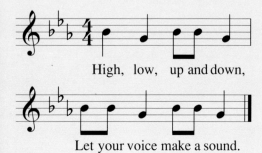

High, low, up and down,

Let your voice make a sound.

Then have each child take a turn making a sound that has an upward or downward movement (for example a siren, a rooster crowing, and so on). The other children imitate each sound. Repeat the melody after each child's sound.

SPECIAL LEARNERS

Some children will benefit from a review of the high/low concept, which was introduced with "The Scarecrow Has a Patch" (Lesson 4). Prepare two cards, one labelled *high* and the other labelled *low*. For the benefit of non-reading children, draw graphic representations of each word around the border of each card. For example, for *high*, draw clouds and for *low*, draw grass. (For visually impaired children, the borders could be made tactually contrasting as well—for example, cotton balls for *high* and ribbon blades of grass for *low*). Have the children take turns mounting one of the cards in an appropriate place on Chart 12 with masking tape, saying the body part or feature at an appropriate pitch level.

LOW

2 TEACHING THE LESSON

1. Review "The Scarecrow Has a Patch" on page 49 to practice high and low. Have the children:
• Move around like floppy scarecrows as they say the refrain.
• Say each verse with a high voice or a low voice, pointing high or low as appropriate.

2. Review "Pumpkin Stew" on page 42. Have the children:
• Sing the song, patting the beat.
• Sing only the words *pumpkin stew,* moving one hand upward as they sing. (Play the pitches D F G on the words *pumpkin stew* as the class sings the song. You may wish to put instrument stick-ons above the pots on Chart 11.)
(You may wish to use Copying Master 2-2 at this time.)
• Identify the melodic direction of the words *pumpkin stew* as low to high, or upward.

Reinforcing the Lesson

Review "E.T.'s Halloween." Look at Chart 14 on page 51 to remember the three sections in the music. Move their hands in an upward direction to show when they hear an upward melodic pattern as the bicycle begins to fly. Then dramatize the music as they listen again.

3 APPRAISAL

The children should be able to identify high and low with pitched and indefinite pitched instruments, singing, speech, and movement.

MORE MUSIC TEACHING IDEAS

Have children who seem very comfortable patting a steady beat take turns playing a steady-beat accompaniment to "Pumpkin Stew." Using a pitched instrument, have each player set his or her own tempo and play G and D together on every beat. If you are using an Orff instrument, remove the bars on each side of the G and D.

SONGBOOK

"Jack-o'-Lantern," page 244 (high and low sounds)
"The Bus," page 266 (high and low sounds)
"Down at the Station," page 268 (high and low sounds)

REVIEW AND EVALUATION

REVIEW

Objectives
To review songs, skills, and concepts learned in Unit 2
To measure the children's ability to:
1. Identify long and short sounds and symbols
2. Identify melody as the tune

Materials
Recordings: "Pumpkin Stew"
"Take a Bite of Music"
"Let's Make a
Jack-o'-Lantern"
"I'll Just Be Myself"
Charts 11 and 13
Wood block, cymbals
Instrument stick-ons
Evaluation Unit 2 Copying Master

TEACHING THE LESSON

Review the songs and concepts in Unit 2 by dramatizing a story. Have the children:
• Listen as you tell the story, singing and performing the activities at the appropriate places. (As the children sing and move, observe individuals and the class as a whole and evaluate how their responses indicate their level of understanding.)

The Scarecrow's Problem
Once upon a time there was a scarecrow hanging on a pole in a cornfield. Every day the scarecrow would move gently in the wind and try to scare the crows away. Each time the scarecrow moved, the crows would fly into the air. But they always came back into the garden to peck at the corn when the wind died down.
• Listen and move to short and long sounds played on a wood block and cymbals, pretending to be scarecrows or crows. The scarecrows move when they hear the long sounds of the cymbals and the crows peck when they hear the wood block.

The scarecrow liked the crows, but not when they were eating the farmer's corn. Then one day an idea popped into the scarecrow's head. "Attention, crows!" the scarecrow called. "Let's make some pumpkin stew so you won't have to eat the farmer's corn!" The crows agreed that the scarecrow's idea was worth a try. So together they collected the ingredients and made a big pot of stew.
• Sing "Pumpkin Stew" on page 42. Use Chart 11 and pretend to make pumpkin stew. Add instrument stick-ons over each pot on the chart. Identify whether each instrument makes a long sound or a short sound.

REVIEW AND EVALUATION

The crows really liked the stew, but the scarecrow did not care for it at all. The crows suggested that the scarecrow take a bite of music.
• Sing "Take a Bite of Music" on page 41, and identify that they are singing the melody or tune.

The scarecrow liked that idea. But since the scarecrow was not having any stew, there was an extra pumpkin left over. The scarecrow wondered, "What will we do with the last pumpkin?" The crows had an answer for that problem as well.
• Sing "Let's Make a Jack-o'-Lantern" on page 43. Use Chart 13 on page 50 as a guide and create an accompaniment using long and short sounds.

The crows had to go back to their nests. After they had gone, the scarecrow worried about what to do the next time the crows came into the garden. Then the scarecrow realized, "I'll just be myself!"
• Sing "I'll Just Be Myself" on page 38, doing the movements with the refrain. Play a cymbal on the long *shine*.

EVALUATION

Evaluation Unit 2 Copying Master can be found in the *Teacher's Resource Book* with full directions for providing an evaluation of the child's progress.

ELEMENTS OF MUSIC	UNIT 3 OBJECTIVES	Lesson 1 CORE Focus: Tone Color and Dynamics	Lesson 2 CORE Focus: Rhythm
Dynamics	Choose appropriate levels of dynamics Explore dynamic possibilities of some classroom instruments	Explore dynamic possibilities of classroom instruments and choose appropriate level to accompany song Sing songs at appropriate dynamic level	
Tone Color	Use four voices Hear solo instruments **Identify the triangle, rhythm sticks, drum, and tambourine by sight and sound**	Identify names of classroom instruments: tambourine, rhythm sticks, drum, triangle Play instrumental accompaniment Improvise with classroom instruments to explore loud and soft sounds	Use classroom instruments for accompaniment
Tempo	Recognize faster/slower		
Duration/ Rhythm	Say, pat, play rhythm of names, short word patterns Compare beat with no beat Walk individually to drum matched to their own natural tempos Sing, hear music with silent beat **Recognize and use the term *beat***	Play rhythm of names of classroom instruments Sing nonmetric song Explore long and short capabilities of classroom instruments	Identify beat Hear term *beat* Use beat in drum accompaniment Sing using "inner hearing"
Pitch	Identify pitches as higher or lower than one another Continue to associate high with small, low with large		
Texture	Continue to use and recognize melody alone and with accompaniment	Hear, sing melody with accompaniment	Hear and use melody alone and with accompaniment
Form	Continue to recognize same/ different Imitating teacher, find and count phrases in a short song Identify introduction of songs Wait for introductions, interludes		
Style	Hear, sing American Indian song, Thanksgiving songs, folk songs, composed songs Hear 20th-century orchestral music	Hear and sing American Indian song, folk song Hear 20th-century orchestral music Compare mood and style of march and lullaby	Hear, sing American Indian song, folk song

PURPOSE Unit 3: Musical Friends

In this unit the children will be introduced to the concept of beat and the names and sounds of some classroom instruments through the use of well-known rhymes and songs, including songs for fall and Thanksgiving. This unit also provides opportunities for the children to use classroom instruments to practice different musical concepts.

SUGGESTED TIME FRAME

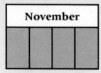

November

FOCUS

Core Lessons 1, 2, 5
• Tone Color and Dynamics
• Rhythm
• Tone Color and Rhythm

Lessons 3, 4, 6
• Pitch
• Tempo
• Rhythm

Lesson 3 Focus: Pitch	Lesson 4 Focus: Tempo	Lesson 5 CORE Focus: Tone Color and Rhythm	Lesson 6 Focus: Rhythm
Use classroom instruments for accompaniment Play a downward scale on bells Make a pitched instrument	Use singing, speaking, whispering, calling voices	Identify and use triangle, tambourine, rhythm sticks, drum Use mouth sound effects with poem	Use singing, speaking, whispering, calling voices
	Identify and use faster/slower tempos		
Practice using beat Play beat on instrument following chart Play on only the strong beat	Practice identifying and keeping beat Walk individually to drum matched to their own natural tempos Sing, hear music with silent beat	Practice identifying and keeping beat Compare beat with no beat Point beat on chart Play the rhythm of instrument names of drum, rhythm sticks, triangle, tambourine Sing song using "inner hearing"	Practice identifying and keeping the beat Practice patting and playing the rhythm of classroom instrument names Sing and play instruments using "inner hearing"
Practice identifying high and low Continue to associate high with small, low with large Play and move to show high and low			
Hear and use melody with accompaniment	Hear, use melody alone and with accompaniment	Hear, use melody alone and with accompaniment	Use melody alone and with accompaniment
	Identify same and different	Identify introduction of songs Wait for introductions, interludes Imitating teacher, find and count phrases in a short song	
Hear, sing folk songs, composed song	Hear, sing folk songs, composed songs	Hear, sing American Indian, folk, composed, Thanksgiving songs	Hear, sing Thanksgiving songs, folk songs, composed songs

BULLETIN BOARD

Make a bulletin board with a Thanksgiving theme. You may wish to title the bulletin board "Musical Friends Get Together." Place a long rectangle in the center of the bulletin board. This represents a table. Put cutouts of characters from some of the songs in the unit, for example, "Hey Diddle Diddle," "The Farmer in the Dell," and "One, Two, Tie My Shoe," seated around the table. You may wish to make these cutouts yourself, or have the children make them. They can draw a place mat for each of the characters, and put these on the table.

LESSON 1

Focus: Tone Color and Dynamics

Related Subjects
American Indians, body parts

Objectives
To identify the names of some classroom instruments
To choose different dynamic levels for classroom instrument accompaniments

Materials
Recordings: "Hush, Little Baby"
"Indian Lullaby"
Comanche Hand Game Song (optional)
"Put Your Finger in the Air"
"Put Your Finger on the Sticks"
Listening—"March" from *Summer Day* Suite, by Sergei Prokofiev
Chart 15
Triangles, rhythm sticks, drums, tambourines
Copying Master 3-1 (optional)

1 SETTING THE STAGE

Review "Hush, Little Baby" on page 14. (Compliment those children who sing the song at an appropriate dynamic level.) Ask the children if they can remember what kind of song "Hush, Little Baby" is (lullaby). Tell them that they are going to learn another lullaby. This lullaby was sung by the Miwok people, an American Indian tribe of central California, to their children.

1, 2
CD 1A, 2A, 2B

Key: D minor   Starting Pitch: G   Scale Tones: *la, do re mi*

Indian Lullaby

Piano Accompaniment on page PA 31   *Miwok Indian*

1. Sleep, my lit-tle one! Sleep, my lit-tle one! My lit-tle squir-rel!

Safe in the tree___ tops the squir-rels are sleep - ing.

All are a - sleep___ in their bas-kets of wil - low.

2. Sleep, my little one! Sleep, my little one! My little cricket!
Safe in the treetops the crickets are sleeping,
All are asleep in their baskets of willow.

3. Sleep, my little one! Sleep, my little one! My little linnet!
Safe in the treetops the linnets are sleeping,
All are asleep in their baskets of willow.

E X T E N S I O N

MORE MUSIC TEACHING IDEAS
Have the children learn "Comanche Hand Game Song." Play the following game when they know the song well. Form two teams. Give one team a stone, or other small object. Both teams stand facing each other. As they sing the song, the team with the stone passes it from child to child behind their backs. At the end of the song the other team members have three tries to guess correctly which child in the opposing team has the stone. If they guess correctly they get a chance to pass the stone.

Comanche Hand Game Song

American Indian folk game

Eh - ka - moh - da,   Eh - ka - moh - da.

Hey hi - ya eh - ka - moh - da, Hey hi - ya eh - ke - moh - da.

Key: C   Starting Pitch: G   Scale Tones: *mi so*

CLASSROOM INSTRUMENTS

CHART
15

2 TEACHING THE LESSON

1. Introduce "Indian Lullaby" to identify dynamic level. Have the children:
• Listen to the song.
• Practice the words of the song. (You may wish to tell the children that a linnet is a small songbird.)
• Listen to the song again and identify its dynamic level (soft).
• Sing the song at the appropriate dynamic level.

2. Introduce Chart 15. Have the children:
• Listen as you play the rhythm of the name of each instrument, one sound for each syllable. Then play or tap the rhythms as they say the names.
• Identify two instruments that have the same rhythm to their names (rhythm sticks and tambourine).
• Explore the dynamic possibilities of these instruments. Classify the sound of each instrument as soft, loud, or soft and loud. (All these instruments can be played soft or loud.)
• Choose one of the instruments to accompany "Indian Lullaby." Decide on an appropriate dynamic level for the accompaniment. (Playing a drum softly is the most suitable accompaniment.)
• Sing "Indian Lullaby" with a few children playing the accompaniment. (You may wish to first play a soft, steady beat as a model while the children sing the song.)

MORE MUSIC TEACHING IDEAS

1. Have the children improvise with soft and loud. Distribute a selection of triangles, rhythm sticks, hand drums, and tambourines to the children. Then choose two children to be leaders. One leader points to an instrument on Chart 15 and the children holding that instrument individually improvise rhythms. (No one plays if the leader is not pointing to the chart.) The other leader sits next to the chart book facing the class. This leader indicates whether the instrument selected plays softly or loudly by holding hands together for soft and holding hands apart for loud. (You may wish to demonstrate the first time.)

2. Explore the long and short capabilities of the drum, triangle, tambourine, and rhythm sticks.

CURRICULUM CONNECTION: LANGUAGE ARTS

Self-Expression—Have the children discuss how "Indian Lullaby" makes them feel. Make a list of their responses on the chalkboard. When everyone who wants to has expressed a feeling, review the responses. Have the class conclude that a song with a soft dynamic level creates a quiet, peaceful feeling.

3. Introduce "Put Your Finger in the Air" to continue practicing dynamic level. Have the children:
• Listen to the song, doing the movements as directed.
• Identify the dynamic level of the song (loud).
• Listen to the song again, singing along as they are able.

4. Introduce "Put Your Finger on the Sticks" to practice identifying instruments. Have the children listen to the song. Identify each instrument on Chart 15 by pointing to that instrument's picture when they hear it mentioned in the song. (You may wish to use Copying Master 3-1 at this time.)

"Put Your Finger on the Sticks"
Put your finger on the sticks, on the sticks;
Put your finger on the sticks, on the sticks;
Put your finger on the sticks,
On the sticks, on the sticks;
Put your finger on the sticks, on the sticks.
(...triangle...
...drum...
...tambourine...)

Key: D   Starting Pitch: F♯   Scale Tones: *ti, do re mi fa so la*

Put Your Finger in the Air

Piano Accompaniment on page PA 32

Words and music by
Woody Guthrie

1. Put your fin-ger in the air, in the air;
2. Put your fin-ger on your head, on your head;

Put your fin-ger in the air; And leave it a-bout a year,
Put your fin-ger on your head; Tell me is it green or red?

Put your fin-ger in the air, in the air.
Put your fin-ger on your head, on your head.

3. Put your finger on your nose, . . .
   And feel the cold wind blow, . . .

4. Put your finger on your chin, . ..
   That's where the food slips in, . . .

5. Put your finger on your cheek, . . .
   And leave it about a week, . . .

6. Put your finger on your finger, . . .
   On your finger, on your finger, . . .

E X T E N S I O N

Reinforcing the Lesson

Review "March" from *Summer Day* Suite. After the class listens to the music, decide on an appropriate dynamic level for a rhythmic accompaniment to this music (soft). Distribute instruments to the children. Have them play their instrument as you point to its picture on Chart 15. (Point to each instrument for sixteen beats before switching to the next one. Repeat the activity to give as many children as possible a turn to play.)

3 APPRAISAL

The children should be able to:
1. Identify the tambourine, hand drum, rhythm sticks, and triangle by name.
2. Play the instruments with "Indian Lullaby" and "March" at appropriate dynamic levels.

MORE MUSIC TEACHING IDEAS

Have the children discuss the feeling of "March," and the musical elements that contribute to this feeling (tempo, dynamics, and so on). Compare the feeling of "March" to that of "Indian Lullaby." Conclude that musical elements such as tempo and dynamics create different feelings and effects with different songs.

SONGBOOK

"Autumn Leaves," page 245 (soft dynamic level)

C O R E
LESSON 2

Focus: Rhythm

Objectives
To identify beat
To become familiar with the term *beat*

Materials
Recordings: "Put Your Finger in the
Air"
"Indian Lullaby"
"Hey Diddle Diddle"
Recorded Lesson—"Pointing
the Beat with 'Hey
Diddle Diddle'"
"The Farmer in the Dell"
Charts 16 and 17
Drum
Copying Masters 3-2, 3-3 (optional)

1 SETTING THE STAGE

Have the children review "Put Your Finger in the Air" on page 58. Encourage the
children to imitate you as you move your
finger to the beat with each verse.

2 TEACHING THE LESSON

**1. Review "Indian Lullaby" on page 56 to
practice beat.** Have the children:
• Sing the song as you softly play the beat
on a drum.
• Recognize that the sounds made by the
drum stayed at the same steady speed.
(Tell the children that the drum played the
beat.)
• Sing the song again as a few children
take turns playing the drum. (Compliment any children who can keep the beat.
See *Extra Help* on page 61.)

"HEY DIDDLE DIDDLE"

E X T E N S I O N

MORE MUSIC TEACHING IDEAS

Have the children practice inner hearing
with "Hey Diddle Diddle." As they pat the
beat together, you indicate whether each
line of the song is to be sung or silent by
saying "sing" or "think," and pointing to
the appropriate picture on Chart 16. Sing
the song several times, with the children
thinking and singing other combinations.
Finish by singing the whole song. (This
activity gives valuable practice with internalizing the beat.)

Key: D   Starting Pitch: A   Scale Tones: *mi so*

Hey Diddle Diddle

Mother Goose Rhyme
Music by M.D.

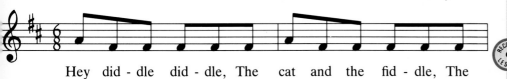

Hey did - dle did - dle, The cat and the fid - dle, The

cow jumped o - ver the moon; The

lit - tle dog laughed to see such sport, and the

dish ran a - way with the spoon.

LESSON 2

2. Introduce "Hey Diddle Diddle" for more practice with beat. Have the children:
- Listen to the song, patting the beat and watching as you point the beat on Chart 16. (Point four beats on each picture.)
- Say the words with you as you or a child who has been patting the beat successfully point the beat.
- Sing the song as you point the beat on the chart.
- Sing the song again as five children pretend to be the five characters in the song. These five children stand in front of the class in the order their characters occur in the song. You stand behind each child or pair of children in turn and indicate four beats over each of their heads as the rest of the class sings. Repeat the activity in order to give other children a turn. (You may wish to use Copying Master 3-2 at this time.)

MORE MUSIC TEACHING IDEAS

Have the children sing "Hey Diddle Diddle" while trying to pat a steady beat. Remove the bars on each side of the low D and A on any bass or alto Orff instrument and play a steady beat on these two bars as the class sings and continues to pat the beat. Have any children who seem completely comfortable in patting the beat while singing the song take turns playing the beat on D and A as the rest of the class sings. The child playing (not the teacher) should set the tempo for the class.

EXTRA HELP

As the children perform any new activity, try to make some kind of positive statement about the way each child performed, such as, "You played the beat correctly. It was exactly with the music." This helps reinforce what is expected of them. Even children who may do the activity incorrectly in some way should be encouraged, for example, if a child had difficulty keeping the beat you might compliment the way she or he held the mallet.

LESSON 2

Reinforcing the Lesson

Introduce "The Farmer in the Dell." Have the children listen to the song as you point the beat on Chart 17. (Point to each figure, moving twice from left to right and top to bottom.) The children can sing along as they are able. Then ask the children to tell you what you were pointing (the beat). Review the sequence of verses in the song with the chart.
(You may wish to use Copying Master 3-3 at this time.)

Play this game: Have the class form a circle. Choose one child to be the farmer. This child stands in the center of the circle. Sing the song, patting or stepping the beat and doing the following movements:
verse 2—The "farmer" chooses a "wife," who comes and stands in the center of the circle.
verse 3—The "wife" chooses a "child," who joins the group in the center of the circle.
verses 4-8—each succeeding character named chooses the next character to join the group in the center of the circle.
verse 9—Everyone except the "cheese" returns to a place in the circle, leaving the "cheese" standing alone.
Play the game again with the "cheese" choosing a new "farmer."

POINT THE BEAT
CHART 17

E X T E N S I O N

SONGBOOK

"Five Fat Turkeys," page 246 (beat)

Key: F   Starting Pitch: C   Scale Tones: *so, do re mi so la*

The Farmer in the Dell

Piano Accompaniment on page PA 34

Singing Game

1. The farm - er in the dell,_____
2. The farm - er takes a wife,_____

the farm - er in the dell,_____
the farm - er takes a wife,_____

Heigh - ho the der - ry - o,
Heigh - ho the der - ry - o,

the farm - er in the dell._____
the farm - er takes a wife._____

3. The wife takes a child.

4. The child takes a nurse.

5. The nurse takes a dog.

6. The dog takes a cat.

7. The cat takes a rat.

8. The rat takes the cheese.

9. The cheese stands alone.

3 APPRAISAL

The children should be able to:
1. Recognize that the sounds made by the drum in "Indian Lullaby" stayed the same.
2. Watch as you point the beat with "Hey Diddle Diddle" and "The Farmer in the Dell" and tell that you were pointing the beat.

LESSON 3

Focus: Pitch

Objectives
To practice identifying high and low
To practice using beat

Materials
Recordings: "Down, Down"
             "Hey Diddle Diddle"
             "Muffin Man"
Chart 16
Bells, xylophone, or other pitched class-
room instruments
Tambourines, rhythm sticks, triangles,
drums
Real or paper leaf
Copying Masters 3-4, 3-5 (optional)

1 SETTING THE STAGE

Introduce "Down, Down" to review the
concept of up and down. Hold a leaf or
a paper cutout of a leaf as high as you can.
Tell the children that you are going to let
the leaf fall. Ask them to predict if the leaf
will fall quickly or slowly. Then have
them watch and listen as you drop the
leaf, singing or saying the words of
"Down, Down." Discuss with the children
how the leaf fell (slowly). Choose one or
two volunteers to move to demonstrate
how the leaf fell. Show the class a pitched
barred instrument that you have turned
so that the lower bars are at the bottom
and the higher bars are at the top. Ask the
children which bars are longer, the lower
bars or the higher bars (lower). Then ask
them which bars will sound higher (the
top) and which will sound lower (the bottom). Discuss how to play a melody so it
moves as the leaf moved when it fell
(slowly and gently from the higher pitches
to the lower pitches).
(You may wish to use Copying Masters 3-4
and 3-5 at this time.)

2B, 3A
CD 2

EXTENSION

COOPERATIVE LEARNING

After the children have watched a demonstration of one child playing a downward
pattern on a pitched instrument while a
few others move downward with the
music, have them practice this skill in
small groups. Assign group membership
randomly. Once the groups are formed,
explain that the first player in each group
will be the one who fits the category you
name (for example, the child with the
longest hair, the person wearing the most
red, and so on). From then on, the instrument player chooses the next member of
the group to have a turn. Watch for and
praise those children who are taking turns
and staying with the group.

KEYBOARD

Reinforce the concept of high/low and
review left and right on the piano. Have the
children remember which is their left
hand, as described in the Keyboard
activity on page 20. Tell them that *L* stands
for *Left* and also for *Low*. Have one child
stand in front of the center of the piano and
play several keys to the left using the left
hand. Identify these sounds as coming
from the lower half of the keyboard. Then
have the child play several keys to the right
using the right hand. Identify these sounds
as coming from the higher half of the keyboard. Give each child a turn to play high
and low sounds on the piano.

Key: C   Starting Pitch: C   Scale Tones: *do re mi fa so la ti do¹*

Down, Down

Piano Accompaniment on page PA 35

Words by Eleanor Farjeon
Music by Fay Ellis

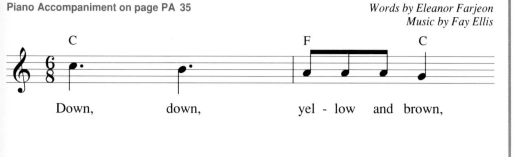

Down,   down,   yel - low   and brown,

The   leaves   are   fall - ing   o - ver the   town.

LESSON 3

Choose one or two volunteers to demonstrate how a leaf falls using the barred instrument. Then have one child play the instrument as the other children pretend to be falling leaves, moving with the melody from high to low.

2 TEACHING THE LESSON

1. Listen and move to "Down, Down" to practice hearing and identifying high to low. Have the children:
• Listen to the song and decide if the melody moves from high to low or from low to high (high to low).
• Echo-say the words after you.
• Listen again and, if you are using the recording, count how many times they hear the melody (four). Notice the faster music at the end of the song, suggesting the wind, followed by music with a definite beat, suggesting raking leaves.
• Listen to "Down, Down" with everyone moving like falling leaves. (Again, if using the recording, remind the children to wait for the introduction to end before moving. They can choose to move on any one of the three times they hear the melody, but must remain in place until the end of the third time. When the wind music begins, the children move about as if blown by the wind. When the raking music begins, you or a child can pretend to rake all the leaves into a pile.)
2. Practice identifying high and low sounds. Have the children:
• Listen as you play a few pitches that are obviously high or low and show by holding their hands high or low whether they think the sounds are high or low.
• Listen as you play from the lowest pitch to the highest pitch and identify how the movement of this melody is different from that of "Down, Down" (it moves from low to high).

MORE MUSIC TEACHING IDEAS

1. For further practice in identifying high and low, play pitches on different instruments. Have the children respond with hand and arm movements, or with crepe paper streamers or scarves. Play the high and low extremes of each instrument for the class before beginning the activity, since high and low judgments are relative to each individual instrument.
2. Have some children who are able play a downward scale on the bells or glockenspiel as the class sings "Down, Down."
3. Have a child move to show high and low as other children play corresponding high and low sounds on pitched classroom instruments.

4. Create a pitched instrument using glasses or bottles of uniform size filled with varying levels of water. (Bottles or jars with lids reduce problems with spilling and evaporation.) Add or subtract the water in each jar until the correct pitch is achieved. Use food coloring or small quantities of tempera paint in each jar to give each pitch of the scale a different color.

CURRICULUM CONNECTION: ART

Showing Melodic Direction—The children can create graphic representations of "Down, Down." Have them each collect eight leaves and glue the leaves in a downward, diagonal pattern from left to right on a piece of paper. (You may wish to draw a diagonal on their papers in advance.) Later, the children can take turns pointing to the leaves one at a time as other children play a barred instrument from the higher pitches to the lower pitches.

LESSON 3

3. Review "Hey Diddle Diddle" on page 61 for more practice with high and low and keeping the beat. Have the children:
• Sing the song, patting the beat on their legs with you.
• Decide on four different places to pat the beat, for example, knees, hips, shoulders, head. Then sing the song, patting on a different place for each four beats as you or a child points to the pictures on Chart 16.
• Sing the song again, playing the beat on a different instrument (rhythm sticks, drum, tambourine, triangle) for each four beats as you or a child points to the pictures on Chart 16.
• Sing or play the song one line at a time, moving to show when the melody moves to higher or lower pitches.
• Sing the song as five children pretend to be the different characters, and a few other children play instruments.

Higher and Lower

MORE MUSIC TEACHING IDEAS

1. Place stick-ons of the tambourine, drum, and triangle above each of the first three pictures on Chart 16 to indicate which instrument plays the beat with which line of "Hey Diddle Diddle." Place stick-ons of all three instruments over the last picture. You can also indicate which instrument plays the beat by having the three instruments in front of the class and pointing to each one in turn as the children sing the song.
2. Play the different instruments only on the higher pitches as the children sing the first three lines of "Hey Diddle Diddle." Play all the instruments together on the last line.

Key: G   Starting Pitch: D   Scale Tones: *so, la, ti, do re mi*

Muffin Man

Piano Accompaniment on page PA 36   *Old English Rhyme and Melody*

1. Oh,   do   you   know   the   muf - fin   man,
2. Oh,   yes,   I   know   the   muf - fin   man,

the   muf - fin   man,   the   muf - fin   man?
the   muf - fin   man,   the   muf - fin   man;

Oh,   do   you   know   the   muf - fin   man
Oh,   yes,   I   know   the   muf - fin   man

that   lives   in   Dru - ry   Lane?
that   lives   in   Dru - ry   Lane.

LESSON 3

Reinforcing the Lesson

Introduce "Muffin Man." Have the children listen to the song. Discuss what muffins are. Listen to the song again and imitate you as you move your hands up and down to show the direction of the pitches of the melody. Then have them listen again, singing along with the second verse.

3 APPRAISAL

The children should be able to:
1. Show that they recognize high and low sounds by using corresponding high and low movements.
2. Move to show understanding of steadily recurring beat with "Hey Diddle Diddle."

SONGBOOK

"Autumn Leaves," page 245 (identify highest and lowest pitches)
"Five Fat Turkeys," page 246 (beat, identify highest and lowest pitches)

LESSON 4

Focus: Tempo

Related Subject
Numbers

Objectives
To practice identifying and using different tempos
To practice identifying same and different
To practice beat

Materials
Recordings: "Little Blue Truck"
"Muffin Man"
"Three Little Muffins"
"Put Your Finger in the
Air"
Copying Master 3-6 (optional)

1 SETTING THE STAGE

Ask the children to start and stop with you as you pat a slow beat. Repeat with a fast beat. Then have them describe the speed of each.

2 TEACHING THE LESSON

1. Review "Little Blue Truck" on page 12 to identify tempo (speed of the beat). Have the children:
• Sing the song.
• Identify how many of the four lyric lines are the same (three) and how many are different (one).
• Sing the song again, patting the beat.
• Identify the speed of the truck (slow, and then very slow).
• Sing the song with the movement.

2. Review "Muffin Man" on page 67 to practice keeping the beat and to recognize same and different. Have the children:
• Listen to the song, patting the beat.
• Tell how each verse is the same and how each is different. (The melodies of each are the same, but the words are slightly different.)
• Sing the song.
• Identify the tempo (medium).
• Play this game when they know the song well. (This is an excellent game to develop independent singing and auditory discrimination, and to monitor singing skills of individual children.) Have one child sit in the front of the room facing away from the class. Have the whole class sing the first verse of the song. Secretly choose another child to sing the second verse. The child in front of the class has three guesses to identify the soloist.

🌐 1A, 2B, 3A
💿 1, 2

E X T E N S I O N

Three Little Muffins

Traditional

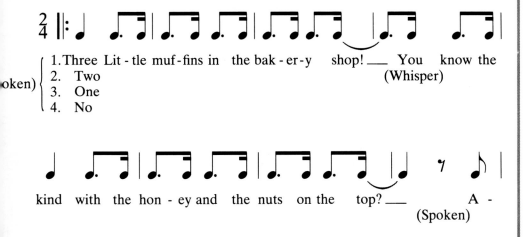

(spoken)
1. Three Lit-tle muf-fins in the bak-er-y shop! __ You know the
2. Two (Whisper)
3. One
4. No

kind with the hon-ey and the nuts on the top? __ A-
(Spoken)

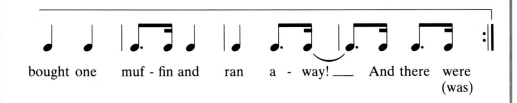

1.,2.,3.

long came a child with a pen-ny to pay, __ And

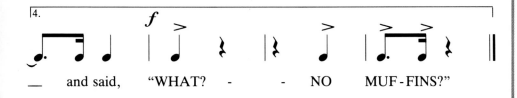

bought one muf-fin and ran a-way! __ And there were
(was)

4.

f

__ and said, "WHAT? - - NO MUF-FINS?"

3. Introduce "Three Little Muffins" to practice fast tempo. Have the children:
• Listen to "Three Little Muffins," imitating you as you do the finger play. (Hold up the appropriate number of fingers for each verse with one hand. On *Along came a child*, "walk" with the first two fingers of the other hand, "take" one finger of the first hand, and run away. On the word *WHAT?* hold both hands out to the side, palms up.)
• Say the poem as soon as they are able. (You may wish to use Copying Master 3-6 at this time.)
• Identify the tempo (fast).

Reinforcing the Lesson

Have several volunteers take turns walking around the room. Match the speed as each child walks by playing the beat on a drum. Have the children pat the beat along with you. Identify the speed of each walk as slow, medium, or fast. Then sing the first verse of "Put Your Finger in the Air" and identify the speed (medium). Sing the whole song doing the movements.

3 APPRAISAL

The children should be able to:
1. Identify different tempos by singing, speaking, and moving.
2. Identify same and different in "Little Blue Truck" and "Muffin Man."
3. Identify beat by patting the beat with songs and poetry.

EXTRA HELP: INDIVIDUAL PARTICIPATION

Children who are reluctant to participate in the individual walking activity may be more willing to do so if you begin by focusing on shoes. Ask the children, "Who is wearing good walking shoes today?" or, "Can we listen to your shoes walk?" This takes the pressure off the child and transfers it to the inanimate shoes.

SONGBOOK

"Uncle Jessie," page 289 (changing tempos)

LESSON 5

Focus: Tone Color and Rhythm

Related Subjects
Numbers, Thanksgiving, American Indians, autumn, shapes

Objectives
To practice identifying and using the tambourine, rhythm sticks, drum, and triangle
To compare beat and no beat

Materials
Recordings: "The Farmer in the Dell"
"One, Two, Tie My Shoe"
"Thank You"
"The Wind"
"Indian Lullaby"
Charts 15, 17, 18, 19, and 20
Tambourines, rhythm sticks, drums, triangles
Copying Masters 1-2, 3-1, 3-3, 3-7, 3-8 (optional)

CD 2

One, Two, Tie My Shoe

Traditional

One,   two,   tie   my   shoe.   Three,   four,

shut   the   door.   Five,   six,   pick,   up   sticks.

Sev-en, eight,   lay them straight. Nine,   ten,   a   big fat hen.

1 SETTING THE STAGE

Without singing, have the children pat a steady beat with you. Then have them identify what they did (pat the beat). Next, have the children imitate you as you pat the beat, changing after every eight beats to a different body part. Encourage them to say the name of the body part each time they pat it.

2 TEACHING THE LESSON

1. Review "The Farmer in the Dell" on page 63 to practice keeping the beat. Have the children:
• Sing the first verse of "The Farmer in the Dell" as you point the beat with the figures on Chart 17.
• Sing the first verse again, pointing to each picture on Chart 17 with you.
(You may wish to use Copying Master 3-3 at this time.)

EXTENSION

VOCAL DEVELOPMENT

Songs with a limited range, such as "One, Two, Tie My Shoe," are valuable for helping the children learn to sing in tune. Explain to the children that this song has only two different pitches. Sing a phrase and have them echo. Make certain that everyone has the starting pitch. If you hear any children singing below the pitch, encourage them to "think higher" and to point to the ceiling. This will reinforce the concept of "higher."

MORE MUSIC TEACHING IDEAS

Play a variation of "The Farmer in the Dell" to practice identifying instruments. Place two drums, two tambourines, two triangles, and two sets of rhythm sticks in the center of the circle before starting the game. Play the game as usual until all the characters are chosen. Before singing the last verse, sing, for example, "The farmer takes a drum. . ." The farmer then picks up the instrument named. Continue naming other characters and instruments until all the characters have an instrument. Then have the characters play an accompaniment with the last verse. (You may wish to use Chart 15 for extra help identifying instruments.) Repeat the game to give other children a turn.

CHART 18

"ONE, TWO, TIE MY SHOE"

LESSON 5

• Identify what they were doing (pointing the beat).
• Form a circle and play the game. (If using the recording, remind the children not to move during the introduction and interludes between the verses.)

2. Introduce "One, Two, Tie My Shoe" to practice beat. Have the children:
• Listen, patting the beat, to the recording or to you singing the song unaccompanied.
• Recognize that they heard only singing. No instruments were playing.
• Sing the song with you, holding up the corresponding number of fingers as each number occurs in the song.
• Sing the song, watching as you point the beat with the figures on Chart 18.
• Sing the song, pointing to each picture on Chart 18 with you.
(You may wish to use Copying Master 3-7 at this time.)
• Identify what they were doing (pointing the beat).
• Sing the song again as different children take turns coming up to the chart and pointing the beat.

MORE MUSIC TEACHING IDEAS

Have the children practice inner hearing with "One, Two, Tie My Shoe." Sing the song while patting the beat, singing only the number names and thinking the rest of each line. Repeat the song, thinking the numbers and singing the rest of each line.

SPECIAL LEARNERS

Children whose physical abilities are limited may be unable to hold up the corresponding number of fingers as they sing the song. They can participate by pointing to a partner's fingers or a drawing. (Make this ahead of time by outlining an outstretched hand.)

LESSON 5

3. Introduce *Thanksgiving* and review the names of classroom instruments. Have the children:

• Look at the picture on Chart 19. Take turns telling what they see, and what they think is going on. (If the children do not relate the painting to Thanksgiving, tell them that the painting is called *Thanksgiving*, and shows a Thanksgiving celebration.)

• Briefly discuss how the activities in the painting relate to their own observances of Thanksgiving.

• Look as you point out the instruments pictured above the painting. Name each instrument and tell the shape of each. Then find similar shapes in the painting. (You may wish to use Copying Master 3-1 at this time.)

• Learn hand signs to represent each instrument:

tambourine	pat one hand with the other
rhythm sticks	tap index fingers
drum	pat legs
triangle	tap thumbs and index fingers together

• Take turns playing each instrument as you point to its picture on Chart 19. (Point to each instrument for at least eight beats before pointing to a different instrument.) The rest of the class indicates the instrument you point to by keeping the beat with the sign for that instrument.

• Show the sign for the instrument they hear as you play each instrument.

FINE ART: THANKSGIVING

 CHART 19

E X T E N S I O N

MORE MUSIC TEACHING IDEAS

1. Have the children play the rhythm of each instrument name, for example, *rhythm sticks* (three syllables).

2. Have the children improvise a piece for four unpitched sounds. Choose four children to be conductors, and assign each of these children one of the instrument hand signs. The other children select either drums, tambourines, rhythm sticks, or triangles, and sit in front of the conductor for their instrument. After each group practices separately with their conductor, improvise a piece, beginning with the first conductor and ending with the fourth. Discuss the results of the improvisation and make suggestions for the next time they do this activity.

Key: E♭   **Starting Pitch: B♭**   **Scale Tones:** *ti, do re mi fa so la*

Thank You

Piano Accompaniment on page PA 37

Music by Franz Schubert

Thank You for the world so sweet,

Thank You for the food we eat,

Thank You for the birds that sing,

Thank You, God, for ev - 'ry - thing.

4. Introduce "Thank You" to practice beat and to identify the sound of the triangle. Have the children:
• Listen to the song, quietly patting the beat.
• Identify phrases by imitating you as you trace an arc in the air for each two-measure phrase.
• Echo the words of each phrase after you. Then say the words of the whole song.
• Listen to the song again.
• Sing the song. (If you are not using the recording, you may wish to play a triangle once at the beginning of each phrase and once at the very end as the children sing.)
• Identify the classroom instrument they heard (triangle).

CURRICULUM CONNECTION: ART

Have the children draw pictures of things for which they are thankful. Encourage them to think beyond material belongings by discussing the three things mentioned in "Thank You" (the world, food, birds). You may wish to label each child's drawing after they are completed and display them around the classroom.

LESSON 5

5. Introduce "The Wind" to introduce beat and no beat. Have the children:
• Look at Chart 20. Notice that the pictures are similar to pictures on the "One, Two, Tie My Shoe" chart (*pick up sticks* and *lay them straight*).
• Identify which picture represents beat and which represents no beat(bottom, no beat; top, beat).
(You may wish to use Copying Master 3-8 at this time.)
• Listen to "The Wind" and show whether it has beat or no beat by patting the beat if it has a beat, or sitting without moving if it has no beat. ("The Wind" has no definite beat.)
• Listen to the poem again, adding appropriate sound effects with mouth sounds or wind chimes. A few children can pretend to be the wind, moving around the room as they dramatize the words of the poem.

Reinforcing the Lesson
Review "Indian Lullaby" on page 56. Have the children show by patting the beat or sitting still whether the song has beat or no beat. (It has a definite beat.) Sing the song again as some children softly play the beat on drums and tambourines.

3 APPRAISAL
The children should be able to:
1. Identify the sound of the tambourine, rhythm sticks, drum, and triangle with appropriate signs.
2. Identify the difference between beat and no beat with movement.

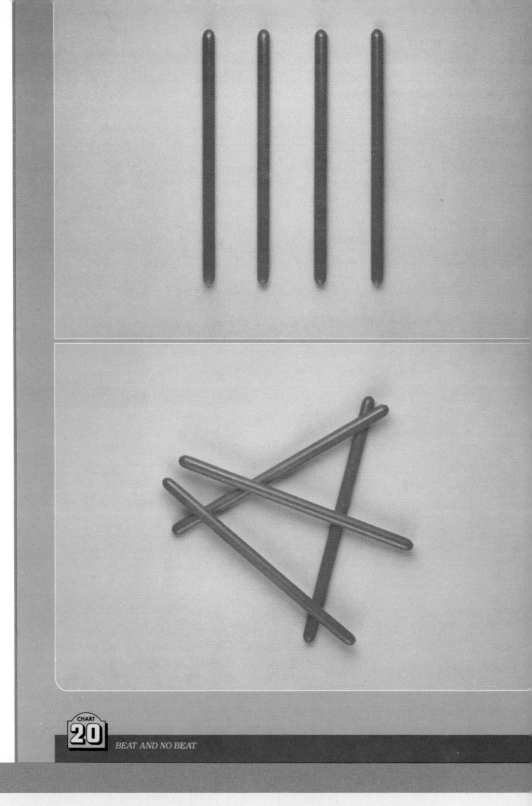

CHART 20

BEAT AND NO BEAT

E X T E N S I O N

SONGBOOK
"Let Us All Be Thankful," page 247 (Thanksgiving)
"Autumn Leaves," page 245 (Autumn)
"Five Fat Turkeys," page 246 (beat, Thanksgiving)

CURRICULUM CONNECTION: ART
Wind Chimes—Wind chimes can be made out of many kinds of materials. A simple wind chime can be made with a coat hanger, plastic fishing line, and sound-producing objects such as shells, small pieces of metal, or big nails. Hang the objects from pieces of fishing line cut to the same length. Hang enough objects so they strike each other when shaken.

CURRICULUM CONNECTION: SCIENCE
Wind Movement—Have the children observe the wind over a five-day period. If weather permits, take a walk outdoors each day. Have the children try to see and feel the wind. Make a chart and record the wind movement for each day as slow, medium, or fast.
(You may wish to use Copying Master 1-2 at this time.)

The Wind

There are many things
    about the wind
    that I do not know.

I have not seen the wind
    and no one has told me where the wind lives,
    or where it is going
    when I hear it
    and when I feel it rushing by.

And something more
    I do not know about the wind.

I do not know if it is angry
    or if it is just playing
    and just doing the things it does for fun.

Sometimes
    the wind gathers sand
    into whirlwinds
    and makes them dance
    over the flat lands
    until they are tired
    and lie down
    to get their breath.

—Indian Poem

LESSON 6

Focus: Rhythm

Related Subjects
Tracing, left to right, top to bottom,
Thanksgiving, numbers

Objective
To practice beat through singing, speech,
playing instruments, and moving

Materials
Recordings: "One, Two, Tie My Shoe"
        "Three Little Muffins"
        "Muffin Man"
        "Thanksgiving Feast"
        "Thank You"
        "Thanksgiving"
Charts 15 and 18
Copying Master 3-7 (optional)

1 SETTING THE STAGE

Review "One, Two, Tie My Shoe" on page
70. Have the children sing the song, first
doing the movements, then patting the
beat. Sing the song again as you point the
beat on Chart 18. Repeat the song, giving
individuals a turn to point the beat on the
chart as the rest of the class traces the numbers in the air.
(You may wish to use Copying Master 3-7
at this time.)

2 TEACHING THE LESSON

**1. Review "Three Little Muffins," page
69, for steady beat.** Have the children:
• Say the poem with the finger play.
• Recognize that they moved and spoke
to a steady beat.
• Dramatize the poem. One child plays
the baker, three play the muffins, and four
play the customers. Repeat the activity in
order to give other children a turn.
**2. Review "Muffin Man" on page 67 to
practice steady beat.** Have the children:

3A

CD 2

Thanksgiving Feast

Pumpkin pie! Gingerbread!
Turkey, stuffing, too!
That's what we'll eat on Thanksgiving Day
and
I'll catch you!

E X T E N S I O N

MORE MUSIC TEACHING IDEAS

Have the children practice inner hearing
with "One, Two, Tie My Shoe," thinking
the numbers instead of singing them as
they pat the beat. Some children play
rhythm sticks in place of singing the numbers and the rest of the class pats the beat.
Repeat the activity to give other children
a turn to play the rhythm sticks.

Thanksgiving

Thank You
for all my hands can hold—
apples red,
and melons gold,
yellow corn
both ripe and sweet,
peas and beans
so good to eat!

Thank You
for all my eyes can see—
lovely sunlight,
field and tree,
white cloud-boats
in sea-deep sky,
soaring bird
and butterfly.

Thank You
for all my ears can hear—
birds' song echoing
far and near,
songs of little
stream, big sea,
cricket, bullfrog,
duck and bee!

—Ivy O. Eastwick

LESSON 6

- Sing the song, patting the beat.
- Recognize that they moved and sang to a steady beat.
- Play the game.

3. Introduce "Thanksgiving Feast" on page 76 to practice beat. Have the children:
- Listen to the poem.
- Name the foods mentioned in the poem (pumpkin pie, gingerbread, turkey, stuffing).
- Echo these words after you as they pat a steady beat. (Use a different kind of voice, for example, whisper, sing, call, and so on, with each word.)
- Play this game: Everyone stands in a circle. Designate something on or near each wall as a safe area. Then choose one child to be "It" and have that child stand in the center of the circle. As everyone says the poem, "It" can move in place on the beat. On the word *you*, "It" tries to tag someone before everyone reaches a safe area. Any child tagged becomes the new "It" and the game continues. (You may wish to have the children crouch down to be safe for a quieter game.)

Reinforcing the Lesson
Review "Thank You" on page 73. Sing the song, quietly patting the beat. Then introduce "Thanksgiving." Listen to the poem, and then have volunteers tell things for which they are thankful. Sing "Thank You" again, taking turns telling things for which they are thankful, or using ideas from "Thanksgiving" as a spoken interlude between repeats of the song.

3 APPRAISAL
The children should be able to:
1. Identify beat by pointing the beat with "One, Two, Tie My Shoe."
2. Show increasing skill performing beat.

MORE MUSIC TEACHING IDEAS
1. Have the children practice patting the rhythms of classroom instrument names as they say them. Try matching the rhythm of each instrument name to the rhythm of a food or word mentioned in "Thanksgiving Feast" (rhythm sticks, tambourine, and triangle—gingerbread or pumpkin pie; drum—too, that's, what, we'll, eat, on, Day, and, I'll, catch, you).
2. Have the children play the food rhythms on the instruments with the same name rhythm. Do this as you or a child points to the different instruments on Chart 15.

SONGBOOK
"Let Us All Be Thankful," page 247 (Thanksgiving)
"Autumn Leaves," page 245 (Autumn)
"Five Fat Turkeys," page 246 (beat, Thanksgiving)

REVIEW AND EVALUATION

REVIEW

Objectives
To review songs, skills, and concepts learned in Unit 3
To measure the children's ability to:
1. Recognize and use the term *beat*
2. Identify the triangle, rhythm sticks, drum, and tambourine by sight and sound

Materials
Recordings: "Hey Diddle Diddle"
"One, Two, Tie My Shoe"
"The Farmer in the Dell"
"Put Your Finger in the Air"
"Put Your Finger on the Sticks"
"Thank You"
Triangle, rhythm sticks, drum, tambourine
Evaluation Unit 3 Copying Master

TEACHING THE LESSON

Review songs and concepts in Unit 3 by dramatizing a story. Have the children:
• Listen as you tell the story, singing and performing the activities at the appropriate places. (As the children sing and move, observe individuals and the class as a whole and evaluate how their responses indicate their level of understanding.)

The Animals' Thanksgiving
• Sing "Hey Diddle Diddle" on page 61, patting the beat.

It was Thanksgiving morning. The cat, the dog, and the cow had been very busy all year acting in their hit play, *Hey Diddle Diddle.* The cat had to play his fiddle every night as the cow performed her famous jumping-over-the-moon stunt. Meanwhile, the dog had to laugh and laugh to keep the people from seeing how the dish-running-away-with-the-spoon trick was done. All three friends were very tired now. They were so tired that they wondered how they would ever find the energy to fix their Thanksgiving dinner. They did not even have the energy to sing their hit song.
• Sing "Hey Diddle Diddle" without any discernible beat. (You will need to guide the children in this activity.) Show by not moving or trying to pat the beat that they do not detect one.

That morning the three friends were so tired that they did not have the energy to do anything. They stood by the window and sang to the people walking along the street.
• Sing "One, Two, Tie My Shoe" on page 70, patting the beat.

REVIEW AND EVALUATION

The farmer who lived in the dell came by with his family and heard the three friends singing. They decided to stop in for a visit with their friends.
• Sing "The Farmer in the Dell" on page 63, patting the beat.

The farmer suggested that everyone play a game to help the three friends feel better.
• Sing "Put Your Finger in the Air" on page 58, doing the movements to the beat.

When they had finished the game the cat admitted that he felt a little better. The farmer's child wanted to play a listening game. The three friends offered the instruments from their show for the game.
• Sing "Put Your Finger on the Sticks" on page 58, showing the hand sign for each instrument as it occurs in the song.

Then the cow suggested a different listening game. Everyone was eager to play.
• Listen, and show the hand sign for the instrument they hear as you play each instrument.

The cat, the dog, and the cow were feeling much better by now, but they were still a little too tired to cook a big dinner. So the farmer and his wife invited them to the house in the dell for Thanksgiving. The three friends happily accepted. Everyone had a wonderful day. Before sitting down to Thanksgiving dinner they all sang "Thank You."
• Sing "Thank You" on page 73, quietly patting the beat.

EVALUATION

Evaluation Unit 3 Copying Master can be found in the *Teacher's Resource Book* with full directions for providing an evaluation of the child's progress.

ELEMENTS OF MUSIC	UNIT 4 OBJECTIVES	Lesson 1 CORE Focus: Classroom Instruments	Lesson 2 CORE Focus: High and Low
Dynamics	Respond to different dynamics when echoing, singing, and speaking	Identify dynamic changes in sections of a song	Vary dynamics in echo patterns
Tone Color	Identify voices of men, women, children Explore instruments for high and low **Name and play jingle bells, wood block, xylophone, glockenspiel, bells, and drum**	Identify and play jingle bells and wood block Play instruments on key words and rhyming syllables Use children's names for words in a song	Explore instruments for high and low Identify and play jingle bells, wood block, xylophone, glockenspiel, bells, and drum Play instruments on rhyming words
Tempo	Recognize, use faster/slower	Sing song faster and slower Move to different tempos	Vary tempo in echo patterns
Duration/ Rhythm	Pat beat with familiar songs and rhymes Echo clap/say short phrases See representation of beats in picture form Sing and hear music containing silent beat Play trotting rhythm pattern (♫) Practice identifying long sounds	Echo phrases of a chant Hear music containing silent beats Pat and play trotting rhythm (♫ ♫) and beat with song Practice identifying long sounds	Hear music containing silent beats
Pitch	Sing songs using high/low **Identify high/low**	Use high/low voices	Sing song with high/low Identify, sing, say, play, see high and low
Texture	Add accompaniment to songs	Hear melody accompanied	Add accompaniment to a song
Form	Find and name same/different sections Follow map showing introduction/interlude/coda Say poem and sing song in AB form	Show recognition of A and B sections of a song	Say poem in AB form
Style	Discover how changes in music elements can change style of music Hear music from operetta Sing spiritual, American and Spanish folk songs, composed songs	Sing a spiritual Sing American folk song	Hear and say phrases with changes in dynamics and tempo Sing traditional English carol Sing Spanish folk song

PURPOSE Unit 4: Holiday Fun

This unit uses seasonal selections to emphasize the musical concepts of playing classroom instruments and identifying high and low while continuing to practice steady beat. Many December holidays are acknowledged, as well as the idea of universal acceptance and understanding.

SUGGESTED TIME FRAME

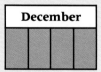

December			

FOCUS

Core Lessons 1, 2, 5
• Classroom Instruments
• High and Low
• Classroom Instruments

Lessons 3, 4, 6
• Steady Beat
• Steady Beat
• Comparing Musical Elements

Lesson 3 Focus: Steady Beat	Lesson 4 Focus: Steady Beat	Lesson 5 CORE Focus: Classroom Instruments	Lesson 6 Focus: Comparing Musical Elements
Play instrumental accompaniment softly Listen and identify dynamic changes	Hear loud/soft	Play loud and soft accompaniments as appropriate	Discuss loud/soft as a musical contrast
Play jingle bells, wood block accompaniment Hear orchestral instruments	Play jingle bells, wood block	Explore instruments for high and low Identify and play jingle bells, wood block, and drum Identify voices of men, women, and children	Identify vocal tone color and high/low as musical contrasts Identify different types of voices (man, woman, child)
		Sing songs with a faster and slower beat	Identify fast/slow as a musical contrast and compare two songs for fast and slow
Keep steady beat by patting, playing instruments, and marching Listen to music containing silent beats while patting beat	Keep beat by patting, marching, and pointing the beat See representation of beats in picture form Sing and hear music containing silent beat Play accompaniment on beat with song	Keep the steady beat on the drum See, play beat from representation in picture form	Keep steady beat by playing instrumental accompaniments Hear music containing silent beats
	Play high and low pitches	Hear and move to high and low Compare voices and instruments for high/low Create and play high and low patterns	Identify high/low as a musical contrast Sing *mi so*
Hear melody accompanied		Add accompaniments to songs	Add accompaniments to songs
Hear, identify, see map of contrasting sections	Improvise for approximate length of a phrase in a poem Hear introduction, interlude, and coda Say poem following phrase mark		Hear song with two sections, one of which repeats Play introduction, interlude, coda
Hear music from operetta Sing spiritual	Hear music from operetta Interpret poems by adding instruments, considering style	Play instruments appropriately with different song styles	Identify musical contrasts that affect style

BULLETIN BOARD

Draw the outline of a bookcase with two shelves. You may wish to decorate the top of the bookcase with holly leaves or other seasonal greenery. Label the top shelf *high* and the bottom shelf *low*. Have the children cut out pictures of things that make high sounds, for example, birds and finger cymbals, and things that make low sounds, for example, trucks and drums. Attach the pictures to the appropriate shelf on the bookcase.

LESSON 1

Focus: Classroom Instruments

Related Subjects
Self-esteem, rhyming words, home and community

Objective
To identify and play jingle bells and the wood block

Materials
Recordings: "This Little Light of Mine"
    "This Little Light of Mine"
    (faster version)
    "The Angel Band"
    "Jack Be Nimble"
    "Hurry, Little Pony"
    Recorded Lesson—"Spanish
      Pronunciation, 'Hurry,
      Little Pony' Verse 3"
Chart 21
Triangle, jingle bells, wood block, drum
Copying Masters 4-1, 4-2, 4-3 (optional)

Vocabulary
jingle bells, wood block

1 SETTING THE STAGE

Introduce "This Little Light of Mine." Have the children listen and identify the rhyming words (*mine, shine*). Have them listen again, making a long arm movement on *mine* and *shine*. Remember a classroom instrument that can make a long sound, such as a triangle, and play it on *mine* and *shine* as they sing. Demonstrate the sound of jingle bells shaking and compare it to the long sound they just played. Identify the new sound as long also. Have them listen to and sing along with the faster version of "This Little Light of Mine," patting the beat to show the faster tempo. Sing again, playing jingle bells on the rhyming words.

3A
CD 2

This Little Light of Mine

Piano Accompaniment on page PA 38   *Spiritual*

This lit-tle light of mine,___ I'm gon-na let it___ shine.___

This lit-tle light of mine,___ I'm gon-na let it___ shine.___

This lit-tle light of mine,___ I'm gon-na let it___ shine.___

Let it___ shine,___ let it___ shine,___ let it___ shine.___

E X T E N S I O N

MORE MUSIC TEACHING IDEAS
After the children know "This Little Light of Mine" well, sing these alternate words to learn more about each other:
Over here is (child's name), I'm gonna let it shine,
She/He likes (something the child likes), I'm gonna let it shine,
She/He doesn't like (something the child doesn't like), I'm gonna let it shine,
Let it shine, let it shine, let it shine.
(You may wish to substitute *him* or *her* for *it*.)

Key: G   Starting Pitch: D   Scale Tones: *so, la, do re mi so*

The Angel Band

Piano Accompaniment on page PA 39

South Carolina Folk Song

1. There was one, there were two,
2. There were four, there were five,
3. There were sev-en, there were eight,

there were three lit - tle an - gels,
there were six lit - tle an - gels,
there were nine lit - tle an - gels,

Ten lit - tle_ an - gels in the band._____

Oh, was - n't that a band?

Sun - day morn - ing, Sun - day morn - ing,

Sun - day morn - ing, Was-n't that a band?

Sun - day morn - ing, Sun - day morn - ing soon?_____

The Angel Band from 36 SOUTH CAROLINA SPIRITUALS by Carl
Diton. Used by permission of G. Schirmer, Inc.

2 TEACHING THE LESSON

1. Introduce "The Angel Band" for prac-tice playing jingle bells and wood block. Have the children:
• Listen to the song, raising their hands each time they hear a number.
• Listen to the song again, with a few chil-dren playing a wood block each time they hear a number.
• Listen to the song again, with a few chil-dren playing jingle bells on the word *angels*.
• Sing the song, with a few children play-ing the wood block part and a few chil-dren playing the jingle bell part. Repeat the activity to give other children a chance to play the instruments.
(You may wish to use Copying Master 4-1 at this time.)

2. Introduce "Jack Be Nimble." Have the children:
• Echo-say the A section of the poem one line at a time.
• Echo the A section again, using a high voice for the first line, and a low voice for the second line.
• Say the A section with you. Then iden-tify and clap the rhyming syllables (*quick, -stick*).
• Say the A section several times as a few children play wood blocks on the rhym-ing syllables.
(You may wish to use Copying Master 4-2 at this time.)

Jack Be Nimble

Ⓐ Jack be nimble, Jack be quick,
Jack jump over the candlestick.

Ⓑ No, no, no, no,
That's not the thing to do!
Don't jump over the candlestick,
You might just burn your shoe!

—adapted by R. DeLelles

EXTRA HELP: ALTERNATE SOUND SOURCES

If jingle bells or a wood block are not available, help the children search for environmental sound sources that make suitable alternatives to these instruments. Inverted paper cups played on a desk top can simulate a wood block. Shaking beans in a covered glass jar can simulate jingle bells. Metal bottle tops flattened with a hammer and nailed loosely to a wooden handle make a substitute jingle stick.

3. Introduce "Hurry, Little Pony." Have the children:

• Listen to the song and identify the animal mentioned in the song (pony). Then identify where the pony and rider are going (town, back home).

• Listen again, gently patting the trotting sound of the pony's hooves on their knees in the A section (the rhythm of the trotting sound, ♫ ♫, is the same as the rhythm of the words *hurry, little* at the beginning of each verse), and patting once on each beat in the B section.

• Designate two places in the room to be town and home respectively. Several children trot to these places during the verses, and stop to pat their pony on the beat during each B section. (You may wish to do this several times so all the children can have an opportunity to move. It also gives them time to become familiar with the song.)

• Listen to the recorded Spanish pronunciation lesson and echo each phrase of verse 3. (See *Pronunciation* guide and translation, below.)

Hurry, Little Pony

Piano Accompaniment on page PA 40

Spanish Folk Song
Words by S.S.

1. Hur - ry, lit - tle po - ny, to the town we go.
2. Hur - ry, lit - tle po - ny, back to home we go.
3. ¡Ar - ré ca - ba - lli - to! Va - mos a Be - lén

Hur - ry lit - tle po - ny, not too fast or slow.
Hur - ry, lit - tle po - ny, not too fast or slow.
Que ma - ña - na es fi - e - sta y pa - sa - do tam - bi - én.

B (*for verses 1 and 2*)

One, two, three, four, five, six, sev-en eight
Po - ny, po - ny, you are great!

B (*for verse 3*)

U - no, dos, tres, cua - tro cin - co, seis, si - e - te, o - cho.

Ar - ré ca - ba - lli - to Us - ted me gus - ta mu - cho.

EXTENSION

PRONUNCIATION

¡Arré caballito!
ä-rā′ kä-bä-yē′ tō

Vamos a Belén.
vä′ mōs ä bā-len′

Que mañana es fiesta
kā män-yä′ nä es fē-es′ tä

y pasado también.
ē pä-sä′ dō täm-bē′ en

Uno, dos, tres, cuatro,
ōō′ nō dōs tres kwä′ trō

cinco, seis, siete, ocho.
sēn′ kō sās sye′ tā o′ chō

¡Arré caballito!
ä-rā′ kä-bä-yē′ tō

Usted me gusta mucho.
ōōs′ ted mā gōōs′ tä mōō′ chō

(Translation:
Hurry, little pony!
We are going to Bethlehem.
Tomorrow is a festival
and also the next day.

One, two, three, four,
Five, six, seven, eight.
Hurry, little pony!
You please me very much.)

MORE MUSIC TEACHING IDEAS

1. Have the children identify the dynamic changes during the introduction and the coda of "Hurry, Little Pony" as getting louder and getting softer. (Play an introduction and coda with appropriate dynamic changes, or use the recording.)
2. Have the children sing "Hurry, Little Pony" at a faster or slower tempo, changing their movement appropriately to match the tempo.

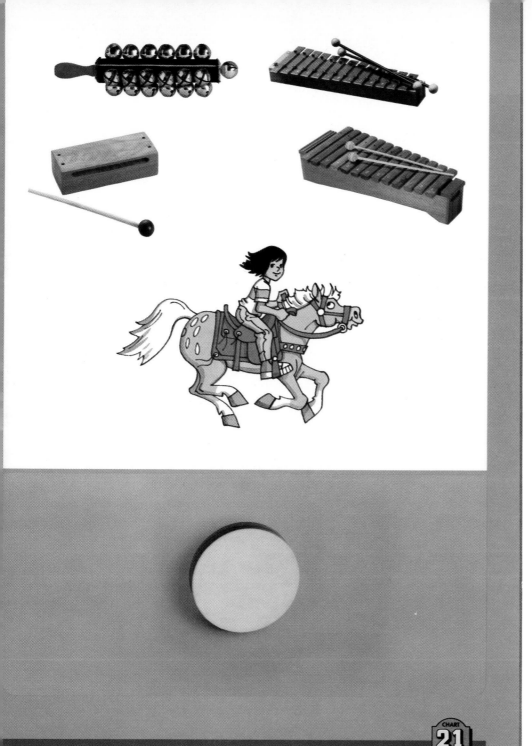

MORE CLASSROOM INSTRUMENTS

CHART 21

4. Play instruments with "Hurry, Little Pony." Have the children:
• Look at Chart 21 and identify the instruments they have already played in this lesson (jingle bells, wood block).
(You may wish to use Copying Master 4-3 at this time.)
• Sing "Hurry, Little Pony" as several children play the trotting rhythm on jingle bells and wood block. (See the orchestration in *More Music Teaching Ideas* for notation.)
• Add a drum on the beat with the B section only.

Reinforcing the Lesson

Have the children form three groups. Sing "Hurry, Little Pony" several times, with Group 1 singing the song, Group 2 trotting like ponies, and Group 3 playing the instrument parts. (You may wish to tell the children they will work with instruments similar to the other instruments pictured on Chart 21 in the next lesson.)

3 APPRAISAL

The children should be able to:
1. Identify pictures of jingle bells and a wood block.
2. Play jingle bells and the wood block with different songs and a poem.

MORE MUSIC TEACHING IDEAS

Have the children learn an accompaniment for the A section of "Hurry, Little Pony." Have them trot to practice the rhythm of the jingle bell and wood block parts. Then have them pat the beat to prepare for playing the xylophone part.

Next, have them pat the rhythm of the rhyming words to prepare for playing the glockenspiel part. Finally, have them pretend to pat a pony on each beat in the B section to prepare for playing the drum part. Use this same patting movement on the drum head, and think the words in their heads as they play.

SONGBOOK

"Jig Jog, Jig Jog," page 274 (pony song; trotting rhythm; add appropriate classroom instruments)
"The Friendly Beasts," page 250 (add appropriate classroom instruments)

LESSON 2

Focus: High and Low

Related Subjects
Taking turns, bilateral movement, rhyming words

Objective
To hear, play, and identify high and low sounds

Materials
Recordings: "Jack Be Nimble"
 "Play Me a Song"
 "We Wish You a Merry
  Christmas"
 "Hurry, Little Pony"
Charts 21 and 22
Jingle bells; wood block; xylophone; glockenspiel or low D, high D, low G, and high G bells; drum
Barred instrument stick-on (optional)
Copying Masters 4-2, 4-4 (optional)

Vocabulary
xylophone, glockenspiel

1 SETTING THE STAGE

Have the children review the A section of "Jack Be Nimble" on page 81, echoing the first line using high voices and the second line using low voices. Echo several times, varying the dynamics and tempo each time. Say both lines, saying the word *Jack* in a high voice and the rest of the words in a low voice. Echo the words to the B section one line at a time, alternating high- and low-pitched voices. (You may wish to use Copying Master 4-2 at this time.)

2 TEACHING THE LESSON

1. Introduce the concept of high and low pitch. Have the children:
• Look at Chart 22 and identify the different positions of the two packages (one is low and one is high).
• Say *low* in a low voice or *high* in a high voice as you randomly point to the high or low package. (You may wish to use Copying Master 4-4 at this time.)
2. Introduce "Play Me a Song" to practice identifying low and high. Have the children:
• Listen to "Play Me a Song." (Point to the low package on the low notes and the high package on the high notes.)
• Listen as you show them low D and high D on a xylophone or other pitched barred instrument. Move to show low or high as you randomly play low D and high D.
• Take turns improvising a piece on low D and high D. (You sing "Play Me a Song," substituting a child's name for the word *children*. That child takes the instrument and improvises a piece of about the length of "Play Me a Song." Repeat the activity,

3A, 3B
CD 2

CHART 22
HIGH AND LOW

E X T E N S I O N

Key: D   Starting Pitch: D   Scale Tones: *do so*

Play Me a Song

Chil - dren, chil - dren, play me a song.

Play on an in - stru - ment all day long.

Key: G   Starting Pitch: D   Scale Tones: *so, la, ti, do re mi fa*

We Wish You a Merry Christmas

Piano Accompaniment on page PA 41

English Carol

We wish you a mer-ry Christ-mas,

We wish you a mer-ry Christ-mas,

We wish you a mer-ry Christ-mas,

And a hap-py New Year.

substituting a different child's name in the song each time. You may also wish to vary the instrument played by substituting an instrument name for the word *instrument* each time.)

3. Introduce "We Wish You a Merry Christmas" to practice identifying higher and lower sounds. Have the children:
• Listen to the song, singing along as they are able.
• Sing the song, watching as you show with hand movements how each *we wish* goes from low to high.
• Sing the song again, mirroring your hand movements to show how each *we wish* goes from low to high.

4. Review "Hurry, Little Pony" on page 82 and add high and low instrument parts. Have the children:
• Review the song, first singing it, and then adding the jingle bell and wood block parts.
• Look at Chart 21 and see what other instruments they can use to accompany the song (xylophone, glockenspiel, and drum).
• Identify high G and low G on the xylophone or resonator bells. Identify the longer bar as low G and the shorter bar as high G. (You may wish to affix the barred instrument stick-on to Chart 22.)
• Pat their knees on the beat as they sing the song. Then have one child play the beat on both G bars together (both hands at the same time). Sing the song with jingle bell, wood block, and xylophone parts.

Reinforcing the Lesson

Have the children identify the rhyming words in "Hurry, Little Pony" (*go* and *slow*). Sing the song, gently tapping shoulders on the rhyming words. Sing the song again as one child plays the high G and low G bars of a glockenspiel or other high-pitched instrument together on the rhyming words. Then add a drum on the beat with the B section. Sing the song several times with the children taking turns playing the parts as the others trot to the music.

3 APPRAISAL

The children should be able to:
1. Echo high and low speaking voices with "Jack Be Nimble."
2. Play high and low pitches with "Play Me a Song" and "Hurry, Little Pony."
3. Move to identify low and high.

SONGBOOK

"My Dreydl," page 248 (take turns spinning a dreydl, or turning as one; rhyming words; high and low)
"Must Be Santa," page 254 (rhyming words)
"The Bus," page 266 (high and low; rhyming words)

LESSON 3

Focus: Steady Beat

Related Subjects
Toys, telling time, Hanukah

Objective
To practice keeping a steady beat

Materials
Recordings: "This Little Light of Mine"
"This Little Light of Mine" (faster version)
"In the Toy Shop"
Listening—"March of the Toys" from *Babes in Toyland* by Victor Herbert
"Hanukah Is Here"
Chart 23
Jingle bells, wood blocks
Copying Masters 4-5, 4-6 (optional)

1 SETTING THE STAGE

Have the children review "This Little Light of Mine" on page 80, using the tempo most appropriate for the class. Sing the song, then remember the rhyming words. Sing the song again, adding jingle bells. Have the children pat the steady beat as they sing the song. Then sing again with a few children softly playing the steady beat on wood blocks and a few others playing jingle bells on the rhyming words.

2 TEACHING THE LESSON

1. Introduce "In the Toy Shop" to practice steady beat. Have the children:
• Listen to the song to discover what time it is, and what is happening. (The clocks are striking midnight, and the wooden soldiers are marching through the toy shop.)
• Listen again, patting the steady beat with alternating hands, like marching.

EXTENSION

CURRICULUM CONNECTION: MATH

Telling Time—Using a clock model with moveable hands, show the children what a clock looks like at midnight. Discuss other times of the day, and show the children those times on the clock. Discuss what might happen in the toy shop at different times of day or night. You may wish to make up additional verses to the song that follow the sequence of time during a day and night. Show the correct time for each verse on the clock. (You may wish to use Copying Master 4-5 at this time.)

In the Toy Shop

Piano Accompaniment on page PA 42

Composer unknown

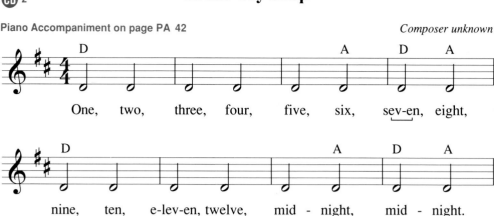

One, two, three, four, five, six, sev-en, eight,

nine, ten, e-lev-en, twelve, mid - night, mid - night.

Mid - night, mid - night, bells are sound - ing;

all the clocks are strik - ing in the town.

Out they come, the wood - en sol - diers,

march-ing through the toy shop, up and down.

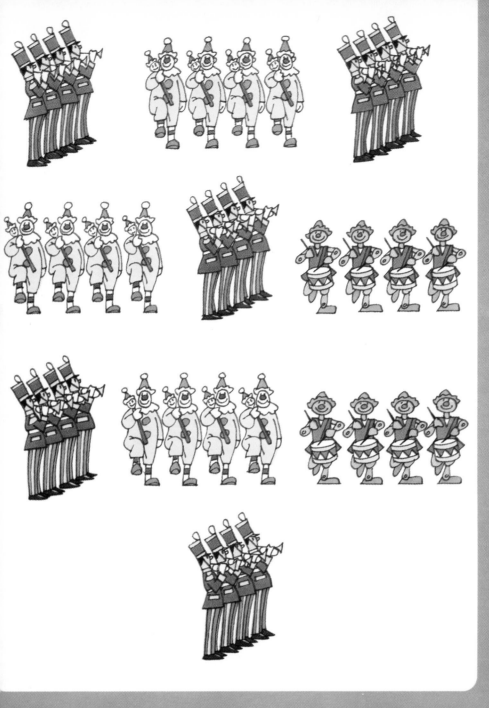

LISTENING MAP: "MARCH OF THE TOYS"
CHART 23

• Listen as you sing the first measure, then sing the second measure. Continue to alternate, listening to you sing a measure, then singing the next measure.
• Sing the song, patting the beat.

2. Introduce "March of the Toys" for moving to a steady beat. Have the children:
• Look at Chart 23, and discuss how many different types of toys they see (three), and what those toys are (trumpeters, clowns, and drummers).
• Listen to "March of the Toys," following the pictures on Chart 23. (You may wish to use Copying Master 4-6 at this time.)
• Discuss what the toys on the map are doing. (The trumpeters are standing still playing trumpets, the clowns are marching, and the drummers are marching and playing drums.)
• Form three groups: trumpeters, clowns, and drummers. Each group decides on a movement, and practices that movement for a minute. Then listen to the music, with each group moving at the appropriate time.
• Identify the movement they were doing as marching, and remember that marching is done to a steady beat.

Reinforcing the Lesson

Preview "Hanukah Is Here" on page 88 to continue practicing steady beat. Have the children pat a steady beat on their knees with you, starting and stopping as you do. Then pat the steady beat as they listen to "Hanukah Is Here."

3 APPRAISAL

The children should be able to keep a steady beat by patting, playing instruments, and marching to different music.

MORE MUSIC TEACHING IDEAS

1. Have the children play a simple accompaniment with "In the Toy Shop." Play alternating low D and high D on a low-pitched instrument throughout the song. Add octave Ds played together after the rhyming words (*town* and *down*). Play a tick-tock sound on a wood block for eight beats as an introduction, followed by a D resonator bell sounding twelve times to indicate it is midnight.
2. Have the children dramatize "In the Toy Shop." They start by pretending to be soldiers or other toys standing on shelves. When the music begins they come to life and march around, returning to their shelves at the end of the song.

3. Have the children form three groups representing the three sections in "March of the Toys," as above. Each group chooses a different instrument to play with their section of the music, for example, trumpeters—wood block, clowns—jingle bells, and drummers—drum. Then listen to the music, with each group playing their instruments on the steady beat at the appropriate time.
4. Have the children listen to "March of the Toys" and identify the dynamic changes in the music. (In general, the basic dynamic plan is soft, loud, soft. However, the section represented by the second group of drummers breaks this pattern because that section is louder than the section before it.)

THE COMPOSER

Victor Herbert (1859–1924)—an Irish-born composer. He came to the United States in 1886 and for a time was the conductor of the Pittsburgh Symphony Orchestra. Herbert is most famous for his operettas, and is known as "the prince of operetta." Among his more than forty operettas are *The Red Mill* and *Naughty Marietta*. "March of the Toys" is from *Babes in Toyland*, which features characters from Mother Goose and fairy tales.

SONGBOOK

"My Dreydl," page 248 (beat)
"Step in Time," page 288 (beat)
"Go Tell It on the Mountain," page 252 (beat)
"El Nacimiento," page 253 (beat)
"Must Be Santa," page 254 (beat)

LESSON 4

Focus: Steady Beat

Related Subjects
Recognizing written names, Hanukah

Objectives
To practice keeping a steady beat
To follow a visual representation of beat

Materials
Recordings: "Play Me a Song"
"Hanukah Is Here"
"Jack Be Nimble"
Listening—"March of the
Toys" from *Babes in
Toyland* by Victor Herbert
Optional Listening—
"Rudolph, the Red-Nosed
Reindeer"
"I Heard a Bird Sing"
(optional)
"Merry Christmas"
(optional)
Charts 23, 24, and 25
Jingle bells, wood block, or pitched instrument
Copying Masters 4-6, 4-7, 4-8 (optional)

1 SETTING THE STAGE

Have the children review "Play Me a Song" on page 84, patting the steady beat as they sing. Substitute a different child's name for the word *children* each time to give individual children an opportunity to play either the jingle bells or wood block, or improvise on low D and high D with a pitched instrument for the length of the song.

Key: D minor   Starting Pitch: D   Scale Tones: *la, ti, do re mi*

3A, 3B
CD 2

Hanukah Is Here

Piano Accompaniment on page PA 44

Words and music by
Suzanne Clayton

1. Light   the   can - dles,   light   the   can - dles,
2. Spin   the   drey - dl,   spin   the   drey - dl,
3. Dance   the   ho - ra,   dance   the   ho - ra,

Light   the   can - dles,   Ha - nu - kah   is   here.
Spin   the   drey - dl,   Ha - nu - kah   is   here.
Dance   the   ho - ra,   Ha - nu - kah   is   here.

E X T E N S I O N

CURRICULUM CONNECTION: READING

Reading Names—Help the children learn to recognize their own printed names. Write each child's name on individual strips of oak tag and place all the strips in a container. Each time you sing "Play Me a Song," substitute the words *this child* for *children*, and hold up one name from the container. The child whose name is on the strip has a turn playing a low and high song.

MORE MUSIC TEACHING IDEAS

1. Have the children play a simple accompaniment with "Hanukah Is Here." Play the steady beat or every other beat on D and A together on a bass xylophone or low bells. Add rhythm instruments with different tone colors on the final rest in each verse, for example, finger cymbals with the first verse, triangle with the second verse, and tambourine with the third verse.

2. Do simple movements with "Hanukah Is Here." During the first verse have one child walk along a row of eight children, tapping one child on the head for every other beat. As the children are tapped, they raise their hands over their heads to imitate a candle being lit. During the sec-

ond verse have the children find their own space and spin like a dreydl. During the third verse have the children walk the beat in a circle, changing direction halfway through the verse. If the class is large enough, have the children form three groups for this activity, with one group moving during each verse.

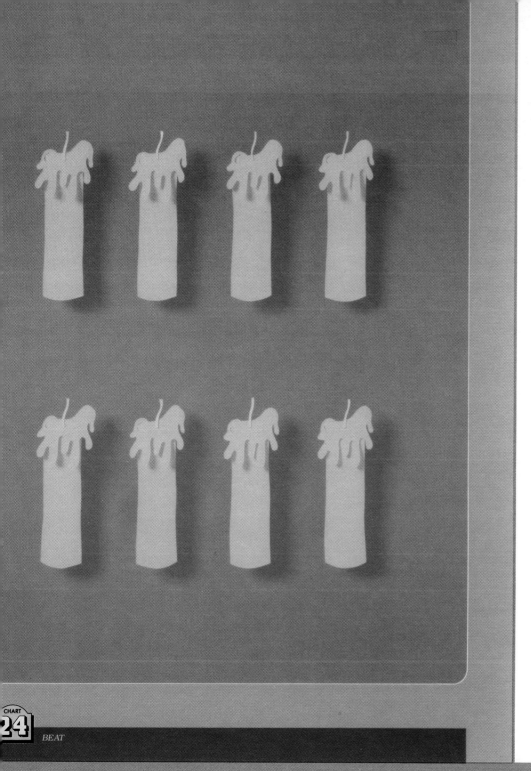

2 TEACHING THE LESSON

1. Teach "Hanukah Is Here" to reinforce beat. Have the children:
• Listen and identify the activities mentioned in the song (lighting candles, spinning the dreydl, dancing the hora).
• Listen to the song again, singing along as they are able.
(You may wish to use Copying Master 4-7 at this time.)
• Pat the steady beat as they sing the song.

2. Introduce a visual representation of beat. Have the children:
• Sing the first verse of "Hanukah Is Here" as you point the beat on Chart 24. (Point to each candle once, left to right and top to bottom, then repeat to point all sixteen beats.)
• Sing the first verse of the song again, pointing to the candles on Chart 24 with you. (You may wish to use Copying Master 4-8 at this time.)

CHART **24**

BEAT

MORE MUSIC TEACHING IDEAS

1. Use the flame stick-ons and have eight children affix their flames to the candles on Chart 24 one at a time on the first eight beats of the song. (Have these children move in front of the chart in a straight line.) Repeat this activity to give other children a turn at the chart.

2. Have several children play unpitched instruments such as triangles or drums as you point to each candle. If some children are very good at this activity, take off some of the flames and have the children play only when you point to a candle that has a flame. (The easiest flame to remove is the last one. Then try removing both the fourth and last flames.)

3. Using the number stick-ons, number the candles from 1 to 8 in order, from left to right, top to bottom. Then repeat the activity in number 2 above, removing some of the flames. After the children have played the pattern, have them tell the number of the beats they did not play.

LESSON 4

3. Review "Jack Be Nimble" on page 81.
Have the children:
• Say the A section, patting the steady beat. Then say the A section again as you trace the arc on Chart 25 with your finger, once during *Jack be nimble, Jack be quick,* and once during *Jack jump over the candlestick.* (Time this movement to last as long as each phrase.)
• Look at the pictures at the bottom of the chart and listen to the second part, or B section, of the poem. Add movements for each picture, for example, shake head back and forth, put both fists on hips, point at each other, point to shoe.
• Say the whole poem, watching as you trace the arcs during the A section, and doing the appropriate movement as you point for four beats to each character at the bottom of the chart during the B section.

Reinforcing the Lesson

Have the children review "March of the Toys," first following the listening map on Chart 23, then marching in time to the music. (You may wish to use Copying Master 4-6 at this time.)

3 APPRAISAL

The children should be able to:
1. Pat, move to, and play the steady beat.
2. Follow a visual representation of beat with "Hanukah Is Here."

CHART 25   PHRASES

EXTENSION

SONGBOOK

"My Dreydl," page 248 (beat)
"Step in Time," page 288 (beat)
"Go Tell It on the Mountain," page 252 (beat)

MORE MUSIC TEACHING IDEAS

Have the children practice internalizing the beat with "Jack Be Nimble." Have them practice saying the A section while jumping the beat. Then have them plan movements for each picture in the B section, doing each movement four times to the beat (shaking head back and forth with hands on each side of head, patting fists on hips, shaking pointed finger, and shaking pointed finger at shoe). Have them say the entire poem with the actions. Then have them repeat the poem with the actions, silently thinking the words of the B section.

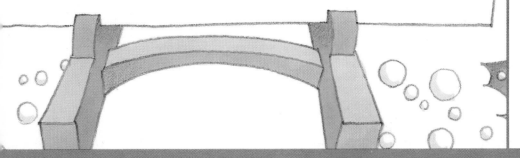

Rudolph, the Red-Nosed Reindeer

Words and music by Johnny Marks

You know Dasher and Dancer, and Prancer and Vixen,
Comet and Cupid and Donner and Blitzen,
But do you recall the most famous reindeer of all?

Rudolph, the red-nosed reindeer, had a very shiny nose
And if you ever saw it, you would even say it glows.
All of the other reindeer used to laugh and call him names.
They never let poor Rudolph join in any reindeer games.

Then one foggy Christmas Eve, Santa came to say,
"Rudolph, with your nose so bright, won't you guide my
    sleigh tonight?"
Then how the reindeer loved him as they shouted out with glee:
"Rudolph, the red-nosed reindeer, you'll go down in history."

MORE MUSIC TEACHING IDEAS

Interpret one of the following poems with the children. First work on speaking together and keeping a steady beat. Then say the poem using different tempos, pitches, and dynamics and determine which style they like best. Try playing instruments at different places in the poem, for example, on the steady beat, on the rhyming words, or play a different instrument at the end of each line.

OPTIONAL LISTENING

The optional listening selection "Rudolph, the Red-Nosed Reindeer" may be used to supplement the lesson's focus on steady beat. You may wish to have some children play jingle bells on the beat.

I Heard a Bird Sing

I heard a bird sing
    In the dark of December
A magical thing
    And sweet to remember.

"We are nearer to Spring
    Than we were in September,"
I heard a bird sing
    In the dark of December.

—*Oliver Herford*

Merry Christmas

I saw on the snow
when I tried my skis
the track of a mouse
beside some trees.

Before he tunneled
to reach his house
he wrote "Merry Christmas"
in white, in mouse.

—*Aileen Fisher*

LESSON 5

Focus: Classroom Instruments

Related Subjects
Christmas, Kwanzaa, auditory discrimination and sequencing

Objectives
To review identifying high and low
To review identifying jingle bells, wood block, and drum

Materials
Recordings: Recorded Lesson—"High and Low Sound Patterns"
"Santa's Coming"
"Kum Ba Yah"
"Jingle Bells"
"Jingle Bells" (slower version; optional)
Charts 22 and 26
Jingle bells, wood block, low-pitched drum
Copying Masters 4-4, 4-9, 4-10, 4-11, 4-12 (optional)

1 SETTING THE STAGE

Have the children look at Chart 22 and listen to "High and Low Sound Patterns." Have them follow the directions on the recording or listen as you play patterns of high and low sounds. Have the children first respond individually to high and low sounds by standing for high and crouching for low. Then have them work in pairs to show the relationship between two pitch examples. Finally, have them work in groups of four to show patterns of four low and high sounds.

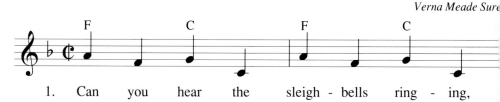

Santa's Coming

Piano Accompaniment on page PA 45

Words and music b
Verna Meade Sure

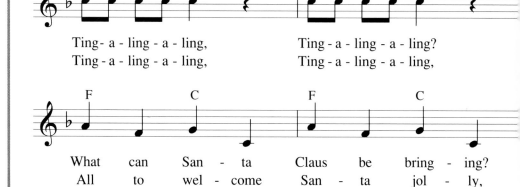

1. Can you hear the sleigh-bells ring-ing,
(2.) trimmed the tree and hung the hol-ly,

Ting-a-ling-a-ling,   Ting-a-ling-a-ling?
Ting-a-ling-a-ling,   Ting-a-ling-a-ling,

What can San-ta Claus be bring-ing?
All to wel-come San-ta jol-ly,

Ting-a-ling-a-ling, ting-a-ling-ling-ling. 2. We've
Ting-a-ling-a-ling, ting-a-   ling-ling-ling.

E X T E N S I O N

COOPERATIVE LEARNING
To help the children learn to work with every classmate, randomly assign the pairs for the Setting the Stage activity. Divide the number of children in the class by two, and count off by that number. Children with the same number are partners. If the children have assigned seats, begin counting with a different child each time and vary your counting design (vertical rows, horizontal rows, around the edges and then into the middle, and so on). In this way after several activities the children will have had many different partners.

MORE MUSIC TEACHING IDEAS
1. Have the children use stick-ons with Chart 22 to create more high and low patterns. Take turns placing four packages in different high and low patterns. Then play their patterns on low F and high F using a pitched instrument or resonator bells. (You may wish to use Copying Master 4-4 at this time.)
2. Have the children add a pitched instrument part to "Santa's Coming" to reinforce the concepts of high and low and steady beat. Have them alternate playing low F and high F on the steady beat throughout the song using a low-pitched instrument such as a bass xylophone. Have them play low F and high F together on the rest after each *ting-a-ling-a-ling* using a higher-pitched instrument such as a glockenspiel.

KEYBOARD
Play a game to review high and low on the keyboard. Have one child point to the boxes on Chart 22 (page 84) four times (for example: low, low, low, high). Have another child play a corresponding pattern on the keyboard, playing the low pitches with the left hand and high pitches with the right hand. The rest of the class should listen to hear if the pattern was played correctly.

Kum Ba Yah

Piano Accompaniment on page PA 46

Traditional

1., 4. Kum ba yah, my Lord, Kum ba yah!
2. Some - one's sing - ing, Lord, Kum ba yah!
3. Some - one's pray - ing, Lord, Kum ba yah!

Kum ba yah, my Lord, Kum ba yah!
Some - one's sing - ing, Lord, Kum ba yah!
Some - one's pray - ing, Lord, Kum ba yah!

Kum ba yah, my Lord, Kum ba yah!
Some - one's sing - ing, Lord, Kum ba yah!
Some - one's pray - ing, Lord, Kum ba yah!

Oh, Lord, ___ Kum ba yah!

MORE MUSIC TEACHING IDEAS

1. Add a high sound, for example, a triangle, at the end of each line of "Kum Ba Yah."

2. If you are using the recording, have the children identify the different vocal tone colors they hear in "Kum Ba Yah" (male, female, and children). Identify the male voice as low and the female voice and children's voices as higher.

2 TEACHING THE LESSON

1. Introduce "Santa's Coming," and review playing jingle bells. Have the children:
• Listen to the song and determine what sound the sleigh bells make (ting-a-ling-a-ling).
• Listen again, raising their hands each time they hear *ting-a-ling-a-ling*.
• Echo-say the words, then echo-sing the song, two measures at a time.
• Sing the song as several children play jingle bells on the words *ting-a-ling-a-ling*. Do this activity several times to learn the words and give each child a chance to play the bells.
• Identify jingle bells as a high-sounding unpitched instrument.

2. Introduce "Kum Ba Yah" and review the sound of the drum. Have the children:
• Listen as you gently play a slow, steady beat on a drum. Then determine that the drum sound is lower than the jingle bell sound. (Be sure the children understand that lower does not mean softer.)
• Listen for the sound of the drum in "Kum Ba Yah."
• Echo the words to "Kum Ba Yah."
• Sing the song several times with a few different children softly playing the beat on a drum each time.

CURRICULUM CONNECTION: SOCIAL STUDIES

Kwanzaa—Kwanzaa is an African American holiday that is celebrated for seven days, beginning on December 26. It is fashioned after a Nigerian harvest celebration. Kwanzaa is a time of giving gifts and thanks.

TEACHER INFORMATION

Music and You uses the term *African American* when referring to Americans of African descent.

LESSON 5

3. Review identifying jingle bells, wood block, and drum by sight. Have the children:

• Look at Chart 26 and determine which instrument they have not used yet in this lesson (wood block).
(You may wish to use Copying Master 4-9 at this time.)

• Follow the chart as three children play jingle bells, a wood block, and a drum as you point to them on the chart.

• Repeat this activity several times to give each child a turn playing an instrument. (You may wish to use Copying Master 4-10 at this time.)

CHART **26** "JINGLE BELLS"

E X T E N S I O N

SPECIAL LEARNERS

When forming groups to play instruments, as in the lesson above, group special learners with more able children. Seat all of the players directly in front of the chart and be sure that you have eye contact with all of the players when you give instructions. If possible, have the special learner repeat the directions to you. Encourage the special learner to play accurately at the correct time, but give him or her extra time to respond. Be sure to compliment *any* children who play their parts correctly.

Key: F   Starting Pitch: A   Scale Tones: *do re mi fa so*

Jingle Bells

Piano Accompaniment on page PA 47

Words and music by
James Pierpont

Jin - gle bells,   jin - gle bells,   jin - gle all the way!

Oh,   what   fun   it   is   to   ride   in   a

one-horse o - pen sleigh!____   one-horse o - pen sleigh!

Reinforcing the Lesson

Have a few children play instruments, following Chart 26, as the class listens to and sings along with "Jingle Bells." Review the words to the song as needed and as time permits.

3 APPRAISAL

The children should be able to:
1. Move to show that they can identify high and low sounds.
2. Identify jingle bells, the wood block, and the drum by sight.

MORE MUSIC TEACHING IDEAS

Have the children:
1. Review "The Farmer in the Dell" on page 63, using these alternate holiday words:
    1. Santa's in the room, Santa's in the room, Hi-ho on Christmas Eve, Santa's in the room.
    2. Santa takes a wife...
    3. The wife takes a child...
    4. The child takes a toy...
    5. The toy takes an elf...
    6. The elf takes Rudolph...
    7. They all do a dance...
    8. Rudolph stands alone...
(You may wish to use Copying Master 4-11 at this time.)

2. Learn "Must Be Santa" on page 254 of the Songbook. (You may wish to use Copying Master 4-12 at this time.)
3. Learn the verse for "Jingle Bells," singing with the slower version on the recording:
Dashing through the snow
In a one-horse open sleigh,
O'er the fields we go,
Laughing all the way;
Bells on bobtail ring
Making spirits bright.
What fun it is to ride and sing
A sleighing song tonight!

SONGBOOK

"Must Be Santa," page 254 (sequencing)
"Go Tell It on the Mountain," page 252 (beat)
"El Nacimiento," page 253 (beat)
"Holiday Song," page 249 (beat)
"My Head and My Shoulders," page 281 (Kwanzaa)
"The Friendly Beasts," page 250 (add classroom instruments)

LESSON 6

Focus: Comparing Musical Elements

Related Subjects
Opposites, Christmas, making comparisons

Objective
To compare songs for different musical contrasts

Materials
Recordings: "Santa's Coming"
"Kum Ba Yah"
"In the Toy Shop"
"Jingle Bells"
Listening—"I'd Like to Teach the World to Sing"
Chart 26
Jingle bells, wood blocks, drums, D resonator bell
Copying Master 4-9 (optional)

1 SETTING THE STAGE

Have the children identify something that is opposite or different from each of these musical concepts—loud (soft), high (low), fast (slow), man's voice (woman's voice, child's voice), melody with accompaniment (melody alone), no beat (steady beat).

2 TEACHING THE LESSON

1. Review "Santa's Coming" on page 92 and "Kum Ba Yah" on page 93 to compare fast and slow tempos. Have the children:
• Listen to both songs and determine which is slower ("Kum Ba Yah").
• Decide if there is any other difference between the two songs (answers will vary).

Key: F   Starting Pitch: D   Scale Tones: *so, la, ti, do re mi fa so*

I'd Like to Teach the World to Sing (In Perfect Harmony)

Words and music by Bill Backer, Billy Davis, Roger Cook, and Roger Greenaway

(for listening only)

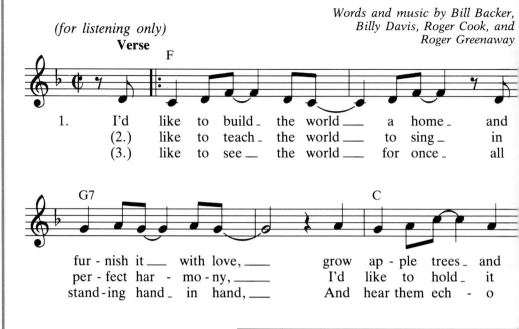

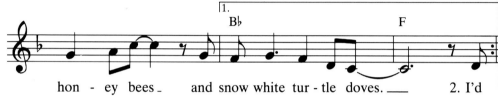

1. I'd like to build the world a home and
(2.) like to teach the world to sing in
(3.) like to see the world for once all

fur-nish it with love, grow ap-ple trees and
per-fect har-mo-ny, I'd like to hold it
stand-ing hand in hand, And hear them ech-o

hon-ey bees and snow white tur-tle doves. 2. I'd
in my arms and
through the hills for

EXTENSION

COOPERATIVE LEARNING

Assign the children randomly to pairs for this entire lesson. Have the pairs discuss answers together before the whole group makes decisions. The pairs should share instruments and take turns playing the assigned parts. By discussing and making decisions together, each child has the opportunity to orally rehearse information and ideas. Encourage sharing, listening, and saying ideas.

keep it com-pa-ny. 3. I'd peace through-out _ the

Refrain

land. That' the song I hear; _ Let the world sing _ to-

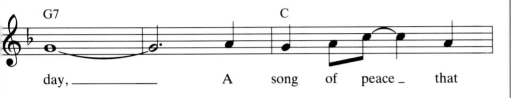

day, _____ A song of peace _ that

ech-oes on _ and nev-er goes _ a-way.

2. Review "In the Toy Shop" on page 86 and "Jingle Bells" on page 95 to compare instrumental accompaniments. Have the children:

• Review "In the Toy Shop," playing a wood block on the steady beat throughout the song to simulate the *tick-tock* sound of a clock, and playing a D resonator bell twelve times each as an introduction, interlude, and coda (ending).

• Review "Jingle Bells," adding the accompaniment suggested by Chart 26. (You may wish to use Copying Master 4-9 at this time.)

• Compare the accompaniments for both songs, and decide which instrument was used with both songs (wood block), and which instruments were only used with one song (resonator bell with "In the Toy Shop," and jingle bells and drum with "Jingle Bells").

• Decide if there are any other differences between the two songs (answers will vary).

Reinforcing the Lesson

Introduce "I'd Like to Teach the World to Sing," and have the children listen for differences within the song. (Answers will vary, but may include different types of voices, different sections, different verses, a refrain that stays the same.) You may wish to have the children learn the words to the refrain by echoing.

3 APPRAISAL

The children should be able to compare and discuss differences and similarities between various musical elements in different songs.

VOCAL DEVELOPMENT

Have the children play this game to help them sing individually. Using a sing-song pattern alternating on *so* and *mi*, sing a question such as "What present would you like?" or "What will Santa bring to you?" to each child. Each child in turn sings his or her wish, and the class echoes the answer. Try to have the children answer in complete sentences, for example, "I would like a bicycle," or "He will bring a puppy."

SONGBOOK

"The Friendly Beasts," page 250 (add classroom instruments)

"Jig Jog, Jig Jog," page 274 (same and different; add classroom instruments and compare effect with "The Friendly Beasts")

"My Head and My Shoulders," page 281 (Kwanzaa; add classroom instruments and compare effect with "The Friendly Beasts")

REVIEW AND EVALUATION

REVIEW

Objectives
To review songs, skills, and concepts learned in Unit 4
To measure the children's ability to:
1. Name and play jingle bells, wood block, xylophone, glockenspiel, bells, and drum
2. Identify high and low

Materials
Recordings: "Santa's Coming"
"Hurry, Little Pony"
"Jack Be Nimble"
"Kum Ba Yah"
"This Little Light of Mine"
"Jingle Bells"
Charts 22 and 26
Jingle bells, wood block, glockenspiel, xylophone, resonator bells, low drum
Holiday package stick-ons
Evaluation Unit 4 Copying Master

TEACHING THE LESSON

Review the songs and concepts in Unit 4 by dramatizing a story. Have the children:
• Listen as you tell the story, singing and performing the activities at the appropriate places. (As the children sing and move, observe and evaluate individuals and the class as a whole as to how their responses indicate their level of understanding.)

Santa's Visit

We were in the living room putting up holiday decorations, when suddenly we heard the faint sound of jingle bells. The sound became louder and louder.
• Sing "Santa's Coming" on page 92, playing jingle bells on the steady beat.

There was a knock at the front door. We answered the door and were surprised to see Santa standing there. We welcomed him in, and asked what he was doing at our house this particular evening. We did not expect him until Christmas Eve.

Santa explained that he was lost. Rudolph was busy at the North Pole, and without Rudolph's red nose to guide the way, he could not find the way back to the North Pole in the fog.

We sat Santa down in a chair, and told him we would try to find a way to solve his problem. Lisa thought the hardware store in town might have something Santa could use. Off she went to town on her little pony.
• Sing "Hurry, Little Pony" on page 82 as one child trots to town and back again. Play the jingle bell, wood block, glockenspiel and xylophone parts.

EXTENSION

MORE MUSIC TEACHING IDEAS

1. This review can be performed as a holiday program for parents or another class in the school. Have the children choose parts and dramatize the story. Costumes can be as simple or elaborate as you wish. One suggestion for a set might be a mural showing a living room at holiday time.
2. Have the children make up their own holiday story using songs from the unit.

REVIEW AND EVALUATION

Lisa came back with a candle and a candlestick. Mother lit the candle, and we gave it to Santa. He shook his head, and told us that a candle would not work because the wind would blow out the flame. We tried to think of something else to do with the candlestick. Jack suggested jumping over it.
• Recite "Jack Be Nimble" on page 81, using high voices for the A section, and low voices for the B section.

Jack was looking high and low for an idea to help Santa. He tried arranging all the presents in different high and low patterns. Each time he rearranged them, he asked someone to play the pattern he had made.
• Using the holiday package stick-ons, have one child arrange low and high patterns on Chart 22. Have other children play the patterns on low D and high D resonator bells.

Santa enjoyed this game, and he even took a turn. But soon he was looking sad again. Father suggested singing a song to cheer Santa up.
• Sing "Kum Ba Yah" on page 93, using good singing voices, and adding a low drum on the steady beat.

When we finished singing, we heard another knock at the door. It was Rudolph. He explained that Santa had been gone so long he had begun to worry. Finally, he went searching for Santa. He was so happy when he saw Santa's sleigh outside our house. Then we all went outside into the dark, and Rudolph turned on his light.
• Sing "This Little Light of Mine" on page 80, playing jingle bells on the rhyming words.

We all wished Santa a safe trip home, and a happy holiday. He gave us a small bag, which we opened. A wood block, jingle bells, and a drum were inside. We played them and sang as Santa headed home to the North Pole.
• Sing "Jingle Bells" on page 95, adding instruments with each line as shown on Chart 26.

EVALUATION

Evaluation Unit 4 Copying Master can be found in the *Teacher's Resource Book* with full directions for providing an evaluation of the child's progress.

RELATED ARTS

A Story Told with Music: A Special Related Arts Lesson

Objectives
To hear a story told with music
To hear vocal tone colors of men, women, and children

Materials
Recordings: Listening—Selections from *Hansel and Gretel* by Engelbert Humperdinck:
"Prelude"
"Susie, Little Susie"
"Brother, Come and Dance with Me"
"Tra-la-la-la"
"There Stands a Little Man"
"The Little Sandman"
"Prayer"
"The Dew Fairy"
"Nibble, Nibble, Mousekin"
"Hocus Pocus"
"Tra-la-la-la"
"Now That We Are Free at Last"
Charts 27, 28, and 29
Hansel and Gretel stick-ons
Copying Master RA-1 (optional)

SETTING THE STAGE

Introduce the story of *Hansel and Gretel*. Have the children look at Chart 27 and watch as you put the stick-on characters of the four people who live in the house (Hansel and Gretel, and their parents) on the chart. Tell the children that the only food in the house is one pitcher of milk. (Put the stick-on pitcher on the table.) Then tell them that "Prelude" will get them ready to hear the rest of the story. Listen to "Prelude."

HANSEL AND GRETEL ACT I

EXTENSION

THE COMPOSER

Engelbert Humperdinck (1854-1921)— German composer of operas and stage music. After studying music in Cologne and Munich, Humperdinck won a music prize which enabled him to travel to Italy. There he met another German composer, Richard Wagner. Much of Humperdinck's music reflects Wagner's influence. In 1893 Humperdinck wrote the fairy-opera *Hansel und Gretel*. The libretto (story) was adapted by his sister, Adelheid Wette, from the fairy tale by the brothers Grimm. *Hansel und Gretel* was an immediate success at its first performance, and has remained popular ever since, especially as entertainment for children.

TEACHING THE LESSON

1. Introduce Act I of *Hansel and Gretel.* Have the children:
• Listen to the story, watching as you move the stick-on figures on Chart 27 appropriately.

ACT I

"Once upon a time there lived a poor family in a tiny house near a great forest. One day the family had no food to eat, so Father went into town to sell brooms. Mother went into the field to gather grass to make more brooms. The children, Hansel and Gretel, stayed at home to help with the housework. They sang a song as they worked."
• Listen to "Susie, Little Susie."
"Hansel and Gretel were hungry, and complained to each other. They tasted the thick cream on top of the pitcher of milk sitting on the table. The thought of the pudding Mother would make with the cream made them so happy they decided to dance."
• Listen to "Brother, Come and Dance with Me."
"Hansel and Gretel were having so much fun they did not see Mother come home. She was very angry because she found them playing instead of working. Mother bumped against the table. Down fell the pitcher of milk. Now there was nothing at all for dinner. Mother was upset, and sent the children into the forest to pick strawberries for dinner. After the children left, Father came home."
• Listen to "Tra-la-la-la."
"Father had sold all his brooms and brought home good things to eat. Mother told him what happened. Father was upset to learn that Hansel and Gretel had

TEACHER INFORMATION

The photographs on this page show Hansel and Gretel standing among the cookie children who have been magically brought back to life after the witch was pushed into the oven. Hilda Harris as Hansel (left) and Gail Robinson as Gretel (right) in the Metropolitan Opera production of *Hansel and Gretel.*

MOVEMENT

When the children know "Brother, Come and Dance with Me" well, have them learn a dance. Choose partners and decide which partner is Hansel and which is Gretel. Then do the following movements.
Brother, come and dance with me (bow or curtsey)
Both my hands I give to thee (clasp hands)
Right foot first, left foot then (move right foot forward and back, then move left foot forward and back)
Turn around and back again (circle in place)
Dancing is so new to me, I'm as clumsy as can be. If you show me what to do, I will try to dance with you. (Hansel sings to Gretel)
Have the children do as the words of the duet suggest, tapping, clapping, and so on. Change partners and repeat the dance.

RELATED ARTS

gone into the forest. A witch who turned children into gingerbread lived there. Mother and Father went off at once to find Hansel and Gretel."

2. Introduce Act II of *Hansel and Gretel*. Have the children:
• Listen to the story, watching as you put the appropriate stick-on figures on Chart 28.

ACT II
"Hansel and Gretel walked deep into the forest, picking and eating strawberries. Gretel sang a song about a flower that looked like a little man."
• Listen to "There Stands a Little Man." "When Hansel and Gretel decided to start for home, they saw that their basket was empty. They had eaten all the strawberries! As they began to look for more, it started to get dark. The forest became strange and scary. They sat down on the grass, tired and frightened. Just then the Sandman appeared."
• Listen to "The Little Sandman." "The Sandman went away, leaving Hansel and Gretel feeling very sleepy and safe. They said their evening prayer before lying down to go to sleep."
• Listen to "Prayer." "As Hansel and Gretel slept near an old log, fourteen angels came to watch over them."

3. Introduce Act III of *Hansel and Gretel*. Have the children:
• Listen to the story, watching as you put the appropriate stick-on figures on Chart 29.

ACT III
"The next morning the Dew Fairy came and shook dewdrops from a flower on the sleeping children to wake them."

CHART **28** HANSEL AND GRETEL ACT II

EXTENSION

CURRICULUM CONNECTION: LANGUAGE ARTS

Dramatization—When the children are familiar with the story of *Hansel and Gretel* have them dramatize scenes from the opera, for example, Hansel and Gretel at home, Father coming home after selling his brooms, Hansel and Gretel lost in the forest, and Hansel and Gretel at the gingerbread house. Have the children try to improvise interesting dialogue. (You may wish to use Copying Master RA-1 at this time.)

HANSEL AND GRETEL *ACT III*

CHART 29

RELATED ARTS

• Listen to "The Dew Fairy."
"Hansel and Gretel awoke to see a beautiful house made of candy and cake. Around the house was a fence made of gingerbread children. Hansel and Gretel tiptoed toward the house and broke a small piece of cake off the roof. As they started to nibble, they heard a voice from inside the house."
• Listen to "Nibble, Nibble, Mousekin."
"Hansel and Gretel were a little frightened, but they were also very hungry. Gretel said the voice was only the wind. They broke off another piece of the house. Then they heard the voice again."
• Listen again to "Nibble, Nibble, Mousekin."
"The witch came to the door of the house and invited Hansel and Gretel inside. When they refused, she sang some magic words that made Hansel and Gretel unable to move."
• Listen to "Hocus Pocus."
"The witch began to prepare the oven to bake Hansel and Gretel into gingerbread as she had done with the other children. She was so happy she took a ride on her broomstick. Then she freed Gretel from the spell and asked her to check the fire. Gretel told the witch that she did not know how, so the witch leaned into the oven to show her. Gretel quickly pushed the witch into the oven and closed the big door. Then Gretel freed Hansel with the witch's magic wand. The big oven exploded and the spell was broken. All the gingerbread children turned back into boys and girls. Just then Father and Mother arrived at the witch's house."
• Listen to "Tra-la-la-la."
"Hansel and Gretel ran to meet their parents. They found the witch turned into a giant gingerbread cookie. Everyone was safe at last."
• Listen to "Now That We Are Free at Last."

ELEMENTS OF MUSIC	UNIT 5 OBJECTIVES	Lesson 1 CORE Focus: Rhythm	Lesson 2 CORE Focus: Tone Color	Lesson 3 Focus: Rhythm	Lesson 4 Focus: Pitch
Dynamics	Hear and use loud and soft				
Tone Color	**Recognize the difference between an instrument of definite pitch and one of indefinite pitch** Hear, see orchestral instruments Continue learning names of classroom instruments	Improvise accompaniment for poem using pitched instrument	Identify pitched and indefinite pitched instruments Add instruments to a poem Identify instruments	Hear orchestral instruments Play a rhythm pattern on triangle	Use instruments to demonstrate high/low and long/short Play song based on a scale on bells Play instruments on rhyming words
Tempo	Identify slow, fast, and changes in tempo	Sing songs that do not change tempo			Move to show slow
Duration/ Rhythm	Review beat, no beat See pictorial representation of beat, silent beat **Recognize notation for a sound one beat long and for a silent beat (♩ , 𝄽)** Sing songs with ♩ ♫ 𝄽	Practice keeping the beat Practice recognizing the difference between beat and no beat Move to show no beat Recognize pictorial representation of beat Practice using basic movements with a song	Practice pointing and keeping the beat See pictorial representation of beat Play ♫ ♩ at the ends of phrases of a song	Practice keeping the beat Tap rhythm of words of poem (♩ ♩ ♩ 𝄽) Use ♩ ♩ ♩ 𝄽 as ostinato with a song Compare and identify longer/shorter sounds Move to show longer/ shorter sounds	Use long/short sounds Play long/short sounds on high and low instruments of indefinite pitch Recognize no beat Move to show no beat Play rhythm of words of a poem on instruments of indefinite pitch
Pitch	Sing songs containing *mi so* (3 5) or *mi so la* (3 5 6) Sing, hear higher/lower See and devise ways to show higher/lower	Sing song containing *mi so la* (3 5 6) Improvise with *mi so* (3 5)	Sing song containing *mi so la* (3 5 6)	Sing song containing *mi so la* (3 5 6) and song based on a scale Move to show how melody goes upward and downward	Devise ways to show higher/lower visually Move to show recognition of higher and lower sounds Explore high and low speaking voices
Texture	Play accompaniments Sing with an ostinato	Add instruments to a poem	Improvise accompaniment to a poem	Sing song with an ostinato	
Form	Find, label same/different Follow visual representation of same/different Identify, use interlude	Recognize that two parts of a song are different (singing in A section, body percussion in B section)		Use rhythm patterns as an interlude between repetitions of a poem	
Style	Listen to orchestral compositions			Listen to orchestral composition of the 18th century	

PURPOSE Unit 5: Winter Days

This unit is intended for use after the December holidays. The musical concepts of recognizing visual representations of and standard notation for a sound that is one beat long and a beat of silence (♩ and 𝄽), and distinguishing between the sounds of pitched and unpitched instruments are presented through the themes of winter and real and make-believe animals.

SUGGESTED TIME FRAME

January					February		
▓	▓	▓	▓	▓			

FOCUS

Core Lessons 1, 2, 5, 6, 9
• Rhythm
• Tone Color
• Rhythm
• Rhythm
• Tone Color and Rhythm

Lessons 3, 4, 7, 8, 10
• Rhythm
• Pitch
• Rhythm and Tempo
• Pitch
• Rhythm

Lesson 5 CORE Focus: Rhythm	Lesson 6 CORE Focus: Rhythm	Lesson 7 Focus: Rhythm and Tempo	Lesson 8 Focus: Pitch	Lesson 9 CORE Focus: Tone Color and Rhythm	Lesson 10 Focus: Rhythm
Hear orchestral instruments **See pictures of orchestral instruments**	Play the beat on classroom instruments Play ♩ ♩ ♩ 𝄽 on classroom instruments	Play ♩ ♩ ♩ 𝄽 on classroom instruments	Use classroom instruments to demonstrate higher and lower **Practice good instrument-playing techniques**	Distinguish between tone qualities of pitched and unpitched instruments Use pitched and unpitched instruments to accompany a song	Accompany a song with pitched and unpitched instruments
		Practice identifying changing tempo			
Practice keeping the beat See representations of beats in picture form See notation for ♩ Follow notation for ♩	Pat and point the beat Practice recognizing notation for a sound one beat long Recognize a pictorial representation for a beat of silence Use a pattern with a beat of silence (♩ ♩ ♩ 𝄽)	Practice identifying and using beat and silent beat	Practice moving to the beat Use a pattern with a beat of silence	See and use pictorial representation and notation for a sound that is one beat long (♩) and for a silent beat (𝄽) **Create rhythms with ♩ and 𝄽**	Practice patting the beat Practice using notation for a sound that is one beat long (♩) and for a beat of silence (𝄽)
	Play a pattern using two pitches		Identify and play higher and lower sounds See and devise ways to show higher and lower visually	**Use inner hearing**	
Identify same and different sections of an orchestral composition				Use movement to show recognition of different sections	Use body percussion and movement to show recognition of different sections
Hear orchestral composition based on children's songs		Listen to descriptive orchestral composition of the 19th century	Listen to descriptive orchestral composition of the 19th century		

BULLETIN BOARD

Set up a bulletin board showing three large quarter notes and a quarter rest. Under each quarter note place a picture of a pitched or an unpitched instrument, for example, a xylophone, a triangle, and a wood block. Leave the space below the quarter rest blank. Put the label *Sound* above the notes and instruments, and put the label *No Sound* above the quarter rest.

LESSON 1

Focus: Rhythm

Related Subjects
Left and right, same and different, winter

Objectives
To practice beat
To practice recognizing the difference between beat and no beat
To recognize visual representations of beat

Materials
Recordings: "Welcome Back to School"
"Icy"
"Teddy Bear"
"Mitten Song"
"One Finger, One Thumb"
(optional)
Charts 30 and 31
Mitten stick-ons
Copying Masters 5-1, 5-2 (optional)

1 SETTING THE STAGE

Introduce "Welcome Back to School." Have the children listen to the song and do the activities described in the A section. Lead the class in the body percussion patterns in the B section. Have the children decide if the A and B sections are the same or different (different).

MORE MUSIC TEACHING IDEAS

Have the children:
1. Make up other verses to "Welcome Back to School," such as *Can you nod? Can you sway?* and so on. Sing the song, doing these new movements.
2. Perform the B section with partners. Have them clap their partner's hands on beats two and four of the third measure.

4B

CD 3

Key: F   Starting Pitch: C   Scale Tones: *so, ti, do re mi fa so la*

Welcome Back to School

Piano Accompaniment on page PA 48

*Words and music by
Randy DeLelles*

Wel-come back to school. __ Can you tap? (tap)

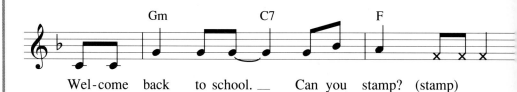

Wel-come back to school. __ Can you stamp? (stamp)

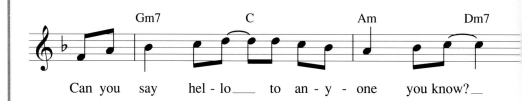

Can you say hel-lo __ to an-y-one you know? __

Can you tap? (tap) And can you stamp? (stamp)

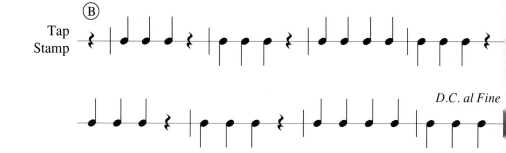

Tap
Stamp

D.C. al Fine

ICY

I slip and I slide
On the slippery ice;
I skid and I glide—
Oh, isn't it nice
To lie on your tummy
And slither and skim
On the slick crust of snow
Where you skid as you swim?

—Rhoda W. Bacmeister

LESSON 1

2 TEACHING THE LESSON

1. Introduce "Icy" to practice recognizing no beat. Have the children:
• Listen to the poem and decide if it has a definite beat or no beat (no beat).
• Think of ways they can move without showing a definite beat. Watch as a few volunteers demonstrate their ideas. Try each idea, first moving parts of their bodies, and then their whole bodies.
• Listen again, moving to show no beat as they dramatize the poem.

MORE MUSIC TEACHING IDEAS

Have the children add instrument sounds to "Icy." Metal instruments such as triangles or glockenspiels can suggest sparkling ice and snow. Play glissandos or random sounds on any *do* pentatonic scale, for example, C D E G A. The children can improvise any way they feel helps express the mood of the poem.

KEYBOARD

Use the keyboard to create sounds for "Icy." Play very high pitches lightly to create a sparkling sound. A glissando, or sliding sound, can be created on either the white or black keys by sliding the backs of the fingers or fingernails over the keys. Holding down the sustaining pedal (the pedal at the right) as they play glissandos will help create a sliding feeling. Have the children experiment with other ways to create sounds that fit the poem.

CURRICULUM CONNECTION: HEALTH

Lead the children in a discussion on playing safely around frozen bodies of water in winter. Important points to emphasize are: always have an adult test the thickness of the ice before playing on it; always be accompanied by an adult when walking across a frozen lake or pond; always play outdoors with a friend. Conclude that playing outdoors in winter is fun, especially when safety rules are followed.

LESSON 1

Teddy Bear

Piano Accompaniment on page PA 50

American Play Son

2. Introduce "Teddy Bear" for practice with beat. Have the children:
• Listen to the first verse and do the movements described in the song.
• Decide if the song has a definite beat (yes).
• Learn the first verse of the song with the movements.
• Look at Chart 30. Sing the song, watching as you point to a bear on each beat, left to right, and top to bottom. (You may wish to use Copying Master 5-1 at this time.)
• Recognize that the pictures on the chart show the movements described in the song, and that each picture represents one beat.
• Learn the second verse and sing both verses with the movements.
• Recognize that the second verse has the same music as the first verse, but the words are different.

1. Ted-dy Bear,   Ted-dy Bear, .   turn   a - round,_____
2. Ted-dy Bear,   Ted-dy Bear,   go   up - stairs,_____

Ted-dy Bear,   Ted-dy Bear,   touch   the   ground.
Ted-dy Bear,   Ted-dy Bear,   say   your   prayers.

Ted-dy Bear,   Ted-dy Bear,   show   your   shoe,_____
Ted-dy Bear,   Ted-dy Bear,   switch   off the   light,_____

Ted-dy Bear,   Ted-dy Bear,   that   will   do.
Ted-dy Bear,   Ted-dy Bear,   say   "Good   night."

CHART
30
KEEPING THE BEAT

CORE
LESSON 1

Reinforcing the Lesson

Introduce "Mitten Song." Have the children listen to the song and tell if it has a definite beat (yes). Look at Chart 31 and watch as you point to one mitten on each beat. Sing the song, pointing at the chart with the beat as you or a child points to the chart. Then have the children look at the bare hands at the bottom of the chart and decide how to put the left and right mitten stick-ons on the hands correctly. Sing the song again, giving a few children turns to point the beat. (You may wish to use Copying Master 5-2 at this time.)

3 APPRAISAL

The children should be able to:
1. Move to show the beat in "Welcome Back to School," "Teddy Bear," and "Mitten Song."
2. Move to show no beat in "Icy," and recognize the difference between beat and no beat.
3. Recognize pictures that represent beat.

Mitten Song

Piano Accompaniment on page PA 51

Words by Mary Louise Alle
Music by Sue Hanl

1. "Thumbs in the thumb place, fin - gers all to - geth - er!"
2. When it is cold, it does - n't mat - ter wheth - er
3. This is the song we sing in mit - ten weath - er;

This is the song we sing in mit - ten weath - er.
Mit - tens are wool, or made of fin - est leath - er.
"Thumbs in the thumb place, fin - gers all to - geth - er!"

EXTENSION

SONGBOOK

"Clap Your Hands," page 267 (beat)
"Epo i tai tai e," page 269 (beat)
"Que Bonito Es," page 286 (same and different phrases)

MORE MUSIC TEACHING IDEAS

Have the children:
1. Take turns singing about their favorite mittens or mittens they wish they had, improvising on *mi* and *so* (3 and 5). These pitches need not be described to the class. The children will imitate you if you use the pitches as a model in the first improvisation. The class can echo each individual response.
2. Move in ways they think appropriate, such as walk, skip, and so on, as they sing "Mitten Song." (Remind the children to stay in their own space as they move around the room.) Select a few children to move individually (walk, skip, hop, and so on) and have the class identify each kind of movement. (It is important

as part of the natural developmental process to have the children identify basic movements as they learn to do them.)

CHART
31

BEAT

MORE MUSIC TEACHING IDEAS

Have the children learn "One Finger, One Thumb." Sing the song and pat, move, or play instruments to reinforce steady beat.

Key: F **Starting Pitch: C** **Scale Tones:** *so, do re mi fa so*

One Finger, One Thumb

Traditional

1. One fin-ger, one thumb, keep mov - ing, One fin-ger, one

thumb, keep mov - ing, One fin - ger, one thumb, keep mov -

ing, And chase your cares a - way. _____ ___ And

chase your cares a - way. _____ And chase _____ your

cares _____ a - way.

2. *one arm, keep moving . . .

3. *one arm, one leg, keep moving . . .

4. *one arm, one leg, wave your hand, keep moving . . .

5. *one arm, one leg, wave your hand,
   stand up, sit down, keep moving . . .

CORE
LESSON 2

Focus: Tone Color

Related Subjects
Alphabet, shapes, sizes

Objectives
To recognize the difference between the sounds of pitched and unpitched classroom instruments
To practice keeping the beat

Materials
Recordings: "Welcome Back to School"
"Stars"
"Twinkle, Twinkle, Little Star"
"The Alphabet Song"
"Teddy Bear"
"Mitten Song"
Charts 30, 31, and 32
Triangle, wood block, drum, bells (or xylophone, glockenspiel)
Enough rhythm sticks or tambourines for the whole class
Copying Masters 5-3, 5-4, 5-5, 5-6 (optional)

1 SETTING THE STAGE

Have the children review "Welcome Back to School" on page 104. Have them listen to the instruments in the accompaniment (xylophones and wood block).

2 TEACHING THE LESSON

1. Introduce "Stars." Have the children:
• Listen to the poem.
• Echo each line of the poem after you.

Stars

Bright stars, light stars,
Shining-in-the-night stars,
Little twinkly winkly stars
Deep in the sky.

Yellow stars, red stars,
Shine-when-I'm-in-bed stars,
Oh, how many blinky stars
Far, far away.

—Rhoda Bacmeister

E X T E N S I O N

EXTRA HELP

To help the children prepare for playing instruments with "Stars," have them first practice identifying where the word *stars* appears in the poem. Ask the children to move their fingertips to suggest the twinkling of a star each time they hear the word *star*. When instruments are added, the children who are not playing may continue this movement.

KEYBOARD

The children can create the sound effects suggested for "Stars" using the high pitches on the keyboard. Have them gently play any two high black keys together each time the word *stars* occurs. After *sky* and *away*, have them play a few random sounds on the black keys. The black keys on the keyboard form a pentatonic (five-tone) scale. Since the tones of this scale blend together pleasingly, it is perfect for improvising melodies or sound effects. Although the pitch relationships of the pentatonic scale can be found in other places on the keyboard, the black keys form the pattern in a visible way, making it easy for children to locate and play.

Key: D   Starting Pitch: D   Scale Tones: *do re mi fa so la*

Twinkle, Twinkle, Little Star

Piano Accompaniment on page PA 52   *Traditional*

Twin-kle, twin-kle, lit-tle star,   How I won-der what you are!

Up a-bove the   world so high,   Like a dia-mond   in the sky.

Twin-kle, twin-kle, lit-tle star,   How I won-der what you are!

• Echo each line of the poem again as one or more children play a triangle on the word *stars* each time it occurs. (You may also wish to have one or more children play a few random sounds after *sky* and *away*. Play these sounds on triangles, or on glockenspiels or bells with only the bars C D E G A on the instrument.)

2. Introduce "Twinkle, Twinkle, Little Star" to hear a pitched instrument and for more practice pointing the beat. Have the children:
• Listen to the song, quietly patting the beat. (You may wish to remind the children that "Twinkle, Twinkle, Little Star" has the same melody as "The Alphabet Song." These words are given below.) (You may wish to use Copying Master 5-3 at this time.)
• Listen to the recording or to you playing with the song, and try to identify the solo instrument (bells). Discuss the sound of the instrument.

THE ALPHABET SONG

A	B	C	D	E		F	G
H	I	J	K	L	M	N	O	P
Q	R	S	and	T		U	V
W		X	and	Y		and	Z.

Now I've said my A - B - C's;
Tell me what you think   of   me!

VOCAL DEVELOPMENT

Among the best vocal models for children are other children who have natural, light, in-tune singing voices. After the children have learned "Twinkle, Twinkle, Little Star," invite one or two volunteers who have well-developed singing skills to stand and sing the song for the rest of the class. Then encourage the other children to sing aloud with the vocal "models" and to try to match their singing quality.

CURRICULUM CONNECTION: ART

Self-Expression—Ask the children to each think of one wish that they would like to have come true and share their wishes with the class. Then have the children draw or trace pictures of stars on yellow construction paper, cut the stars out, and draw pictures about their wishes on one side. You can write each child's wish on the other side of the star. Display the stars around the classroom. (You may wish to use Copying Master 5-4 at this time.)

LESSON 2

• Sing the song as you point to one star for each beat on Chart 32.

• Sing the song again as one or two children take turns pointing the beat on the chart. (You may wish to use Copying Master 5-5 at this time.)

3. Review "Teddy Bear" on page 106 for more practice with beat and to identify instruments. Have the children:

• Review the song with the movements.

• Sing the first verse again as one or two children take turns pointing the beat on Chart 30.

• Watch as you place several classroom instruments in front of the class (triangle, wood block, drum, rhythm sticks, tambourine, glockenspiel or bells). (At least one should be a pitched instrument.) Then listen as you sing "Teddy Bear" substituting an instrument name for each movement, for example, "Teddy Bear, Teddy Bear, point to the triangle," and so on. Point to the appropriate instrument as they hear its name. (You may wish to use Copying Master 5-6 at this time.)

4. Review "Mitten Song" on page 108 to practice playing the beat. Have the children:

• Choose instruments and sing the song, playing the beat as you point the beat on Chart 31. (Some children can move, such as walk, skip, and so on, as others play. Then switch parts.)

CHART
32
POINT THE BEAT

E X T E N S I O N

COOPERATIVE LEARNING

Have the children point to Copying Master 5-5 in pairs, sharing one paper between them. By limiting the resources, partners will be required to cooperate. In addition, moving to the beat jointly will help unsure learners move along with the steady beat. For this activity, you may wish to pair skilled and less-skilled beat keepers. Repeat this activity several times to strengthen the skill of keeping the steady beat.

MORE MUSIC TEACHING IDEAS

Have the children:

1. Play an instrument identification game with movement. Have the children move when they hear a pitched instrument, such as bells or a glockenspiel, and freeze when they hear an unpitched instrument, such as a triangle. Repeat the game with other sets of pitched and unpitched instruments, such as a xylophone and a wood block.

2. Play the rhythm ♫ ♩ on unpitched instruments, such as tambourines or drums, each time ♫ ♩ occurs in "Welcome Back to School."

LESSON 2

Reinforcing the Lesson

Have the children play an instrument identification game. Put a selection of different instruments out of sight of the class. After you play an instrument, have the children take turns identifying each instrument you play by coming up and playing that same instrument. Ask the children to think and discuss why they can tell the difference between the sounds of two instruments. (Accept any reasonable answers, for example, a xylophone sings and a wood block talks. A more accurate answer is that a xylophone has definite pitches at different levels of high and low, and a wood block does not.)

3 APPRAISAL

The children should be able to:
1. Recognize different instruments by their sounds.
2. Point the beat with reasonable accuracy with "Twinkle, Twinkle, Little Star" and "Teddy Bear," and play the beat with "Mitten Song."

CURRICULUM CONNECTION: MATH

Use different instrument shapes to practice identifying the names of geometric shapes, such as a drum for a circle, a wood block for a rectangle, a triangle for a triangle, and so on. Use instruments of different sizes, such as drums and triangles, to practice identifying smaller and larger. You may wish to use instrument and geometric shape stick-ons on the inside front cover of the Big Book to reinforce this concept.

SONGBOOK

"Jig Jog, Jig Jog," page 274 (beat; add pitched and unpitched instruments)
"He Had a Dream," page 256 (Martin Luther King Day)

LESSON 3

Focus: Rhythm

Related Subjects
Colors, animals, winter

Objectives
To practice keeping the beat
To practice identifying short and long

Materials
Recordings: "It Fell in the City"
  "The Snow Man"
  "Teddy Bear"
  "The Secret of the Polar
    Bear"
  Listening—"Frosty the
    Snow Man"
  Listening—"Sleigh Ride"
    from *German Dances*
    K. 605 by Wolfgang
    Amadeus Mozart
Jingle bells, triangles
Six colored pieces of poster board or construction paper—black, red, blue, green, gray, and yellow—each glued or taped to a same-sized piece of white poster board or construction paper
Copying Masters 5-7, 5-8, 5-9 (optional)

1 SETTING THE STAGE

Place the six colored papers or poster boards backed with white where the class can see them. Have the children listen to "It Fell in the City" to identify what fell (snow) and what colors are mentioned (black, red, blue, green, gray, yellow). Read the poem again. As each color is mentioned, have one child identify that colored card and turn the card over, "turning it to white." Each time the words *all turned white* occur, the class says those words and taps the rhythm ($^4_4$ ♩ ♩ ♩ 𝄽).

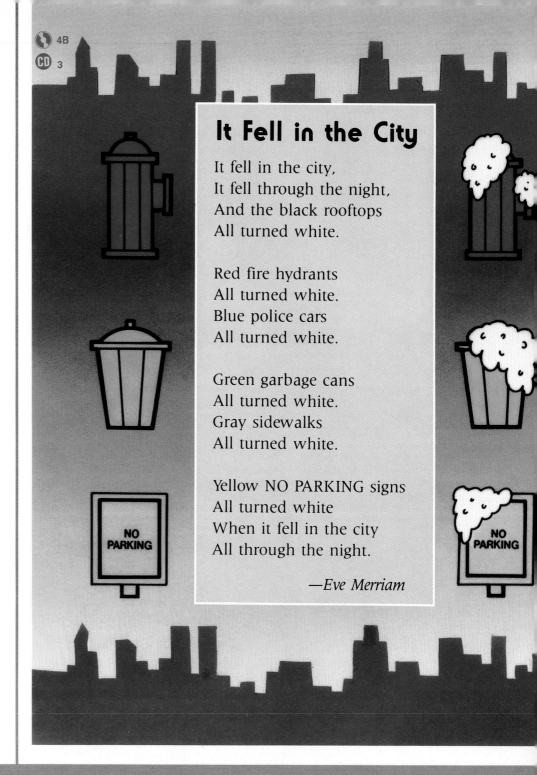

It Fell in the City

It fell in the city,
It fell through the night,
And the black rooftops
All turned white.

Red fire hydrants
All turned white.
Blue police cars
All turned white.

Green garbage cans
All turned white.
Gray sidewalks
All turned white.

Yellow NO PARKING signs
All turned white
When it fell in the city
All through the night.

—*Eve Merriam*

E X T E N S I O N

Key: C   Starting Pitch: C   Scale Tones: *do re mi fa so la ti do¹*

The Snow Man

Words and music by
Lillian Willse Brown

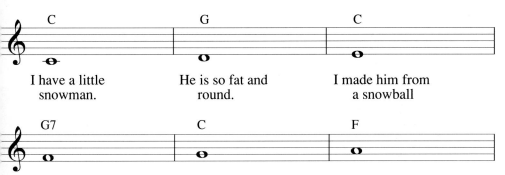

I have a little
snowman.

He is so fat and
round.

I made him from
a snowball

I rolled upon the ground.   I gave him eyes, a nose,   a nice warm scarf of red,
a mouth,

I put some buttons on his coat,   A hat upon his head.

Watch   him   as   he   melts   to   the   ground.

LESSON 3

2 TEACHING THE LESSON

1. Introduce "The Snow Man" to practice tapping a rhythm pattern. Have the children:
• Listen to the song.
• Practice the words. (You may wish to use Copying Master 5-7 at this time.)
• Sing the song, patting the beat.
• Form two groups. Group 1 taps the rhythm of *all turned white* (⁴₄ ♩ ♩ ♩ 𝄾) with each measure as Group 2 sings the song. Switch parts and sing the song again.

MORE MUSIC TEACHING IDEAS

Have the children sing "The Snow Man," moving to show the upward and downward melodic direction. (You may wish to use Copying Master 5-8 at this time.)

CURRICULUM CONNECTION: ART

Have the children make paper snowmen. Stuff paper lunch bags with newspaper and tape them closed. Then paint the bags white. When the paint is dry, tie a piece of string around each bag to form a head. Paint faces, and give the snowmen hats, scarves, buttons, and so on, using paper, scraps of cloth, or other available materials.

LESSON 3

2. Review "Teddy Bear" on page 106 to practice playing a rhythm pattern. Have the children:
- Sing the song with the movements.
- Discuss various kinds of real bears, including the polar bear.
- Tap the rhythm of *all turned white* as they sing the song.
- Have a few children play the rhythm on triangles as the class sings the song with the movements.

3. Introduce "The Secret of the Polar Bear" to practice tapping two different rhythm patterns. Have the children:
- Tap the *all turned white* rhythm with you four times.
- Change the words of the rhythm pattern to *ice is nice*.
- Echo you as you say:

  long johns

Then say the pattern with you four times. (You may need to explain that long johns are long, heavy undergarments worn during the winter.)
- Decide which pattern has longer sounds *(long johns)*.
- Write the words for both chants on the chalkboard and see who can read all or part of them.
- Draw two long dashes under *long johns* and three shorter dashes under *ice is nice*.
- Pat both rhythms on their knees or on the floor.
- Listen to "The Secret of the Polar Bear." Identify the animal in the poem.
- Echo the poem line by line.
- Say the poem two times, saying *long johns* and *ice is nice* two times each as an interlude.
- Remind the children to stay in their own space as they move around the room. Then have a few children move like polar bears as the rest of the class says the poem with the interlude.

The Secret of the Polar Bear

The secret of the polar bear
Is that he wears long underwear.

—*Dennis Lee*

E X T E N S I O N

CURRICULUM CONNECTION: SCIENCE

Bears—are among the largest land mammals. Because of their small eyes and ears bears do not see or hear as well as some other animals. However, their sense of smell is excellent. While most animals walk or run on their toes, a bear puts its foot completely on the ground with each step. Bears usually live alone, and most sleep, or *hibernate*, during the winter. There are many different kinds of bears, including brown bears, grizzly bears, black bears, and polar bears. Polar bears inhabit the regions surrounding the North Pole. Their thick, white fur protects them from the cold and helps them blend in with the ice and snow. Polar bears are very good climbers and swimmers.

MORE MUSIC TEACHING IDEAS

Have the children:
1. Sing "Teddy Bear," substituting the words *polar bear* for *teddy bear*.
2. Listen as you play longer and shorter sounds on the piano or other instrument, and respond by moving forward on long sounds and backward on short sounds.
3. Form two groups. Group 1 says "The Secret of the Polar Bear" as Group 2 says the *ice is nice* rhythm. Then switch parts. Repeat the activity using the *long johns* rhythm as an ostinato.
4. Form three groups. Group 1 says the poem as Groups 2 and 3 each say one of the ostinatos. Say the ostinatos one at a time before saying the poem. Have some children move like bears during this activity.

Key: C   Starting Pitch: G   Scale Tones: *do re mi fa so la ti do¹ re¹*

Frosty the Snow Man

Words and music by
Steve Nelson and Jack Rollins

(For listening only)

1. Frosty the snow man was a jolly happy soul,
   With a corn cob pipe and a button nose
   and two eyes made out of coal.

   Frosty the snow man is a fairy tale, they say,
   He was made of snow but the children know
   how he came to life one day.

   There must have been some magic in that old silk hat they found.
   For when they placed it on his head he began to dance around.

   Oh, Frosty the snow man was alive as he could be,
   and the children say he could laugh and play
   just the same as you and me.

2. Frosty the snow man knew the sun was hot that day,
   So he said, "Let's run and we'll have some fun
   now before I melt away."

   Down to the village, with a broomstick in his hand,
   Running here and there all around the square
   sayin', "Catch me if you can."

   He led them down the streets of town right to the traffic cop.
   And he only paused a moment when he heard him holler, "Stop!"

   For Frosty the snow man had to hurry on his way
   But he waved good-bye sayin', "Don't you cry,
   I'll be back again some day."

   Thumpety thump thump, thumpety thump thump,
   Look at Frosty go.
   Thumpety thump thump, thumpety thump thump,
   Over the hills of snow.

LESSON 3

4. Introduce "Frosty the Snow Man" for more practice with rhythm patterns. Have the children:
• Listen to the song, patting the steady beat.
• Listen again, tapping the *all turned white* pattern ($^4_4$ ♩ ♩ ♩ 𝄾) as an accompaniment.

Reinforcing the Lesson

Introduce "Sleigh Ride" from *German Dances* K. 605 by Wolfgang Amadeus Mozart for more practice moving to a steady beat. Have the children decide how to play steady beat with jingle bells. Then have them listen to the music. When they hear bells, have them move to the beat as if they were riding in a horse-drawn sleigh. When they do not hear bells, have them stand in place and move to the beat by swaying, waving their arms back and forth, and so on. Recognize that they heard several different melodies in the composition. (You may wish to use Copying Master 5-9 at this time.)

3 APPRAISAL

The children should be able to:
1. Keep the beat by patting with "The Snow Man" and moving with "Sleigh Ride."
2. Recognize longer and shorter sounds in different rhythm patterns.

MORE MUSIC TEACHING IDEAS

Have the children listen to "Frosty the Snow Man" and sing *Frosty* each time it occurs at the beginning of a phrase. Have them show that these pitches move from high to low by moving a hand from high to low. You may wish to have them sing more of the song as they are able.

THE COMPOSER

Wolfgang Amadeus Mozart (volf' gang ä-mä-dā' əs mōt' särt) (1756-1791)—was born in Salzburg, Austria. His great musical talent was evident at a very young age. When Mozart was still a child, his father took him and his older sister, Nannerl, on concert tours all over Europe. In 1781 Mozart settled in Vienna. He wrote operas, symphonies, chamber music, piano music, sacred music, and many other works. "Sleigh Ride" is the third in a set of three *German Dances* which Mozart wrote in 1791.

SONGBOOK

"Goin' to the Zoo," page 270 (repeated rhythm patterns; animals)
"He Had a Dream," page 256 (Martin Luther King Day)

LESSON 4

Focus: Pitch

Objectives
To identify and use high and low
To show higher and lower with hand signs
and body movement

Materials
Recordings: "The Snow Man"
           "The Secret of the Polar
             Bear"
           Listening— Sounds of
             Humpback Whales
Glockenspiel or resonator bells
Drum and triangle (or other unpitched
classroom instruments that have low or
high sounds)
Copying Masters 5-7, 5-10, 5-11, 5-12
(optional)

1 SETTING THE STAGE

Have the class listen as one child plays low
C and high C on a glockenspiel or bells.
Help the class identify which sound is
lower and which is higher. Review "The
Snow Man" on page 115 and decide if it
starts and ends low or high (low). Have
them sing the song, using body movement to show how the melody moves
from low to high and back to low. (You
may wish to use Copying Masters 5-7 and
5-10 at this time.)

2 TEACHING THE LESSON

**1. Review "The Secret of the Polar Bear"
on page 116 for more practice identifying
high and low.** Have the children:
• Explore ways to use low and high
pitches as they say the poem.
• Review tapping and saying the two
rhythm ostinatos *long johns* and *ice is nice,*
remembering which has long sounds (*long
johns*) and which has short sounds (*ice
is nice*).
• Try saying *long johns* with a low voice
and *ice is nice* with a high voice.
• Choose one instrument that makes a
low sound and one that makes a high
sound, for example, drum and triangle.
• Take turns playing the *long johns* rhythm
on the low instrument and the *ice is nice*
rhythm on the high instrument.
• Form three groups. One or more children in Groups 1 and 2 play one of the
rhythms as the rest of their group says
the appropriate chant. Group 3 says the
poem. Perform in the following order.
A *long johns* twice on a drum
B *ice is nice* twice on a triangle
C "The Secret of the Polar Bear" twice
(You may wish to use Copying Master 5-11
at this time.)

The Whales Off Wales

With walloping tails, the whales off Wales
Whack waves to wicked whitecaps.
And while they snore on their watery floor,
They wear wet woolen nightcaps.

EXTENSION

MORE MUSIC TEACHING IDEAS

Have the children:
1. Play "The Snow Man" on bells. Give
each of eight children a mallet and one
resonator bell of the C scale. Have each
child play his or her bell as you point to
them in order of ascending pitch while the
rest of the class sings the song.
2. Pat the rhythm of "The Secret of the
Polar Bear." Then take turns playing the
rhythm on a drum or other unpitched
instrument as a few children play the *long
johns* and *ice is nice* ostinatos.
3. Move like a slow, lumbering bear and
chant the *long johns* rhythm as a few children say "The Secret of the Polar Bear."

The whales! the whales! the whales off Wales,
They're always spouting fountains.
And as they glide through the tilting tide,
They move like melting mountains.

—*X. J. Kennedy*

2. Introduce Sounds of Humpback Whales to hear high and low. Have the children:
• Listen and try to identify the source of the sounds they hear (whales).
• Listen as you tell them about the song of the humpback whale (see *Curriculum Connection*, below).
• Listen again, showing with hand and arm movements when they hear high or low sounds. (You may wish to use Copying Master 5-12 at this time.)
• Recognize that the whale songs have no steady beat.

Reinforcing the Lesson

Introduce "The Whales Off Wales" for more practice listening for high and low. Have the children listen to the poem. (As you are reading the poem, use mostly low vocal inflections.) Then discuss the poem and decide whether they heard mostly low sounds or high sounds (low). Have the children decide how whales move (high and low as they surface to breathe and then dive back down; smoothly, fluidly as they swim; and so on). Then listen to the poem, moving appropriately. (Remind the children to be aware of others as they move.) If time permits, have the children move like whales as they listen to Sounds of Humpback Whales.

3 APPRAISAL

The children should be able to:
1. Identify high and low sounds with hand signs and body movement.
2. Identify high- and low-sounding instruments and use them appropriately with "The Secret of the Polar Bear."

MORE MUSIC TEACHING IDEAS

Discuss rhyming words at the end of each line in "The Whales Off Wales" (*whitecaps, nightcaps, fountains, mountains*). Some children may be able to identify rhyming words within the lines (*tails, Wales; snore, floor; glide, tide*). Listen to the poem, with a few children taking turns playing low-pitched instruments, such as a bass xylophone, a large drum, and so on, on these words.

CURRICULUM CONNECTION: SCIENCE

Whales—are huge sea animals that look like fish, but are really mammals, like dogs, cats, and elephants. One kind of whale, the blue whale, is the largest animal that has ever lived. Some whales, like the humpbacks, make sounds that resemble singing. Individual songs can last as long as thirty minutes. In ancient times sailors thought the songs of the whales were mermaids singing.

SONGBOOK

"Baby Beluga," page 264 (whales)

C O R E
LESSON 5

Focus: Rhythm

Objectives
To follow notation for a sound that is one beat long
To recognize same and different

Materials
Recordings: "Twinkle, Twinkle, Little Star"
"London Bridge"
Listening—*Children's Symphony* (first movement) by Harl McDonald
Charts 32, 33, and 34
Triangles
Copying Masters 5-5, 5-13, 5-14 (optional)

1 SETTING THE STAGE

Review "Twinkle, Twinkle, Little Star" on page 111. Have the children sing the song as one child points the beat on Chart 32. Sing the song again and identify the part that has a different melody (the middle). Remind the children that each star on the chart represents one beat. (You may wish to use Copying Master 5-5 at this time.)

2 TEACHING THE LESSON

1. Introduce standard musical notation for a sound that is one beat long. Have the children:
• Look at Chart 33 as you tell them that this chart shows one way a sound that is one beat long can be written in music. (You may wish to use Copying Master 5-13 at this time.)
• Sing "Twinkle, Twinkle, Little Star" as you point the beat on Chart 33. (You may wish to remind the children that "Baa, Baa, Black Sheep" has the same melody as "Twinkle, Twinkle, Little Star.") Have a few children play triangles on the beat.

BEAT NOTATION

CHART 33

E X T E N S I O N

COOPERATIVE LEARNING

After the children have been introduced to Chart 33 and have seen a demonstration of playing triangles with "Twinkle, Twinkle, Little Star," have them work in groups of three to practice performing the song. Assign the roles of pointer, triangle player, and singer. Give each group Copying Master 5-13 and a triangle. Explain that the pointer is to point the beat on the copying master while the singer sings and the triangle player accompanies. Have them switch roles until each child has tried each part. You may wish to begin by guiding a demonstration group through this process. Have successful groups perform for the class. Skills to encourage are sharing limited resources and switching roles.

Key: D   Starting Pitch: A   Scale Tones: *do re mi fa so la*

London Bridge

Piano Accompaniment on page PA 54

Traditional

1. Lon - don Bridge is fall - ing down, fall - ing down, fall - ing down.

Lon - don Bridge is fall - ing down, My fair la - dy.

. Build it up with iron bars . . .

. Iron bars will bend and break . . .

. Build it up with needles and pins . . .

. Needles and pins rust and bend . . .

. Build it up with silver and gold . . .

. Silver and gold I've not got . . .

LESSON 5

2. Introduce "London Bridge" to practice keeping the beat. Have the children:
• Listen to the song.
• Review the sequence of verses.
• Sing all the verses of "London Bridge" as different children point the beat and a few others play the beat on triangles.
• Play the traditional game (see below) if time permits, singing the song and trying to walk the beat as best they can.

PLAYING "LONDON BRIDGE"

Choose two children to form the bridge. One child is secretly designated silver, and the other gold. The two children join hands, holding them up high to form an arch. The other children form a line and walk under the bridge in single file as they sing the song. On the word *lady*, the children forming the bridge drop their arms and catch the child passing under the arch at that time. The captured child is asked to choose salt or pepper. If the child chooses salt he or she is rocked slowly back and forth; if the child chooses pepper he or she is rocked quickly back and forth. Then the captive is asked to secretly choose silver or gold, and stands behind the appropriate child. Continue the game until all the children have been captured.

Traditionally the silver and gold teams have a tug of war to determine the winner. (If you prefer not to have a tug of war, the side with the most captured children at the end is the winner.)

LESSON 5

3. Introduce *Children's Symphony* **(first movement) by Harl McDonald to practice keeping the beat and identifying same and different.** Have the children:
• Listen and identify familiar melodies in the music ("London Bridge" and "Twinkle, Twinkle, Little Star" or "Baa, Baa, Black Sheep").
• Signal when they hear familiar melodies by patting the beat.
• Listen again, singing along with the familiar melodies as they are able.
• Look at Chart 34 and decide how it fits the music (each picture represents a different melody; the drums represent brief interludes played by percussion instruments). Listen to the music again, following the chart to see if the pictures fit the music the way they determined. (You may wish to use Copying Master 5-14 at this time.)
• Decide which parts of the music are the same (the first and third) and which is different (the second). Notice how the chart shows this with same and different pictures representing each section.

34

LISTENING MAP: CHILDREN'S SYMPHONY *(First Movement)*

E X T E N S I O N

THE COMPOSER

Harl McDonald (1899-1955)—American composer, was born on a ranch in the Rocky Mountains near Boulder, Colorado. He studied music in California and Germany. McDonald moved to Philadelphia, where he taught at the University of Pennsylvania. He became manager of the Philadelphia Orchestra, which premiered most of his works. Much of McDonald's music was inspired by historical American subjects. *Children's Symphony* uses familiar childhood melodies in a symphonic setting.

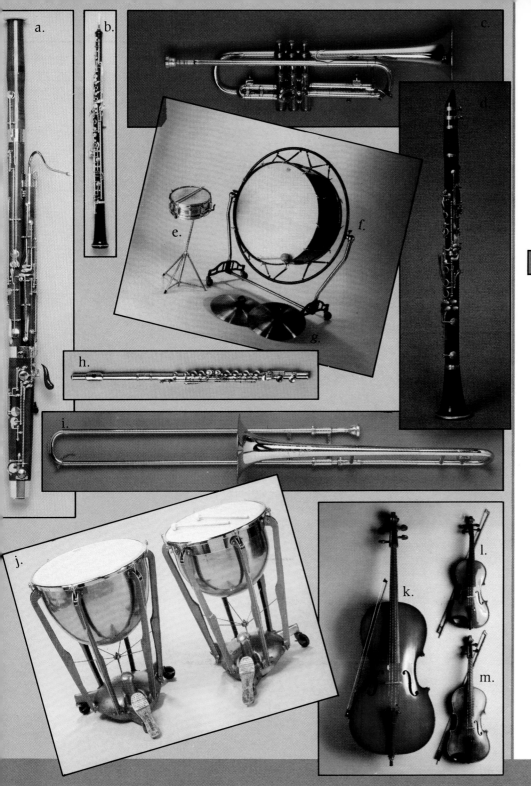

Reinforcing the Lesson

Form two groups and listen to *Children's Symphony* (first movement) again. Group 1 moves in a predetermined way, such as walking the beat, when they hear "London Bridge." Group 2 moves in a contrasting way, such as standing in place and swaying on the beat, when they hear "Twinkle, Twinkle, Little Star."

3 APPRAISAL

The children should be able to:
1. Point the beat using visual representations of and standard music notation for a sound that is one beat long.
2. Recognize and move to identify same and different sections in *Children's Symphony*.

MORE MUSIC TEACHING IDEAS

Show the class pictures of instruments and have individuals name as many of the instruments as they can. (You may wish to use the pictures on page 123. The instruments pictured are: a. bassoon, b. oboe, c. trumpet, d. clarinet, e. snare drum, f. bass drum, g. cymbals, h. flute, i. trombone, j. timpani, k. cello, l. violin, m. viola.) Tell the children any names they do not know. Then listen to the first movement of *Children's Symphony* and have the children identify as many of the instruments they hear as they can. You may wish to identify each instrument for the children by pointing to its picture when you hear it.

COOPERATIVE LEARNING

To form random groups for the Reinforcing the Lesson activity, "count off" around the class using the words *star* and *bridge*. All "bridge" children walk the steady beat when they hear "London Bridge." All "star" children sway in place when they hear "Twinkle, Twinkle, Little Star." After practicing the movements, have the groups meet and discuss other appropriate ways to move to their sections of *Children's Symphony* (first movement). Skills to encourage are forming a group, listening to and sharing ideas, and selecting an appropriate activity.

SONGBOOK

"Old Dan Tucker," page 282 (same and different)
"Step in Time," page 288 (steady beat)
"Uncle Jessie," page 289 (notation for sounds one beat long)

CORE
LESSON 6

Focus: Rhythm

Related Subjects
Left and right, cooking, rhyming words, square

Objectives
To practice recognizing musical notation for a sound that is one beat long
To recognize visual representation of a beat of silence
To identify a beat of silence and use it in a rhythm pattern

Materials
Recordings: "Mitten Song"
             "Popping Corn" (version 1)
             "Square Dance"
Charts 31, 33, and 35
Mitten stick-ons
Wood blocks or rhythm sticks

1 SETTING THE STAGE

Have the children review "Mitten Song" on page 108, patting the beat. Watch as one child puts the stick-on mittens over the hands on Chart 31. Sing the song again, pointing the beat as one child points the beat on the chart. Then look at Chart 33 and have the children remember that this chart shows musical notation for a sound that is one beat long. Sing the song several times as groups of children play the beat on wood blocks or rhythm sticks. Repeat this activity until all the children have a turn playing instruments.

SILENT BEAT

CHART 35

EXTENSION

Key: G   Starting Pitch: G   Scale Tones: *so, ti, do re*

Popping Corn

Piano Accompaniment on page PA 55

*Words and music by
Lynn Freeman Olson*

Sharply

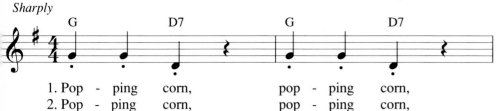

1. Pop - ping   corn,   pop - ping   corn,
2. Pop - ping   corn,   pop - ping   corn,

Hear   it   bang   and   sput - ter!   Pop - ping   corn,
Nois - y   when   you   heat   it!   Pop - ping   corn,

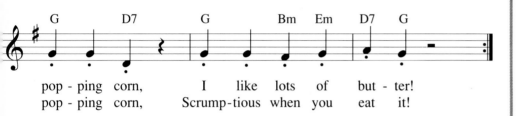

pop - ping   corn,   I   like   lots   of   but - ter!
pop - ping   corn,   Scrump-tious   when   you   eat   it!

2 TEACHING THE LESSON

1. Introduce a visual representation of a beat of silence. Have the children:
• Look at the top of Chart 35. Notice that the first three pots contain popped corn and that the last pot is empty.
• Remember that many of the pictures on charts they have seen represent a sound that is one beat long.
• Decide what the empty pot might represent (a beat of silence).

2. Introduce "Popping Corn" (version 1) and tap a rhythm pattern that contains a beat of silence. Have the children:
• Listen to the song to discover if they were right about what the empty pot represents.
• Listen again, raising their hands whenever a beat of silence occurs in the melody.
• Echo the words after you in rhythm, noticing the beats of silence and identifying the rhyming words (*sputter, butter, heat it, eat it*).
• Listen to the song, singing along as they are able.
• Follow as you point the beat from left to right, patting when you point to a full pot and moving their hands apart when you point to the empty pot. Repeat the resulting rhythm pattern, ♩ ♩ ♩ 𝄽, several times.
• Listen to the song, patting the new rhythm pattern.
• Sing the song as a few children play the pattern on wood blocks or rhythm sticks.

MORE MUSIC TEACHING IDEAS

Have the children:
1. Sing "Popping Corn," substituting tapping for the words *popping corn*.
2. Take turns individually singing the words *popping corn* on G G D.
3. Play G G D using bells or other pitched instruments whenever the words *popping corn* occur in the song. If possible, hold the instrument vertically so the highest pitches are also the highest physically.

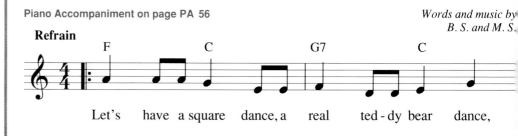
CORE

LESSON 6

Reinforcing the Lesson

Introduce "Square Dance." During the verses have the children pat, stamp, or nod the ♩ ♩ ♩ ♪ rhythm pattern they used with "Popping Corn." Have them form a square. Then listen to the song again, moving three steps forward, bowing, and moving three steps backward and bowing with the ♩ ♩ ♩ ♪ pattern. You may wish to have the entire class move in one large square first, and then have groups of eight children each form squares in traditional square dance formation, or do the dance in a circle, moving to the left for eight steps and then to the right for eight steps.

Square Dance

Piano Accompaniment on page PA 56

Words and music by
B. S. and M. S.

Let's have a square dance, a real ted-dy bear dance,

Let's have a square dance, a bear square dance.

Verse

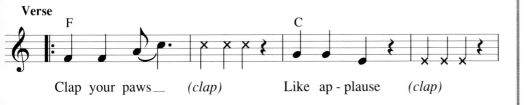

Clap your paws___ *(clap)*   Like ap - plause   *(clap)*

Go   up and down   like the   old   see - saws.

2. Stamp your feet. *(stamp)* What a beat! *(stamp)*
   Move all around to the teddy bear beat.

3. Nod your head, *(nod)* As I said. *(nod)*
   Keep on a-nodding 'til it's time for bed.

3 **APPRAISAL**

The children should be able to:
1. Recognize musical notation for a sound that is one beat long.
2. Recognize visual representation of a beat of silence.
3. Identify a beat of silence in a rhythm pattern, and move to or play the pattern with different songs.

SONGBOOK

"Goin' to the Zoo," page 270 (silent beat)
"Little Spotted Puppy," page 276 (silent beat)

LESSON 7

Focus: Rhythm and Tempo

Related Subjects
Bath, bubbles, left and right, circle

Objectives
To practice identifying and using beat and a beat of silence
To practice identifying changing tempos

Materials
Recordings: "Popping Corn" (version 1)
"Popping Corn" (version 2)
"Before the Bath"
"The Bubble Bath"
"Looby Loo"
Listening—"Soap Bubbles" from *Children's Games* by Georges Bizet
"After My Bath"
Chart 35
Wood blocks or rhythm sticks (optional)

1 SETTING THE STAGE

Review "Popping Corn" (version 1; slower tempo) on page 125. Tap the ♩ ♩ ♩ ♩ pattern as you point the beat on Chart 35. Remember that the empty pot represents a beat of silence. Sing the song, patting the rhythm pattern. (You may wish to have a few children who did not have a turn before play the pattern on wood blocks or rhythm sticks.) Then have the children sing the whole song (version 2; with *accelerando*), speeding up the tempo at the end and moving to imitate corn popping.

BEFORE THE BATH

It's cold, cold, cold,
And the water shines wet,
And the longer I wait,
The colder I get.

I can't quite make
Myself hop in
All shivery-cold
In just my skin.

Yet the water's warm
In the tub I know.
So—1, 2, 3
And in I GO!

—*Corinna Marsh*

EXTENSION

THE BUBBLE BATH

Take some bubbles, pour them in . . . . *SPLASH SPLASH SPLASH SPLASH SPLASH SPLASH SPLASH SPLASH*

Stirrrrrrrrrr in the water back and forth . . .

watch the bubbles growING . . . GROWING . . . .
watch the bubbles goING . . . . GOING . . . .

POP   POP   POP

POPPING HERE . . . . POPPING THERE
IN THE AIR . . . . EVERYWHERE

POPPING HERE . . . . POPPING THERE
IN THE AIR . . . . EVERYWHERE

Watch the bubbles going, going, watch the bubbles
slowing, slowing,   DOWN
                       DOWN
                          DOWN

Now we can jump IN!

SPLASH

— *Millie Burnett*

2 TEACHING THE LESSON

1. Introduce "Before the Bath" to practice a rhythm pattern with a beat of silence. Have the children:
• Listen to "Before the Bath" and identify places where the ♩ ♩ ♩ ♪ pattern might fit *(1, 2, 3; cold, cold, cold)*.
• Listen to the poem again, patting on those words when they occur.
• Listen again, softly patting or playing the pattern throughout the poem as an ostinato.

2. Introduce "The Bubble Bath" for more practice playing a pattern with a silent beat. Have the children:
• Stand up and form a circle. Imagine that there is a big bathtub in the center of the circle in which they are going to prepare a bubble bath.
• Listen to "The Bubble Bath," showing with appropriate movements when they hear the ♩ ♩ ♩ ♪ pattern *(splash, splash, splash, pop, pop, pop,* and *down, down, down)*. Carefully jump into the "bathtub" at the end of the poem.

CURRICULUM CONNECTION: SCIENCE

Have the children experiment making bubbles. (If weather permits, you may wish to do this activity outside.) Prepare a solution of water and liquid soap in a large, flat container. Have the children take turns making bubbles by dipping a variety of different-sized objects with holes in them into the solution and blowing, or having the wind blow on them. Observe how the bubbles float and move in the air.

LESSON 7

3. Introduce "Looby Loo" for more practice keeping a beat. Have the children:

• Remain standing in the circle. Pretend to test the water in the bathtub to make sure it is not too hot or too cold by moving their hands back and forth in the center of the circle.

• Listen to "Looby Loo," doing the movements on the beat with you, and singing along as they are able. End by sitting down in the circle and pretending they are now sitting in the bathtub.

4. Introduce "Soap Bubbles" from *Children's Games* by Georges Bizet. Have the children:

• Imagine that they are bubbles in a bubble bath.

• Watch as one or two volunteers pretend to move like bubbles (gently, delicately, smoothly; with arms rounded out to the sides, in front, or overhead).

• Practice moving like bubbles, trying not to bump into one another.

• Listen to "Soap Bubbles," moving around freely like bubbles. (Have the bubbles gently land on the very last note.)

• Decide if the beat in "Soap Bubbles" stayed the same or if it became slower and faster. (It becomes slightly slower and faster throughout. You may wish to have the children listen and move again to determine this.)

• Listen to "Soap Bubbles" again, moving to show the tempo changes as they are able. (You may wish to refer to the biography of Georges Bizet on page 4 at this time.)

Looby Loo

Piano Accompaniment on page PA 57   *English Singing Game*

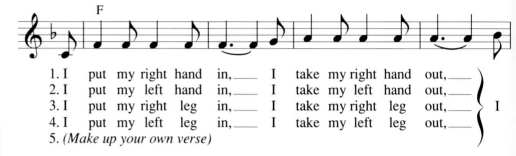

EXTENSION

SPECIAL LEARNERS

For the child with special needs, movement to music can be a wonderful or difficult experience. Plan the lesson so that the special child is protected from ridicule. Talk with the entire class about the importance of working together and helping one another in a considerate way. Have able children model desired types of movement and then have the children tell the good points of each. If space or unpredictable behavior is a problem, have only a few children move at a time. If socially unacceptable behavior occurs, try to alter it first by a look, a facial expression, or a gesture. Reinforce desired behavior through praise or reward (such as letting the child select a favorite song or go first at an activity).

AFTER MY BATH

After my bath
I try, try, try
to wipe myself
till I'm dry, dry, dry.

Hands to wipe
and fingers and toes
and two wet legs
and a shiny nose.

Just think how much
less time I'd take
if I were a dog
and could shake, shake, shake!

—*Aileen Fisher*

LESSON 7

Reinforcing the Lesson

Have the children pretend to get out of the bathtub, take an imaginary towel, and dry themselves off. Do this first in free pantomime, and then to the rhythm of the ♩ ♩ ♩ ♩ pattern. Have them listen to "After My Bath," pretending to dry themselves off to the rhythm of the pattern.

3 APPRAISAL

The children should be able to:
1. Visually identify, pat, play, and move to a rhythm pattern containing a silent beat.
2. Move to show changing tempos in "Popping Corn" and "Soap Bubbles."

SONGBOOK

"Uncle Jessie," page 289 (changing tempos)

LESSON 8

Focus: Pitch

Related Subjects
Bath, bubbles, left and right, circle, safety

Objectives
To see and devise ways to visually show higher and lower
To practice moving to the beat

Materials
Recordings: "Before the Bath"
Recorded Lesson—"Melodic Direction in 'Looby Loo' "
"Looby Loo"
"The Bubble Bath"
Listening—"Soap Bubbles" from *Children's Games* by Georges Bizet
Listening—"Splish Splash" by Bobby Darin
C D E G A resonator bells or pitched, barred instruments with only C D E G A bars left on
Copying Masters 5-15, 5-16 (optional)

1 SETTING THE STAGE

Have the children stand in a circle and pretend there is a large bathtub in the center. Listen to "Before the Bath," patting the ♩♩♩ ♪ pattern. Say the poem again, alternately patting and tapping the pattern as they watch and imitate you.

2 TEACHING THE LESSON

1. Review "Looby Loo" on page 130 to move to the beat and identify higher to lower pitches. Have the children:
• Listen to the refrain, moving to the beat.
• Sing *on a Saturday night* in the last two measures of the refrain and decide if it starts on a higher pitch and goes lower, or starts on a lower pitch and goes higher. (It starts on a higher pitch and goes lower.) (You may wish to use Copying Master 5-15 at this time.)
• Think of a way to move to show the direction of the melody when they sing the song, for example, hold their noses and pretend to lower themselves into the bathtub by gradually bending their knees.
• Sing the song, doing the movements suggested in each verse, and adding their own movements to show the melodic direction of the last two measures of the refrain.

5A, 5B
CD 3

E X T E N S I O N

THE COMPOSER

Bobby Darin (1936-1973)—American pop singer and composer, was born Robert Walden Cassoto in the Bronx, New York. As a child he learned to play piano, drums, and guitar. After working as a composer of radio commercials, he began to record his own compositions. Many of these songs, including "Queen of the Hop," "Dream Lover," and "Splish Splash," became very popular in the 1950s and 1960s. However, Bobby Darin's biggest recorded hit, "Mack the Knife," is from *The Threepenny Opera* by Kurt Weill.

LESSON 8

2. Review "The Bubble Bath" on page 129 for playing higher and lower sounds. Have the children:
• Pretend to test the water in the bathtub to make sure it is not too hot or too cold.
• Listen to "The Bubble Bath," showing with appropriate movements when they hear the ♩ ♩ ♩ ♪ pattern. Carefully jump in the tub at the end of the poem.
• Move to the poem as a few children add the following sound effects using C D E G A resonator bells or pitched, barred instruments with only C D E G A bars:
a. Play any two pitches together on *splash, splash, splash* and *pop, pop, pop*
b. Play high and low sounds on *popping here, popping there*
c. Play glissandos, sliding from higher to lower pitches, on *down, down, down*
(You may wish to use Copying Master 5-16 at this time.)
3. Review "Soap Bubbles" for listening for higher and lower. Have the children:
• Listen, moving like bubbles to show the changes in tempo.
• Listen again, moving to show the melodic changes from higher to lower and lower to higher.

Reinforcing the Lesson

Introduce "Splish Splash." Have the children listen to the music and move to the beat. You may wish to have them move freely, or mirror you as you pat the beat with both hands on your head, shoulders, knees, and so on.

3 APPRAISAL

The children should be able to:
1. Identify and move to show higher and lower sounds in "Looby Loo," "Soap Bubbles," and "The Bubble Bath."
2. Move to the beat in "Looby Loo" and "Splish Splash."

MORE MUSIC TEACHING IDEAS

"The Bubble Bath" provides an opportunity to help the children develop producing good tones on Orff instruments. Have the children experiment on the instruments to find ways to produce the sounds suggested by the poem. Before playing these sounds with the poem, practice trying to produce a good tone. On the word *pop*, play in the middle of the bar with a gentle popping motion. Practice glissandos by sliding up and down the bars from low to high and back again. Use the glissandos with *down, down, down*. Gently move the mallets around the bars in small circles to create the sound of splashing water. Use this sound as an introduction to the poem. Practice alternating low and high sounds and play them with *popping here, popping there.*

SONGBOOK

"Marching Round the Levee," page 280 (circle game)
"The Bus," page 266 (downward moving patterns)
"Little Red Caboose," page 278 (upward moving patterns)

CORE
LESSON 9

Focus: Tone Color and Rhythm

Related Subjects
Sleeping habits, animals

Objectives
To distinguish between the sounds of pitched and unpitched instruments
To recognize and use notation for a sound that is one beat long and a beat of silence

Materials
Recordings: "Popping Corn" (version 2)
"Never Sleep Late Anymore"
"My Little Puppy"
Recorded Lesson—"Notation for a Silent Beat"
Listening—"The Teddy Bears' Picnic"
Charts 35, 36, and 37
Resonator bells or other pitched instruments, triangles
Dog, quarter note, and quarter rest stick-ons
Copying Masters 5-17, 5-18, 5-19 (optional)

1 SETTING THE STAGE

Review "Popping Corn" on page 125. Have the children look at Chart 35 and pat the rhythm pattern suggested by the pots (♩ ♩ ♩ 𝄽), remembering that the last beat in the pattern is silent. The children should learn to "feel" the beat of silence by holding their hands out to their sides each time the beat of silence occurs. Have them sing the song again, tapping the rhythm pattern throughout.

CHART
36
PITCHED AND UNPITCHED INSTRUMENTS

EXTENSION

Never Sleep Late Anymore

no Accompaniment on page PA 58

Words and music by
George Winston and Robert Kersey

Oh,   just let   me get up in the   ear - ly   morn,

Just let   me get up in the   ear - ly   morn,

Just let   me get up in the   ear - ly   morn   and I'll

nev - er sleep   late   an - y - more._____

LESSON 9

2 TEACHING THE LESSON

1. Introduce "Never Sleep Late Anymore." Have the children:
• Look at Chart 36 and name the instruments on the chart (xylophone and triangle). Decide what the boy in the picture is doing (waking up). (You may wish to use Copying Master 5-17 at this time.)
• Listen to the song.
• Listen again, singing along as they are able.

2. Learn an instrument accompaniment for "Never Sleep Late Anymore." Have the children:
• Sing the song, tapping on the words *just* and *early morn* each time they occur in the song.
• Form two groups. Sing the song, with Group 1 patting on *just* and Group 2 patting on *early morn*.
• Sing the song again, with a child from Group 1 playing G and D together on bells or other pitched instrument on *just*, and a child from Group 2 playing a triangle on *early morn*.
• Sing the song with the bells and triangle as the class taps at the end of each phrase (after *morn* and *-more*).
• Repeat the song with the instruments, with another child playing G and G¹ together on a different pitched instrument at the end of each phrase.
• Identify instruments by sound with their eyes closed, by patting when they hear you play a pitched instrument and making a triangle shape with their fingers when they hear you play a triangle.

MORE MUSIC TEACHING IDEAS

Play three additional sounds on G and D on *never, late,* and *-more* during the last phrase of "Never Sleep Late Anymore" using a glockenspiel or other pitched instrument.

CORE

LESSON 9

3. Introduce "My Little Puppy" and musical notation for a rest. Have the children:
• Listen to the song, mirroring the movements with you. (Movements are shown on page 138.)
• Listen again, singing along as they are able.

My Little Puppy

Piano Accompaniment on page PA 60

Words and music b
Elizabeth Deutsc

Verse

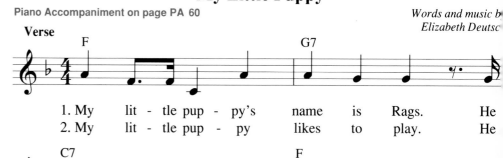

1. My   lit - tle pup - py's   name   is   Rags.   He
2. My   lit - tle pup - py   likes   to   play.   He

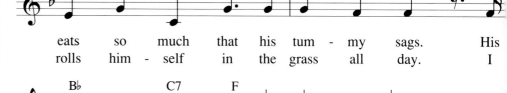

eats   so   much   that   his   tum - my   sags.   His
rolls   him - self   in   the   grass   all   day.   I

ears   flip - flop   when his   tail   wig - wags,   And   when   he   walks,   he
whis - tle   but   he____   won't o - bey,   He   al - ways   runs   the

Refrain

zigs   and   zags.
oth - er   way.   Flip - flop,   wig - wag,   zig - zag!

Flip - flop,   wig - wag,   zig - zag!   He   does - n't   have   an - y

ped - i - gree,   But   I   love   him   and   he   loves   me.

EXTENSION

NOTES AND RESTS

CHART 37

4. Introduce musical notation for a beat of silence. Have the children:

• Watch as you place a dog stick-on over each of the doghouses on Chart 37. Then gently bark and pat on the beat as you point the beat with the dogs on the chart.

• Watch as you remove the last dog in each row. Discover that the empty doghouses represent beats of silence. Pat the resulting rhythm, feeling the beats of silence by holding their hands out to their sides on those beats. Recognize that the pattern is the same as the one they used with "Popping Corn."

• Watch as you replace each dog with a quarter note stick-on and put rest stick-ons in the empty doghouses. Remember that each note represents one beat, and determine that a rest is a musical sign for a beat of silence. Perform the rhythm as you point the beat. (You may wish to use Copying Master 5-18 at this time.)

Reinforcing the Lesson

Introduce "The Teddy Bears' Picnic." Have the children listen, tapping the rhythm pattern notated on Chart 37 as you point. Have the children listen again, skipping or galloping when they hear the A section, stepping in place for the B section, and pretending to sleep at the end.

3 APPRAISAL

The children should be able to:

1. Close their eyes and distinguish between the sounds of pitched and unpitched instruments by patting when they hear a pitched instrument and making a triangle shape with their fingers when they hear an unpitched instrument.

2. Recognize and use notation for a beat of silence by patting when they see a quarter note and holding their hands out to their sides when they see a rest.

MORE MUSIC TEACHING IDEAS

Have the children:

1. Sing "My Little Puppy" with a few volunteers acting out the parts of the puppy and the owner. Switch roles and repeat the activity.

2. Create their own combinations of sounds and silences by directing you to arrange notes and rests in different patterns on Chart 37. Then perform the resulting rhythms. (You may wish to use Copying Master 5-19 at this time.)

3. Use these combinations of sounds and silences to accompany songs or listening selections on unpitched instruments. If the music has more than one section, play rhythms on different instruments with each section.

4. Review "Teddy Bear" on page 106. Sing the song and do the movements. Then, sing the song, patting the beat. Finally, help the children develop inner hearing by singing only the words *teddy bear* each time they occur, and acting out the rest of each line as they think the words:

SONGBOOK

"Little Spotted Puppy," page 276 (a song about a dog)

LESSON 10

Focus: Rhythm

Objective
To recognize and use notation for a sound that is one beat long and notation for a beat of silence

Materials
Recordings: "The Teddy Bears' Picnic"
"My Little Puppy"
"Never Sleep Late Anymore"
"Square Dance"
Chart 37
Pitched instruments, triangles
Quarter note and quarter rest stick-ons

1 SETTING THE STAGE
Review "The Teddy Bears' Picnic." Have the children watch as you place three notes and one rest over the doghouses in each row on Chart 37. Tap the rhythm. Listen to "The Teddy Bears' Picnic," tapping the rhythm as you point the beat in the A section and marching to the beat in the B section. Pretend to fall asleep at the end of the song.

2 TEACHING THE LESSON
1. Review "My Little Puppy" on page 136 to practice beat. Have the children:
• Sing the song, patting the beat during the verses and doing the movements during the refrains.
• Choose partners and dramatize the song. One child in each pair is the dog and the other child is the owner. Switch roles and repeat the activity.
2. Review "Never Sleep Late Anymore" on page 135 and review the accompaniment. Have the children:
• Sing the song.

E X T E N S I O N

COOPERATIVE LEARNING
After using Chart 37 with the dog, note, and rest stick-ons as a class, have the children divide into small groups to create new rhythm patterns that may be tapped or played with "Square Dance." Distribute one set of Copying Masters 5–18 and/or 5–19 to each group. Have them arrange and rearrange either the dogs or the notes and rests until they agree upon a pattern. Practice the pattern together until they can clap it twice through without stopping. Then have each group perform its pattern for the class. Paste the patterns in place and save them. Try a different pattern each day with "Square Dance."

138 UNIT 5

MOVEMENT FOR "MY LITTLE PUPPY"

(Underlined words have dramatic action.)

Verse 1

My little puppy's name is Rags.

He eats so much that his tummy sags.

His ears flip flop, when his tail

 wig wags,

And when he walks, he zigs and zags.

Refrain

 Flip flop wig wag,

 zig zag!

 Flip flop wig wag,

 zig zag!

He doesn't have any pedigree,

 But I love him, and he loves me.

Verse 2

My little puppy likes to play.

He rolls himself in the grass all day.

I whistle, but he won't obey,

He always runs the other way.

LESSON 10

• Sing the song, patting on the words *just* and *early morn* each time they occur in the song.

• Form two groups. Sing the song, with Group 1 patting on *just* and Group 2 patting on *early morn*.

• Sing the song again, with a child from Group 1 playing G and D together on bells or other pitched instrument on *just*, and a child from Group 2 playing a triangle on *early morn*.

• Sing the song with the bells and triangle as the class pats at the end of each phrase (after *morn* and *-more*).

• Repeat the song with the instruments, with another child playing G and G' together on a different pitched instrument at the end of each phrase.

• Repeat the activity to give a turn playing instruments to as many children as possible.

Reinforcing the Lesson

Review "Square Dance" on page 126. Have the children sing the song, doing the movements as if they were teddy bears. Then, using only the top row of doghouses on Chart 37, place three notes and a rest over the doghouses to match the rhythm pattern they used during "Square Dance." (You may wish to have them practice with the dog stick-ons first, then replace the dogs with the notes and a rest.) Repeat the song if time permits.

3 APPRAISAL

The children should be able to identify notation for a sound that is one beat long and notation for a beat of silence by patting when they see a quarter note and holding their hands out to their sides when they see a rest.

SONGBOOK
"Little Spotted Puppy," page 276 (a song about a dog; steady beat; beat of silence)

REVIEW AND EVALUATION

REVIEW

Objectives
To review songs, skills, and concepts learned in Unit 5
To measure the children's ability to:
1. Recognize notation for one beat of sound and notation for one beat of silence
2. Recognize the difference between pitched and unpitched classroom instruments

Materials
Recordings: "Welcome Back to School"
   "Teddy Bear"
   Listening—"The Teddy Bears' Picnic"
   "Popping Corn"
   "Never Sleep Late Anymore"
   "Square Dance" .
   "My Little Puppy"
   "Mitten Song"
Charts 35 and 37
Pitched and unpitched classroom instruments
Evaluation Unit 5 Copying Master

TEACHING THE LESSON

Review the songs and concepts in Unit 5 by dramatizing a story. Have the children:
• Listen as you tell the story, singing and performing the activities at the appropriate places. (As the children sing and move, observe and evaluate individuals and the class as a whole as to how their responses indicate their level of understanding.)

The Teddy Bears' Visit
It was a special day at school. The Teddy Bears were coming to visit. Everyone got together to sing a song welcoming the Teddy Bears.
• Sing "Welcome Back to School" on page 104. Follow the directions in the A section and do the body percussion in the B section. Recognize that the pattern they tapped and stamped in the B section contained a beat of silence.

Since these were performing Teddy Bears, everyone was eager to see them do their tricks. The Teddy Bears asked everyone to move and play a game with them.
• Review "Teddy Bear" on page 106. Sing the song and do the movements. Then close their eyes and listen as you play a pitched or an unpitched instrument on the beat. Take turns identifying the instrument you played.

After playing the game the Teddy Bears were hungry. Everyone decided to make some popcorn for a snack.
• Look at Chart 35 and pat the rhythm pattern suggested by the pots (♩ ♩ ♩ 𝄽).

E X T E N S I O N

MORE MUSIC TEACHING IDEAS
This review can be used to plan a special Visitors' Day, giving the children the experience of behaving appropriately with guests. Have the children "invite" their teddy bears or other toys to school. The toys can share all the daily routines. Use or adapt the activities suggested by the Review lesson. You may also wish to use other songs and activities in the unit, such as "London Bridge," "The Snow Man," "The Secret of the Polar Bear," "Looby Loo," and "Splish Splash." Props such as invitations, place cards, achievement certificates, and memory books can be made. The children can fill in their names and their toys' names, and take them home as souvenirs.

REVIEW AND EVALUATION

Indicate the beat of silence by holding their hands out to their sides when it occurs.
• Sing "Popping Corn" on page 125, patting the rhythm pattern.

The Teddy Bears really enjoyed the popcorn. It reminded them of the day the Teddy Bears all had their picnic.
• Watch as you place three quarter notes and one rest over each row of doghouses on Chart 37. Then pat the rhythm they see. Listen to "The Teddy Bears' Picnic," patting the rhythm pattern during the A sections and marching in place during the B section. Pretend to fall asleep at the end.

The Teddy Bears said that even though they are always tired after their picnic, they never sleep late.
• Sing "Never Sleep Late Anymore" on page 135. Play the instrumental accompaniment. Then close their eyes and listen as you play a pitched or an unpitched instrument, patting softly if they hear a pitched instrument and forming a triangle with their fingers if they hear an unpitched instrument.

Next, the Teddy Bears decided to lead everyone in a square dance.
• Form one large square or smaller squares of groups of eight and sing "Square Dance" on page 126. Do the ♩ ♩ ♩ ♩ rhythm pattern according to the directions in each verse.

The Teddy Bears shared a story about the funny little puppy that lives with them.
• Sing "My Little Puppy" on page 136, doing the movements. Read an eight-beat rhythm that you construct on Chart 37 using quarter notes and quarter rests, for example, ♩ ♩ ♩ ♩ ♩ ♩ ♩ and pat or play it as an interlude or an ostinato with the song.

It was time for the Teddy Bears to go home. Before they left, they made sure they were wearing their mittens.
• Sing "Mitten Song" on page 108. Then watch as you change the rhythm on the top row of Chart 37 to ♩ ♩ ♩ ♩. Pat the rhythm as they sing "Mitten Song" again.

Everyone said "Good-bye" and "Thank you" to the Teddy Bears as they left. It was such a nice visit. Everyone hoped that the Teddy Bears would visit again some day.

EVALUATION

Evaluation Unit 5 Copying Master can be found in the *Teacher's Resource Book* with full directions for providing an evaluation of the child's progress.

ELEMENTS OF MUSIC	UNIT 6 OBJECTIVES	Lesson 1 CORE Focus: Tone Color	Lesson 2 CORE Focus: Higher and Lower
Dynamics	Use loud/soft appropriately	Use loud/soft appropriately	Use loud/soft appropriately
Tone Color	Continue to learn names of classroom instruments **Identify four types of voices (whispering, singing, speaking, calling)** Hear trumpet, tuba, piano, band Hear symphony orchestra	Identify four types of voices (whispering, singing, speaking, calling)	Practice identifying four types of voices (whispering, singing, speaking, calling) Hear piano Use instruments to enhance mood of poem
Tempo	Experience and use appropriate tempos	Experience and use appropriate tempos	Experience and use appropriate tempos Move to show tempo change in poem
Duration/ Rhythm	Aural/oral experiences with ♩, ♫, 𝄽 (echoing, singing songs, using ostinatos, finding words that fit basic combinations) Hear, sing, use strong beat Practice basic locomotor movements	Hear, sing, use strong beat Practice basic locomotor movements Echo three-note patterns	Hear, sing strong beat
Pitch	See *mi so* (3 5) in pictorial notation (sing with words, point) for known song **Recognize higher/lower** Sing and hear clear examples of upward/downward Sing known songs showing *mi so* (3 5) with higher/lower arm movements	Sing and hear clear examples of upward/downward	Recognize higher/lower Move to show higher/lower Identify lower of two pitches
Texture	Perform melody with rhythm and/or speech ostinato Recognize a melody with accompaniment		
Form	**Identify same/different** Create short melodic or rhythmic compositions by combining short patterns created by individual children		Hear same/different in listening selection
Style	Hear and review comparing lullaby and march styles Hear music of the 18th, 19th, and 20th centuries	Hear contemporary vocal piece that uses American Indian words Sing spiritual	Hear music from the 19th and 20th centuries

PURPOSE Unit: 6 Same and Different

This unit is designed to be taught during February. Through a variety of songs and listening selections, the children will experience ways of using their voices, identifying whispering, singing, speaking, and calling; recognizing higher and lower; and identifying same and different.

SUGGESTED TIME FRAME

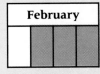

February

FOCUS

Core Lessons 1, 2, 5
• Tone Color
• Higher and Lower
• Same and Different

Lessons 3, 4, 6
• Higher and Lower
• Rhythm
• Rhythm

Lesson 3 Focus: Higher and Lower	Lesson 4 Focus: Rhythm	Lesson 5 CORE Focus: Same and Different	Lesson 6 Focus: Rhythm
Hear trumpet, tuba, orchestra, piano	Continue to learn names of classroom instruments	Practice identifying the four voices Use pitched instruments for higher and lower identification practice Hear and identify voices of a man and a child **Play original tunes on G and B♭**	Listen to a band Name some instruments in a band
Experience and use appropriate tempos	Experience and use appropriate tempos	Experience and use appropriate tempos	
Practice basic locomotor movements Practice keeping the beat	Practice rhythms containing ♩ and 𝄽 Practice basic locomotor movements	Sing song with ♩ and ♫	Move to the beat Play an ostinato pattern with a song Practice using notation for ♩ and 𝄽 Practice basic locomotor movements
Recognize higher/lower Hear clear examples of upward and downward **Practice upward and downward by playing short segments of a song** **Practice inner hearing**	Practice identifying higher/lower	Practice identifying higher/lower Identify and sing echoes **Singing game with individual singing** **Sing part of song with *mi* and *so* (3 5)** **Play original tunes on B♭ and G bells**	
	Perform melody with rhythm and/or speech ostinato		Perform melody with ostinato and identify as melody with accompaniment
	Create introduction, interlude, coda by combining short rhythmic segments	Identify same and different **Echo movement** **Show same and different by dramatizing an orchestral selection**	Identify same and different Sing echoes
Hear parts of 18th-century concerto and 20th-century suite		Hear orchestral music of the 18th and 20th centuries	Hear music of the 20th century Identify differences between lullaby and march

BULLETIN BOARD

Set up a bulletin board titled "Same and Different" to provide the children with a visual means to practice this concept. Put sets of two or three items in various areas around the bulletin board. These items can relate to winter and February holidays, for example, snowflakes, lace-edged hearts, pictures of Abraham Lincoln and George Washington, pictures relating to Black History Month, Chinese New Year, and so on. Some sets should have pictures that are all the same, and some should have pictures that are different.

Focus: Tone Color

Related Subjects
Days of the week, Black History Month, water

Objective
To identify four different kinds of voices (whispering, singing, speaking, calling)

Materials
Recordings: "Hello, There"
Listening—*Miniwanka, or The Moments of Water* by R. Murray Schafer
"Rain" (optional)
"Zion's Children"
Chart 38
Copying Masters 6-1, 6-2 (optional)

1 SETTING THE STAGE
Introduce "Hello, There." Have the children listen to the song and identify the kind of voice they hear (singing). Then have them think of other things voices can do (whisper, speak, call). Listen to "Hello, There" again, singing the echoes each time they occur.

Hello, There!

Piano Accompaniment on page PA 62   *Traditional*

Hel - lo, there! (Hel - lo, there!) How are you? (How are you?)

It's so good (It's so good) To see you. (To see you.)

We'll sing and (We'll sing and) be hap-py (be hap-py)

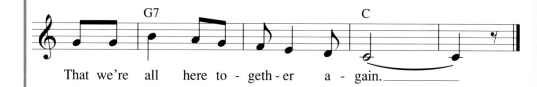

That we're all here to - geth - er a - gain. _____

E X T E N S I O N

MORE MUSIC TEACHING IDEAS
Play this game to practice tone matching and tone quality identification. Have the children sit in a circle. Choose one child to be "It," and have that child sit in the center of the circle with eyes closed. Then the rest of the class sings "Hello, There." Designate another child to sing the echoes as a solo. At the end of the song the child who is "It" tries to guess who sang the echoes. The game continues with the child who sang becoming the new "It."

Key: F   Starting Pitch: C   Scale Tones: *so, la, do re mi so la*

Zion's Children

Piano Accompaniment on page PA 63

African American Spiritual

Old   Zi - on's   chil - dren   march-ing   a - long,

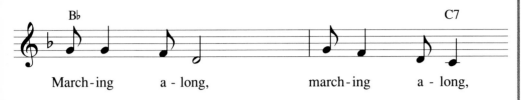

March-ing   a - long,   march-ing   a - long,

Old   Zi - on's   chil - dren   march-ing   a - long,

Talk-ing a - bout   the wel - come   day.

LESSON 1

3. Introduce "Zion's Children" to practice using singing voices. Have the children:
• Listen to the song, patting the beat.
• Identify the kind of voice they hear (singing).
• Listen to the song, singing along as they are able.
• Sing the song, marching in follow-the-leader style with you or a child as leader.

Reinforcing the Lesson
Have the children listen to you give examples of the four kinds of voices, identifying which one they hear by pointing to the appropriate picture on Chart 38. (You may wish to have a few volunteers give the examples.) (You may wish to use Copying Master 6-1 at this time.)

3 APPRAISAL
The children should be able to hear examples of speaking, whispering, calling, and singing voices and identify which kind of voice they heard by pointing to the appropriate picture on Chart 38.

MORE MUSIC TEACHING IDEAS
1. Have the children call out the days of the week, following each with two pats on the beat (repeat Sunday at the end). Then sing "Zion's Children," chanting and patting this as an interlude between verses. Repeat this activity using speaking and whispering voices, and singing on *so mi*.
2. You may wish to have the children learn the following Valentine's Day songs in the Songbook: "I Made a Valentine," page 258; "The Best of Friends," page 259. (You may wish to use Copying Master 6-2 at this time.)

CURRICULUM CONNECTION: SOCIAL STUDIES
Spirituals—songs that have a religious or "spiritual" meaning. The oldest spirituals were not written down, but passed on from singer to singer. Spirituals were first sung by Africans brought to the United States as slaves. These songs expressed their troubles and their hope for a better life after death. Spirituals can be slow or fast, and are often accompanied by hand clapping.

SONGBOOK
"Uncle Jessie," page 289 (Black History Month)
"Peanut Butter," page 284 (four voices)
"I Made a Valentine," page 258 (tone color of a child singing)
"The Best of Friends," page 259 (Valentine's Day song)

LESSON 2

Focus: Higher and Lower

Related Subjects
Snow, numbers

Objectives
To identify and use higher and lower
To practice identifying whispering, speaking, singing, and calling voices

Materials
Recordings: "Cynthia in the Snow"
Listening—Prelude in C♯ Minor, Opus 28, No. 10 by Frédéric Chopin
"Hello, There"
Recorded Lesson—"Listening for Higher and Lower"
Listening—*Acadian Songs and Dances* (fourth movement) by Virgil Thomson
Charts 39 and 40
Pitched barred instrument
Copying Masters 6-3, 6-4, 6-5 (optional)

1 SETTING THE STAGE

Introduce "Cynthia in the Snow." Have the children listen to the poem and identify the kinds of voices they hear (speaking, whispering).

5B, 6A
CD 4

Cynthia in the Snow

It SUSHES,
It hushes
The loudness in the road.
It flitter-twitters,
And laughs away from me.
It laughs a lovely whiteness,
And whitely whirs away,
To be
Some otherwhere,
Still white as milk or shirts.
So beautiful it hurts.

—*Gwendolyn Brooks*

E X T E N S I O N

CURRICULUM CONNECTION: ART

Paper Snowflakes—Give each child a sheet of white, one-ply paper toweling. Have the children fold their towels in half, and in half again. Cut sections out of the towels, being careful not to cut away all the folded edges. You may wish to dip the edges of the cut towels into small bowls of different watered-down food colorings that you prepared ahead of time. Open each towel very carefully and allow them to dry. Mount the finished "snowflakes" on colored paper and display them in the classroom. (You may wish to use Copying Master 6-3 at this time.)

MORE MUSIC TEACHING IDEAS

1. Have the children discuss different ways to move to "Cynthia in the Snow," such as calmly and quietly with the first three lines, slightly increasing the speed of the movement with lines four through seven, and becoming more serene with the last four lines. Then have them use these ideas as they listen to the poem.
2. Decide on a few places where certain instruments, such as a glockenspiel or a triangle, could be added to enhance the mood of the poem, for example, at the very beginning, at the ends of phrases, on the word *whirs*, at the very end, and so on. As the class listens to the poem, you or a child conduct the instrument players by pointing to the appropriate instrument at its designated place in the poem, or place

stick-ons of the instruments on the inside front cover of the Big Book and point to them.

HIGHER AND LOWER

CHART 39

LESSON 2

2 TEACHING THE LESSON

1. Introduce identifying higher and lower.
Have the children:

• Watch as you position a pitched barred instrument on end with the longer bars at the bottom.

• Listen as you play each pitch from lowest to highest and back to lowest.

• Listen as you play only the highest and lowest pitches.

• Look at Chart 39. Notice that one snowflake is higher than the other.

• Watch as individual children or pairs of children come up to the chart and listen, pointing to the appropriate snowflake on the chart as you or another child randomly plays either the highest or lowest pitch. (You may wish to use Copying Master 6-4 at this time.)

• Listen again, indicating whether they hear a high or low pitch by crouching on a low pitch, and standing on tiptoe with their arms stretched high on a high pitch.

MORE MUSIC TEACHING IDEAS

1. Have the children move to show higher and lower as they listen to *Miniwanka, or The Moments of Water.*
2. Have the children take turns playing lower and higher pitches as you or a child point to the higher and lower snowflakes on Chart 39.

COOPERATIVE LEARNING

After listening to the highest and lowest pitches on a barred instrument, have the children work in pairs or small groups to decide whether you are playing the highest or lowest pitch. By discussing their answers with one another, they will form a consensus opinion. This activity requires the oral rehearsal of the concept higher/lower. It also requires that the children defend a position when there is a difference of opinion. Help the children discuss differing ideas among one another without getting angry. Explain that they can agree to disagree.

KEYBOARD

Use the keyboard to reinforce the concept of high/low. Review playing low pitches to the left with the left hand, and high pitches to the right with the right hand. Then have the children work in pairs, with one child pointing to the high and low snowflakes in random order as the other child reacts immediately, playing the correct side of the keyboard. Have them switch roles. This type of reaction exercise helps the children understand the relationship between a visual symbol and its related sound.

CORE
LESSON 2

2. Introduce Prelude in C♯ Minor, Opus 28, No. 10 by Frédéric Chopin. Have the children:
• Show how they would move if they were falling snowflakes, turning gently as they go from high to low. Assume an interesting shape as they land. (You may wish to tell the children that no two snowflakes are alike, and suggest that they each try to make their shape as individual as possible.)
• Show how they would move if the wind swirled the snowflakes back up into the air to turn and fall again.
• Listen to Prelude in C♯ Minor, Opus 28, No. 10 and notice how the music moves from high to low.
• Discuss how the previous movement activity could be used to show high and low in the music.
• Listen to the music again, doing these movements.

3. Review "Hello, There" on page 142 for more practice identifying high and low. Have the children:
• Listen to the song, singing the echoes. (Have them notice that they are using their singing voices.)
• Listen to the pitches for the words *hello, there* to tell if the second pitch is higher, lower, or the same as the first and third pitches (lower).
• Do the same for the other three-note patterns that are echoed throughout the song. (The second pitch is lower in each group of three throughout.)
• Decide on the melodic direction of the last line. (It starts high and goes lower.)
• Listen to the song again, singing all the echoes, and singing the last line all together, as they are able.
• Practice using their calling voices as they say *hello, there* in two groups.

CHART
40

LISTENING MAP: ACADIAN SONGS AND DANCES *(Fourth Movement)*

EXTENSION

THE COMPOSER

Frédéric Chopin (shō′ pan) (1810-1849)—Polish composer and pianist. Chopin is one of the few composers who wrote almost exclusively for solo piano. In his use of the rhythms of Polish folk dances such as the mazurka and the polonaise, he was one of the first nationalistic composers. He was a master of small forms, excelling in such genres as the waltz, nocturne, and prelude. His études brought the study of technical problems to the level of great art. Today Chopin is regarded as one of the most influential composers of piano music.

THE COMPOSER

Virgil Thomson—American composer and music critic, was born in Kansas City, Missouri, in 1896. In 1925 he moved to Paris, where he became influenced by Erik Satie and other modern French composers. He returned to the United States in 1940. Two of Thomson's most famous works are the operas *Four Saints in Three Acts* and *The Mother of Us All*. Thomson also pioneered in writing music for motion pictures. His score to the film *Louisiana Story* won the Pulitzer prize in 1948. Two orchestral suites were drawn from this score, including *Acadian Songs and Dances*.

Four Themes from *Acadian Songs and Dances*
(Fourth Movement)

Virgil Thomson

Theme 1: ♩=66

mp

Theme 2:

f

Theme 3:

f

Theme 4: ♩.=66

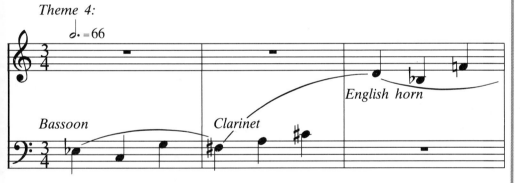

Bassoon — Clarinet — English horn

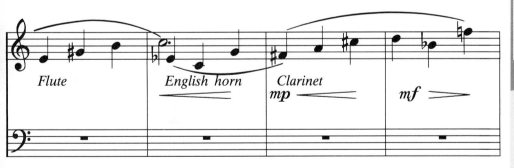

Flute — English horn — Clarinet — *mp* — *mf*

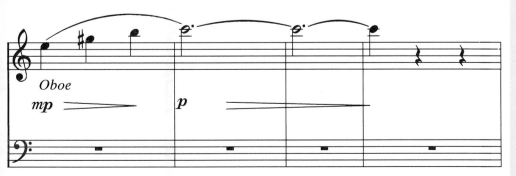

Oboe — *mp* — *p*

Four themes from *Acadian Songs and Dances* (fourth movement) by
Virgil Thomson. Used by permission of G. Schirmer, Inc.

Reinforcing the Lesson

Introduce *Acadian Songs and Dances* (fourth movement) for more practice identifying higher and lower. Have the children lightly pat the beat as they listen. Then have them look at Chart 40 as they listen again, watching as you point to the picture that corresponds to each theme. (The raccoon walking is Theme 1; the raccoon swimming is Theme 2; the raccoon dancing is Theme 3; the alligator swimming is Theme 4; the alligator sneaking up on the raccoon is when all the themes repeat; the raccoon escaping is the very end of the piece.) Have them identify which picture you pointed to with the lower theme (the first picture of the alligator). Have them tell you what they think is the story of the music. (You may wish to use Copying Master 6-5 at this time.)

3 APPRAISAL

The children should be able to:
1. Move to identify higher and lower pitches.
2. Identify whispering and speaking voices in "Cynthia in the Snow," and singing and calling voices in "Hello, There."

SONGBOOK

"The Bus," page 266 (downward moving patterns)
"Little Red Caboose," page 278 (upward moving patterns)
"The Best of Friends," page 259 (strong beat; downward moving patterns)

LESSON 3

Focus: Higher and Lower

Related Subjects
Valentine's Day, Presidents' Day

Objectives
To practice identifying higher and lower
To practice keeping the beat

Materials
Recordings: "When the Flag Goes By"
Listening—Concerto for
Trumpet and Orchestra
(second movement) by
Michael Haydn
Listening—"Effie Joins the
Carnival" and "Effie
Goes Folk Dancing" from
Suite No. 1 for Tuba and
Piano by Alec Wilder
"Mail Myself to You"
Charts 41, 42, and 52
Copying Masters 5-10, 6-6, 6-7, 6-8, 6-9,
6-10, 6-11, 6-12 (optional)

1 SETTING THE STAGE

Have the children look at Chart 41 and
identify pictures that might represent
pitches that go higher (three ascending
flags). Have a few volunteers play or sing
three pitches that go higher.

6A

CD 4

"WHEN THE FLAG GOES BY"

CHART 41

EXTENSION

Key: C   Starting Pitch: C   Scale Tones: *do re mi so la do¹*

When the Flag Goes By

Piano Accompaniment on page PA 64

Words and music by
Lynn Freeman Olson

1. When the flag goes by, hold it high!
2. When you hear this song, sing out strong!

Wave it for our coun - try!
Sing it for our coun - try!

When the flag goes by, hold it high!
When you hear this song, sing out strong!

And cheer when the flag goes by!
And cheer when the flag goes by!

2 TEACHING THE LESSON

1. Introduce "When the Flag Goes By" to practice identifying pitches that go higher. Have the children:

• Listen to the song as you point to one line of pictures on Chart 41 for each line of the song. (You may wish to point to each of the three ascending flags on the words *hold it high*.)
• Practice the words as you point to the pictures on the chart. (You may wish to use Copying Master 6-6 at this time.)
• Listen again, singing along as they are able. Pretend to wave a small flag back and forth on the beat, holding it higher on the words *hold it high*. (You may wish to use Copying Master 6-7 at this time.)
• Sing the song, marching with their flags.

MORE MUSIC TEACHING IDEAS

1. Have the children sing "When the Flag Goes By" and take turns playing the pitches E G C' on resonator bells each time the words *hold it high* occur in the song. Compare the relative sizes of the three bells (the highest bell is shortest). Then take turns playing the pitches C D E D C on resonator bells each time the words *when the flag goes by* occur in the song. Again, compare the relative sizes of the three bells (the highest bell is shortest). (You may wish to use Copying Master 5-10 at this time.)
2. Have the children practice inner hearing with "When the Flag Goes By." Sing the song while patting the beat, thinking the words *hold it high* each time they occur

in the song. Then sing the song again, thinking the words *when the flag goes by* each time they occur in the song.

LESSON 3

2. Introduce Concerto for Trumpet and Orchestra (second movement). Have the children:
• Look at the picture of the trumpet on Chart 52 on page 198 as you point to it. (You may wish to use Copying Master 6-8 at this time.)
• Briefly discuss brass, the material out of which the trumpet is made. (You may wish to tell the class that the sound of brass instruments is made by buzzing the lips into the mouthpiece.)
• Listen to Concerto for Trumpet and Orchestra (second movement).

E X T E N S I O N

CURRICULUM CONNECTION: SCIENCE

Brass—a metal formed by mixing melted copper and zinc. The melted brass can be poured directly into forms to harden or made into blocks, called ingots, for storage. Brass has been used for thousands of years. The ancient Romans were the first to use brass widely. They made many things from brass, including coins, pots, and decorations. Today, brass is used to make hardware, jewelry, pots, candlesticks, flatware, and much more. Ask the children to name things they have seen that are made of brass. The brass in brass musical instruments contains a lot of zinc, which makes it strong and hard.

THE PERFORMER

Wynton Marsalis, notable black American trumpet player, was born in New Orleans in 1961. After studying at the Juilliard School in New York City, Marsalis played with jazz bands, including touring with his own quintet. He also performs music from the classical repertoire and has achieved success playing trumpet concertos such as Concerto for Trumpet and Orchestra by Michael Haydn.

3. Introduce "Effie Joins the Carnival" and "Effie Goes Folk Dancing" from Suite No. 1 for Tuba and Piano for more practice listening for high and low. Have the children:
• Listen as you tell them that they are going to hear music about an elephant named Effie. Try to imagine the elephant in each situation (at a carnival, going folk dancing) as they listen. (You may wish to use Copying Master 6-9 at this time.)
• Listen to "Effie Joins the Carnival" and "Effie Goes Folk Dancing" and identify the sound of the tuba. Notice that the tuba is a lower-sounding instrument than the trumpet. (You may wish to use Copying Master 6-10 at this time.)
• Listen again, marching with "Effie Joins the Carnival," and skipping with "Effie Goes Folk Dancing."

MORE MUSIC TEACHING IDEAS
Have the children:
1. Dramatize "Effie Joins the Carnival" and "Effie Goes Folk Dancing."
2. Take turns skipping in small groups to "Effie Goes Folk Dancing."
3. Have the children draw pictures of Effie as they listen to the music.

THE PERFORMER
Harvey Phillips, American tuba player, was born in Aurora, Missouri, in 1929. As a young man he played with the Ringling Brothers and Barnum & Baily Circus Band. Phillips later studied at the Juilliard School and the Manhattan School of Music in New York City. He has played with various groups in New York City, and was a founding member of the New York Brass Quintet. Because there had not been much music written for tuba, Phillips commissioned works for tuba from a number of composers, including Alec Wilder, who wrote Suite No.1 for Tuba and Piano.

THE COMPOSER
Michael Haydn (hī' dən) (1737-1806)—Austrian composer, younger brother of composer Franz Joseph Haydn. He studied composition mainly by reading books. A prolific composer, Michael Haydn wrote symphonies, stage music, concertos, chamber music, and church music.
Alec Wilder (1907-1980)—American composer known for both his popular and serious music. He wrote many pieces for children. Suite No. 1 for Tuba and Piano is one of several works Wilder dedicated to noted tuba player Harvey Phillips and his family. Mr. Phillips says that above all else Wilder loved "music, nature, and children."

LESSON 3

4. Introduce "Mail Myself to You." Have the children:
• Mirror you as you move to dramatize the words to the refrain of "Mail Myself to You" without the music.
• Try to guess what the song is about.
• Listen to the refrain as they mirror your movements again. Look at Chart 42, echoing the words of the refrain as you point to the corresponding picture. (You may wish to use Copying Master 6-11 at this time.)
• Listen to the whole song, acting out the words while mirroring you, and singing along with the refrain as they are able.

Key: D   Starting Pitch: A   Scale Tones: *do re mi fa so la*

Mail Myself to You

Piano Accompaniment on page PA 66

Words and music by Woody Guthrie

EXTENSION

CURRICULUM CONNECTION: SOCIAL STUDIES

Mailing Letters—Discuss why letters are in envelopes, and why the name and address of the person to whom the letter is being sent should be printed on the outside of the envelope. Then print each child's name and address on an envelope. Using these addressed envelopes, have the children pretend to be mail carriers, and deliver the mail to their classmates. You may wish to plan a class trip to the local post office. (You may wish to use Copying Master 6-12 at this time.)

MORE MUSIC TEACHING IDEAS

Reinforce the concept of downward melodic movement. Have the children figure out that the last line of "Mail Myself to You" stays on the same pitch for four pitches, then moves downward. Ask them to find a way to show how this melody moves through body movement. Have them take turns playing the last line of the song on a bell set or Orff instrument.

CHART
42
"MAIL MYSELF TO YOU"

LESSON 3

Reinforcing the Lesson

Listen to the refrain of "Mail Myself to You" again and identify which line on Chart 42 has pitches that go higher (the third, *stick some stamps on top of my head*).

3 APPRAISAL

The children should be able to:
1. Identify pitches that get higher and lower.
2. Move to keep a steady beat.

SONGBOOK

"My Valentine," page 260 (Valentine's Day)
"America," page 262 (patriotic)
"Old Dan Tucker," page 282 (favorite song of Lincoln)

LESSON 4

Focus: Rhythm

Related Subject
Presidents' Day

Objectives
To practice rhythms using ♩ and ♪
To identify and use classroom instruments
To practice identifying higher and lower

Materials
Recordings: "When the Flag Goes By"
"George Washington"
Recorded Lesson—"Learning to Skip"
Listening—"Walk on Down the Road"
"The Farmer in the Dell"
"Mail Myself to You"
Charts 41 and 42
Classroom instruments
Quarter note and quarter rest stick-ons
Copying Masters 6-13, 6-14 (optional)

1 SETTING THE STAGE

Have the children review "When the Flag Goes By" on page 151. Look at Chart 41 as they sing the song, waving or pretending to wave a flag on the beat and raising the flag on *hold it high*. Remember that the pitches go higher on these words. Sing the song again, marching to the beat, waving and holding up their flags as they march. Recognize that they are marching to the beat.

2 TEACHING THE LESSON

1. Introduce "George Washington" to practice identifying higher and lower. Have the children:
• Listen to the song.
• Listen to the song again, singing along as they are able.
• Decide if the pitches of *Washington* in the first two measures move higher or lower (lower).
• Sing the song again, using one hand to show how the melody moves on these three pitches.
• Sing the song again, following a leader and marching around the room.

2. Identify and play classroom instruments. Have the children:
• Watch as you construct the rhythm pattern ♩ ♩ ♩ ♪ on the inside front cover of the Big Book using quarter note and quarter rest stick-ons. Recognize this rhythm as a pattern they have used before.
• Pat the rhythm. (You may wish to use Copying Master 6-13 at this time.)
• Take turns identifying classroom instruments by listening as you name an instrument and picking up the correct instrument from a group of instruments.
• Tap or play the rhythm pattern on classroom instruments as an ostinato with "George Washington."

George Washington

Piano Accompaniment on page PA 68

Words and music by Lynn Freeman Olson

f George Wash-ing-ton! George Wash-ing-ton!

He was a great, great, man.

When A-mer-i-cans won-dered who could lead them,

they said, "George Wash-ing-ton can!"

EXTENSION

MORE MUSIC TEACHING IDEAS

Have the children pat the rhythms of different presidents' names, for example,

A - bra - ham   Lin - coln

Combine four of these name rhythms to create an introduction, interlude, or coda for "George Washington."

COOPERATIVE LEARNING

Have the children work in groups of four to identify classroom instruments. Have each group form a circle with several instruments placed in the center. All groups may have the same instrument selection, or you may give different instruments to each group. As you say an instrument name, the group members should determine whether or not they have the instrument and, if they do, identify it. By working in groups, children who are not sure of instrument names will have support learning the names. Encourage group members to give information to those who are not sure.

LESSON 4

3. Introduce "Walk on Down the Road" to practice walking and skipping. Have the children:
• Stand in a scatter formation with sufficient space around each of them.
• Practice going from walking to skipping by walking with "bouncy heels." (See *Movement* below.)
• Practice walking and skipping with "Walk on Down the Road."

4. Review "The Farmer in the Dell" on page 63. Have the children:
• Listen to the song while patting the beat.
• Sing the song and play the game, substituting skipping for standing.

Reinforcing the Lesson

Review "Mail Myself to You" on page 154. Sing the entire song, doing movements suggested by the words. Sing just the refrain, looking at Chart 42 as you point four beats on each picture. Then watch as you put the rhythm pattern ♩ ♪ ♩ ♪ on the inside front cover of the Big Book using the quarter note and quarter rest stick-ons. Pat the new pattern. Sing the refrain again as a few children play this pattern as an ostinato. If time permits, repeat the activity to give other children a turn to play. (You may wish to use Copying Master 6-14 at this time.)

3 APPRAISAL

The children should be able to:
1. Correctly read and pat notation for rhythms containing ♩ and ♪.
2. Identify and use classroom instruments.
3. Correctly identify higher and lower in "When the Flag Goes By" and "George Washington."

MOVEMENT

A keen awareness of the body's center of gravity must be developed in order to maintain good body alignment and insure equal development of both sides of the body. A natural progression of walking with "bouncy heels" leads gradually to letting each foot come off the ground, and this produces a skip—easily and naturally. Frequent repetitions of this sequence help strengthen the equal involvement of both sides of the body while reinforcing the basic coordination needed for skipping. (*Note:* Students may need many reminders to "give each foot a chance to skip.")

SONGBOOK

"My Valentine," page 260 (Valentine's Day; silent beat)
"America," page 262 (patriotic)
"Old Dan Tucker," page 282 (favorite song of Lincoln)

LESSON 5

Focus: Same and Different

Related Subjects
Animals, lullabies

Objectives
To identify same and different
To practice identifying higher and lower
To practice identifying whispering, speaking, singing, and calling voices

Materials
Recordings: Listening—"Echo" from Divertimento in E♭, by Franz Joseph Haydn
"Lullabye"
Listening—*Acadian Songs and Dances* (fourth movement) by Virgil Thomson
Recorded Lesson—"Listening for Themes in *Acadian Songs and Dances*"
"Teddy Bear"
"Zion's Children"
Charts 40 and 43
G and B♭ resonator bells
Copying Masters 6-5, 6-15 (optional)

1 SETTING THE STAGE

Have the children echo you as you say short statements, imitating the kind of voice you use (whispering, speaking, singing, or calling). Then have them tell you which voice you used. Have one child answer a question. Have the class decide if the child said the same thing as you (the echo), or said something different (the answer).

4B, 5B, 6A, 6B

CD 3, 4

Key: F   **Starting Pitch: A**   **Scale Tones:** *so, la, ti, do re mi fa so*

Lullabye

Piano Accompaniment on page PA 69

Words and music by B. S. and M. S.

Lul - la-bye, (lul - la-bye,) lul - la-bye,

(lul - la-bye,) My sleep - y lit - tle one,

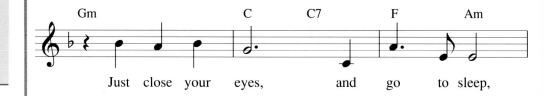

Just close your eyes, and go to sleep,

E X T E N S I O N

THE COMPOSER

Franz Joseph Haydn (hī′ dən) (1732-1809)—Austrian composer. As a young man he wrote music at the court of Prince Esterhazy (es′ tər-häz-ē), a great music lover. During a visit to London in 1791 Haydn composed his famous *Surprise* Symphony. Haydn wrote many kinds of music, including over 150 Divertimentos. He wrote 104 symphonies and developed the symphony as a musical form. For this reason, Haydn is called the "father of the symphony." He also established the basis of the modern orchestra.

MORE MUSIC TEACHING IDEAS

1. Have the children do echo movements. Stand in front of the children and have them watch you move, moving with you. Then have them stand still as you move, and imitate your movements after you have finished. Move only your hands and arms at first. Try this activity with "Echo," with you moving on each phrase and the children imitating your movements on the echoes.
2. Have the children sing "Where Is Thumbkin?" on page 22. Have them notice that the music repeats. Have them identify the parts that are echoes (measures 1 and 2, 3 and 4, 7 and 8). Then have them notice that measures 5 and 6 are a question and answer. Sing the song with one child hiding and singing the

echoes and answers. Have different children hide for each verse.
3. Sing questions to different children and have them answer after you. Encourage them to sing their responses.

(go   to sleep,)   go   to sleep,   (go   to sleep,)

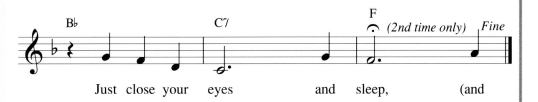

Just close your   eyes   and   sleep,   (and

I know you're tired___   you've had a bus - y

sleep.)   I know you're   tired___   you've

2 TEACHING THE LESSON

1. Introduce "Echo" from Divertimento in E♭ by Franz Joseph Haydn. Have the children:
• Listen and decide if they hear echoes or answers (each phrase is echoed exactly).
• Listen again, raising their hands when they hear each echo.

2. Introduce "Lullabye" to hear and sing echoes. Have the children:
• Listen for echoes in the song.
• Listen again, singing the echoes when they occur.
• Tell what kind of voices performed the song (man's and child's).

EXTRA HELP

If the children need help sensing when ''their part'' (the echo) occurs, have them listen to ''Lullabye'' once more, practicing the echo parts by ''mouthing the words.'' This will also provide an extra hearing of the tune, increasing the likelihood of their singing with pitch accuracy.

LESSON 5

3. Review *Acadian Songs and Dances* **(fourth movement) to listen for same and different.** Have the children:
• Look at Chart 40 on page 148 and listen for repeated melodies in the music as you point to the picture that corresponds to each theme.
• Remember which picture represents the low sounds (the alligator alone).
• Listen again, pointing toward the chart with you. (You may wish to use Copying Master 6-5 at this time.)
• Listen to each theme, and think of a movement to do (walking, swimming, or dancing) that corresponds to the way the raccoon is moving in each picture.
• Listen again, doing the different movements with each theme. (You may wish to have them imitate you.)

4. Review "Teddy Bear" on page 106 and play it on bells. Have the children:
• Sing the song, doing the movements.
• Decide which words are the same (*teddy bear, teddy bear*).
• Sing only the first *teddy bear* and decide if the third note is lower or higher than the first two (lower).

day. It's time to go to sleep, To-

had a bus-y day. It's time to

mor-row you can play. *D.C. al Fine* So

go to sleep, To-mor-row you can play.

CURRICULUM CONNECTION: LANGUAGE ARTS

Visual Discrimination and Reading Readiness—Cut out a variety of different patterns from old wallpaper sample books. Make sure there are two samples of each pattern. Mount each pattern sample on a 3″ × 5″ index card and place the cards in a small bag or box. Have each child pick a card from the container. When all the children have a card, have them find which child has a card with the same pattern as theirs. As the children become more proficient at identifying same and different, play the game with letters and shapes on the index cards in place of the patterns. (You may wish to use Copying Master 6-15 at this time.)

MORE MUSIC TEACHING IDEAS

Have the children dramatize *Acadian Songs and Dances* (fourth movement). Choose one child to be the alligator. Then listen to the music, with the rest of the class doing the raccoon movements in place as you point to each picture on Chart 40. Have the children freeze on the low music as the alligator stealthily moves around the room. When the low and high music sound together, indicating the chase, have the alligator tap the nearest child. That child pretends to swim away as the alligator gives chase. On the last note, the alligator freezes and the raccoon escapes. Repeat the activity to give different children a chance to play the alligator. (You may wish to have only one child play each role at first, as the rest of the class watches.)

HIGHER AND LOWER

CHART 43

LESSON 5

• Look at Chart 43 and determine why the third teddy bear at the top of the chart is positioned lower than the other two (to show that the third pitch is lower).

• Sing the song again as you point to one bear on each pitch. Repeat, giving a few children turns pointing to the bears.

• Determine how to play the pitches on *teddy bear* with bells (play B♭ twice and G once).

• Sing the song as a few children take turns playing the B♭ and G bells on the words *teddy bear* each time they occur in the song. (Have a different child play the bells on each line.)

• Play a high-low identification game. Listen as you randomly play sets of two pitches on the B♭ and G bells, crouching down if the second pitch is lower, standing on tiptoe with arms overhead if the second pitch is higher, or standing with arms at their sides if both pitches are the same.

Reinforcing the Lesson

Review "Zion's Children" on page 145 for more practice identifying same and different. Have the children sing the song and decide which parts are the same (measures 1 and 2 are the same as measures 5 and 6). Sing the song, marching behind a leader.

3 **APPRAISAL**

The children should be able to:

1. Identify same and different aurally and with movement.
2. Identify higher and lower aurally, visually, and with movement.
3. Identify and use whispering, speaking, singing, and calling voices.

MORE MUSIC TEACHING IDEAS

1. Have the children sing "Teddy Bear," showing the higher-higher-lower pattern with arm movements each time it occurs in the song.

2. Have the children substitute pitch syllables *so so mi* for the words *teddy bear* each time they occur in the song.

3. Take turns playing their own original tunes on the G and B♭ bells.

SONGBOOK

"Que Bonito Es," page 286 (same and different phrases)

"Old Dan Tucker," page 282 (same and different parts; favorite song of Lincoln)

"The Bus," page 266 (downward moving patterns)

"Little Red Caboose," page 278 (upward moving patterns)

"Peanut Butter," page 284 (four voices)

"I Made a Valentine," page 258 (same and different phrases)

LESSON 6

Focus: Rhythm

Related Subject
Bands

Objectives
To practice moving to a beat
To practice identifying same and different
To practice rhythms with ♩ and 𝄽
To name some band instruments

Materials
Recordings: "Here Comes the Band"
"George Washington"
Listening—*Children's March*
by Edwin Franko
Goldman
"Lullabye"
"When the Flag Goes By"
Chart 41
Classroom instruments
Quarter note and quarter rest stick-ons
Copying Masters 6-6, 6-13, 6-16 (optional)

1 SETTING THE STAGE

Have the children listen to "Here Comes the Band" and name the instruments mentioned in the poem (tuba, flute, trombone, trumpet). (You may wish to use Copying Master 6-16 at this time.) Then have them try to name other instruments that are used in a band (cymbals, saxophones, clarinets, drums, and so on). Have them name the kind of music that a band usually plays (march). Have them name marchlike songs that they know ("Zion's Children," "When the Flag Goes By," and so on).

2 TEACHING THE LESSON

1. Review "George Washington" on page 156 to practice same and different. Have the children:
• Sing the song, patting the beat.
• Recognize that only measures 1 and 2 are the same.

2. Introduce *Children's March* by Edwin Franko Goldman to listen for familiar melodies. Have the children:
• Listen and determine if they hear one melody or different melodies (different) and if they hear familiar songs (yes).

Here Comes the Band

The band comes booming down the street,
The tuba oomphs, the flutes tweet tweet;

The trombones slide, the trumpets blare,
The baton twirls up in the air.

There's "oohs!" and "ahs!" and cheers and clapping—
And I can't stop my feet from tapping.

—William Cole

E X T E N S I O N

EXTRA HELP

If the children need more preparation in distinguishing same and different, have them look at the picture on page 162 in your book to find the band members who are the same. Have them also find examples of same and different in the classroom.

The order of familiar melodies
heard in *Children's March*
is as follows:

"Mary Had a Little Lamb"

"Jingle Bells"

"Sing a Song of Sixpence"

"The Farmer in the Dell"

"Here We Go Round the Mulberry Bush"

"Hickory Dickory Dock"

"Three Blind Mice"

"Rock-a-bye Baby"

"Pop! Goes the Weasel"

"London Bridge"

• Identify as many of the familiar songs in *Children's March* as they can (see the list provided on this page).
• Stand in a circle and listen to *Children's March* again, marching around the circle to the beat, and changing directions each time a new melody begins.
3. Review "Lullabye" on page 158. Have the children:
• Listen to "Lullabye," singing along on the echoes as they are able.
• Name some ways that "Lullabye" is different from *Children's March* (softer, slower, more restful, and so on).

Reinforcing the Lesson
Look at Chart 41 and review "When the Flag Goes By" on page 151. Using the quarter note and quarter rest stick-ons, construct the rhythm pattern ♩ ♩ ♩ 𝄽 on the inside front cover of the Big Book. Have the children read the notation and practice the pattern. Then form two groups. Sing the song, with one group marching and the other group playing the rhythm pattern as an ostinato on classroom instruments. Have them recognize that they are playing an accompaniment. Have the groups switch parts and repeat the activity. (You may wish to use Copying Masters 6-6 and 6-13 at this time.)

3 APPRAISAL
The children should be able to:
1. Move to the beat with increasing skill and accuracy.
2. Identify different melodies in *Children's March* and same parts of the melody in "George Washington."
3. Recognize notation for a rhythm pattern and play that pattern as an ostinato.
4. Name some band instruments.

MORE MUSIC TEACHING IDEAS
1. Have the children play rhythm instruments on the beat with *Children's March* or "Zion's Children." You may wish to put instrument stick-ons on the inside front cover of the Big Book and point to each instrument to direct the children when to play.
2. Decide on movements to do with each melody in *Children's March*, for example, moving back and forth like a clock pendulum with "Hickory Dickory Dock," pretending to rock a baby on the beat with "Rock-a-bye Baby," and so on. Have the children jump each time they hear the *pop* music in "Pop! Goes the Weasel." Listen to the music, doing the different movements as each new melody begins.

THE COMPOSER
Edwin Franko Goldman (1878-1956)— American bandmaster and composer. As a teenager he studied composition with Antonín Dvořák in New York. He became cornet soloist with the Metropolitan Opera orchestra when he was seventeen. He formed his first band in 1911. In 1918 he began the Goldman Band outdoor concerts in New York's Central Park. Goldman composed over 100 marches, including *On the Mall* and *Children's March*.

SONGBOOK
"Que Bonito Es," page 286 (same and different phrases)
"Old Dan Tucker," page 282 (same and different parts; favorite song of Lincoln)

REVIEW AND EVALUATION

REVIEW

Objectives
To review songs, skills, and concepts learned in Unit 6
To measure the children's ability to:
1. Identify four types of voices (whispering, singing, speaking, calling)
2. Recognize higher and lower
3. Identify same and different

Materials
Recordings: "Hello, There"
             "Zion's Children"
             "Lullabye"
Chart 38
Bells or other pitched instrument
Evaluation Unit 6 Copying Master

TEACHING THE LESSON

Review the songs and concepts in Unit 6.
Have the children:
• Listen as you read the lesson, singing and performing the activities at the appropriate places. (As the children sing and move, observe and evaluate individuals and the class as a whole as to how their responses indicate their level of understanding.)

Look and Listen
Today you are going to learn how to use your eyes and ears to look and listen carefully. Look at these four pictures and name the kind of voice shown in each picture.
• Look at Chart 38 on page 143 and identify speaking, whispering, calling, and singing voices. Take turns coming up to the chart and pointing to each kind of voice as you name it.

Now that you have named four ways we can use our voices, listen carefully to each kind of voice.
• Either as a group or individually, listen as you or a child demonstrates examples of the four kinds of voices, and identify which one they hear by pointing to the appropriate picture on Chart 38.

You did well finding four ways to use the voice. Now use your listening skills to find higher and lower sounds. Listen carefully as I play two different pitches. If the second pitch is higher than the first, stand on tiptoe with arms stretched up high. If the second pitch is lower than the first, crouch down low to the ground.
• Listen and move appropriately as you play three or four sets of two different pitches on resonator bells or another pitched instrument. (Watch for children who respond accurately to the different pitches.)

REVIEW AND EVALUATION

You can sing songs and show higher and lower pitches with your hand. As we sing "Hello, There," think about whether the last part, *all here together again,* goes higher or lower. Show what you think with hand movements that go higher or lower when we sing that part.
• Sing "Hello, There" on page 142. As they sing, show with hand movements that the last part goes lower. (Do this with them.)

Another listening skill you should have is being able to hear repeated sound patterns. There is a repeated sound pattern in "Zion's Children." Each time you hear it, raise your hand.
• Sing "Zion's Children" as they march around in a circle. They should raise their hand each time they sing the words *old Zion's children.*

Use your listening skills to find different sections in "Lullabye." Pretend to rock a baby and sing the echoes when you hear that section. When you hear a different melody, pretend to sleep.
• Identify the different sections in "Lullabye" by pretending to rock a baby during the first section and by pretending to sleep during the second section.

You have used your eyes and ears well to look and listen today.

EVALUATION

Evaluation Unit 6 Copying Master can be found in the *Teacher's Resource Book* with full directions for providing an evaluation of the child's progress.

ELEMENTS OF MUSIC	UNIT 7 OBJECTIVES	Lesson 1 CORE Focus: Tone Color	Lesson 2 CORE Focus: Same and Different	Lesson 3 Focus: Same and Different	Lesson 4 Focus: Tone Color
Dynamics	Use, hear different dynamic levels	Use, hear different dynamic levels			
Tone Color	Vary tone color using body percussion and classroom instruments **Identify flute, piccolo, violin**	Choose classroom instruments for their particular tone color Identify piccolo, flute, and violin	Identify the violin	Hear the violin	Use classroom instruments to represent characters in a story Identify piccolo, flute, and violin
Tempo	Practice locomotor movements at different tempos	Identify and move at slow and fast tempos Move at quick tempo	Practice walking a moderate tempo		
Duration/ Rhythm	Recognize rhythm of locomotor movements Devise pictures of one and two equal sounds to a beat Do four-beat patterns Sing, use ² and ² meters	Practice steady beat Sing song in ² meter	Practice steady beat Hear one and two sounds to a beat Do simple four-beat movement patterns Sing song in ² meter	Do simple four-beat patterns Create different four-beat responses to teacher's four-beat patterns (Q/A) Sing songs in ² meter	Sing a song in ² meter
Pitch	Practice using two-note patterns: *mi so* (3 5) Hear, sing, play three-note patterns: *mi so la* (3 5 6) **Identify upward/downward Create, play upward/ downward patterns**		Use *mi so* (3 5) in a song Hear upward and downward melodic patterns	Use *mi so* (3 5) in a song Play *mi so* (3 5) question/answer patterns	
Texture	Perform melody with rhythm and/or speech ostinato Hear melody with accompaniment	Add accompaniment to a poem	Play an accompaniment with a melody		Perform melody with an accompaniment
Form	Identify same/different phrases and sections **Create question/answer patterns**	Identify sections by change in tone color Identify question and answer in a poem	Identify same/different Identify question/answer patterns	Identify same/different Identify and tap question/answer patterns	
Style	Move to show style and elements of music	Hear music of the 19th century Hear Portuguese folk melody	Move to show same and different Hear music of the 18th century	Move to show same and different sections Hear music of the 18th century	Move to show the character of a 19th-century listening selection

PURPOSE Unit 7: Move into Spring

This unit is designed to be taught during early spring. Through songs and listening selections that focus on animals and plants in spring, the children will experience identifying some orchestral instruments, creating responses to question-and-answer patterns, and identifying upward and downward melodic patterns. The children will also focus on movement, beginning with their own space, continuing into moving through space, and finally identifying several different kinds of movement.

SUGGESTED TIME FRAME

March	April

FOCUS

Core Lessons 1, 2, 5, 6, 8
• Tone Color
• Same and Different
• Rhythm and Movement
• Upward and Downward
• Upward and Downward

Lessons 3, 4, 7, 9, 10
• Same and Different
• Tone Color
• Same and Different
• Beat and Strong Beat
• Two Sounds to a Beat

Lesson 5 CORE Focus: Rhythm and Movement	Lesson 6 CORE Focus: Upward and Downward	Lesson 7 Focus: Same and Different	Lesson 8 CORE Focus: Upward and Downward	Lesson 9 Focus: Beat and Strong Beat	Lesson 10 Focus: Two Sounds to a Beat
	Use pitched classroom instruments	Hear solo piano	Hear piccolo, flute, and violin Play pitched classroom instruments	Use and vary body-percussion sounds	Play unpitched percussion instruments
Practice locomotor movements at different tempos		Move to different tempos	Move to fast and slow in a song	Hear and do body-percussion patterns to fast and slow tempos	Hear fast and slow tempos
Sing songs with changing meters Identify rhythm of locomotor movements	Play different response to a short melodic pattern Sing a song with ²⁄ and ²⁄. meters Move to rhythm of locomotor movements	See pictorial representation of duration Identify and move to rhythm patterns of locomotor movements	See pictorial representation of duration Sing song in ²⁄.	See pictorial representation of beat and strong beat Create simple ostinato patterns Distinguish between beat and strong beat	Devise and see pictorial representations of beat and two sounds to a beat Create and do simple four-beat patterns Sing songs in ²⁄ and ²⁄. meters Practice keeping beat
	Identify upward/downward visually Move to show upward/downward Play upward/downward patterns Create upward/downward question/answer patterns	Identify melodic direction as same or different	Sing a song with *mi so la* (3 5 6) Play *mi so la* upward and downward Visually, aurally, and through movement identify upward and downward	Sing upward and downward patterns in a song	Sing a song with *mi so la* (3 5 6)
	Hear melody with accompaniment	Hear and sing melodies with accompaniment	Do a simple body-percussion accompaniment with a song	Do and create simple body-percussion accompaniments showing beat and strong beat	Create and do simple body-percussion and unpitched-percussion instrumental accompaniments
Identify sections by changes in rhythm patterns	Identify melodically same and different phrases	Identify same and different phrases/sections Move to show AB and ABA forms			
Sing English folk song	Sing English folk song	Hear music of the 19th century	Hear music of the 19th century	Sing traditional songs	Sing traditional songs

BULLETIN BOARD

Construct a background showing a spring meadow with a pond and some trees. As the children learn the songs and poems in the unit, add the following pictures from each to the scene: the animals in "The Secret Song"; the lark; pictures from "Spring"; the Quakers; children doing different movements; butterflies, flowers, ducks, and turtles in upward and downward patterns; children on a seesaw. At the end of the unit, you may wish to use the bulletin board as a focus for the review lesson.

Move into Spring

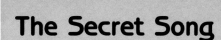

C O R E
LESSON 1

Focus: Tone Color

Objectives
To use the tone colors of classroom instruments to create an expressive accompaniment
To recognize that the piccolo, flute, and violin play music that is generally high in pitch
To identify sections of music that have different tone colors

Materials
Recordings: "The Secret Song"
             Listening—"The Lark Song"
             from *Scenes of Youth* by
             Peter Ilyich Tchaikovsky
             Listening—"Indo Eu"
             (Portuguese folk dance)
             "Spring Is Here" (optional)
Chart 44
Assorted classroom instruments
Copying Masters 7-1, 7-2 (optional)

1 SETTING THE STAGE

Have the children listen to the poem "The Secret Song" twice. The first time have them identify the characters who answered the questions (spider, fish, pigeon, owl, fox). The second time have them move to dramatize each question. Discuss the tempo of their movements, and determine whether each of their movements was fast or slow (answers will vary). (You may wish to use Copying Master 7-1 at this time.)

E X T E N S I O N

COOPERATIVE LEARNING
After the children have worked with "The Secret Song," tell them that the poem describes small beautiful things that are sometimes overlooked. Have the children work in small groups to look for such things in their environment. They may collect objects or make pictures of those they cannot collect, such as living creatures and large branches. Have them arrange and fasten the items and/or pictures on a long sheet of paper. Then choose a soft instrument sound for each item. As a group member points to each item one at a time, the others play the corresponding sounds. Encourage the conductor to point from left to right, so the children will be "reading the score." Hang the groups' papers around the room.

The Secret Song

Who saw the petals
    drop from the rose?
I, said the spider,
But nobody knows.

Who saw the sunset
    flash on a bird?
I, said the fish,
But nobody heard.

Who saw the fog
    come over the sea?
I, said the sea pigeon,
Only me.

Who saw the first
    green light of the sun?
I, said the night owl,
The only one.

Who saw the moss
    creep over the stone?
I, said the gray fox,
All alone.

—Margaret Wise Brown

2 TEACHING THE LESSON

1. Add appropriate instruments to "The Secret Song." Have the children:

• Choose an instrument that reflects the tempo and character of each question, such as a triangle for the rose petals, a cymbal tapped with a wooden mallet for the sunset, a rubbed drumhead for the fog, finger cymbals for the first green light, and sand blocks for the moss.

• Say the poem as a few children move and a few others play the instruments.

• Choose instruments for each of the animals who answered the questions, such as a guiro or scraper for the spider, jingle bells for the fish, an upward glissando on a pitched instrument for the pigeon, a hand drum for the owl, and a tambourine for the fox.

• Choose four children for each stanza. Two play the instruments for the question and answer, and two do the movements. (Have the child doing the answer movement watch and come toward the child doing the question movement.)

MOVEMENT

Watch as the children move to show styles and characteristics of animals, events, and musical elements. For positive reinforcement, point out and compliment those children who are sensitive to the characteristics they are dramatizing. Whenever possible, give every child a chance to try out each character.

LESSON 1

2. Introduce "The Lark Song." Have the children:
• Listen to "The Lark Song" and determine which of the characters in "The Secret Song" this music might be about, and why. (Have the children give specific reasons drawn directly from the music for their answers, for example, the high pitch suggested the spider, or the quick, fluttery parts suggested the pigeon. Accept any reasonable answers.)
• Look at Chart 44 and identify the lark as the subject of the music. (You may wish to use Copying Master 7-2 at this time.)
• Look at the pictures of the piccolo, flute, and violin. Name any they may already know. Say the name of each instrument several times after you.
• Listen to the music again and determine that these instruments are all fairly high in pitch.
• Move to "The Lark Song," being certain to respect each other's space. (You may wish to have small groups take turns moving, rather than have the whole class move at once.)

CHART
44
SOLO ORCHESTRAL INSTRUMENTS

E X T E N S I O N

THE COMPOSER

Peter Ilyich Tchaikovsky (pē' tər il' yich chī-kof' skē) (1840-1893)—a Russian who became one of the leading composers of his day. The ballet *The Nutcracker* is one of his best-known works. Other well-known Tchaikovsky ballets are *Swan Lake* and *The Sleeping Beauty.* He also wrote symphonies, concertos, operas, songs, and chamber music. Tchaikovsky's music is full of beautiful melodies, many of which he drew from his Russian folk music heritage.

Key: F   Starting Pitch: F   Scale Tones: *so₁ la₁ ti₁ do re mi fa so la*

Indo Eu

Piano Accompaniment on page PA 72   *Portuguese Dance Melody*

(For listening only)

La la la la la la la la la la la la la

La la la la la la la la la la la la. Fine

La la la la la la la la la la la la la

La la la la la la la la la la la la la. D.C. al Fine

Reinforcing the Lesson

Introduce the Portuguese folk dance "Indo Eu." Have the children listen to the music, raising their hands when they hear the instruments change. (The form of "Indo Eu" is ABABABA. Instrument changes indicate the beginning of each new section.) Then have the children form a circle. Circle to the left during each A section, and stop and pat the beat during each B section.

3 APPRAISAL

The children should be able to:
1. Choose classroom instruments to play with "The Secret Song" based on tone color characteristics.
2. Say the names of the piccolo, flute, and violin, and determine that all three instruments are high in pitch.
3. Identify sections in "Indo Eu" by hearing tone color changes.

MORE MUSIC TEACHING IDEAS

Have the children listen to "Spring Is Here" and identify the sound of the flute heard in the accompaniment. Have them sing the song as they are able.

Key: D   Starting Pitch: A   Scale Tones: *mi so*

Spring Is Here

Chant

Spring is here, spring is here. Birds and flow-ers now ap-pear.

SONGBOOK

"Peanut Butter," page 284 (four voices)

SAME AND DIFFERENT

Same and different,
Same and different,
We are all
the same and different.

—*Carol Bitcon*

CORE
LESSON 2

Focus: Same and Different

Objectives
To identify same and different characteristics in people
To identify same and different sections of music through movement
To identify question-and-answer patterns

Materials
Recordings: "Same and Different"
Listening—"Indo Eu"
(Portuguese folk dance)
Listening—"Spring" from
The Four Seasons by Antonio
Vivaldi
"Quaker, Quaker"
"Lemonade" (optional)
Charts 45 and 46
Question mark and period stick-ons
Copying Masters 7-3, 7-4, 7-5 (optional)

1 SETTING THE STAGE

Have the children echo-say "Same and Different." Then say the whole chant, patting the steady beat. Have them each think of some way they are all the same, such as, they are the same because they all have heads, they all go to the same school. Then have them think of ways they are different, such as, some of them are boys and some are girls, they have different names, and so on. Alternate saying the chant with individual children describing one way they are same or different.

2 TEACHING THE LESSON

1. Review "Indo Eu" on page 169 and learn a dance. Have the children:
• Listen to the song and remember how the sections are different (different melodies and different accompaniments).

EXTENSION

COOPERATIVE LEARNING

In small groups, have the children sit in a circle and discuss ways they are the same and different from one another. Give each child three bingo chips, paper clips, or other small items. Each time they share an idea, they put one item into the center of the circle. When all their items are used, they must wait to give another idea until everyone else's are also used. This strategy gives slower speakers a chance to share. After each group has suggested many ideas, form a class circle and have each child say one way he or she is the same or different from others in the room. Keep going around the circle until there are no more ideas. After the first time around, anyone may pass.

LESSON 2

• Learn the dance without the music.
A section—Circle for sixteen beats.
B section—One child moves for four beats. Everyone repeats that movement for the next four beats. The child to the left of the first child does a different movement for the next four beats, and the class repeats the new movement for the last four beats.
• Do the whole dance with the music.
• Identify that they were doing the same movement when echoing and different movements for each new leader during the B sections of "Indo Eu."

2. Introduce "Spring" from *The Four Seasons* by Antonio Vivaldi for more practice with same and different. Have the children:
• Look at Chart 45 and identify pictures that are the same and different. (You may wish to use Copying Master 7-3 at this time.)
• Discuss the story the pictures suggest.
• Listen to the music, raising one hand each time they think they hear the theme that represents the tree.
• Identify one instrument used in "The Lark Song" that is also used in "Spring" (violin). (You may wish to use Copying Master 7-4 at this time.)
The form of "Spring" is as follows:
A section—full theme played by strings (tree in sun)
B section—trills by high strings (birds)
A section—partial theme (tree)
C section—low strings (brook)
A section—partial theme (tree)
D section—low strings rumbling, fast violin part (storm)
A section—partial theme (tree)
E section—longer string section with violin solos (sun)
A section—partial theme (tree)

THE COMPOSER

Antonio Vivaldi (an-tō' nē-ō vi-väl' dē) (1678-1741)—Italian composer. Born in Venice, he studied violin with his father, who was a professional musician. When he was twenty-six, Vivaldi became the music director of a conservatory in Venice. Many of his vocal works were written for the students there. Vivaldi also wrote many operas. But he is best known for his instrumental music, in particular his violin concertos. *The Four Seasons* are the first four in a series of twelve violin concertos called *The Contest Between Harmony and Invention.* Each season's concerto is accompanied by a descriptive poem, also written by Vivaldi.

C O R E
LESSON 2

Reinforcing the Lesson

Show the children pictures of a question mark and a period. Explain that a question mark is used at the end of a written question, and a period is used at the end of a statement. (It may be helpful to spend time reviewing what a question is and that an answer is usually a statement.) Introduce "Quaker, Quaker" and have the children echo each line as you point to the question mark on lines 1 and 3 and the period on lines 2 and 4. Then look at Chart 46 and sing the song as you point to the pictures of the woman for the questions and the pictures of the man for the answers. The questions and answers differ from each other. (You may wish to use the question mark and period stick-ons to reinforce this concept.)
(You may wish to use Copying Master 7-5 at this time.)

3 APPRAISAL

The children should be able to:
1. Tell how they are the same and different from each other.
2. Identify same and different sections in "Indo Eu" verbally and through movement.
3. Identify question-and-answer patterns in "Quaker, Quaker."

Quaker, Quaker

American Folk Song

"Quak-er, Quak-er, how is thee?" "Ver-y well,   I thank thee."

"How's thy neigh-bor next to thee?" "I don't know, I'll go and see."

E X T E N S I O N

SONGBOOK

"Uncle Jessie," page 289 (two contrasting sections)
"Little Spotted Puppy," page 276 (same and different phrases)
"Baby Beluga," page 264 (two contrasting sections)

MORE MUSIC TEACHING IDEAS

1. Have the children accompany "Quaker, Quaker" with two different pitched instruments to reinforce the question and answer phrases in the song. Play D and A together on the steady beat. The first instrument, for example, an alto xylophone, plays during the two question phrases and the second instrument, for example, a soprano xylophone, plays during the two answer phrases.
2. Have the children play questions and answers in pairs on unpitched or pitched instruments. Each pair chooses two different instruments and decides who will play the questions and who will play the answers. It is not important at this time to have questions and answers of the same length. It is important for each child to wait until the other is finished before beginning.

CURRICULUM CONNECTION:
LANGUAGE ARTS

Language—One way groups of people differ is in the way they speak. The Quakers speak English, but some of the words they use are not standard usage. Explain the meanings of the words *thee* (you) and *thy* (your) to help the children better understand "Quaker, Quaker." Ask if any of the children speak more than one language, or know words in other languages. Have these children share some words with the rest of the class.

CHART
46
SAME AND DIFFERENT

MORE MUSIC TEACHING IDEAS

Have the children learn "Lemonade" to
practice using *so* and *mi.*

Lemonade

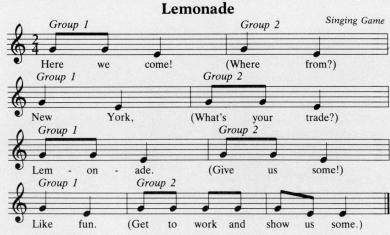

Group 1   *Group 2*   Singing Game

Here   we   come!   (Where   from?)

Group 1   *Group 2*

New   York,   (What's   your   trade?)

Group 1   *Group 2*

Lem - on - ade.   (Give   us   some!)

Group 1   *Group 2*

Like   fun.   (Get   to   work   and   show   us   some.)

Key: C major   Starting Pitch: G   Scale Tones: *mi so*

LESSON 3

Focus: Same and Different

Objectives
To distinguish between echoes and answers when responding to four-beat patterns

To practice identifying same and different sections and phrases

To practice identifying and playing question-and-answer patterns

Materials
Recordings: "Quaker, Quaker"
  Recorded Lesson—"Echoes and Answers"
  Listening—"Spring" from *The Four Seasons* by Antonio Vivaldi
  "Old MacDonald"
Charts 45 and 46
Question mark and period stick-ons
Copying Masters 7-3, 7-6 (optional)

1 SETTING THE STAGE

Have the children review "Quaker, Quaker" on page 172. Echo each line after you. Then sing the song, pointing to the appropriate pictures on Chart 46 for the questions and answers. You may wish to use the question mark and period stick-ons to reinforce question and answer.

2 TEACHING THE LESSON

1. Play a question-and-answer game with "Quaker, Quaker." Have the children:

• Sit in a circle. One child faces you as you sing the question phrases in "Quaker, Quaker" to that child. That child sings the answer phrases back to you.

• The first child turns to the next child to the left around the circle and sings the questions. The second child sings the answers.

• Repeat this activity completely around the circle. (You may wish to draw a period on a flash card and a question mark on another. Have the child singing the questions hold the question mark flash card, and the child singing the answers hold the period flash card. Pass the flash cards from child to child as the game progresses around the circle. Or, give each child a set of flash cards and have them hold up their question mark cards when they hear questions and their period cards when they hear answers.)

• Identify the answers as different from the questions.

EXTENSION

MORE MUSIC TEACHING IDEAS

1. Sing "Quaker, Quaker." Improvise a sixteen-beat B section for the song, using two different pitched instruments, such as a soprano and alto glockenspiel. You play a question on the pitches A and F♯ for four beats. Have a child play an answer on A and F♯ for four beats using a different rhythm or melodic pattern than yours. You play the same question again, and the child plays another answer. Sing "Quaker, Quaker" again. Tell the children this form (song-improvisation-song) is called ABA.

2. Use classroom objects to illustrate ABA form, for example, lay out a pencil, a book, and a pencil. Have the children find and lay out their own ABA examples. (You may wish to use Copying Master 7-6 at this time.)

Key: G   Starting Pitch: G   Scale Tones: *so, la, do re mi*

Old MacDonald

Piano Accompaniment on page PA 74   *Traditional*

1. Old   Mac - Don - ald   had   a   farm.

Ee - i - ee - i - oh.   And   on   that farm he

had   some chicks.   Ee - i - ee - i - oh.   With a

chick,   chick   here,   and   a   chick,   chick   there,

(No repeat on Verse 1)

Here a chick,   there a chick,   Ev - 'ry-where a chick,   chick,

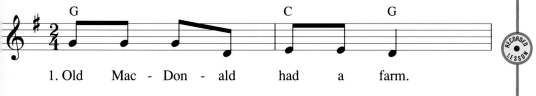

Old Mac-Don - ald   had   a farm,   Ee - i - ee - i - oh.

2. . . .ducks. . .quack, quack,. . .chick, chick here, chick, chick there. . .
3. . . .pigs. . .oink, oink,. . .quack, quack here, quack, quack there. . .
4. *(Make up a verse)* . . .oink, oink here, oink, oink there. . .

SONGBOOK

"Jig Jog, Jig Jog," page 274 (same and different phrases)
"Que Bonito Es," page 286 (same and different phrases)

LESSON 3

2. Practice echoing and answering. Have the children:
• Echo-tap four-beat patterns after you. (Use combinations of quarter notes, quarter rests, and two eighth notes.)
• Tap back a pattern that is different from yours, to answer rather than echo.
• Individually tap back patterns after you, echoing or answering as they choose. The rest of the class decides whether each individual echoed or answered your pattern.

3. Review "Spring" for more practice identifying same and different sections. Have the children:
• Look at Chart 45 on page 171 and identify the pictures that are the same. (You may wish to use Copying Master 7-3 at this time.)
• Listen to the music, raising one hand when they hear the music for the A section.
• Dramatize the story on the chart as they listen to the music again.

Reinforcing the Lesson

Introduce "Old MacDonald." Have the children join in singing as they are able. Find parts of the song that are always the same (*ee-i-ee-i-oh*) and parts that are different (the animal sounds). Think of different animals to add new verses to the song. The children who suggest an animal should also decide what sound to use for that animal.

3 APPRAISAL

The children should be able to:
1. Identify and distinguish between echoes and answers by responding with different four-beat patterns when asked to sing and tap four-beat answers.
2. Identify same and different in "Spring" and "Old MacDonald."
3. Identify and sing question-and-answer patterns in "Quaker, Quaker."

LESSON 4

Focus: Tone Color

Objectives
To review identifying some orchestral instruments
To use classroom instruments to help tell a story

Materials
Recordings: "Old MacDonald"
Listening—"The Lark Song" from *Scenes of Youth* by Peter Ilyich Tchaikovsky
"Learning"
Chart 44
Pitched and unpitched classroom instruments
Copying Masters 7-2, 7-4, 7-7, 7-8, 7-9 (optional)

1 SETTING THE STAGE

Have the children review "Old Mac-Donald" on page 175. Then sing the song, adding unpitched classroom instruments, for example, rhythm sticks for *chick*, a guiro or other scraper for *quack*, and a scraped drum for *oink*. (You may wish to use Copying Master 7-7 at this time.)

2 TEACHING THE LESSON

1. Review "The Lark Song" to practice identifying instruments by sight and sound. Have the children:
• Look at Chart 44 on page 168 and identify the instruments (piccolo, flute, violin). (You may wish to use Copying Masters 7-2, 7-4, and 7-8 at this time.)
• Review the reasons why the composer may have used those instruments. (The instruments seem to describe the size, fluttery movement, and song of a lark.)
• Choose either the piccolo, flute, or violin. Raise one hand each time they hear that instrument.

E X T E N S I O N

CURRICULUM CONNECTION: SCIENCE

The Lark—a small bird known for its melodious song. Larks are dull-colored, usually grayish brown streaked with black. Most larks have tufts of feathers, called crests, on their heads. They can be found all over the world, except in the coldest areas. Most larks live on the ground, but a few perch on bushes or posts. They walk rather than hop. Many larks are strong fliers, and often sing while in flight. One of the most famous species of lark is the skylark, which is common in Europe.

LEARNING

Once there were three eggs in a small nest.
Peck, peck, peck.
One bird, two birds, three tiny birds came out of the eggs.
Peep, peep, peep.
Mother bird fed her baby birds.

Baby raccoons were on the ground.
Scratch, scratch, scratch.
They gobbled their food.

Baby fish were swimming in the lake.
They were following the big fish.
Swish, swish, swish.
The fish were learning to swim.

All the babies were learning their lessons.

Mother bird pushed her babies to the side of the nest.
It was time to learn to fly.
Flop, flop, flop.
They couldn't.
Then flap, flap, flap.
Up they flew.

Father raccoon climbed a tree.
The babies tried to follow.
Then, one by one, they climbed up, up, up.

The baby fish were learning to swim together.
One fish swam away, then swam back to the group.
Another fish swam away, then came back.
Then all the fish were swim, swim, swimming together.

Everyone was tired.
So they all snuggle, snuggle, snuggled and took a nap.

—S.S.

LESSON 4

• Move to "The Lark Song." Start by pretending to sit in their nests. Then pretend to fly, showing how the music moves. Fly back to their nests at the end of the music. (Encourage the children to anticipate the ending so they are back in their nests when the music ends.)

2. Introduce "Learning." Have the children:
• Listen as you explain that they are going to play instruments to help tell a story.
• Choose either a pitched or unpitched instrument, whichever you think is appropriate, for each of the characters in the story—three baby birds, mother bird, baby raccoons, baby fish, big fish, father raccoon. Also add sounds on the repeated words: *peck, peep, scratch, swish, flop, flap, up, swim, snuggle.* (Set up barred pitched instruments using C D E G A, C pentatonic. If using a piano, only play the black keys, F♯ pentatonic.)
• Listen to the story, playing the appropriate instrument as each character is mentioned. (Be sure to leave plenty of time to play each instrument as you tell the story.) (You may wish to use Copying Master 7-9 at this time.)

Reinforcing the Lesson

Compare the high-pitched instruments used in "The Lark Song" to the instruments chosen to represent the birds in "Learning." Help the children realize that in both cases certain instruments were chosen because a character suggested a particular tone color.

3 APPRAISAL

The children should be able to:
1. Identify the piccolo, flute, and violin by sight.
2. Choose classroom instruments with specific tone colors to represent characters in a story.

MORE MUSIC TEACHING IDEAS

1. After the children know the story of "Learning" well, have them try to tell the story using instruments only.
2. Have the children dramatize "Learning." Form three groups: birds, raccoons, and fish. Practice the different movements mentioned in the story that are appropriate for each group. Choose one child in each group to be the parent. Then listen to the story with each group moving at the appropriate time, and all snuggling together for a nap at the end. (You may wish to use Copying Master 7-9 at this time.)

EXTRA HELP: ALTERNATE INSTRUMENTS

If classroom instruments are not available, use sound sources from around the classroom as alternate instruments. Specify that these items should be ones that cannot be damaged. Remind the children that these items are not just for making noise, and that all sounds should be made with musical intent.

SONGBOOK

"Down at the Station," page 268 (use classroom instruments for train sound effects)
"Little Red Caboose," page 278 (use classroom instruments for train sound effects)

CORE
LESSON 5

Focus: Rhythm and Movement

Objectives
To identify their own space for movement
To explore and identify locomotor movements
To identify rhythm patterns of six locomotor movements

Materials
Recordings: "My Place"
           "I Can Get from Here to There"
           Recorded Lesson—
              "Rhythms of Locomotor Movements"
           "Rig-a-Jig-Jig"
Chart 47
Square piece of paper or fabric
Small object such as an eraser or counter for each child in the class
Copying Master 7-10 (optional)

1 SETTING THE STAGE

Have each child choose a small object to represent himself or herself. Place the square piece of fabric or paper on a flat surface where everyone can see it. Have the children take turns putting their objects on the square in a space where there is plenty of room around it. When all the children have placed their objects, help them notice that the objects have space between them. Then put the objects away and have the children position themselves in the available open space to create a similar arrangement.

My Place

Words and music by Danai Gagné
Adapted

This is my place. This is my space.   No one else but me.

E X T E N S I O N

I Can Get From Here to There

I can get from here to there,
I can get most anywhere.
I can travel all through space,
And I can come back to my place.

—Jacque Schrader

2 TEACHING THE LESSON

1. Introduce "My Place" to identify each child's own space. Have the children:
• Identify the space in which they are positioned as their own by looking around the room for nearby objects, such as a window or a cabinet.
• Explore their space by reaching high, low, and all around themselves without moving their feet. (Be sure each child has enough room to stretch in all directions without touching anyone else. You may wish to divide the class into smaller groups if space is limited.)
• Echo "My Place" one line at a time, adding the following movements.

first line: point to the floor where they are
second line: stretch arms upward, to the sides, and down
third line: shake finger emphatically

• Sing the song with the movements.

2. Introduce "I Can Get from Here to There" to practice moving carefully. Have the children:
• Listen to the poem.
• Echo-say the poem one line at a time, then say the whole poem.
• Say the poem as one child moves around the others, returning to his or her own space by the word *place*.
• Say the poem several more times as other individuals or small groups repeat the activity. (Try to have as many children as possible move. Encourage them to make interesting paths that explore all the available empty space. Make sure they give themselves enough time to get back to their own spaces without running. They should always be aware of the others around them.)

MORE MUSIC TEACHING IDEAS

Have the children move to "The Lark Song," considering the paths of the other children as they move about the room. Have them start in their own space, and return to it by the end of the music.

SPECIAL LEARNERS

Some special learners may have difficulty in returning to place by the end of the poem. Help them by first trying the sequence with sound cues instead of the poem. For example, have the children move away from their starting places when they hear a wood block and return to place when they hear a triangle. Encourage them to move in curved lines as well as straight lines. Some children may be able to experiment with zig-zag, dotted, or "squiggly" lines. Moving with a helpful partner may provide a more successful experience for some children.

LESSON 5

3. Introduce rhythms that are long, short, or combinations of long and short. Have the children:

• Look at Chart 47 and identify the movements pictured (walking, running or jogging, jumping, hopping, skipping, and galloping).

• Try each movement, considering the other children's spaces as they explore.

• Discuss whether the rhythm of each movement is long, short, or a combination of long and short. (You may wish to use Copying Master 7-10 at this time.)

BEAT DIVISIONS   CHART 47

E X T E N S I O N

KEYBOARD

After walking in the classroom, have the children "take a walk" up and down the keyboard. Beginning on the bottom key, have them play every white and black key in order all the way to the top of the keyboard (88 keys) and then back down.

Key: C   Starting Pitch: G   Scale Tones: *re mi fa fi so la ti do¹*

Rig-a-Jig-Jig

Piano Accompaniment on page PA 75

English Folk Song

As   I   was   walk - ing   down   the   street,

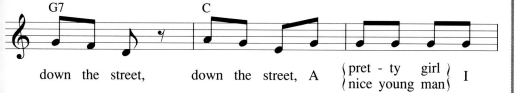

down   the   street,   down   the   street,   A {pret - ty   girl } I
                                                                 {nice young man}

chanced to   meet   Hi - O!   Hi - O!   Hi - O!

Rig - a - jig - jig   and   a - way   we   go,   a -

way   we   go,   a - way   we   go,   Rig - a - jig - jig and a -

way   we   go,   Hi - O!   Hi - O! __ Hi - O! _____

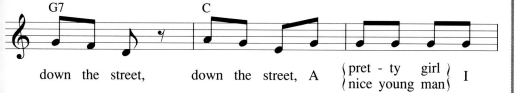

C O R E
LESSON 5

Reinforcing the Lesson

Introduce "Rig-a-Jig-Jig." Have the children listen to the song, walking around the room during the first section, and changing to skipping or galloping when the rhythm changes. Then have one child walk around the room during the first section, and choose a partner and skip or gallop during the second section. Repeat the song, with both children walking during the first section, and both choosing new partners during the second section. Continue this activity until everyone is moving. Help the children realize that walking represents long, even sounds, and skipping or galloping represents a combination of long and short sounds.

3 APPRAISAL

The children should be able to:
1. Show that they can identify their own space by moving away from and back to it.
2. Walk, jog, hop, jump, gallop, and skip as indicated in the lesson.
3. Identify rhythm patterns of locomotor movements as consisting of long, short, or long and short sounds.

SONGBOOK

"Epo i tai tai e," page 269 (long and short sounds)

"Down at the Station," page 268 (use locomotor movements to move as one or more trains)

"Little Red Caboose," page 278 (use locomotor movements to move as one or more trains)

"Step in Time," page 288 (use locomotor movements to move to the beat)

"Goin' to the Zoo," page 270 (use locomotor movements to move to the beat)

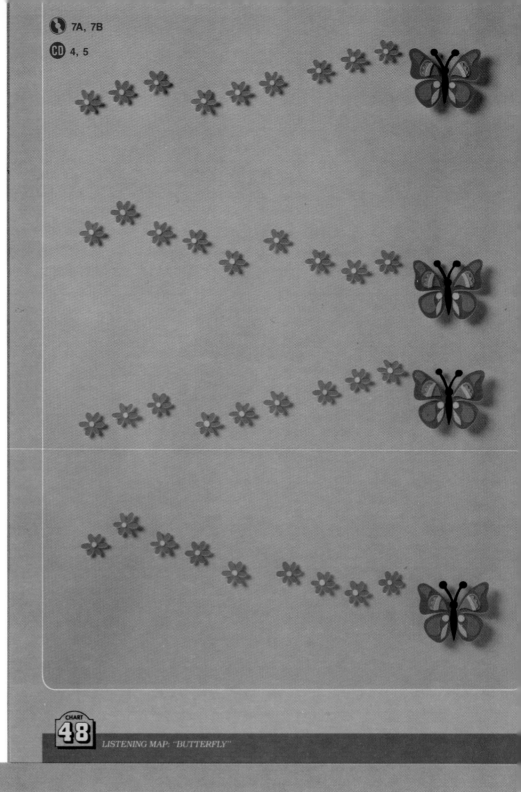

CHART **48**

LISTENING MAP: "BUTTERFLY"

LESSON 6

Focus: Upward and Downward

Objectives
To see, hear, and move to upward and downward melodic patterns
To identify and play upward and downward patterns

Materials
Recordings: "Butterfly"
Recorded Lesson—
"Upward and
Downward"
"Rig-a-Jig-Jig"
Chart 48
Pitched classroom instruments
Copying Masters 7-11, 7-12 (optional)

1 SETTING THE STAGE

Have the children review finding their own space. Review the rules for moving around the room. Have the children walk around the room, considering the other children's spaces as they move. Then have them each choose one spot in the room and walk to that spot, crouching lower and lower as they walk. Then have them return to their original space, stretching taller and taller. Identify this movement as moving downward and upward.

2 TEACHING THE LESSON

1. Introduce "Butterfly" to reinforce upward and downward. Have the children:
• Look at Chart 48 and identify the direction of each group of flowers on each line.
• Listen to "Butterfly," moving their hands to show the melodic direction as you point to the chart. (Each flower and butterfly is one pitch of the song.)
• Discover that measures 1–4 and 9–12 have the same melodic pattern. (You may wish to use Copying Master 7–11 at this time.)

E X T E N S I O N

MORE MUSIC TEACHING IDEAS
Have the children review "Spring Is Here" on page 169 to reinforce high and low. Have them sing the song and stand to show the high pitch and bend their knees to show the low pitch.

Butterfly

Piano Accompaniment on page PA 77

Words and music by
Lynn Freeman Olson

But-ter-fly, but-ter-fly, where do you roam?

Whose luck - y gar - den do you call your home?

But-ter-fly, but-ter-fly, why won't you stay?

Why are you al - ways flut-ter-ing a - way?

LESSON 6

• Move like butterflies, using hands or bodies to show upward downward patterns.
2. Show phrases in "Butterfly." Have the children:
• Sit with partners you assign them.
• Listen to the song while looking at Chart 48. (You may wish to use Copying Master 7–11 at this time.)
• Decide who will move during lines 1 and 3 and during lines 2 and 4.
• Sit facing their partners and listen to "Butterfly" again. Group 1 moves one hand like a butterfly during lines 1 and 3, group 2 moves during lines 2 and 4.
• Listen again, moving through the room. Group 1 moves through the room during lines 1 and 3, landing on the last word of each line. Group 2 moves during lines 2 and 4, landing next to their partners on the last word of each line.
3. Play upward and downward questions and answers. Have the children:
• Listen and watch as you play five-note stepwise upward or downward patterns. Identify the direction of each pattern.
• Take turns playing an answer to your question by playing the pitches you played in reverse order.

Reinforcing the Lesson
Review "Rig-a-Jig-Jig" on page 181. Have the children listen to the words *down the street* each time they occur in the song and identify the melodic direction as downward. Play the game.

3 **APPRAISAL**
The children should be able to:
1. Identify upward and downward patterns in "Butterfly" by sight and sound, and show them by moving.
2. Play upward and downward patterns as answers to musical questions.

MORE MUSIC TEACHING IDEAS
After the children have played upward and downward questions and answers with you, have them work in pairs. Give one pitched instrument to each pair and have them play upward and downward questions and answers to each other. After a short period of time have several pairs who are good at this activity play their questions and answers for the rest of the class. (You may wish to use Copying Master 7-12 at this time.)

SPECIAL LEARNERS
Help the children in each pair focus on the chart lines to which they are to respond by labeling them. Use two red squares (from Stick-On Sheet 6) to label lines 1 and 3 and two yellow circles (from Stick-On Sheet 7) to label lines 2 and 4. Assign one shape to each member of the pair.

SONGBOOK
"Ah! Les Jolis Papillons," page 263 (upward and downward; butterflies)

LESSON 7

Focus: Same and Different

Objectives
To identify same and different phrases, sections, and movements
To review identifying long and short

Materials
Recordings: "Butterfly"
"Clickety Clack"
Listening—"The Wild Horseman" from *Album for the Young*, Book 1 by Robert Schumann
Charts 47 and 48
Copying Masters 7-11, 7-13 (optional)

1 SETTING THE STAGE

Have the children review "Butterfly" on page 183. Use Chart 48 to help identify the melodic direction of the song. Remember that lines 1 and 3 have the same melodic pattern. Create movement as a class or in pairs that shows the same and different parts of the song, for example, flutter around the room during lines 1 and 3, gently open and shut wings while resting on an imaginary flower during line 2, and fly away during line 4. (You may wish to use Copying Master 7-11 at this time.)

2 TEACHING THE LESSON

1. Introduce "Clickety Clack" and identify repeated words. Have the children:
• Listen to the song and identify the words that repeat (*going to the city and it won't come back*).
• Listen again, singing *going to the city and it won't come back* each time it occurs.
• Add these movements to the B section.

woo, woo   pull the train whistle
clickety clack   pat your knees
this old train is loaded down   "chug" with arms

EXTENSION

VOCAL DEVELOPMENT

The octave leap from the last note of the A section to the first note of the B section (from *back* to *Woo*) and the leap of a seventh between the fourth and fifth measures of the B section (between *down* and *Woo*) present a challenge. To help the children sing these intervals, tell them to raise their hands above their heads as though they were shooting a basketball through a hoop. This encourages them to approach the note lightly from above instead of straining for it from below.

Clickety Clack

Piano Accompaniment on page PA 78

Music by Hap Palmer
Words by Martha and Hap Palmer

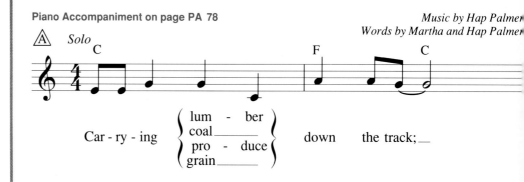

A Solo
Car-ry-ing { lum - ber / coal___ / pro - duce / grain___ } down the track;__

Group
Go-ing to the cit-y and it won't come__back. won't come__back.

B All
Woo, woo, click-e-ty clack, This old train__ is__

load-ed down.＿ Woo, woo, click-e-ty clack,

This old train＿ is＿ cit-y bound.＿

• Dramatize the song. Have several children form a train and move around the room during the A section. During the B section stop and do the movements. (You may wish to use Copying Master 7-13 at this time.)

2. Review identifying the rhythm of walking. Have the children:

• Look at Chart 47 on page 180 and review the movements. Remember that skipping and galloping have a combination of long and short sounds, and the other movements have all long or all short sounds.

• Decide which picture shows the movement they did during the A section of "Clickety Clack" (probably walking). Determine that walking has a long sound.

Reinforcing the Lesson

Introduce "The Wild Horseman" from *Album for the Young*, Book 1 by Robert Schumann. Have the children determine whether they would use the same movement they used with "Clickety Clack" (no). Determine that they would use either galloping or skipping. Listen again for different sections in the music. Describe how they are the same or different. (There are three sections, ABA: the A sections sound the same; the B section sounds lower.) Form two groups to show the form of the piece. One group gallops or skips during the A sections and the other gallops or skips during the B section.

3 APPRAISAL

The children should be able to:

1. Identify same and different by sight, sound, and through movement.
2. Identify, compare, and move to show all long sounds in "Clickety Clack" and a combination of long and short sounds in "The Wild Horseman."

MORE MUSIC TEACHING IDEAS

Have the children work in pairs to show the question-and-answer phrases in each section of "The Wild Horseman." Have partners sit facing one another with space between them. The first partner moves hands on the floor during the question phrases, the second partner does the same during the answer phrases. Then do the activity moving around the room. The first partner moves away from the second partner during the question phrases, and the second partner joins the first during the answer phrases.

THE COMPOSER

Robert Schumann (shoo′ män) (1810-1856)—German composer. He is one of the great composers of art songs and piano compositions. As a young man he studied to be a lawyer, but gave that up to devote his time to music and writing. He married the daughter of his piano teacher. Schumann wrote some of his most famous song cycles in the year following his marriage. Among these are *Woman's Love and Life* and *Poet's Life*. His many piano works include *Papillons, Carnaval,* and *Scenes from Childhood. Album for the Young* is a collection of pieces for piano students.

SONGBOOK

"Jig Jog, Jig Jog," page 274 (same and different phrases)

"Que Bonito Es," page 286 (same and different phrases)

C O R E
LESSON 8

Focus: Upward and Downward

Objectives
To identify upward and downward melodic direction by sight and sound
To play upward and downward melodic patterns

Materials
Recordings: Listening—"The Lark Song" from *Scenes of Youth* by Peter Ilyich Tchaikovsky
"The Ducklings"
"Peter Cottontail"
"See-saw, Margery Daw"
Chart 49
Pitched classroom instruments
Arrow stick-ons
Copying Masters 7-14, 7-15, 7-16 (optional)

1 SETTING THE STAGE

Review "The Lark Song." Have the children listen to the music, raising one hand when they hear very high pitches towards the end of the music, and again when they hear the downward melodic pattern at the very end of the music.

2 TEACHING THE LESSON

1. Practice identifying upward and downward melodic patterns. Have the children:
• Listen as you or a child plays an upward or downward melodic pattern on E G A and point upward or downward as appropriate to identify the melodic direction. (After doing this a few times, hide the instrument and have the children identify the melodic direction aurally rather than visually.)
• Repeat this activity to give each child a chance to play a pattern.

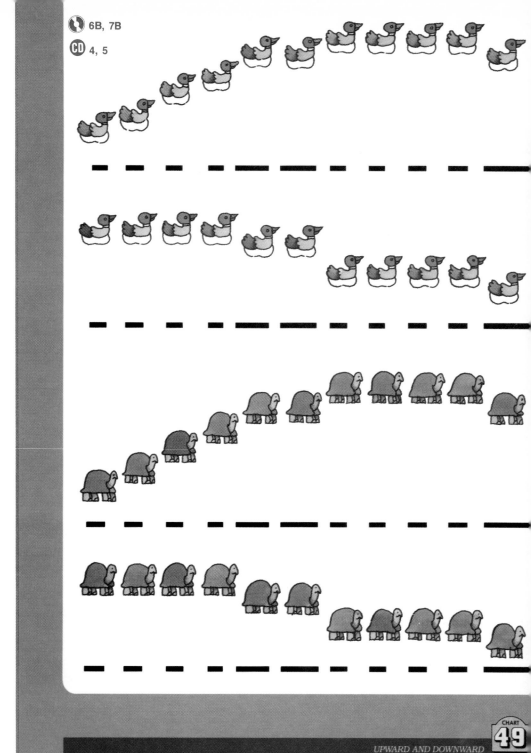

UPWARD AND DOWNWARD

CHART 49

E X T E N S I O N

COOPERATIVE LEARNING

Have the children practice playing and identifying upward and downward patterns in small randomly assigned groups. One child plays a pattern, and the remaining group members decide whether the pattern was upward or downward. The player should carefully check the group answer for accuracy. Each child plays two or three patterns and then appoints another player from within the group. The groups should only ask for your help if no group member has the answer to their problem. Encourage the skills of taking turns, coming to consensus agreement, explaining to others, and solving problems within the group.

KEYBOARD

Have the children practice playing and identifying upward and downward patterns on the keyboard. Beginning on any pitch, have a child play four to eight keys stepwise, moving upward. Then have another child play a pattern that moves downward. The class should decide the direction in which each pattern moved. After this activity, several children could work together at the keyboard to create an upward/downward piece.

EXTRA HELP

To prepare the children for encountering repeated tones in "The Ducklings," page 187, extend the upward and downward activity so that it includes experiences with repeated tones—tones that do not go upward or downward.

Key: C and C minor   Starting Pitch: C   Scale Tones: C: *do re mi fa so la*
C minor: *la₁ ti₁ do re mi fa*

The Ducklings

Piano Accompaniment on page PA 80   *Adapted*

See the lit - tle   duck - lings   Swim-ming here and   there.

Heads are in the   wa - ter,   Tails are in the   air.

Slower

There's a lit - tle   tur - tle,   Swim-ming down be - low—

D.C. al Fine

Tries to catch the   duck - lings,   But he is too   slow.

LESSON 8

2. Introduce "The Ducklings" to practice identifying melodic direction. Have the children:

• Listen for upward and downward melodic patterns in the song.

• Listen again, showing what they hear by moving one hand upward or downward with the melody. (Be sure to keep your hand still to encourage them to use their listening skills. This way, you can also see who understands the concept.)

• Look at Chart 49 to check their hand movements.

• Listen to the song again, watching as you point to one picture for each syllable. (You may wish to use the stick-on arrows to reinforce the concept of upward and downward at this time.)
(You may wish to use Copying Master 7-14 at this time.)

• Form two groups, ducklings and turtles. Then dramatize the song, each group moving at the appropriate time. (The children may enjoy making their own duck or turtle puppets out of construction paper and using the puppets to dramatize "The Ducklings.")
(You may wish to use Copying Master 7-15 at this time.)

CURRICULUM CONNECTION: SCIENCE

Animal Families—Ducks and turtles are both animals with backbones (vertebrates). Baby ducks and baby turtles both hatch from hard-shelled eggs. Both ducks and turtles can swim in the water, as fish do, but they need to breathe air, as we do, in order to live. But ducks are classed as birds and turtles are classed as reptiles, two different kinds of animals.

C O R E
LESSON 8

3. Introduce "Peter Cottontail" for more practice identifying melodic direction. Have the children:
• Listen to the song, singing along as they are able.
• Listen to the words *Easter bonnet too* and identify the melodic direction as downward.
• Sing the song, moving their hands to show the downward melodic pattern. (You may wish to use Copying Master 7-16 at this time.)

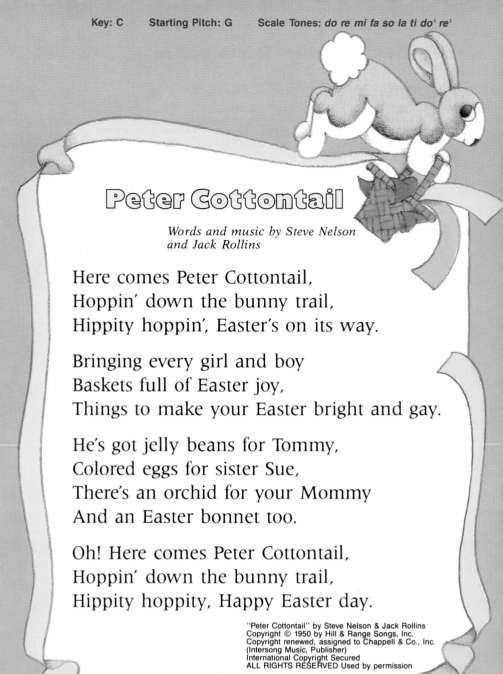

Peter Cottontail

Words and music by Steve Nelson and Jack Rollins

Here comes Peter Cottontail,
Hoppin' down the bunny trail,
Hippity hoppin', Easter's on its way.

Bringing every girl and boy
Baskets full of Easter joy,
Things to make your Easter bright and gay.

He's got jelly beans for Tommy,
Colored eggs for sister Sue,
There's an orchid for your Mommy
And an Easter bonnet too.

Oh! Here comes Peter Cottontail,
Hoppin' down the bunny trail,
Hippity hoppity, Happy Easter day.

E X T E N S I O N

SPECIAL LEARNERS

Visual learners will benefit from seeing a picture of the melody for *Easter bonnet too.* Simple line drawings of hats could be mounted on the chalkboard or a flannel board to show the downward direction of this melody. Encourage the children to point to the hats as they sing.

Key: C   Starting Pitch: G   Scale Tones: *mi so la*

See-saw, Margery Daw

Piano Accompaniment on page PA 81   *Traditional*

Swaying

See - saw,   Mar - ger - y Daw,

Jack   shall have a new mas - ter,

He   shall have but a pen - ny a day,

be - cause he can't work an - y fast - er.

Reinforcing the Lesson

Introduce "See-saw, Margery Daw." Have the children echo-sing the song with you. Then have them pat the beat as they sing the whole song. Have them identify the melody of *new master* and *-y faster* as going downward. Have a few children play this downward pattern using A G E on a pitched instrument as the rest of the class sings the song.

3 APPRAISAL

The children should be able to:
1. Identify upward and downward melodic patterns by sight and sound.
2. Play upward and downward melodic patterns.

SONGBOOK

"The Bus," page 266 (downward)
"Ah! Les Jolis Papillons," page 263 (upward and downward)
"Little Red Caboose," page 278 (upward)

Key: F   Starting Pitch: A   Scale Tones: *do di re ri mi fa*

LESSON 9

Focus: Beat and Strong Beat

Objectives
To practice keeping a steady beat
To distinguish between beat and strong beat
To identify strong beats visually in sets of two

Materials
Recordings: "Apples and Bananas"
"Little Ducky Duddle"
"The Ducklings"
Charts 50 and 51
Duck stick-ons
Copying Masters 7-17, 7-18, 7-19 (optional)

1 SETTING THE STAGE

Have the children pat a steady beat with you, being careful to start, stop, and keep the same tempo as you do. After starting a few times, keep the beat going. Begin chanting *one, two, one, two,* and so on, and have the children join in. Have them think of something to do other than patting when they say *two,* such as tapping their shoulders. Practice this new pattern, alternating patting and tapping shoulders as they chant, until they feel comfortable with it.

Apples and Bananas

Piano Accompaniment on page PA 82   *Traditional*

2. I like to āt, āt, āt, āt.
   I like to āt āpples and bānānās . . .

3. I like to ēt . . . ēpplēs and bēnēnēs . . .

4. I like to īt . . . īpples and bīnīnīs . . .

5. I like to ōt . . . ōpples and bōnōnōs . . .

6. I like to ūt . . . ūpples and būnūnūs . . .

 STRONG BEAT

LESSON 9

1. Introduce "Apples and Bananas." Have the children:
• Echo the first verse of the song, alternating patting and tapping shoulders on the beat.
• Listen as you sing the song and substitute long *a* as follows:
I like to āt, āt, āt, āt.
I like to āt, āpples and bānānās.
• Sing the song with the new vowel sounds while continuing to pat and tap the beat.
• Repeat the song, changing the substituted long *a* vowel sounds to long *e, i, o,* or *u* in each verse. (You may wish to use Copying Master 7-17 at this time.)

2. Introduce strong beat. Have the children:
• Look at Chart 50.
• Do the pat-tap body percussion.
• Tell how Chart 50 and the body percussion are related. (Both patterns are in sets of two, and can be counted *one, two, one, two.*)
• Tell how the first beat in each two-beat set is different from the second (it is stronger).

LESSON 9

3. Introduce "Little Ducky Duddle" and create a new two-beat pattern. Have the children:

• Experiment with different two-beat body percussion patterns of their own until they each find one they like.

• Echo each new pattern, one at a time.

• Choose one new pattern they all like and can do comfortably.

• Do this pattern with you as they echo "Little Ducky Duddle" in four-beat segments.

• Sing the song several times as small groups take turns moving like ducks.

Little Ducky Duddle

Piano Accompaniment on page PA 83   *Traditional*

Lit-tle Duck-y Dud-dle went wad-ing in a pud-dle,

went wad-ing in a pud-dle quite small. "Quack, quack!"

Said he, "It does-n't mat-ter how much I spash and splat-ter,

I'm on - ly a duck-y af-ter all. Quack, quack!"

EXTENSION

BEAT AND SILENT BEAT

CHART **51**

LESSON 9

4. Compare beat and strong beat in "Little Ducky Duddle." Have the children:
• Look at Chart 51 as they sing "Little Ducky Duddle." Pat the beat as you point to the ducks on the chart.
• Sing the song again, patting the beat. (You may wish to use Copying Master 7-18 at this time.)
• Determine that they are patting the steady beat, and decide how they could show only the strong beat (pat on the first and third ducks in each line). (You may wish to use the duck stick-ons at this time. Create a strong-and-weak-beat pattern using ducks with open bills on the first and third beats and ducks with closed bills on the second and fourth beats. The children can either pat or quack on the strong beats.)
• Sing the song twice, patting all the beats the first time, and only patting the strong beats the second time.

Reinforcing the Lesson
Have the children think of another duck song ("The Ducklings"). Sing the song, patting either the beat or the strong beat as you point to Chart 51. Have a few children individually pat beat or strong beat as the class sings. Then have the class decide whether that child patted the beat or the strong beat.

3 APPRAISAL
The children should be able to:
1. Pat the steady beat with reasonable accuracy.
2. Distinguish between beat and strong beat by doing a pat-tap movement to show strong beat or patting only on the strong beat.
3. Pat the strong beat and tap or rest on the weak beat when shown patterns in sets of two.

MORE MUSIC TEACHING IDEAS

1. Have the children add an unpitched instrument accompaniment to "Little Ducky Duddle" that reinforces beat and strong beat. Have a few children softly play wood blocks or hand drums on the beat. Then add a guiro or other scraping sound on the strong beat and a triangle or cowbell on each *quack*. Have the class sing the song with this accompaniment.
2. Have the children use the duck stick-ons, combining ducks with open and closed bills, to create a four-beat rhythm pattern. Have them quack or pat for each duck with an open bill, and be quiet for each duck with a closed bill. Have them quack or play the pattern as an ostinato with "Little Ducky Duddle." (You may wish to use Copying Master 7-19 at this time.)

SONGBOOK

"My Head and My Shoulders," page 281 (strong beat)
"Old Dan Tucker," page 282 (strong beat)
"Uncle Jessie," page 289 (strong beat)

LESSON 10

Focus: Two Sounds to a Beat

Objectives
To practice steady beat
To follow pictures showing one sound to a beat and two equal sounds to a beat

Materials
Recordings: "See-saw, Margery Daw"
"Little Ducky Duddle"
"The Ducklings"
"Cobbler, Cobbler, Mend My Shoe" (optional)
"Clickety Clack"
Charts 49 and 51
Unpitched classroom instruments
Duck stick-ons
Copying Masters 7-20, 7-21 (optional)

1 SETTING THE STAGE

Review "See-saw, Margery Daw" on page 189. Have the children pat a steady beat as you sing the song. Then have them pat and sing along with you. Have them find other ways to keep the beat that remind them of a see-saw. Watch as several children demonstrate their ideas. Then have everyone try their ideas together.

2 TEACHING THE LESSON

1. Review "Little Ducky Duddle" on page 192 for more practice with steady beat.
Have the children:
• Sing the song with you, patting the steady beat as they follow Chart 51.
• Choose an instrument on which to play the steady beat, such as a wood block.
• Sing the song as a few children play the steady beat on the instruments.

2. Review "The Ducklings" on page 187 to identify two equal sounds to a beat. Have the children:
• Follow Chart 49 as they sing the song.

duck   **swimming**

E X T E N S I O N

MORE MUSIC TEACHING IDEAS

Have the children learn "Cobbler, Cobbler, Mend My Shoe" and review "Lemonade" on page 173 for more practice with songs having one and two sounds to a beat. (You may wish to use Copying Master 7-20 at this time.)

Cobbler, Cobbler, Mend My Shoe

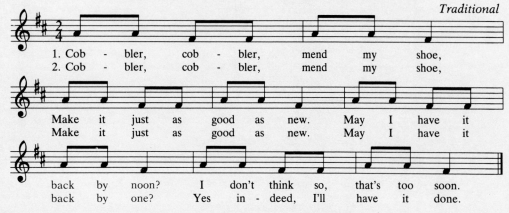

Traditional

1. Cob - bler, cob - bler, mend my shoe,
2. Cob - bler, cob - bler, mend my shoe,

Make it just as good as new. May I have it
Make it just as good as new. May I have it

back by noon? I don't think so, that's too soon.
back by one? Yes in - deed, I'll have it done.

Key: D   Starting Pitch: A   Scale Tones: *mi so*

• Say the word *duck* when you hold up one finger, and *swimming* when you hold up two fingers together.
• Divide into two groups. As they pat the beat, group 1 says *duck* and group 2 says *swimming* once on every beat.
• Identify *duck* as one sound to a beat and *swimming* as two sounds to a beat.

3. Identify one sound to a beat and two equal sounds to a beat with pictures. Have the children:
• Think of pictures that could show the difference between one sound to a beat and two equal sounds to a beat, for example, a whole apple and an apple in halves.
• Look at the duck and two-ducks stick-ons and decide they can be used to show one sound and two equal sounds to a beat.
• Create several four-beat patterns using combinations of two ducks and one duck. (These patterns can be constructed on the inside front cover of the Big Book.) Read the patterns, saying *duck* for the one-duck square and *swimming* for the two-duck square. (You may wish to use Copying Master 7-21 at this time.)

Reinforcing the Lesson

Review "Clickety Clack" on page 184. Have the children think of train sounds that have one sound to a beat, such as *toot*, and two sounds to a beat, such as *chug-a*. Make up a four-beat pattern using these two sounds, for example, *chug-a chug-a toot toot*.

3 APPRAISAL

The children should be able to:
1. Keep the steady beat with different songs.
2. Follow pictures of one sound to a beat and two equal sounds to a beat and say word patterns that match the pictures.

MORE MUSIC TEACHING IDEAS

1. Have the children play their rhythm patterns on unpitched instruments. Use them as ostinatos with different songs.
2. Have the children say their patterns as they listen to "Clickety Clack." Review the words, and have half the class say the rhythm pattern as the other half sings the song. Then switch parts. (You may wish to use the dot stick-ons to show this new pattern.)
3. Have the children form two groups. Group 1 sings "The Ducklings" while Group 2 says one of the four-beat rhythm patterns as an ostinato.

4. Have the children use the shoe stick-ons to construct four-beat rhythm patterns on the inside front cover of the Big Book. Read the patterns, saying *shoe* for the one-shoe square and *cobbler* for the two-shoe square.

SONGBOOK

"Los Pollitos," page 279 (one and two sounds to a beat)
"Clap Your Hands," page 267 (one and two sounds to a beat)

REVIEW AND EVALUATION

REVIEW

Objectives

To review songs, skills, and concepts learned in Unit 7

To measure the children's ability to:

1. Identify some solo orchestral instruments (violin, flute, and piccolo)
2. Identify upward and downward direction of the melody
3. Create different responses to question-and-answer patterns

Materials

Recordings: Listening—"Spring," from *The Four Seasons* by Antonio Vivaldi

Listening—"The Lark Song" from *Scenes of Youth* by Peter Ilyich Tchaikovsky

Listening—"Sounds of the Flute, Piccolo, and Violin"

"Rig-a-Jig-Jig"

"The Ducklings"

"Butterfly"

"The Secret Song"

Unit 7 Evaluation (Instrument Sounds)

Charts 44, 48, and 49

Pitched and unpitched classroom instruments

Copying Master 7-2 (optional)

Evaluation Unit 7 Copying Master

TEACHING THE LESSON

Review the songs and concepts in Unit 7 by dramatizing a story. Have the children:

• Listen as you tell the story, singing and performing the activities at the appropriate places. (As the children sing and move, observe and evaluate individuals and the class as a whole as to how their responses indicate their level of understanding.)

A Spring Walk

It's a beautiful day for a walk outside. Let's go together. Listen to the music and walk every time you hear the first section or a section that sounds the same as the first section. Stand still when you hear a different section.

• Listen to "Spring," walking every time they hear the A section, and standing still during the other sections.

Listen! Can you hear the lark singing? Can you see it? How does it move?

• Listen to "The Lark Song," moving to show the melodic contour.

What instruments played "The Lark Song"?

• Look at Chart 44 on page 168 and say the name of each instrument as you randomly point to each picture several times.

REVIEW AND EVALUATION

• Listen to "Sounds of the Flute, Piccolo, and Violin" and point to the appropriate instrument on the chart. (You may wish to use Copying Master 7-2 at this time.)

The sun feels so good, and the air is so warm, I'm going to continue to walk. I'll be looking for somebody to walk and skip with me.
• Listen to "Rig-a-Jig-Jig" as you walk during the A section. Then choose one child to skip with you during the B section. During the next A section you both walk alone, and then both choose a partner for the B section. Continue until everyone is walking and skipping. (Watch for children who move appropriately.)

Look at the pretty little pond. Can you see the little ducklings swimming everywhere? And the turtles down there?
• Look at Chart 49 on page 186 and review the upward and downward melodic direction of "The Ducklings."
• Sing "The Ducklings," moving one hand in the air to show the melodic direction.

Look at the two butterflies over there in the flowers. Watch how one moves from flower to flower, and the other follows.
• Look at Chart 48 on page 182. Identify the first and third lines as the same and the second and fourth lines as different.
• Form two groups and listen to "Butterfly." Group 1 moves during lines 1 and 3, and group 2 moves during lines 2 and 4.

Let's play our own questions and answers. I'll play a question, and you play an answer that is different from my question. Then I'll play the same question again, and you give me another answer.
• Listen to the four-beat question, then play a different answer. (Do this as an individual activity. Give each child two opportunities to play answers, using pitched or unpitched instruments.)

If you listen carefully to this poem you can hear all sorts of questions and answers outside that have their own special sounds.
• Listen to "The Secret Song," playing instruments that reflect the character of each question and answer in the poem.

Thank you for coming outside with me on this beautiful spring day.

EVALUATION
Evaluation Unit 7 Copying Master can be found in the *Teacher's Resource Book* with full directions for providing an evaluation of the child's progress.

UNIT 8 • OVERVIEW

ELEMENTS OF MUSIC	UNIT 8 OBJECTIVES	Lesson 1 CORE Focus: Tone Color	Lesson 2 CORE Focus: Beat and Strong Beat	Lesson 3 Focus: Tempo	Lesson 4 Focus: Strong Beat
Dynamics	Recognize and use loud/soft, louder/softer		Hear louder/softer beats		Play a soft pattern
Tone Color	**Identify trumpet, timpani, flute, and violin** Use various vocal and instrumental tone qualities Practice the four voices Listen to children, men	Create body-percussion sounds Practice identifying trumpet, flute, and violin Identify the timpani Identify the four voices and use two of them Hear children	Create body-percussion patterns that show strong beat Do songs with speaking and singing parts Hear children	Hear flute, violin, trumpet, and timpani	Use different instrumental tone colors to show beat and strong beat Hear flute and trumpet Use speaking and singing voices Hear children's and men's voices
Tempo	Hear, use different tempos	Hear different tempos		Identify slow, medium, and fast tempos	Bounce balls at different tempos
Duration/ Rhythm	Learn songs in $\frac{2}{2}$ $\frac{2}{2}$. and $\frac{4}{4}$ Hear song in $\frac{3}{8}$ Practice patting rhythm or beat of songs, poems **Show identification of strong beat in music with two beats per measure** **Recognize two equal sounds to a beat**	Sing songs in $\frac{2}{8}$	Sing songs in $\frac{2}{8}$ Show identification of strong beat visually and through movement and ball bouncing Hear songs with two equal sounds to a beat	Sing songs in $\frac{2}{8}$ Bounce balls to show strong beat and practice keeping a steady beat	Sing songs, do chants in $\frac{2}{8}$ Identify and play strong beat
Pitch	Sing song with three pitches: *mi so la* (3 5 6) Practice identifying upward/downward		Sing songs with three pitches: *mi so la* (3 5 6)	Sing song with three pitches: *mi so la* (3 5 6)	
Texture	Continue identifying melody alone or with accompaniment Sing songs with rhythm or speech ostinatos	Identify appropriate accompaniments for a song Use rhythmic ostinatos Create and sing an ostinato	Use rhythmic ostinato patterns Play bordun on strong beat		Play accompaniments with songs
Form	Discover same/different phrases and sections Label short ABA forms		Identify different sections of a song	Identify different verses of a song by tempo	Identify sections by tone color
Style	Identify several elements that affect musical style Sing African song Hear Japanese song Hear music in Asian style	Hear tone colors of instruments and found sounds that affect style	Experience strong beat as an element of music that affects style		Identify beat and strong beat in Japanese song

PURPOSE Unit 8: Sounds All Around

This unit is designed to be taught during the period from late spring through the end of the school year. Through poems, listening selections, and songs that emphasize games and movement, the children will experience identifying instrumental tone color, beat and strong beat, and recognizing two equal sounds to a beat. The children will also review the musical elements they have learned throughout the year and use this information to compare music from different cultures.

SUGGESTED TIME FRAME

April	May	June

FOCUS

Core Lessons 1, 2, 5, 6, 9
• Tone Color
• Beat and Strong Beat
• Rhythm
• Pitch
• Tempo and Tone Color

Lessons 3, 4, 7, 8, 10
• Tempo
• Strong Beat
• Pitch
• Style
• Musical Elements

Lesson 5 CORE Focus: Rhythm	Lesson 6 CORE Focus: Pitch	Lesson 7 Focus: Pitch	Lesson 8 Focus: Style	Lesson 9 CORE Focus: Tempo and Tone Color	Lesson 10 Focus: Musical Elements
			Hear loud and soft	Hear loud and soft	Hear loud and soft
Use different tone colors of classroom instruments to show different rhythms	Use pitched classroom instruments	Use speaking and singing voices	Hear orchestral instruments Hear men's and children's voices	Hear piano, flute, trumpet, violin, and timpani Use singing voices	Hear orchestral instruments and piano Use singing and speaking voices
		Hear, use different tempos	Hear fast and slow music	Practice identifying slow, medium, and fast	Show tempo contrast in movement
Sing songs in $\frac{2}{4}$ Pat the beat and tap the rhythm of songs Identify two equal sounds to a beat Arrange objects for rhythmic dictation using ♩ and ♫	Sing songs in $\frac{2}{4}$ Hear a song with one and two equal sounds on a beat	Sing song in $\frac{2}{4}$ and song in $\frac{4}{4}$ Hear song in $\frac{3}{4}$	Sing song in $\frac{4}{4}$	Sing song in $\frac{4}{4}$	Sing songs in $\frac{4}{4}$ $\frac{2}{4}$ and $\frac{3}{4}$ Practice steady beat Hear song in $\frac{3}{4}$ Say speech ostinato with a song
Sing song with three pitches (*mi so la*) Play improvised melodies on *mi so la* (3 5 6)	Practice identifying and playing upward and downward	Hear *mi so la* in a song Practice identifying upward/downward Create melodies using C D E G A	Hear upward/downward	Hear upward/downward Play downward patterns	Practice identifying upward and downward Play upward/downward patterns and show direction graphically
	Play upward/downward accompaniment with a song	Create upward melody to accompany a chant			Sing melody alone and melody with accompaniment Say a speech ostinato with a song
Do a song-rhythms-song form and identify it as ABA	Do song-instrument-song form and identify it as ABA		Identify solo-group form Hear ABA form	Identify sections by tempo change Hear and see representation of ABA form	
Experience rhythm as an element that affects musical style		Sing African song	Identify elements of music in Asian style Sing African song Hear a 19th-century orchestral piece	Hear 20th-century piano piece	Identify several musical elements that affect style

BULLETIN BOARD

Put a large circle on the bulletin board with the words *Sounds All Around* in the center of the circle. Have the children draw or cut out pictures of as many sound sources as they can identify, including environmental sounds, body percussion sounds, instruments, animal sounds, and so on. Attach these pictures around the circle according to categories.

LESSON 1

Focus: Tone Color

Objectives
To identify the trumpet, flute, violin, and timpani by sight and sound
To identify vocal, body-percussion, and classroom-instrument sounds that can be used as accompaniments

Materials
Recordings: Recorded Lesson—"What Instrument Do You Hear?"
"Ourchestra"
"Draw a Bucket of Water"
"Bow, Wow, Wow!"
Charts 38 and 52
Copying Masters 6-1, 8-1, 8-2 (optional)

1 SETTING THE STAGE

Have the children listen as you describe the physical characteristics of a trumpet. Then have them each tell a partner what instrument they think you described. Tell them that the children who identified the trumpet were correct. Repeat, describing a flute and a violin.

2 TEACHING THE LESSON

1. Review identifying the flute, violin, and trumpet, and identify the timpani. Have the children:
• Look at Chart 52 and identify the flute, trumpet, and violin as you point to them. (Point to the timpani to see if anyone knows the name of those instruments.)
• Learn the name *timpani*. (You may wish to use Copying Master 8-1 at this time.)
• Listen to the sound of each instrument. Then listen to the sounds in random order, identifying which one they hear by pointing to the correct picture on Chart 52. (You may wish to use Copying Master 8-2 at this time.)

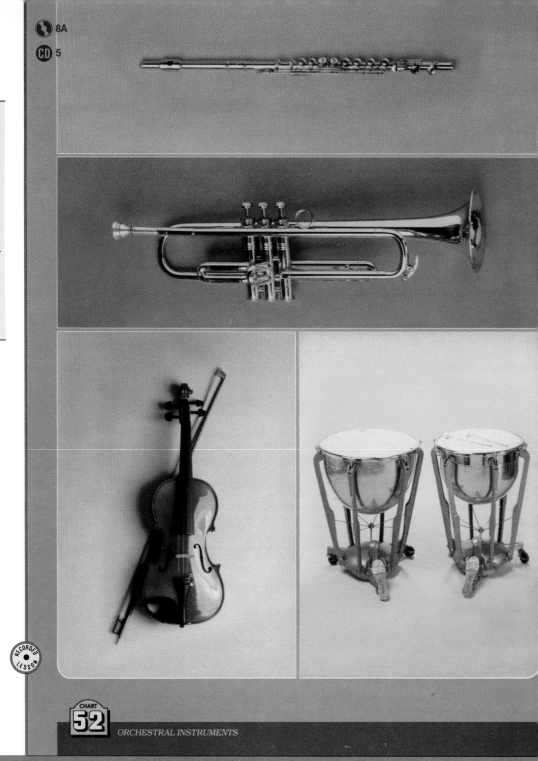

CHART **52** ORCHESTRAL INSTRUMENTS

E X T E N S I O N

OURCHESTRA

So you haven't got a drum, just beat your belly.
So I haven't got a horn—I'll play my nose.
So we haven't any cymbals—
We'll just slap our hands together.
And though there may be orchestras
That sound a little better
With their fancy shiny instruments
That cost an awful lot—
Hey, we're making music twice as good
By playing what we've got!

—*Shel Silverstein*

2. Introduce "Ourchestra" to review sounds the children can make without instruments. Have the children:
• Listen to "Ourchestra" and identify the instruments mentioned in the poem (drum, horn, cymbals).
• Discuss the meaning of the poem. (When instruments are not available, or you don't know how to play them, you can still make music using the sounds around you.)
• Think of different ways to make instrument-like sounds using body percussion. Then have each child take a turn making her or his own sound for four beats, with the class echoing each four beats.

MORE MUSIC TEACHING IDEAS

Help the children prepare for a summer of music-making by making them aware of the sound sources around them. Have them put together a book called *Sounds All Around* that includes pictures of things they can use to make sounds, such as hands tapping or patting, feet stamping, spoons, pots and pans, and so on.

MAKING INSTRUMENTS

Have the children make instruments out of found objects. Encourage the children to experiment and use their imaginations. The following are some suggestions to get started. Make a drum out of a can with a plastic lid. (Remove the bottom of the can to make the sound more resonant.) Make shakers by putting rice, macaroni, or beans in a covered container. Make rhythm sticks out of lengths of dowel, or collect sticks from outside. Metal sounds can be made by hitting a small saucepan lid with a striker, or hitting a hanging metal object such as a large bolt with another metal object. Use two pot lids for cymbals. Experiment with strikers until you find some that make pleasing sounds.

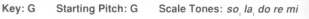

CORE
LESSON 1

3. Introduce "Draw a Bucket of Water" and review the four ways to use the voice. Have the children:
• Look at Chart 38 on page 143 and remember the four ways to use the voice (speaking, singing, whispering, and calling). (You may wish to use Copying Master 6-1 at this time.)
• Listen to "Draw a Bucket of Water" and determine the two ways the voice is used in the song (singing and speaking).
• Echo-sing the song one phrase at a time.
• Listen to the song again, singing as much as they are able.

Draw a Bucket of Water

African American Play Party Game

Draw   a   buck - et   of   wa   -   ter

for   my   on - ly   daugh   -   ter.

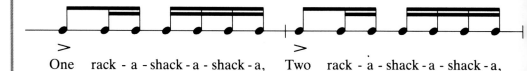

One   rack - a - shack - a - shack - a,   Two   rack - a - shack - a - shack - a,

Three   rack - a - shack - a - shack - a,   Four   rack - a - shack - a - shack - a.

Let   this   old   { la - dy / man____ }   un - der ___

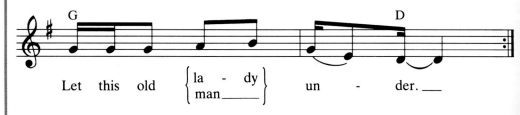

Let   this   old   { la - dy / man____ }   un - der. ___

EXTENSION

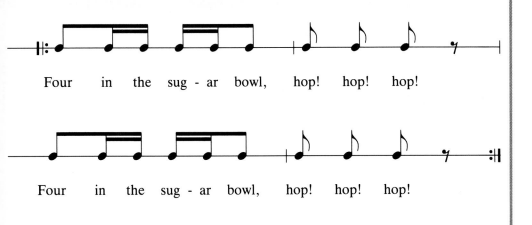

Four in the sug-ar bowl, hop! hop! hop!

Four in the sug-ar bowl, hop! hop! hop!

Key: D   Starting Pitch: D   Scale Tones: *do re mi so la*

Bow, Wow, Wow!

Traditional

"Bow, wow, wow!"   "Whose dog art thou?"

"Lit-tle Tom-my Tuck-er's dog. Bow, wow, wow!"

Reinforcing the Lesson

Introduce "Bow, Wow, Wow!" Have the children listen to the song and discuss the kinds of tone colors they might use as accompaniments with this song. (Any of the tone colors discussed in this lesson can work as an accompaniment.) Play an instrumental accompaniment similar to the one on the recording. Make up a spoken ostinato, for example,

Bow   wow   bow wow wow

Try playing this pattern using body-percussion sounds.

3 APPRAISAL

The children should be able to:
1. Identify the trumpet, flute, violin, and timpani by sight and sound.
2. Identify several tone colors that can be used as accompaniments with a song.

MORE MUSIC TEACHING IDEAS

Have the children play the following accompaniment with "Bow, Wow, Wow!" using Orff instruments or other pitched classroom instruments.
Bass Xylophone:

Play octave Ds on a glockenspiel with the rests at the ends of the first, second, and fourth lines.

SONGBOOK

"Peanut Butter," page 284 (four voices)
"The Bus," page 266 (add different body-percussion sounds, "found" sounds, or classroom-instrument sounds on the repeated words in each verse)

CORE
LESSON 2

Focus: Beat and Strong Beat

Objective
To practice identifying, moving to, and playing beat and strong beat

Materials
Recordings: "Bow, Wow, Wow!"
"Draw a Bucket of Water"
"Bounce High, Bounce Low"
"One, Two, Three, Four, Five"
Charts 50 and 53
Drums, rhythm sticks
Rubber ball

1 SETTING THE STAGE

Have the children listen as you play a steady beat on a drum, patting the beat with you. Then have them walk the steady beat, making their own paths around the room. Have the children walk again, this time only stepping on every other beat. Determine that they are stepping on the strong beat. Count *one*, two, *one*, two, and have partners create patterns that show strong beat, for example, pat knees on *one*, tap partner's hands on *two*. (Play *one* on the drumhead and *two* on the rim to help the children stay together.)

2 TEACHING THE LESSON

1. Review "Bow, Wow, Wow!" on page 201 for practice playing beat and strong beat. Have the children:
• Look at Chart 50 on page 191 to review strong beat.
• Take turns playing rhythm sticks on the steady beat and drums on the strong beat.
• Start a pat-tap pattern, and sing "Bow, Wow, Wow!"

EXTENSION

SPECIAL LEARNERS

Some children may have difficulty in identifying and stepping on only the strong beat during the Setting the Stage activity. To assist these children, have the class sit in place and listen as you play a clear loud-soft pattern on a drum. Have them say *loud-soft* as you play. Then have them say *loud-soft* again, patting on *loud* each time. Finally, have them say *one-two* as you play, patting on *one*. Have the children count with you again, making a large motion with both hands in a different direction on *one* each time (reaching up high, reaching to one side, reaching forward, and so on). This practice will help them be better able to step only on the strong beat.

8A
CD 5

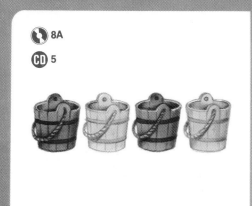

1 2 3 4

STRONG BEAT
CHART 53

LESSON 2

• Sing the song doing the patterns they created with their partners. Choose one pattern and do it all together.

• Sing the song with some doing the pattern and some playing the instruments.

2. Review "Draw a Bucket of Water" on page 200 for more practice identifying strong beat. Have the children:

• Look at Chart 53 and echo-sing the first line of the song four beats at a time, as you point to the pictures of the buckets.

• Identify the reason the color on some of the pictures in the top row is darker (they represent the strong beats).

• Echo the rest of the song, following the pictures on the chart.

• Form groups of four and learn the game. (You may wish to demonstrate first with one group of four.) Each group forms a square, facing in.

Part 1 (*draw a bucket of water*)—Partners across the square hold hands and gently push and pull back and forth with a sawing movement.

Part 2 (*one rack-a-shack-a-shack-a*)—Partners do the same movement as in part 1 on each number, and hold their position during *rack-a-shack-a-shack-a*.

Part 3 (*let this old lady under*)—One at a time, each set of partners encircles one other person in the group with their arms. Do this four times until the whole group is within the square.

Part 4 (*four in the sugarbowl*)—Each group jumps together to the left on each *hop*.

SPECIAL LEARNERS

For children who need some extra preparation for the "Draw a Bucket of Water" game, demonstrate the pulling motion with just two children at first. Have them keep one foot in front of the other with both feet flat on the floor, to brace themselves as they pull back and forth. Have another couple join them and demonstrate the entire game. Then have each of these two couples join with a new couple to form two sets for the next repetition. Continue in this way until the entire class is involved. If holding hands is a problem, provide colorful pieces of material or leather, about one foot in length, to take the place of joined hands.

CORE
LESSON 2

3. Introduce "Bounce High, Bounce Low" for more practice with strong beat. Have the children:
• Echo-sing "Bounce High, Bounce Low," doing a pat-tap pattern.
• Echo again, doing the pats and thinking the taps.
• Recognize that they were patting the strong beat.
• Pretend to bounce a ball with both hands on the strong beats.
• Form a circle and bounce a ball around the circle on the strong beat, bouncing on *one* as they say *"one,* two, *one,* two." Then bounce the ball on the strong beat as they sing "Bounce High, Bounce Low."

Bounce High, Bounce Low

Traditional

Bounce high,   Bounce low,   Bounce the ball to   Shi - loh!

EXTENSION

MORE MUSIC TEACHING IDEAS

Have the children play an accompaniment with "Bounce High, Bounce Low." Using any pitched instrument, play D and A together on the strong beat. Have several children play this accompaniment as the rest of the class bounces a ball on the strong beat.

Key: C   Starting Pitch: G   Scale Tones: *mi so la*

One, Two, Three, Four, Five

Traditional

Ⓐ

One, two, three, four, five. Once I caught a fish a - live.

Six, sev - en, eight, nine, ten. Then I let him go a - gain.

Ⓑ *(spoken)*
Solo I (question)   Solo II (answer)

Why did you let it go? Be - cause it bit my fin - ger so!
Which fin - ger did it bite? The lit - tle fin - ger on my right!

Reinforcing the Lesson

Introduce "One, Two, Three, Four, Five." Have the children do a pat-tap pattern with you as they echo-sing the song two measures at a time. Identify the whole pattern as keeping the beat, and the pats only as the strong beats.

3 APPRAISAL

The children should be able to identify beat and strong beat visually, with movement, and by playing instruments.

SONGBOOK

"My Head and My Shoulders," page 281 (beat and strong beat)
"Old Dan Tucker," page 282 (beat and strong beat)
"Uncle Jessie," page 289 (beat and strong beat)
"Step in Time," page 288 (beat and strong beat)

LESSON 3

Focus: Tempo

Objectives
To review identifying slow, medium, and fast tempos
To hear the sound of the trumpet, flute, violin, and timpani

Materials
Recordings: "Walk to School"
"Bounce High, Bounce Low"
Recorded Lesson—"Slow, Medium, and Fast"
"I'll Race You Down the Mountain"
Chart 3
X and O stick-ons
Star stick-on
Rubber balls

1 SETTING THE STAGE

Have the children review "Walk to School" on page 4. Sing the song, patting the beat. Then look at Chart 3 and review walking slow, medium, and fast. Have a child put an X on the picture showing slow, a star on the picture showing medium, and an O on the picture showing fast. Choose partners and sing and walk the beat three times, first at a slow tempo, then at a medium tempo, and finally at a fast tempo.

2 TEACHING THE LESSON

1. Review "Bounce High, Bounce Low" on page 204 to practice keeping a steady beat at different tempos. Have the children:
• Pat the steady beat of a bouncing ball. (You or one child can bounce the ball.)
• Identify the tempo of the bouncing ball as slow, medium, or fast.

1A, 8A
CD 1, 5

E X T E N S I O N

Key: G   Starting Pitch: D   Scale Tones: *so, la, ti, do re mi*

I'll Race You Down the Mountain

Piano Accompaniment on page PA 84

Words and music by
Woody Guthrie and Marjorie Mazia

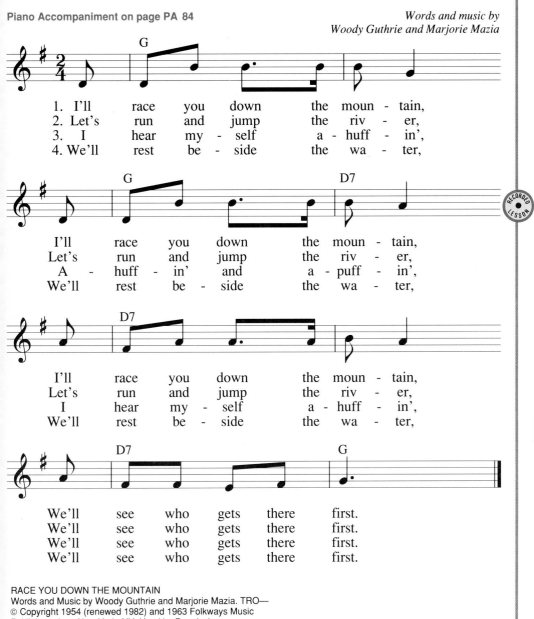

1. I'll   race   you   down   the   moun - tain,
2. Let's   run   and   jump   the   riv - er,
3. I   hear   my - self   a - huff - in',
4. We'll   rest   be - side   the   wa - ter,

I'll   race   you   down   the   moun - tain,
Let's   run   and   jump   the   riv - er,
A - huff - in'   and   a - puff - in',
We'll   rest   be - side   the   wa - ter,

I'll   race   you   down   the   moun - tain,
Let's   run   and   jump   the   riv - er,
I   hear   my - self   a - huff - in',
We'll   rest   be - side   the   wa - ter,

We'll   see   who   gets   there   first.
We'll   see   who   gets   there   first.
We'll   see   who   gets   there   first.
We'll   see   who   gets   there   first.

LESSON 3

• Sing "Bounce High, Bounce Low" at the tempo of the bouncing ball.
• Repeat the activity a few times, giving other children a chance to choose different tempos at which to bounce the ball. (You may wish to explain to the children that when bouncing a ball, the closer to the ground a ball is bounced the faster it will bounce.)
2. Review the sounds of the flute, violin, trumpet, and timpani. Have the children:
• Listen to music played by different instruments at different tempos, and move to show the beat at each tempo.

Reinforcing the Lesson

Introduce "I'll Race You Down the Mountain." Have the children listen to the song and identify the activities in each verse (racing, running and jumping, huffin' and puffin', resting). Identify the tempo of each verse and create movements to go with them, first using only their fingers, and then using their whole bodies. Perform these movements as they sing the song.

3 APPRAISAL

The children should be able to:
1. Listen and move to identify the tempo of different songs as slow, medium, or fast.
2. Identify the sounds of the trumpet, flute, violin, and timpani.

SONGBOOK

"Uncle Jessie," page 289 (contrasting tempos)
"Little Red Caboose," page 278 (changing tempo)

LESSON 4

Focus: Strong Beat

Objectives
To practice identifying and playing the strong beat
To review the sound of the trumpet, flute, and violin

Materials
Recordings: "Little Ducky Duddle"
"One Potato, Two Potato"
Listening—"Sakura"
"Draw a Bucket of Water"
Charts 50 and 53
Unpitched classroom instruments
Copying Master 8-3 (optional)

1 SETTING THE STAGE

Review "Little Ducky Duddle" on page 192. Have the children listen to the song twice, first patting the steady beat, and then patting the strong beat. Sing the song, pointing to Chart 50 on page 191. Identify the steady beat (all the rectangles) and the strong beat (the first and third rectangles). Then choose one unpitched instrument to play the steady beat and another to play the strong beat. Sing "Little Ducky Duddle" as a few children play the instruments. Repeat the activity to give others a turn to play.

2 TEACHING THE LESSON

1. Introduce "One Potato, Two Potato" to practice strong beat. Have the children:
• Stand in a circle and extend one hand in a fist into the center of the circle. Watch and listen as you go around the inside of the circle and tap one fist on each strong beat as you say the chant.
• Recognize that you were tapping on the strong beat.
• Repeat the chant several times. The child whose hand is tapped on the word *more* exchanges places with the person in the center of the circle and taps the strong beat the next time. (You may wish to have the child tapped on *more* leave the circle and play an unpitched instrument on the strong beat.)
(You may wish to use Copying Master 8-3 at this time.)

ONE POTATO, TWO POTATO

One potato, two potato,
Three potato, four,
Five potato, six potato,
Seven potato, more.

—Traditional

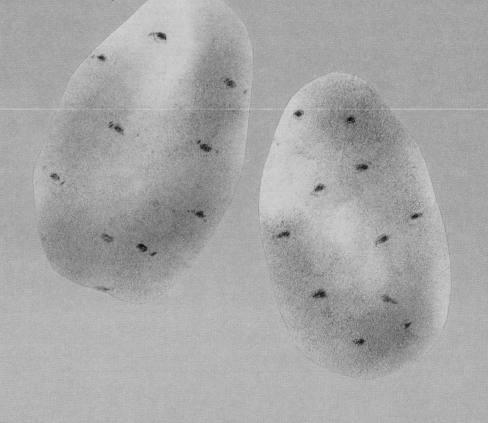

EXTENSION

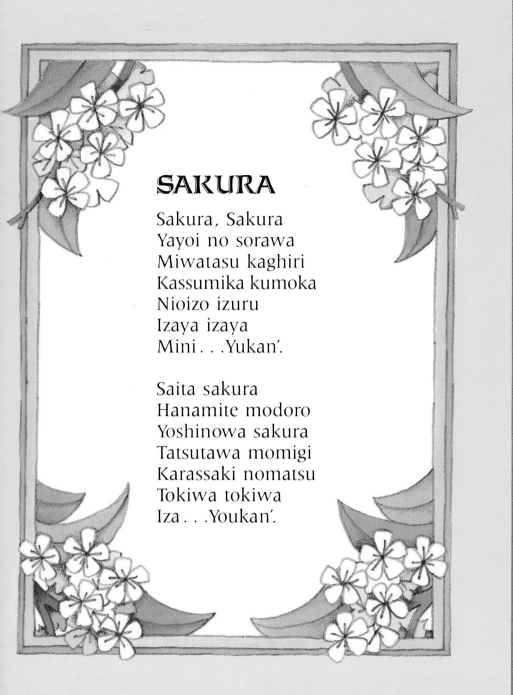

SAKURA

Sakura, Sakura
Yayoi no sorawa
Miwatasu kaghiri
Kassumika kumoka
Nioizo izuru
Izaya izaya
Mini. . .Yukan'.

Saita sakura
Hanamite modoro
Yoshinowa sakura
Tatsutawa momigi
Karassaki nomatsu
Tokiwa tokiwa
Iza. . .Youkan'.

2. Introduce "Sakura" for more practice feeling beat and hearing tone color. Have the children:
• Listen to "Sakura" and make up a soft pattern of one, two, or four beats.
• Discuss the form of the piece and the different tone colors.

Introduction	harpsichord
	flute, violins,
	trumpet and flute
	together
	violins
Verse 1	children, men,
	children and men
	together
Interlude	trumpet and flute
Verse 2	children and men
	together
Coda	trumpet and flute

• Form four groups. Each group will listen for one of the following: flute, trumpet, children, or men.
• Listen to "Sakura" again, softly patting the strong beat when they hear the tone color of their group's name. Sometimes one group pats alone, and sometimes two groups pat together.

Reinforcing the Lesson
Review "Draw a Bucket of Water" on page 200. Have the children look at Chart 53 on page 202 to see the pictures showing strong beat and to review the sequence of movements in the game. Then form groups of four and play the game on page 203.

3 APPRAISAL
The children should be able to:
1. Identify strong beat and play the strong beat with different musical selections.
2. Show that they recognize the flute, trumpet, and violin by moving with one of these featured tone colors.

MORE MUSIC TEACHING IDEAS
1. Have the children review "Bounce High, Bounce Low" on page 204 and practice keeping the strong beat with bouncing balls. Work with partners, bouncing, rolling, or tossing a ball back and forth on the strong beat at different tempos. Change the words to match the activity.
2. Have the children remain in the four groups they formed for "Sakura" and softly play every other beat on unpitched instruments as they listen to the music. Assign one instrument for each group: trumpet, flute, children, men.

COOPERATIVE LEARNING
To form the four listening groups for "Sakura" and to reinforce the concept of tone color, use four color names to assign the children to groups. Have four children each name a color. List their suggestions on the chalkboard. "Count off" around the class, having each child say the next color in order, for example: red, orange, purple, blue; red, orange, purple, etc. All "reds" form a group, and so on. On another occasion, have the children think of different categories they can use to divide into groups.

SONGBOOK
"My Head and My Shoulders," page 281 (beat and strong beat)
"Old Dan Tucker," page 282 (beat and strong beat)
"Uncle Jessie," page 289 (beat and strong beat)
"Step in Time," page 288 (beat and strong beat)

LESSON 5

Focus: Rhythm

Objective
To identify two equal sounds in a beat

Materials
Recordings: "Little Ducky Duddle"
"One, Two, Three, Four, Five"
Charts 51 and 54
Unpitched classroom instruments
Duck stick-ons
Copying Masters 7-21, 8-4, 8-5 (optional)

1 SETTING THE STAGE

Review "Little Ducky Duddle" on page 192. Have the children sing the song as you point the beat on Chart 51 on page 191. Identify the ducks on the chart as each representing one beat. Have the children think of a one-syllable word, for example, *duck* or *quack*, that they can say as you point to each duck. Then show the children the stick-ons with two ducks in one square.

Have the children think of a word in the song with two equal sounds that they can say for these beats (*little*, *Ducky*, and *wading* are possibilities). Have a few children come up and put two-duck squares over some of the ducks on the chart. Then have the class read the new rhythms saying the one- and two-syllable words they chose. (You may wish to use Copying Master 7-21 at this time.) Sing the song, say the new rhythms, and sing the song again. Identify this form as ABA.

2 TEACHING THE LESSON

1. Review "One, Two, Three, Four, Five" on page 205 to identify two equal sounds in one beat. Have the children:

• Echo the song, patting the steady beat.
• Echo the song again, tapping the rhythm of the words.
• Sing the song, tapping the rhythm of the words.
• Look at Chart 54, singing the song as you point to one fish tank on each beat. Notice that some fish tanks contain one fish, and some contain two. (You may wish to use Copying Master 8-4 at this time.)
• Read the rhythm on the chart, saying *fish* for each tank containing one fish, and *bubble* for each tank containing two fish.
• Sing the song, tapping the rhythm of the words as you point the beat on the chart. Notice that the number of fish in each tank corresponds to how many times they tapped on each beat. (You may wish to use Copying Master 8-5 at this time.)

CHART 54 *TWO EQUAL SOUNDS TO A BEAT*

E X T E N S I O N

MORE MUSIC TEACHING IDEAS

Have the children play the rhythm of the B section of "One, Two, Three, Four, Five" on unpitched instruments. Then, using any available Orff instruments, have the children who seem able play the rhythm of the B section on the G bar. Then have them play the rhythm on any combination of E and G. Finally, have them play the rhythm on any combination of the E, G, and A bars. Some children may be able to work in pairs, with the first child improvising on the question and the second on the answer. Use two different instruments for this question-answer improvisation.

2. Identify one- and two-syllable names of children in the class. Have the children:
• Take turns saying and tapping the rhythm of their first names, with the rest of the class echoing each name.
• Identify the children with one-syllable names (they only tapped once).
• Identify the children with two-syllable names (they tapped twice).
• Identify the number of syllables in the names of the rest of the children.
• Choose a one-syllable name and a two-syllable name from the class and read the rhythm on Chart 54 again, saying the one-syllable name when they see one fish in a tank and the two-syllable name when they see two fish in a tank.
• Choose two different unpitched instruments and read the rhythm on Chart 54 again, playing once on one instrument for each one-fish tank, and twice on the other instrument for each two-fish tank.

Reinforcing the Lesson
Have the children think of things in different categories that have one- and two-syllable names, such as kinds of flowers (rose, tulip), animals (cat, kitten), colors (blue, purple), or other categories that interest them. Read the rhythm on Chart 54 using these names.

3 APPRAISAL
The children should be able to identify words that have one sound and two equal sounds to a beat, and visually identify symbols for a beat with one or two sounds.

MORE MUSIC TEACHING IDEAS
Put four identical containers, such as apple sauce jars, in front of the class. Establish that each container represents one beat. Have the children use objects such as pencils, tongue depressors, or stirrers to take rhythmic dictation. Have them listen as you say a four-beat rhythm pattern of one- and two-syllable names, for example, *Jim, Jim, Sally, Jim.* Then watch as one child arranges the objects in the containers to show the correct number of sounds in each beat. Have the children try to put their objects in a line that shows the four beats with the correct number of sounds in each beat (I I II I), matching the pattern in the containers. Say the pattern as an ostinato with a song such as "Little Ducky Duddle."

KEYBOARD
Use the keyboard to reinforce the concept of two equal sounds to a beat. Have two or three children at a time stand at the keyboard and play the black keys only. First have them play as you say "duck, duck, duck, duck . . . ," moving their finger to a different black key on each beat. Then have them play two sounds to a beat as you say "duck-ling, duck-ling, duck-ling, duck-ling . . . ," again moving to different black keys for every strike. Remind them to use a light touch.

SONGBOOK
"Los Pollitos," page 279 (one and two sounds to a beat)
"Clap Your Hands," page 267 (one and two sounds to a beat)

LESSON 6

Focus: Pitch

Objective
To practice identifying upward and downward melodic direction

Materials
Recordings: "Robin Redbreast"
"My Oak Tree"
"Bow, Wow, Wow!"
Charts 55 and 56
Pitched classroom instruments
Copying Masters 8-6, 8-7 (optional)

1 SETTING THE STAGE

Have the children point up and then point down. Then have them listen to "Robin Redbreast" and tell what directions are mentioned in the poem (up and down). Discuss what happens in the poem in terms of upward and downward movement. (You may wish to use Copying Master 8-6 at this time.)

8A
CD 5

Robin Redbreast

Little Robin Redbreast
    Sat upon a tree,
Up went kitty cat,
    And down went he;
Down came kitty,
    And away Robin ran;
Says little Robin Redbreast,
    "Catch me if you can."

—*Mother Goose*

E X T E N S I O N

LOW

HIGH

UPWARD AND DOWNWARD

LESSON 6

2 TEACHING THE LESSON

1. Review playing upward and downward on pitched instruments. Have the children:

• Look at Chart 55. Identify the highest and the lowest bars on the instrument and the direction to play upward (left to right) and to play downward (right to left).

• Watch as you or a child demonstrates playing upward on an instrument one pitch at a time, from the lowest to the highest pitches.

• Take turns playing upward and downward on as many different instruments as are available. Repeat this activity until everyone has had a turn to play.

• Listen to "Robin Redbreast," playing upward or downward patterns on the instruments after each line as appropriate.

SPECIAL LEARNERS

Left and right can be difficult concepts for some children of Kindergarten age. Show them how to form an *L* by looking at the backs of their hands and extending the left thumb and forefinger. Help them associate the letter *L* with *Left* and notice that the left hand plays the *Low* sounds on the *Longest* bars of the xylophone.

COOPERATIVE LEARNING

To give many children a chance to play instruments in a short amount of time, divide the class into as many groups as you have different pitched instruments, for example: xylophone, glockenspiel, piano, electronic keyboard. Place the instruments in different areas of the room, having each group assemble around one instrument. All group members should take a turn playing an upward pattern, then a downward pattern. Other group members should monitor for accuracy. When all children have had a turn, each group moves clockwise around the room to the next instrument. In this way, each child will have a chance to play a variety of instruments upward and downward.

KEYBOARD

Have the children play the upward and downward instrument patterns in this lesson on the keyboard, using either the black keys, white keys, or a combination of both.

2. Introduce "My Oak Tree" for more practice identifying upward and downward melodic patterns. Have the children:
• Listen to the song and identify the melodic direction of measures 1–12 as first going upward, and then downward.
• Look at Chart 56 and identify the acorn pattern as going upward from left to right. (You may wish to use Copying Master 8-7 at this time.)
• Identify the tree in the song (oak) and the kind of nut that grows into an oak tree (acorn). Discuss other nuts that grow into trees, such as chestnut, pecan, and so on.
• Listen to the song again and pretend to be acorns buried in the ground. Curl up as small as possible, and then slowly grow into a tall oak tree, waving their arms and fingers like branches blowing in the wind.

Key: C   Starting Pitch: C   Scale Tones: *do re mi fa so la ti do¹*

My Oak Tree

Piano Accompaniment on page PA 85

Music by M. Angelo
Words by Barbara J. Braun

I   saw a lit - tle   a - corn,   ly - ing on the   ground.

I   put it in my   pock - et,   Told Dad - dy what I'd   found.

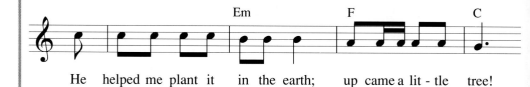

He   helped me plant it   in the earth;   up came a lit - tle   tree!

Just   see what we have   grown, My   Dad - dy and   me! *An   oak tree!*

E X T E N S I O N

MORE MUSIC TEACHING IDEAS

1. Have the children play an upward and downward accompaniment on the strong beat with "My Oak Tree." Play upward from C to C¹ and then downward from C¹ to C, one pitch on each strong beat. Have a few children play this upward and downward pattern as the class sings the song.

2. Compare "My Oak Tree" with "The Snow Man" on page 115.

LESSON 6

Reinforcing the Lesson

Review "Bow, Wow, Wow!" on page 201. Sing the song, showing the melodic direction with hand movements. Have the children stand in a single circle and face a partner. Have them learn the following movements.

Line 1: stamp three times (alternating feet)

Line 2: pat three times, then join hands with partner

Line 3: change places with partner, then drop hands

Line 4: jump-turn halfway around to face a new partner

(Repeat until everyone is back with their original partners.)

3 APPRAISAL

The children should be able to show upward and downward melodic direction through movement and by playing upward and downward patterns on classroom instruments.

MORE MUSIC TEACHING IDEAS

When the children are comfortable tapping the rhythm of "Bow, Wow, Wow!" have them play the rhythm of the song on unpitched percussion instruments. The children can take turns playing the rhythm as an interlude between repetitions of the song. Identify the song-instrument-song form as ABA.

CURRRICULUM CONNECTION: SCIENCE

Windowsill Garden—Discuss how plants grow from seeds. Then have the children plant a variety of seeds in individual containers and put them on a sunny windowsill. Each child should care for his or her own plant. Over the next few weeks have the children observe their plants growing. Lead occasional discussions about how the plants differ from one another in size, color, and shape. (You may wish to have the children take their plants home at the end of the school year.)

SONGBOOK

"Ah! Les Jolis Papillons," page 263 (upward and downward)

"The Bus," page 266 (upward and downward)

"Los Pollitos," page 279 (upward and downward)

"Happy Birthday," page 272 (upward and downward)

LESSON 7

Focus: Pitch

Objective

To practice identifying high and low, and upward and downward

Materials

Recordings: Listening—"Merry-Go-Round"
Recorded Lesson—"Upward and Downward in 'Merry-Go-Round' "
"My Oak Tree"
"One Potato, Two Potato"
"Che Che Koolay"

Chart 55 and 56

Pitched classroom instruments

1 SETTING THE STAGE

Have the children look at Chart 55 on page 213 and identify the high end and the low end of the instrument. Then identify which direction to play getting higher and which to play getting lower. Have the children listen as a few children play stepwise patterns that get higher or lower, pointing thumbs up if the pattern gets higher and thumbs down if the pattern gets lower.

2 TEACHING THE LESSON

1. Introduce "Merry-Go-Round" for more practice with upward and downward. Have the children:

• Listen as you play upward and downward patterns on a high-pitched classroom instrument.

• Listen to "Merry-Go-Round" and identify an amusement park ride that has horses and moves upward and downward (a merry-go-round).

• Listen as you play measures 1–3 of "Merry-Go-Round" on a pitched instrument (E G G E G G G E G G).

• Show upward and downward by bending their knees for the lower pitches and standing for the higher pitches as you play measures 1–3.

• Listen as you play measures 9–11 (D G G D G G G D G G).

• Show upward and downward by using the movement above as you play measures 9–11.

• Listen to "Merry-Go-Round" and show upward and downward using the movement above each time these patterns occur (measures 1–3, 9–11, 17–19).

2. Review "My Oak Tree" on page 214 for strong beat and to practice playing upward and downward melodic patterns. Have the children:

• Echo-sing the song two measures at a time, patting the steady beat.

• Echo-sing the song again, patting the strong beat.

Merry-Go-Round

Piano Accompaniment on page PA 86

Words and music by B. S. and M. S.

(For listening only)

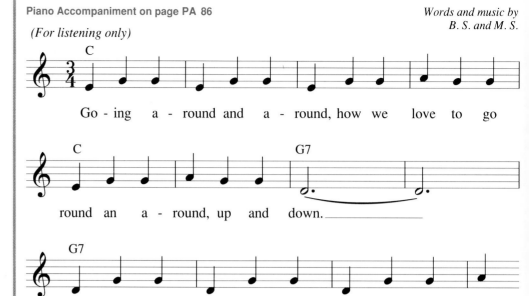

Go - ing   a - round and   a - round, how   we   love   to   go

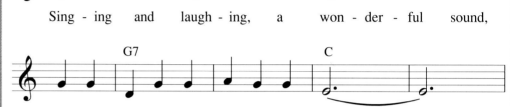

round   an   a - round, up   and   down._____

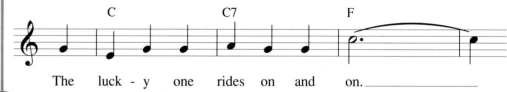

Sing - ing   and   laugh - ing,   a   won - der - ful   sound,

as   we   go round and   round, up   and   down._____

Ev - 'ry - one   reach - es   to   take   the   brass   ring,

The   luck - y   one   rides   on   and   on._____

EXTENSION

MORE MUSIC TEACHING IDEAS

1. When the children are familiar with "Merry-Go-Round," have them create their own merry-go-round music. Have them play upward and downward patterns on a glockenspiel with only the C D E G A bars on. Randomly play triangles and finger cymbals to give the sound more sparkle. This activity can be done in groups of six, with three children moving and three children playing. Switch roles so each child has a turn moving and playing.

2. Have the children divide into as many groups as there are pitched instruments. Have each group say "Che Che Koolay" together, with each group member taking a turn improvising either an upward or downward melody to the rhythm of the words. Then discuss whether each melody was an accurate presentation of upward or downward.

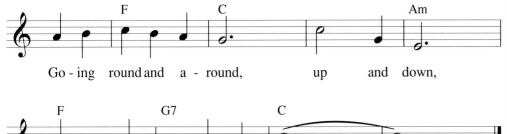

Go - ing round and a - round, up and down,

on the mer - ry - go - round._____

Key: F   Starting Pitch: A   Scale Tones: *so, do re ri mi fa so*

Che Che Koolay

Singing game from Ghana

Solo   Group   Solo   Group

Che-che koo-lay, che-che koo-lay, Che-che Ko-fee sa che-che Ko-fee sa

Solo   Group   Solo   Group

Ko-fee sa-lan-ga, Ko-fee sa-lan-ga. Ka-ka-shee lan-ga, ka-ka-shee lan-ga.

Solo   Group

Koom - ma-dye - day, Koom - ma-dye - day.

• Identify that they patted the beat first and just the strong beat the second time.
• Sing the song, patting the strong beat.
• Look at Chart 56 on page 215 and sing the song as one child points to the acorns to demonstrate the upward melodic direction.
• Play an upward scale from C to C'. Play a downward scale from C' to C.
• Sing the song as a few children play the upward and downward scales, playing the pitches on each strong beat. Repeat the C' before changing from the upward to the downward scale.

3. Review "One Potato, Two Potato" on page 208 for more practice playing upward and downward melodies. Have the children:
• Echo-say the rhyme, tapping on each number and the word *more*.
• Say the rhyme, tapping as before.
• Say the rhyme as a few children play the tapped words beginning on low C and going up the scale. (You may wish to have a different child play each pitch on individual resonator bells.)

Reinforcing the Lesson

Introduce "Che Che Koolay." Have the children listen to the song. Then listen again, putting one hand on the floor when they hear the lowest pitches (the third measure), and raising one hand when they hear the highest pitches (the last measure). Have them listen again, moving their whole bodies.

3 APPRAISAL

The children should be able to identify upward and downward and high and low by sight and sound, through movement, and by playing instruments.

PRONUNCIATION

Che-che koo-lay, Che-che Ko-fee sa
chā-chā kōo-lā   chā-chā kō-fē sä

Ko-fee sa-lan-ga, Ka-ka-shee lan-ga
kō-fē sä-lan-gä Kä-kä-shē lan-gä

Koom-ma-dye-day
kōom-ma-dī-dā

(Translation:
I give thanks for good thoughts,
for clothes for my shoulders,
for food for my stomach.
I will dance for you.)

SONGBOOK

"Ah! Les Jolis Papillons," page 263 (upward and downward)
"The Bus," page 266 (upward and downward)
"Los Pollitos," page 279 (upward and downward)
"Happy Birthday," page 272 (upward and downward; high and low)

LESSON 8

Focus: Style

Objective
To identify and compare musical elements in music of different cultures

Materials
Recordings: "Che Che Koolay"
　　　　　Listening—"Laideronette, Empress of the Pagodas" from *Mother Goose Suite* by Maurice Ravel
　　　　　Listening—"Sakura"
Chart 57

1 SETTING THE STAGE

Have the children think about different musical elements they can use to describe a piece of music. First have partners exchange ideas, and then tell their ideas to the class. Help the children remember the elements they have focused on in class, such as loud and soft, fast and slow, instruments and voices, long and short, beat and rhythm, high and low, upward and downward, melody alone and melody with accompaniment, same and different. Ask if they think these elements are in music all around the world (yes).

2 TEACHING THE LESSON

1. Review "Che Che Koolay" on page 217 to hear a song from Africa. Have the children:

• Listen as you tell them that "Che Che Koolay" is a song from Ghana, a country in Africa. Then listen to the song and identify any of the musical elements they discussed.

• Listen to you say the solo part and then echo each two beat-pattern until they are comfortable with the words.

FINE ART: *An Empress of Ch'ien Lung*. Unidentified Artist. THE METROPOLITAN MUSEUM OF ART. NY

E X T E N S I O N

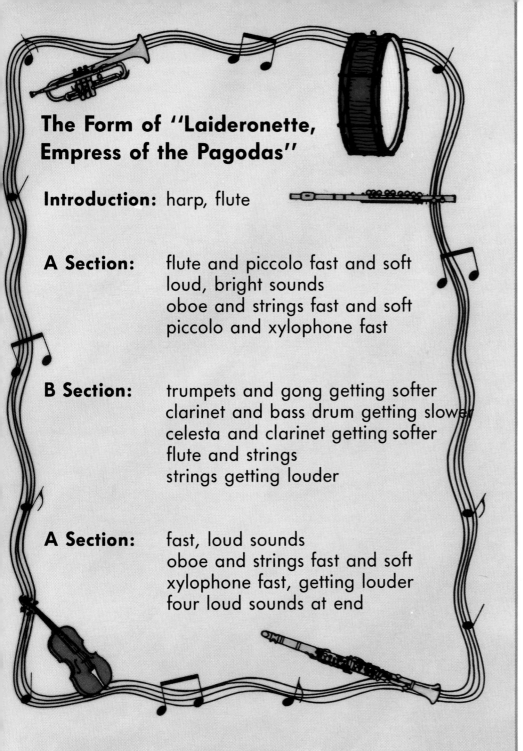

The Form of "Laideronette, Empress of the Pagodas"

Introduction: harp, flute

A Section: flute and piccolo fast and soft
loud, bright sounds
oboe and strings fast and soft
piccolo and xylophone fast

B Section: trumpets and gong getting softer
clarinet and bass drum getting slower
celesta and clarinet getting softer
flute and strings
strings getting louder

A Section: fast, loud sounds
oboe and strings fast and soft
xylophone fast, getting louder
four loud sounds at end

• Listen to the song, singing the echo part.
• Sing the song several times with different children improvising movements during the solos, and the class imitating the movements during the echoes.
• Identify this form as solo-group, and identify the group part as an exact echo of the solo part.
2. Introduce "Laideronette, Empress of the Pagodas" to hear music in a Far-Eastern style. Have the children:
• Look at Chart 57. Identify the woman in the picture (a Chinese empress).
• Speculate how music about this empress might sound, using the terms discussed at the beginning of the lesson. (You may need to ask questions, for example, will the music be loud or soft, will it have long sounds or short sounds, and so on.)
• Listen to "Laideronette, Empress of the Pagodas." Then discuss the musical elements they heard in the music, and decide if these elements were similar to their speculations.

Reinforcing the Lesson

Have the children review "Sakura" on page 209 and identify musical elements that sound the same or different from those in "Laideronette, Empress of the Pagodas." (Both have a Far-Eastern sound, both use strings and flute; "Sakura" has singing and "Laideronette, Empress of the Pagodas" does not. You may wish to tell the children that "Sakura" is an authentic Japanese folk song while "Laideronette, Empress of the Pagodas" is written in a Far-Eastern style by a French composer. Accept all reasonable answers.)

3 APPRAISAL

The children should be able to identify and compare musical elements in music from different cultures.

THE COMPOSER

Maurice Ravel (mor-ēs′ rä-vel′) (1875-1937)—French composer, who had a special talent for choosing instruments to produce the sounds he wanted. He was also much admired as a pianist, and was one of the great innovators in piano composition. Some of Ravel's best-known works are the ballets *Daphnis et Chloé* and *Bolero*, the opera *L'Enfant et les sortilèges (The Spellbound Child)*, and the orchestral works *La Valse* and Piano Concerto in D for Left Hand. *Mother Goose Suite* was originally written as a piano duet and later orchestrated by Ravel. "Laideronette, Empress of the Pagodas" is one of five movements from this suite.

CURRICULUM CONNECTION: LITERATURE

The inspiration for "Laideronette, Empress of the Pagodas" was the story "The Green Serpent" by Marie D'Aulnoy, found in *Tales of My Mother Goose* by Charles Perrault. In the story, pagodas are small creatures with bodies of precious stones. They entertain using tiny instruments made of almond and walnut shells.

CURRICULUM CONNECTION: ART

Have the children make pagodas by forming pipe-cleaner figures, placing a paper snowflake over the head of each figure. Have them tie a string to the pipe-cleaner head and move the puppet as they listen to "Laideronette, Empress of the Pagodas."

SONGBOOK

"Los Pollitos," page 279 (Ecuadorian song)
"Epo i tai tai e," page 269 (Maori song)
"Ah! Les Jolis Papillons," page 263 (French song)

C O R E
LESSON 9

Focus Tempo and Tone color

Objectives
To review identifying slow, medium, and fast tempos
To review identifying the flute, trumpet, violin, and timpani

Materials
Recordings: Recorded Lesson—"Tempo and Tone Color"
Listening—"Boa Constrictor"
Listening—*The Cat and the Mouse* by Aaron Copland
"Going on a Picnic"
Charts 47, 52, 58, and 59
A and B stick-ons
Copying Masters 8-2, 8-8 (optional)

1 SETTING THE STAGE

Have the children listen as you clap a steady beat at a slow, medium, and fast tempo, and identify each tempo.

2 TEACHING THE LESSON

1. Listen to "Tempo and Tone Color" to identify tempos and tone colors. Have the children:

• Look at Chart 52 on page 198 and identify the four instruments (flute, trumpet, violin, timpani). (You may wish to use Copying Master 8-2 at this time.)

• Listen to "Tempo and Tone Color" and identify the tempo and the tone color of each example.

Example 1	fast	flute
Example 2	slow	trumpet
Example 3	medium	timpani
Example 4	fast	violin

• Listen again, moving one part of their bodies at the appropriate tempo for each example.

Slow

Medium

Fast

E X T E N S I O N

COOPERATIVE LEARNING

To identify the instruments on Chart 52, page 198, have the children work in pairs or small groups to tell each other the names of as many instruments on the chart as they are able. Then tell them the name of each instrument. If they or their partner named it correctly, they should shake hands. This brief activity allows each child to orally rehearse the names of the instruments.

CHART
58
SEQUENCING

2. Introduce "Boa Constrictor" to identify a slow tempo. Have the children:

• Listen to the song and talk about what they think a boa constrictor is (a large snake).

• Listen to the song again and identify which body part mentioned in the song is not shown in the pictures on Chart 58 (thighs). (Ask a volunteer to make up a movement for the class to do for thighs.)

• Listen again, and point to each body part as it is mentioned.

• Sing the song, imitating the movements shown on the chart and using the new movement the class decided on for thighs.

• Decide if the song is slow, medium, or fast (slow).

LESSON 9

3. Introduce *The Cat and the Mouse* for more practice identifying fast and slow tempos. Have the children:

• Pat the beat as they listen to the first part of the music, and identify the tempo as fast.

• Look at Chart 59 and notice that the two pictures of the cat and mouse in the triangle are the same and the picture in the circle is different. Identify the form of the pictures as ABA. Use the A and B stick-ons to identify the picture at the bottom of the chart as representing an ending. (You may wish to use Copying Master 8-8 at this time.)

• Listen to the music and follow the chart. Determine if the tempo of the music remains fast throughout (it changes from fast to slow to fast).

• Identify the activities of the cat and mouse in A (cat chasing mouse) and B (cat and mouse dancing) and the ending (mouse getting away from the cat).

• Determine what kind of movement is appropriate for the fast parts of the music (jogging, hopping, jumping). Refer to Chart 47 on page 180 if necessary.

• Form pairs and dramatize *The Cat and the Mouse* as they listen to it again. Remember that the cat does not catch the mouse. Switch parts and repeat the activity. (You may wish to do this a few pairs at a time.)

LISTENING MAP: THE CAT AND THE MOUSE

CHART 59

THE COMPOSER

Aaron Copland—one of the outstanding modern American composers, was born in Brooklyn, New York, in 1900. Many of his works use native folk songs and rhythms to evoke early American life. His ballets *Billy the Kid, Rodeo,* and *Appalachian Spring* are considered masterpieces of American dance theater. Copland has written music for orchestra, chamber groups, voice, and piano. *The Cat and the Mouse,* for solo piano, was Copland's first published work.

Key: F   Starting Pitch: F   Scale Tones: *so, la, do re mi so*

Going on a Picnic

Piano Accompaniment on page PA 88

Words and music by
Lynn Freeman Olson

Go - ing on a pic - nic in the park to-day—

If it does - n't rain there's time to play.

Did you bring the ___ ____? Yes, I brought the ___ ____!

Read - y for a pic - nic, here we go!

LESSON 9

Reinforcing the Lesson

Introduce "Going on a Picnic." Have the children pat a moderate walking tempo. Echo the first part of "Going on a Picnic" as they pat, and identify the tempo as medium. Then have the children each tell you something that they would like to bring on a picnic. Then you ask each child if he or she brought that item to the picnic, for example, "Did you bring the salad?" and the child answers "Yes, I brought the salad." Have everyone sing the last line together. Then sing the song with different children answering the questions you ask, or have the children take turns asking questions, with the rest of the class answering together.

3 APPRAISAL

The children should be able to:
1. Identify slow, medium, and fast tempos verbally and with movement.
2. Identify the flute, trumpet, violin, and timpani by sight and sound.

VOCAL DEVELOPMENT

This call and response song provides an opportunity for you to work with children who are having difficulties singing in tune. If a child sings the question incorrectly, take a few moments to try to remediate the problem. Start by singing the question phrase on "loo" and ask the child to echo you. (The "oo" vowel sound is often effective in helping children match pitch.) If the child sings the phrase on "loo" correctly, have him or her go back to singing the words. This process, which should be carried out in a relaxed and encouraging manner, will focus the children's attention on the skill of singing in tune.

MORE MUSIC TEACHING IDEAS

Reinforce the concept of downward melodic movement. Have the children identify the melodic direction of the melodic segments *Did you bring the_____ _____?* and *Here we go!* in "Going on a Picnic" (downward). Have the children sing each segment while showing the downward melodic direction with movement. Have them take turns playing each segment on pitched instruments.

SONGBOOK

"Los Pollitos," page 279 (Ecuadorian song; tempo and instrumental tone colors on recording)
"Epo i tai tai e," page 269 (Maori song; tempo and instrumental tone colors on recording)
"My Head and My Shoulders," page 281 (Zulu song from Africa; tempo)
"Ah, Les Jolis Papillons," page 263 (French song; tempo and instrumental tone colors on recording)

Key: G   Starting Pitch: G   Scale Tones: *so, la, do re mi*

LESSON 10

Focus: Musical Elements

Objective
To review identifying tempo, form, and pitch

Materials
Recordings: "Going on a Picnic"
Listening—"Merry-Go-Round"
"Charlie Over the Ocean"
Listening—*The Cat and the Mouse* by Aaron Copland
Listening—"Boa Constrictor"
Listening—"Laideronette, Empress of the Pagodas" from *Mother Goose Suite* by Maurice Ravel
"Eight Balloons"
Chart 60
Copying Master 8-9 (optional)

1 SETTING THE STAGE

Review "Going on a Picnic" on page 223. Have the children think of things they need to take along on a picnic. Then sing the song, using these items in the question-and-answer part.

2 TEACHING THE LESSON

1. Review "Merry-Go-Round" on page 216 to review upward and downward. Have the children listen to "Merry-Go-Round" and show upward and downward by bending their knees for the lower pitches and standing for the higher pitches in measures 1–3, 9–11, and 17–19.

2. Introduce "Charlie Over the Ocean" for more practice with beat. Have the children:

• Remain in the circle and sit facing towards the center. Echo-sing the song, two measures at a time. Have small groups or soloists sing the solo part.

• Play this game as they stand in a circle: Choose one child to be the leader. The leader walks outside the circle, singing the solo part. The class sings the echo. At the end of the song, the leader touches a child on the shoulder. The child who was touched walks and tries to catch the leader, who attempts to return to the empty place. The game continues as the child who was touched becomes the new leader.

Charlie Over the Ocean

Singing Game

Char - lie o - ver the o - cean,   (Char - lie o - ver the

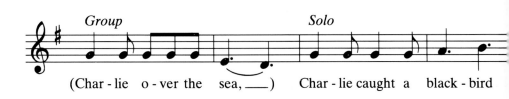

o - cean)   Char - lie o - ver the sea, ___

(Char - lie o - ver the sea, ___)   Char - lie caught a black - bird

Group   Solo   Group

(Char - lie caught a black - bird) Can't catch me. _ (Can't catch me. _)

EXTENSION

MORE MUSIC TEACHING IDEAS
Have the children add a rhythm ostinato to "Charlie Over the Ocean." Form two groups. Group 1 says:

O - cean   Char - lie - o

as Group 2 sings the song with a leader. Switch parts and repeat the activity.

MORE MUSIC TEACHING IDEAS
Have the children identify the melodic direction of the first two measures of "Charlie Over the Ocean" (stays the same, then moves upward). Have them show this melodic direction in movement as they sing. Provide pitched instruments and have the children take turns playing the segment. Repeat this procedure with each two-measure segment of the melody. Have the children find a way to show the melodic direction of each segment in a pictorial or graphic way. (For example, for each two-measure melodic segment, draw a line on the chalkboard to represent an ocean wave that stays the same, moves upward, or moves downward.)

SONGBOOK

Identify musical elements of songs from the Songbook section that have become special favorites of the class.

LESSON 10

3. Use musical elements as guides for interpreting different music. Have the children:

• Divide into three groups. Each group will dramatize either *The Cat and the Mouse*, "Boa Constrictor," or "Laideronette, Empress of the Pagodas." Choose the music they wish to dramatize, or assign a number one through three to each piece and then count off by threes to form groups.

• Review the elements in each piece and decide on movements appropriate for the piece they are going to dramatize.

• Dramatize their pieces, one at a time, as the other groups watch.

• Discuss how the musical elements in each piece influenced the movements they used with each dramatization.

Reinforcing the Lesson

Introduce "Eight Balloons." Have the children look at Chart 60 as they listen to the poem. Then have some act out how each balloon might move. Have them sit down and echo the last four lines of the poem after you. (You may wish to use Copying Master 8-9 at this time.)

Eight Balloons

Eight balloons no one was buyin'
All broke loose one afternoon.
Eight balloons with strings a-flyin'
Free to do what they wanted to.
One flew up to the sun—POP!
One thought highways might be
    fun—POP!
One took a nap in a cactus pile—POP!
One stayed to play with a careless
    child—POP!
One tried to taste some bacon
    fryin'—POP!
One fell in love with a
    porcupine—POP!
One looked close in a crocodile's
    mouth—POP!
One sat around 'til his air ran out—
    WHOOSH!
Eight balloons no one was buyin'—
They broke loose and away they
    flew,
Free to float and free to fly
And free to pop where they wanted
    to.

—*Shel Silverstein*

3 APPRAISAL

The children should be able to describe musical elements that are important characteristics of different pieces of music and create movements that are appropriate for each piece.

REVIEW AND EVALUATION

REVIEW

Objectives
To review songs, skills, and concepts learned in Unit 8
To measure the children's ability to:
1. Identify trumpet and timpani, and practice identifying flute and violin
2. Show identification of strong beat in music with two beats per measure
3. Aurally recognize two equal sounds to a beat

Materials
Recordings: "Draw a Bucket of Water"
"One, Two, Three, Four, Five"
"My Oak Tree"
"Bounce High, Bounce Low"
Listening—"Sounds of the Trumpet, Flute, Violin, and Timpani"
Unit 8 Evaluation (Instrument Sounds)
Charts 53, 54, 55, and 56
Pitched classroom instruments
Rubber ball
Evaluation Unit 8 Copying Master

TEACHING THE LESSON

Review the songs and concepts in Unit 8 by dramatizing a story. Have the children:
• Listen as you tell the story, singing and performing the activities at the appropriate places. (As the children sing and move, observe and evaluate individuals and the class as a whole as to how their responses indicate their level of understanding.)

Going to the Park
It's a beautiful day today. Why don't we go to the park? There are lots of games we can play at the park. Let's take a walk there. Follow me: one, two, one, two.
• Walk on the beat around the room as you clap or play a steady beat. (Watch for children who are able to keep a steady beat.)

Well, here we are at the park. That walk made me thirsty, how about you? Let's go over to the well and draw a bucket of water.
• Sing "Draw a Bucket of Water" on page 200. Look at Chart 53 on page 202 and remember that the pictures with the darker color in the top row represent the strong beats. Form groups of four and play the game on page 203.

Here comes a child who has just gone fishing. Let's find out if the fishing trip was successful.

REVIEW AND EVALUATION

• Sing "One, Two, Three, Four, Five" on page 205. Have one child ask the questions and another child give the answers in the B section. Read the rhythm of the song on Chart 54 on page 210, saying *fish* for a tank with one fish, and *bubble* for a tank with two fish. (Watch for children who can accurately tap and say the rhythm from the chart.)

There are two people standing nearby looking at a small tree. Can you tell me what is special about that tree?
• Sing "My Oak Tree" on page 214, moving to show the upward and downward melodic direction. Look at Chart 56 to review upward melodic direction. Then look at Chart 55 on page 213 to review which direction to play upward and downward. Listen as the children take turns playing five-pitch upward and downward patterns on the strong beat, pointing up if the pitches go upward, and pointing down if the pitches go downward.

I brought a ball with me to the park. Why don't we go over to the pavement and play a game. First we'll pretend to bounce a ball as we sing the song, and then play the game with my ball.
• Sing "Bounce High, Bounce Low" on page 204, pretending to bounce a ball on the strong beat. Then form a circle and bounce a ball around the circle on the strong beat as they sing the song again. (Watch for children who can mime bouncing a ball on the strong beat.)

It's time to go home. We're going to leave the park in four groups—flutes, trumpets, violins, and timpani. Each group will leave when it hears its instrument.
• Form four groups and identify each group as flutes, trumpets, violins, or timpani. Then listen to "Sounds of the Trumpet, Flute, Violin, and Timpani" and return to their seats as they hear the appropriate instrumental tone color. (Watch for children who recognize the instrumental tone colors.)

Our trip to the park was fun. Let's do it again sometime soon.

EVALUATION

Evaluation Unit 8 Copying Master can be found in the *Teacher's Resource Book* with full directions for providing an evaluation of the child's progress.

MUSICAL

"Raggedy Ann and Raggedy Andy Visit Amazing Amazo"

Objectives
To stage and perform a play through speech, singing, and movement
To improvise dialogue to dramatize a story

Materials
Recordings: "Love Is the Magic Word"
"I Am Amazo"
"Mixity Maxity Klippity Klack" (verse 1)
"Mixity Maxity Klippity Klack" (verse 2)
"Anyone Can Make a Mistake"
"Love Is the Magic Word" (verse 1)

1 SETTING THE STAGE

Ask the children to imagine what they might see and do in a magician's workshop. Then tell them that they are going to hear a story about the day Raggedy Ann and Raggedy Andy visited Amazo the Magician. (You may wish to have the children listen to the story with the songs first, and then use the suggestions below as a guide for dramatizing the play.)

 9A
CD 5

Raggedy Ann and Raggedy Andy™ Visit Amazing Amazo

a musical based on the book
Raggedy Ann and Andy and the Absent-Minded Magician

by Jean Bethell

Script by Michael Treni   Words and music by Barbara Staton

Cast

Raggedy Ann	Narrator(s)
Raggedy Andy	Magic Show Audience and Performers
Amazo	Chorus

Scene: A spooky-looking house along a tree-lined path. One wall of the house is cut away so the room inside can be seen. The room is filled with birdcages, mirrors, fishbowls, handcuffs, fans, decks of cards, drums, trumpets, and balloons. Prominent in the room is a large red sign with gold letters. The sign reads AMAZO THE MAGICIAN. At the beginning of the play this room is concealed behind a curtain.

EXTENSION

CURRICULUM CONNECTION: LITERATURE

Raggedy Ann and Raggedy Andy—These rag dolls are popular characters of children's stories. Raggedy Ann, the doll, was patented in 1915 by New York City writer and political cartoonist Johnny Gruelle. The doll was originally found in an attic and belonged to Gruelle's daughter Marcella. He wrote stories about the doll to entertain the girl while she was sick. *Raggedy Ann Stories*, the first book, was published in 1917. Gruelle later introduced a Raggedy Andy doll in response to readers' requests. Both dolls have red yarn hair, shoe-button eyes, and red-and-white striped legs. They have been featured in hundreds of books by Gruelle and others, as well as in musical plays, movies, and television shows.

COSTUME SUGGESTIONS

Dress Raggedy Ann and Raggedy Andy to look as much like the original characters as possible. Simple wigs can be made out of red yarn. Both characters should wear red-and-white striped stockings. Raggedy Ann wears a blue dress with red polka dots (or a red-and-blue print dress) covered by a white pinafore, and bloomers. Raggedy Andy wears a red-white-and-blue plaid or checkered shirt with a wide collar, droopy bow tie, baggy, bell-bottomed pants, and a sailor hat. Amazo should have a magic wand and eccentric clothing, including a cape. Other costumes can be created by the children as a related arts project. These costumes can tie in with the magic acts described in the

play, or to a magic act of their own invention. Encourage the children to use their creative talents the best way they can.

SCENERY AND PROPS

Determine the arrangement of the room in Amazo's house by the kind of magic acts he will perform. A large screen or curtained doorway should be at one end of the room for children who will be "appearing" and "disappearing" to hide behind. The room should also contain seats for the magic show audience, a large red sign reading AMAZO THE MAGICIAN in gold letters, a magic book, a top hat, and other assorted objects such as birdcages, mirrors, fishbowls, handcuffs, fans, decks of cards, drums, trumpets, and balloons.

Key: B♭   Starting Pitch: B♭   Scale Tones: *mi fa so la ti do¹*

Love Is the Magic Word

Piano Accompaniment on page PA 89   *Words and music by B. S.*

1. Love   is   the   ma-gic word.__   Love   is   the
2. Hold my hand   and   come with me.__   Let's go   see   what

ma-gic word.__   It   makes your trou-bles   go   a-way__
we can see.__   No   mat-ter what the   day may bring,__

Just to hear some-bod-y say,__   "I   love you,   I
We can han-dle   an-y-thing.__ You're my   friend,   I'm

love you,"   And   that's like ma-gic to   me.
your friend.   Oh,   I   like be-ing with you.

MUSICAL

2 TEACHING THE LESSON

1. Introduce "Love Is the Magic Word."
Have the children:
• Imagine that they are taking a walk with Raggedy Ann and Raggedy Andy.
• Listen to the beginning of the story and become familiar with the song.

CURRICULUM CONNECTION: LANGUAGE ARTS

Creative Writing—Have the children make up their own stories about Raggedy Ann and Raggedy Andy. You may wish to use the Raggedy Ann and Raggedy Andy stick-ons with Charts 27 and 28 in the Big Book to provide backgrounds for the stories.

MUSICAL

2. Read the story up to the next song and introduce "I Am Amazo." Have the children:

• Listen to the story and the song.

• Improvise what Raggedy Ann and Raggedy Andy might say to each other when they enter the magician's workshop.

• Listen to the song again and pretend to be Amazo by acting out the words, for example, swirl an imaginary cape and take a bow, wave an imaginary magic wand, pull a rabbit out of a hat. Point to themselves on the words *that's me*.

(The scene is empty during the first verse of the song. The AUDIENCE for the magic show is sitting behind the curtain. The CHORUS sings off to one side. During the second verse RAGGEDY ANN and RAGGEDY ANDY enter and walk hand in hand toward the house. At the end of the song the NARRATOR enters and stands at the opposite side of the scene.)

NARRATOR: One day Raggedy Ann and her brother, Raggedy Andy, took a walk. They stopped in front of a spooky-looking house. They had never seen it before.

RAGGEDY ANN: I wonder if anyone lives here?

NARRATOR: Before Raggedy Ann could stop him, Raggedy Andy knocked on the front door. Immediately the door opened wide.

(The front door opens. AMAZO steps out.)

NARRATOR: There stood a funny old man wearing a large cape.

AMAZO: Hello! Hurry and be seated. The neighbors are all here, and the show is about to begin. I mustn't keep my audience waiting.

RAGGEDY ANN
RAGGEDY ANDY } What show?

(Amazo motions Raggedy Ann and Raggedy Andy inside and shuts the door. The curtain pulls back to reveal the audience seated in the living room.)

NARRATOR: Raggedy Ann and Raggedy Andy stepped inside the house. They saw people seated in the room waiting for the show to begin. The room was filled with all kinds of interesting things. There were birdcages, mirrors, fishbowls, handcuffs, fans, decks of cards, drums, trumpets, and balloons. Then they saw a big red sign with sparkly gold letters. The sign read AMAZO THE MAGICIAN. Amazo stepped into the center of the room and swirled his cape about.

AMAZO: Presenting Amazo, the greatest magician on Earth!

Key: G   Starting Pitch: G   Scale Tones: *so, la, ti, do re mi*

I Am Amazo

Piano Accompaniment on page PA 90

Words and music by B. S.

I am A - ma - zo,   the   most a - maz - ing A - ma - zo.

I   will   a - maze   you   with   each   trick,
I'll   pull   a   rab - bit   from   this   hat,

So   watch   me   wave   this   ma - gic   stick,
I'll   turn   a   mouse   in - to   a   cat,

And   you will cer - tain - ly   a - gree with   me._____
I   bet you nev - er   thought of   do - ing   that._____

I'm A - maz - ing,   A - maz - o,   that's   me.

MUSICAL

3. Read the story up to the next song and introduce "Mixity Maxity Klippity Klack." Have the children:

• Listen to the story and imagine how they would do each magic trick. (You may wish to have some children play the magic objects in the performance. Encourage them to use all their talents in the best way. For example, a child who likes to dance could play the puppet who is turned into a dancing clown, and other children holding colorful scarves could perform movements to suggest the scarves flying like butterflies. These children hide behind a curtain or screen until it is time for them to appear. You may have them appear from behind Amazo's cape. Have them disappear again after the song, or remain onstage and react to what is happening.)

• Practice reacting to lines such as "Raggedy Andy disappeared." Do this first as a group and then have volunteers react individually.

• Listen to the first verse of "Mixity Maxity Klippity Klack," singing along as they are able to become familiar with the words and rhythm.

• Think of other ways to react to what is happening in the story, for example, dance happily in a circle around Raggedy Andy when he finally reappears. (The main characters, together with all the magic performers onstage, form a circle around Raggedy Andy and skip to the left as they sing the first verse of the song.)

• Make up other words that fit this rhythm.

NARRATOR: Amazo began to demonstrate his magic tricks. He made incredible things appear out of nowhere! He turned a puppet into a dancing clown. He made beautiful scarves fly like butterflies.

AMAZO: For my next trick I will try to make an object disappear. *(holds up the object)* I just need someone to hold this for me while I say the magic words.

RAGGEDY ANDY: May I hold it?

(Raggedy Andy walks up to Amazo. Amazo hands Raggedy Andy the object. Raggedy Andy holds the object in front of Amazo.)

NARRATOR: Amazo said the magic words.

AMAZO Abracadabra, you're gone!

(Raggedy Andy hides with the object.)

NARRATOR: All at once both the object and Raggedy Andy disappeared. Raggedy Ann was horrified! Amazo looked amazed.

RAGGEDY ANN: Now look what you've done. You made my brother disappear.

(Amazo picks up a large book and begins to flip through it.)

NARRATOR: Amazo began to leaf through the pages of a big leather book. He just could not seem to remember the right magic words when he needed them.

AMAZO: Olo, solo, bolo, boo? No. See saw, hee haw, bippety bop? No. Humpty Dumpty, do re mi? No.

NARRATOR: Nothing seemed to bring back Raggedy Andy.

AMAZO: Aha, got 'em! Mixity maxity klippity klack.

(Raggedy Andy comes out of hiding.)

NARRATOR: Suddenly there stood Raggedy Andy! Raggedy Ann was so happy to see him. She gave him a big hug.

(Raggedy Ann hugs Raggedy Andy.)

NARRATOR: Everyone sang the magic words.

Key: B♭   Starting Pitch: B♭   Scale Tones: *re mi fa so la ti do¹*

Mixity Maxity Klippity Klack

Piano Accompaniment on page PA 92

Words and music by B. S.

1. Mix - i - ty max - i - ty   klip - pi - ty klack,
2. Mix - i - ty max - i - ty   klip - pi - ty klack,

Mix - i - ty max - i - ty   klip - pi - ty klack,_____
Mix - i - ty max - i - ty   klip - pi - ty klack,   A -

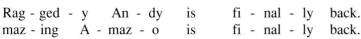

Rag - ged - y   An - dy   is   fi - nal - ly   back.
maz - ing   A - maz - o   is   fi - nal - ly   back.

Mix - i - ty max - i - ty   klip - pi - ty klack.
Mix - i - ty max - i - ty   klip - pi - ty klack.

MUSICAL

- Listen to the part of the story when Amazo disappears and finally reappears.
- Sing and dance in a circle around Amazo just as they did when Raggedy Andy reappeared.

4. Read Raggedy Andy's apology and introduce "Anyone Can Make a Mistake." Have the children:

- Listen to "Anyone Can Make a Mistake" and become familiar enough with the song to say the words at the end. (You may wish to discuss the idea that when people remember to use such words as *please, thank you,* and *I'm sorry,* they will find that other people are nicer to them in return. These words can work magic, too.)

5. Read the end of the story and review the first verse of "Love Is the Magic Word." Have the children:

- Listen to the end of the story.
- Sing the first verse of "Love Is the Magic Word," swaying together from side to side on the beat (two beats to a measure).

6. Prepare for the play. Have the children:

- Decide who is going to play the different parts. (You may wish to assign parts, or hold "auditions." If the Narrator's part is too long for one child to handle, you may wish to divide the part among several children, or read it yourself.)
- Practice saying their lines in character. Discuss what type of voice each character might have.
- Practice the lines until they can all say their lines on cue.
- Decide on where each character enters and exits during the play and practice each character's movements.
- Rehearse the performance. (As the children rehearse have them perform as if they had an audience.)
- Perform the play.

RAGGEDY ANDY: Where was I? The last thing I remember was Amazo saying, *(looking at Amazo)* "Abracadabra, you're gone."

(Amazo hides with the book.)

NARRATOR: As Raggedy Andy said the magic words, Amazo disappeared with the book.

RAGGEDY ANN: Now you've done it. Amazo *and* the book are gone!

RAGGEDY ANDY: What can we do? We don't know the magic words.

RAGGEDY ANN: Maybe we can remember them. Let's see, was it mixity mixity klippity klap? No. Maxity mixity klappity klick? No.

NARRATOR: Everyone tried hard to think of the magic words. Just as they had said almost everything possible, Raggedy Ann remembered.

RAGGEDY ANN: Mixity maxity klippity klack!

(Amazo comes out of hiding.)

NARRATOR: All at once Amazo and the book appeared. Everyone was so glad to see Amazo. They sang and danced around him.

Reprise: "Mixity Maxity Klippity Klack" (verse 2)

RAGGEDY ANDY: I'm sorry, Amazo. I didn't mean to make you disappear. It won't happen again.

AMAZO: Quite all right, young man. We all make mistakes.

Key: C   Starting Pitch: E   Scale Tones: *do re mi fa so la do'*

Anyone Can Make a Mistake

Piano Accompaniment on page PA 93   *Words and music by B. S.*

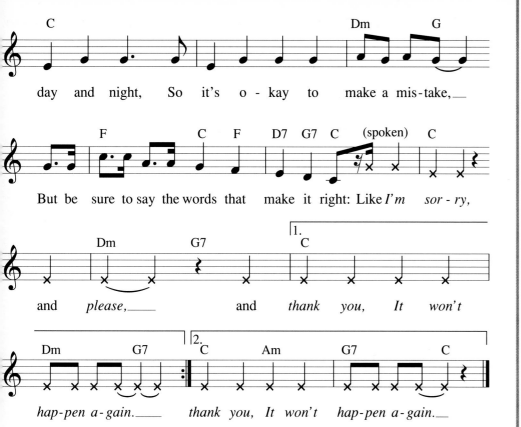

day and night, So it's o-kay to make a mis-take,—

But be sure to say the words that make it right: Like *I'm* *sor-ry*,

and *please,*— and *thank you,* It won't

hap-pen a-gain.— *thank you, It won't hap-pen a-gain.*—

3 APPRAISAL

The children should be able to:
1. Stage and perform a play through speech, singing, and movement.
2. Improvise speaking parts in the play as they dramatize the story.

RAGGEDY ANN: Thank you for the wonderful magic show.
RAGGEDY ANDY: Please let us come back again sometime.
NARRATOR: It had been a wonderful day for everyone. Raggedy Ann and Raggedy Andy joined in singing with all their new friends.
Reprise: "Love Is the Magic Word" (verse 1)

The End

MUSICAL

"Hats"

Objective
To perform a play using speech, song, dance, costumes, and instruments

Materials
Recordings: "Hats for Sale!"
"Lullaby"
"No Hats in Sight"
"The Peddler's Song"
"Monkey See, Monkey Do"
Indian bells or finger cymbals, drum, wood block, xylophone
Copying Master M-1 (optional)

1 SETTING THE STAGE
Have the children discuss what they might find in a jungle (trees, streams, wild animals, and so on).

2 TEACHING THE LESSON

1. **Introduce *Hats*.** Have the children:
• Listen to the story and the songs.
• Identify the characters (Peddler, Elephant, Birds, Monkeys, Wise Woman) and discuss the plot.

 9A

CD 6

Hats
(A Traditional Folk Tale)

Script adaptation by Marilyn Davidson and Karen Abramson Mazur
Words and music by Karen Abramson Mazur

CAST

Narrator	Birds
Peddler	Monkeys
Elephant	Chorus
Wise Woman	

Scene: A jungle in southeast Asia. A large tree is center stage. There is a stream nearby. The CHORUS is seated on both sides of the stage, facing the audience. The NARRATOR enters and walks downstage right and stays there throughout the play.

NARRATOR: Once upon a time, in a country far away, there lived a peddler. This peddler was famous far and wide for selling beautiful hats, which he made himself. The hats were made of the finest materials and came in colors of the rainbow—red, orange, yellow, green, blue, and violet. Each year everyone looked forward to the first day of the fair. On that day, and that day only, the peddler would pile all the hats he had made during the year into two large baskets, place the baskets on top of his elephant, and travel to the village to sell the hats.

(The PEDDLER enters from the back of the auditorium with the ELEPHANT, who is carrying two baskets of hats. They walk slowly to the stage during the song.)

NARRATOR: As the peddler started on his long journey to the village, he sang a song to tell everyone he was coming to sell his hats.

EXTENSION

CASTING SUGGESTIONS
The Peddler should be a boy or girl with a strong, clear speaking voice and the ability to sing a simple phrase alone. The Wise Woman and the Peddler must be able to memorize some dialogue. The Elephant should be able to bend over and walk on all fours whenever possible. Use a minimum of twelve Monkeys and three Birds. Have an adult or an older child be the Narrator.

COSTUME SUGGESTIONS
The children in the Chorus should wear a wide variety of bright colors or flowered prints. The Narrator can wear street clothes, or a simple costume suggesting the Far East, such as a long robe and a turban. The Peddler can wear baggy pants, a bright, oversized shirt tied with a rope belt, and sandals. The Elephant can wear a grey shirt and pants. Make large, floppy ears out of grey construction paper. A cardboard tube from a used roll of paper towels can be tied to the head to make a trunk. A strip of grey construction paper, oaktag, or a length of rope painted grey can be used as a tail. The Monkeys can wear brown pants and pullover shirts. Cut out ears from brown construction paper and attach them to a loop of brown construction paper that fits snugly on the head. Curled lengths of brown oaktag or construction paper can be used as tails. The Birds can wear blue pants and shirts or leotards covered with crepe-paper feathers.

Key: C   Starting Pitch: G   Scale Tones: *do re mi fa so la ti do*[1]

Hats for Sale!

Piano Accompaniment on page PA 94

Words and music by
Karen Abramson Mazur

Hats for sale!   Hats for sale!   I have man-y hats for sale.

Hats for sale!   Hats for sale!   Man-y fine   hats.   *Fine*

Vio - let,   blue,   green,   or-ange, yel-low, red;

They   will   fit   on   an - y   head.   Buy   one of each,   *D.C. al Fine*

buy   them   for fun;   Rain-bow col-ors   ev - 'ry   one!

2. Introduce "Hats for Sale!" Have the children:
• Listen to the song.
• Echo-say the words, two measures at a time.
• Echo-sing the song, two measures at a time.
• Listen to the song and show the direction of the melody with their hands. (You may wish to have the children imitate you.) Notice that the end of the song is the same as the beginning.
• Sing the song as one child plays Indian bells or finger cymbals.

SCENERY AND PROPS

A tree should be prominent in center stage, constructed so as to be sturdy enough to support the Monkeys. Student desks with green crepe-paper or construction-paper leaves attached could be used as a tree. Hang leaves or streamers from the tree to give the illusion of more foliage. Complete the scene with construction-paper or papier-mâché rocks and bright flowers. (You may wish to paint a colorful backdrop depicting a jungle, or showing a village in the distance.) Hats can be made from 12″ × 18″ sheets of folded consruction paper. (Simple, folded hats will stack easily in the Peddler's baskets.) There should be at least two hats of each color. Use two straw baskets to hold the paper hats.

MUSICAL

3. Introduce "Lullaby." Have the children:
- Listen to the song.
- Listen again, swaying from side to side on the strong beat.
- Echo-say the words, four measures at a time.
- Echo-sing the song, four measures at a time.
- Sing the song.
- Learn the dance (directions in music).
- Sing the song and do the dance.
- Sing the song and do a slightly silly version of the dance.

CURRICULUM CONNECTION: SCIENCE

Monkeys—are small, lively animals that live mostly in the tropical areas of Central and South America, Africa, and Asia. Monkeys belong to the highest order of mammals, the *primates*, and rank among the most intelligent animals. There are about two hundred different kinds of monkeys. Some monkeys spend their entire lives in trees, while others live on the ground. All monkeys live in groups called *troops*. These troops can contain as many as one hundred or more monkeys.

NARRATOR: The peddler traveled for a long time, until the sun was high in the sky. Both he and the elephant became very hot and tired.

(The Peddler and the Elephant come onstage.)

NARRATOR: As they were nearing the village, they came to a large tree beside a cool, flowing stream.

PEDDLER: Elephant, you and I are very hot and tired. Let us nap in this shade until the sun is lower in the sky. Then we can go into the village to sell the hats.

(The Peddler takes the baskets of hats off the Elephant, spreads them on the ground, and looks thoughtfully at them during the Narrator's speech.)

NARRATOR: Carefully, the peddler took the baskets of hats off the elephant's back and spread them out on the ground, just in case a customer should happen to come by. He thought about how beautiful the hats looked in their rainbow colors of red, orange, yellow, green, blue, and violet. He sat down, leaned against the tree and looked and looked at them until he fell asleep.

(The Peddler sits down, leans against the tree, and pulls his own hat down over his eyes. The Elephant lies down next to the Peddler. They both fall asleep. The BIRDS enter and flutter over to the sleeping Peddler to examine the hats.)

NARRATOR: As the peddler and the elephant slept, some little birds came along. They saw the hats and liked them so much that they sang a song to help the peddler and the elephant sleep.

(The Birds flutter to stage left and dance during the song.)

Key: C   Starting Pitch: C   Scale Tones: *do re mi fa so la ti do¹*

Lullaby

Piano Accompaniment on page PA 96

*Words and music by
Karen Abramson Mazur*

Sleep,   oh,   sleep,   Time   to   rest
Movements: Step   Hop   Step   Hop   Flutter around in small circle
*   right   right   left   left*

Like   the   ba - by   birds   in   their   nest.
Form circle, move clockwise, fluttering wings

Let the sun - shine warm your face.
Raise arms in a circular motion, place hands on cheeks

All is qui - et in this place,
Hold arms over head and sway side to side

Sleep, oh, sleep, Sleep, oh, sleep,
Step *Hop* *Step* *Hop* *Flutter around in small circle*
right *right* *left* *left*

Sleep, sleep, sleep.
Both arms right *Both arms left* *Crouch on floor in sleeping position*

MUSICAL

4. Introduce the chant "No Hats in Sight."
Have the children:
• Echo-say the first two measures, then the next two measures.
• Learn the order of the colors and say the "color" measures in rhythm.
• Form two groups. Everyone says one "color" measure, followed by Group 1 saying the Peddler's part and Group 2 saying the Monkeys' part.
• Echo-say the last two measures.
• Say the complete chant as one child plays the Peddler's part on a drum and another child plays the Monkeys' part on a wood block.

NARRATOR: The peddler did not know that a large family of very mischievous monkeys lived in the tree. These monkeys, like all monkeys, would do anything they saw anyone else doing.

(The MONKEYS quietly creep onto the stage. The Birds flutter away, frightened, as the Monkeys imitate the Birds' dance.)

Reprise: "Lullaby"

NARRATOR: Now these monkeys loved hats. They saw that the peddler had a hat on his head. So each monkey took one of the peddler's wonderful hats and put it on.

(Each Monkey takes a hat and puts it on. Then they all quietly climb up into the tree branches.)

NARRATOR: When the peddler and the elephant awoke, they had a big surprise!

(During the chant the Peddler uses a different gesture each time he says What shall I do? such as throwing out his arms or holding his head. The Monkeys imitate each movement, repeating the words after the Peddler. Play the rhythm of these words on a drum each time the Peddler says them, and on a wood block each time the Monkeys say them. The Elephant sways back and forth sympathetically. The Peddler does not see or hear the Monkeys. The Elephant looks up, sees the Monkeys, and tries without success to get the Peddler to look at them.)

No Hats in Sight

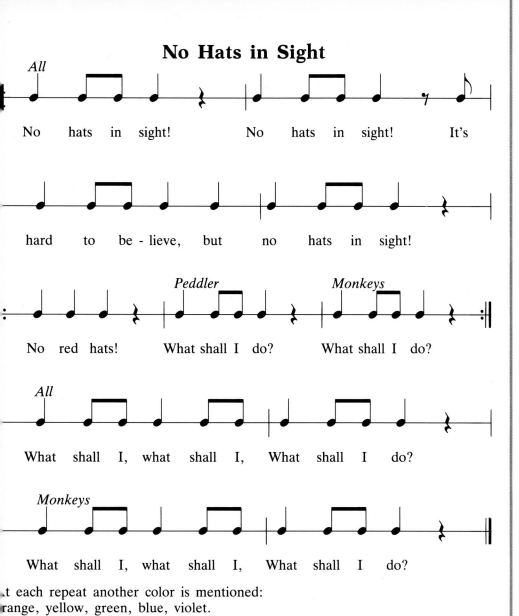

All

No hats in sight! No hats in sight! It's

hard to be - lieve, but no hats in sight!

No red hats! *Peddler* What shall I do? *Monkeys* What shall I do?

All

What shall I, what shall I, What shall I do?

Monkeys

What shall I, what shall I, What shall I do?

t each repeat another color is mentioned:
range, yellow, green, blue, violet.

MUSICAL

5. Introduce "The Peddler's Song." Have the children:
• Listen to the song.
• Echo-say the words, two measures at a time.
• Echo-sing the song, two measures at a time.
• Sing the song as they are able.
• Choose one child to sing the Peddler's part and a small group to sing the Monkeys' part.
• Sing the song and listen as the selected children sing measures 5 and 6.

6. Introduce "Monkey See, Monkey Do." Have the children:
• Listen to the song.
• Echo-say the words, two measures at a time.
• Tap the rhythm of the song as they listen to it again.
• Echo-sing the song, two measures at a time.
• Sing the song.
• Practice playing the descending glissando used in the play on a xylophone.

7. Dramatize the story. Have the children:
• Discuss the different ways that the Elephant, Birds, and Monkeys move. Compare these movements to how the people in the play move.
• Dramatize the story as they listen to it again. (Choose three children to be the Peddler, Elephant, and Wise Woman. Small groups can be the Birds, Monkeys, and Chorus. When they can act out the story well, have the children perform it for other classes or parents.) (You may wish to use Copying Master M-1 at this time.)

3 APPRAISAL

The children should be able to perform a play using speech, song, dance, costumes, and instruments.

(The Monkeys all laugh and chatter, holding their stomachs or placing their hands over their mouths. The Peddler finally looks up and seems them.)

PEDDLER: *(shaking one fist at the Monkeys)* You naughty monkeys, give me back my hats!

(Monkeys each shake one fist at the Peddler.)

PEDDLER: *(shaking both fists at the Monkeys)* You naughty monkeys, give me back my hats!

(Monkeys each shake both fists at the Peddler.)

PEDDLER: *(shaking both fists and jumping up and down)* You naughty monkeys, give me back my hats!

(Monkeys each shake both fists at the Peddler and jump up and down.)

Key: C   Starting Pitch: C   Scale Tones: *do re mi fa so la do¹*

The Peddler's Song

Piano Accompaniment on page PA 98

Words and music by
Karen Abramson Mazu

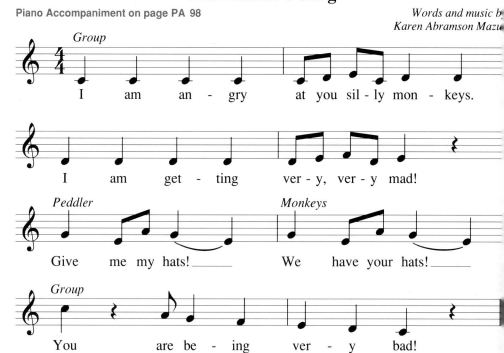

(WISE WOMAN enters and sees the Peddler jumping up and down.)

NARRATOR: Just then, a wise woman came along. She could not understand why the peddler was so angry.

WISE WOMAN: What is wrong? Why are you jumping around? It is much too hot!

PEDDLER: I am a hatmaker. All year I have been making hats to sell in the village.

WISE WOMAN: If they are like the one you are wearing, they are very fine hats indeed! Why should that make you angry?

PEDDLER: Look up in this tree, and you will see!

(The Wise Woman looks up and sees the Monkeys. She begins to laugh.)

PEDDLER: How can you laugh? My children will have no food to eat if I have no hats to sell!

WISE WOMAN: I will get your hats back for you. I know all about monkeys. Haven't you ever heard the saying, "Monkey see, monkey do?"

(The Peddler shakes his head.)

WISE WOMAN: Just watch!

Key: C   Starting Pitch: G   Scale Tones: *mi so la*

Monkey See, Monkey Do

Traditional

Mon-key see,   mon-key do.   Mon-keys do the same as you!

(At the end of the song, the Wise Woman makes gestures at the Monkeys, such as scratching her head, clapping her hands, jumping up and down, and so on. The Monkeys imitate each movement. Finally the Wise Woman grabs the Peddler's hat off his head and throws it on the ground. The Monkeys do the same, accompanied by a descending glissando played on a xylophone. All the hats are now on the ground within reach. The Wise Woman and the Peddler pick up the hats and put them back into the baskets.)

PEDDLER: You do know a lot about monkeys. Thank you! Please, take one of the hats for yourself, any color you like, as a gift from me.

WISE WOMAN: Thank you! I will!

(The Wise Woman picks out a hat, puts it on her head, and waves goodbye as she continues on her way. The Peddler puts the baskets back on the Elephant and they slowly begin to walk off.)

NARRATOR: So the peddler put the baskets of hats back on the elephant and they both continued on to the village, where the peddler sold all of his beautiful hats.

Reprise: "Hats for Sale"

The End

SONGBOOK

"Jack-o'-Lantern"

TEACHING THE SONG

Have the children pretend they are big, round jack-o'-lanterns swaying on the strong beat as they sing the song. Identify these movements as long. Listen for the rhyming words (*sight* and *night,* and *vine* and *shine*). Notice that the rhyming words occur on long sounds. Choose an unpitched instrument that can make a long sound, such a triangle, to play on these words.

Key: D   Starting Pitch: D   Scale Tones: *do re mi fa so la do*

Jack-o'-Lantern

Piano Accompaniment on page PA 99

German Folk Song
Words by Lois Holt

1. Jack - o' - lan - tern,   jack - o' - lan - tern,
2. You were once   a   yel - low pump - kin

You are   such   a   fun - ny   sight.
Grow - ing   on   a   stur - dy   vine.

As   you   sit   there   in   the   win - dow,
Now   you   are   a   jack - o' - lan - tern

Look - ing   out   at   the   night.
See   the   can - dle - light   shine.

EXTENSION

NOTEWORTHY

strong beat
long and short
playing classroom instruments
Use with pages 41, 47, 49, 51, 53.

Autumn Leaves

Piano Accompaniment on page PA 100   *Anonymous*

Au - tumn leaves are fall - ing,   Nights are grow - ing chill,

Ma - ple leaves are turn - ing red a - long   the   hill.

E X T E N S I O N

SONGBOOK

"Autumn Leaves"

TEACHING THE SONG

Have the children listen to the song, softly patting the steady beat. Listen again and identify the three signs of autumn in the song (falling leaves, chilly nights, leaves turning colors). Echo-sing each phrase. Then sing the song, patting the beat. Choose three unpitched instruments, such as a drum, triangle, and rhythm sticks. Softly play one instrument on the beat with each sign of autumn as they sing the song. Identify the melodic direction of the last line as high to low.

NOTEWORTHY

steady beat
playing classroom instruments
melodic direction
Use with pages 59, 67, 74, 77.

"Five Fat Turkeys"

TEACHING THE SONG

Have the children listen to the song and identify the rhyming words (*we, tree,* and *see; around* and *found*). Echo-sing the song four measures at a time as they pat the steady beat. When the children know the song well, choose one child to be the cook. The cook sits with eyes closed so that five turkeys can be chosen. (The turkeys stay seated with the rest of the class.) The turkeys sing the song. The cook tries to guess which five children are the turkeys. Give other children a chance to be the cook and the turkeys.

CD 6

Five Fat Turkeys

Piano Accompaniment on page PA 101

Traditional

Five fat tur-keys are we,_____

We slept all night in a tree._____

When the cook came a-round we could-n't be found,

So that's why we're here, you see._____

NOTEWORTHY

steady beat
rhyming words
small group singing
Use with pages 62, 67, 74, 77.

Let Us All Be Thankful

Piano Accompaniment on page PA 102

Traditional Melody
Words by M. S.

Let us all be thank - ful on this Thanks - giv - ing Day.

May good health and love and peace be here to stay.

SONGBOOK

"Let Us All Be Thankful"

TEACHING THE SONG

Have the children echo-say the words as they pat the beat. Then echo-sing the song one phrase at a time, showing the melodic direction with one hand. Identify the melodic direction of the first phrase as upward and the melodic direction of the second phrase as downward. Identify the rhyming words (*day* and *stay*). Have one child play a triangle on the rhyming words as the class sings the song.

EXTENSION

NOTEWORTHY
steady beat
rhyming words
melodic direction
Use with pages 74, 77.

SONGBOOK

"My Dreydl"

TEACHING THE SONG

Ask if anyone knows what a dreydl is (a special top children play with during Hanukah). Have the children stand in a scatter formation. As they listen to the song, patting the beat, you move among them. As you touch each child, that child begins to spin. The children stop spinning when you touch them again.

Have the children notice the downward direction of the melody in measures 2, 4, and 6, and the upward direction of the melody in measure 8.

Key: C   Starting Pitch: G   Scale Tones: *do re mi fa so la ti do'*

My Dreydl

Piano Accompaniment on page PA 102

Music by S. E. Goldfarb
Words by S. S. Grossman

1. I have a lit-tle drey-dl, I made it out of clay;
2. My drey-dl's al-ways play-ful, It loves to dance and spin.

And when it's dry and read-y, Then drey-dl I shall play.
A hap-py game of drey-dl, Come play, now let's be-gin.

O drey-dl, drey-dl, drey-dl, I made it out of clay;
O drey-dl, drey-dl, drey-dl, It loves to dance and spin.

O drey-dl, drey-dl, drey-dl, Now drey-dl I shall play.
O drey-dl, drey-dl, drey-dl, Come play, now let's be-gin.

E X T E N S I O N

NOTEWORTHY

steady beat
creative movement
cultural tradition
upward and downward
Use with pages 85, 87, 90.

9B
 6

Holiday Song

Piano Accompaniment on page PA 104

Round from England
Words by B. S.

God   bless   all   good   friends   here,

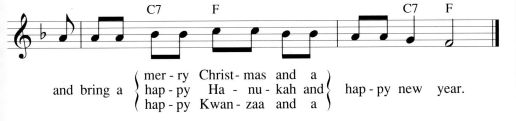

and bring a   { mer-ry Christ-mas and a }
           { hap-py Ha-nu-kah and } hap-py new year.
           { hap-py Kwan-zaa and a }

SONGBOOK

"Holiday Song"

TEACHING THE SONG

Have the children pat the steady beat as they echo-sing the song one measure at a time. Then sing the song, patting the beat. Sing the song three times, first playing the beat on the wood block, then on jingle bells, and finally on both instruments together.

E X T E N S I O N

MORE MUSIC TEACHING IDEAS

Have one child play alternating low and high F on every other beat throughout the song, using a pitched instrument. (The child will be playing half notes.)

NOTEWORTHY

steady beat
playing unpitched instruments
low and high
Use with page 95.

SONGBOOK

"The Friendly Beasts"

TEACHING THE SONG

Have the children listen to the song and identify the animals and what each of them did to help Jesus (the donkey carried Jesus' mother to Bethlehem; the cow gave Jesus her manger for a bed; the sheep gave Jesus wool for a blanket). Dramatize the song with three children playing the donkey, the cow, and the sheep. Have each child enter at the appropriate verse and stand around a box representing the manger. Then have the children echo-say the words one phrase at a time. Have them find parts of the song that have the same words (first and last phrases). Sing the song as they are able.

9B

CD 6

Key: E♭   Starting Pitch: E♭   Scale Tones: *ti, do re mi fa so la*

The Friendly Beasts

Piano Accompaniment on page PA 104

Traditional English Carol

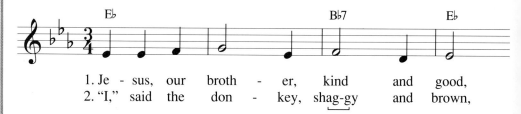

1. Je - sus, our broth - er, kind and good,
2. "I," said the don - key, shag-gy and brown,

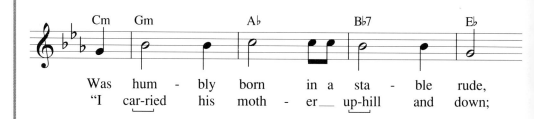

Was hum - bly born in a sta - ble rude,
"I car-ried his moth - er up-hill and down;

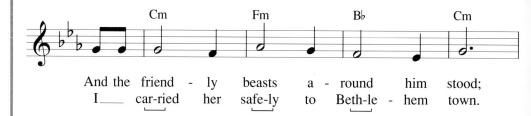

And the friend - ly beasts a - round him stood;
I car-ried her safe-ly to Beth-le - hem town.

EXTENSION

NOTEWORTHY

seasonal song
creative movement
same and different
Use with pages 83, 95, 97.

Je - sus, our broth - er, kind and good.
I," said the don - key, shag-gy and brown.

3. "I," said the cow, all white and red,
   "I gave him my manger for a bed;
   I gave him my hay to pillow his head.
   I," said the cow, all white and red.

4. "I," said the sheep with the curly horn,
   "I gave him my wool for his blanket warm;
   He wore my coat on Christmas morn.
   I," said the sheep with the curly horn.

SONGBOOK

"Go Tell It on the Mountain"

TEACHING THE SONG

Have the children pat the beat as they listen to the song. Then continue patting the beat as they echo-sing the song two measures at a time. Sing the song, patting the beat. Point the beat on Chart 26 (page 94) as they sing. Then sing the song with a few children playing the instruments shown on the chart.

Key: F   Starting Pitch: A   Scale Tones: *so, la, do re mi*

Go Tell It on the Mountain

Piano Accompaniment on page PA 106

African American Spiritual

Go,   tell   it on   the   moun - tain,

O - ver___ the hills   and   ev - 'ry - where.

Go,   tell   it on   the   moun - tain,

Our   heav'n - ly   Lord___   is   born.

E X T E N S I O N

NOTEWORTHY

steady beat
playing classroom instruments
Use with pages 87, 90, 95.

Key: A minor   Starting Pitch: A   Scale Tones: *mi si la ti do*ˡ

9B

6

El Nacimiento

Piano Accompaniment on page PA 107

Puerto Rican Folk Song

San Jo- sé y Ma- rí- a____

a Be- lén lle- ga- ron,____

Pi- die- ron po- sa- da____

y se la ne- ga- ron.____

SONGBOOK

"El Nacimiento"

TEACHING THE SONG

Have the children listen to the song and notice that it is sung in a language other than English (Spanish). The title "El Nacimiento" means "Manger Scene." The words mean "Saint Joseph and Mary arrived in Bethlehem. They asked for lodging and they were refused." Have eight houses around the room for a small group of children to visit. Have them walk the steady beat from house to house, singing the song. Have the children take turns being in the houses or being in the movement group. At first the group is refused entrance at each house, but then is let in. This dramatization is based on the Mexican custom of *Las Posadas*.

EXTENSION

PRONUNCIATION

El Nacimiento
el nä-si-myen′ tō

San José   y María
sän hō-sā′ ē mä-rē′ ä

a Belén   llegaron,
ä be-len′ ye-gä′ ron

Pidieron   posada
pē-dyer′ on pō-sä′ dä

y se la negaron.
ē se lä ne-gä′ ron

(You may wish to use the Recorded Lesson for the children to practice the Spanish words.)

NOTEWORTHY

steady beat
creative dramatization
Use with pages 87, 95.

SONGBOOK

"Must Be Santa"

TEACHING THE SONG

Have the children listen to the song. When they are familiar with the song, add the following movements with each of the rhyming word patterns.

special night—hold hands high
beard that's white—stroke beard

cap on head—hand on top of head
suit that's red—indicate jacket

ho, ho, ho—both hands on stomach
cherry nose—touch nose

reindeer sleigh—hands next to head with fingers spread out
come our way—beckon on each word
(You may wish to use pictures to illustrate the sequence of the rhyming word patterns. Put the pictures on the chalkboard or on a visual from top to bottom.) Sing the song with the movements.

Key: G   Starting Pitch: D   Scale Tones: *so, la, ti, do re mi fa*

Must Be Santa

Piano Accompaniment on page PA 108

Words and music by
Hal Moore and Bill Fredricks

1. Who's got a beard that's long and white?
2. Who's got boots and a suit of red?

San-ta's got a beard that's long and white.
San-ta's got boots and a suit of red.

Who comes a-round on a spe-cial night?
Who wears a long cap on his head?

San-ta comes a-round on a spe-cial night,
San-ta wears a long cap on his head,

MUST BE SANTA
Words and Music by Hal Moore and Bill Fredricks. TRO—
© Copyright 1960 (renewed 1988) Hollis Music, Inc., New York, NY.
Used by Permission.

EXTENSION

NOTEWORTHY

cumulative song
action song
Use with pages 85, 87, 95.

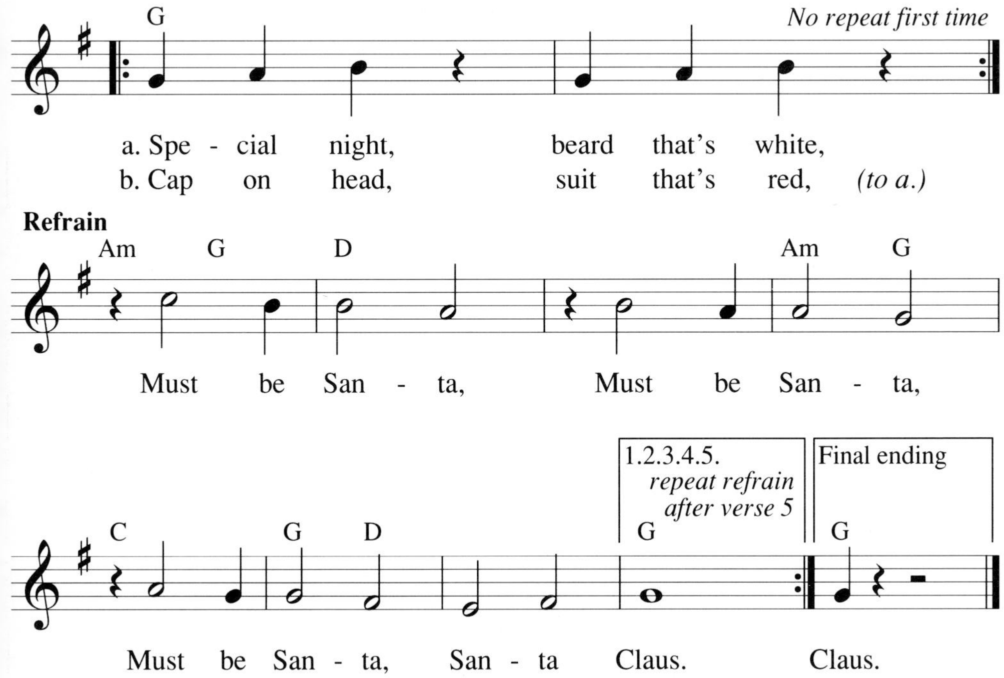

No repeat first time

G

a. Spe - cial   night,   beard   that's   white,
b. Cap   on   head,   suit   that's   red,   *(to a.)*

Refrain

Am   G   D   Am   G

Must   be   San - ta,   Must   be   San - ta,

1.2.3.4.5. *repeat refrain after verse 5*	Final ending
G	G

C   G   D

Must   be   San - ta,   San - ta   Claus.   Claus.

3. Who's got a great big cherry nose?
Santa's got a great big cherry nose.
Who laughs this way, "Ho, ho, ho!"
Santa laughs this way, "Ho, ho, ho!"
c. Ho, ho, ho, cherry nose, *(to b.)*

4. Who very soon will come our way?
Santa very soon will come our way.
Eight little reindeer pull his sleigh,
Santa's little reindeer pull his sleigh,
d. Reindeer sleigh, come our way, *(to c.)*

5. Dasher, Dancer, Prancer, Vixen,
Comet, Cupid, Donner, Blitzen,
Dasher, Dancer, Prancer, Vixen,
Comet, Cupid, Donner, Blitzen, *(to d.)*

Key: G   Starting Pitch: G   Scale Tones: *so, la, do re mi*

SONGBOOK

"He Had a Dream"

TEACHING THE SONG

Have the children softly pat a steady beat as they listen to the song. Discuss the meaning of the words in each section of the song. Listen again, raising one hand each time they hear a new section begin. Decide on a different way to keep the beat for each section, for example, pat the first section, tap shoulders for the second section, join hands and step around a circle to the left for the third section, tap shoulders for the fourth section, link arms and sway to the beat for the fifth section, and tap shoulders for the sixth section. Play different unpitched instruments on the beat in each section.

He Had a Dream

Piano Accompaniment on page PA 110

Words and music by
Ruth Manier

1. He want-ed ev-'ry-bod-y__ to have the same free-dom.
2. He want-ed ev-'ry-bod-y__ to join__ hands to-geth-er.

He want-ed ev-'ry-bod-y__ to have the same free-dom.
He want-ed ev-'ry-bod-y__ to join__ hands to-geth-er.

He want-ed ev-'ry-bod-y__ to have the same free-dom.__
He want-ed ev-'ry-bod-y__ to join__ hands to-geth-er.__

This was his dream.

% Refrain

Doc - tor King,__ Doc - tor King,__

Doc - tor King__ was a civ - il rights lead - er,

EXTENSION

NOTEWORTHY

steady beat
movement to a steady beat
Martin Luther King Day
playing unpitched instruments
identifying sections of a song
Use with pages 113, 117.

Doc - tor King,__ Doc - tor King,__

He had a dream.

Fine

3. Let's all love each oth - er and live like broth-ers,

Let's all love each oth - er and live like broth-ers,

Let's all love each oth - er and live like broth-ers,

and make his dream come true.

D.C. al Fine

CURRICULUM CONNECTION: SOCIAL STUDIES

Dr. Martin Luther King, Jr. (1929-1968)— American civil rights leader, was a Baptist minister. He spent his life working to end discrimination against African Americans in the United States through peaceful means. His philosophies and powerful speaking voice won him the support of millions of people of all races. His most famous speech, "I have a dream," was given from the steps of the Lincoln Memorial to a crowd of more than 200,000 people during the 1963 March on Washington, D.C. In 1965 Dr. King was awarded the Nobel Peace Prize for his work.

SONGBOOK

"I Made a Valentine"

TEACHING THE SONG

Have the children listen to the song, to see if they hear any phrases (lines) of the song that are the same. Have them echo-sing each phrase to figure out that the first two are exactly the same and the last one begins the same way. Have them identify the singing voice as that of a child.

I Made a Valentine

Piano Accompaniment on page PA 113

Words and music by Lynn Freeman Olson

EXTENSION

NOTEWORTHY

same and different phrases
tone color of child singing
Use with pages 145, 161.

The Best of Friends

Piano Accompaniment on page PA 114

Words and music by
Helen Taylor

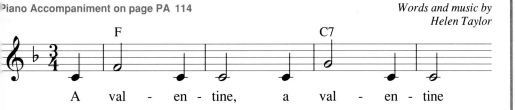

A val - en - tine,   a   val - en - tine

I   give   to   you   to   say _____

that   we   are   friends,   the   best   of   friends,

to - day   and   ev - 'ry - day. _____

EXTENSION

SONGBOOK

"The Best of Friends"

TEACHING THE SONG

Have the children pat the strong beat as they listen to the song in preparation for passing a valentine around a circle. Have them join in singing as soon as they are able and continue to pat the strong beat. When they can keep together fairly well, have them sit close together in a circle and pass a valentine from one child to the next on the strong beat.

To reinforce higher and lower pitches in the melody, have the children move one hand to show how the melody moves on the words *we are friends* and *best of friends.* (Each example moves downward.)

NOTEWORTHY
strong beat
downward
Use with pages 145, 149.

SONGBOOK

Key: G   Starting Pitch: D   Scale Tones: *so la ti do re mi fa s*

My Valentine

Piano Accompaniment on page PA 116

Words and music by
Edith Savage

"My Valentine"

TEACHING THE SONG

Have the children listen to the song and notice the beats of silence. Have them listen again, tapping on the beat of silence that comes just before the word *making* each time it occurs in the song. (You may wish to have the children point to someone in the room on the word *you*.) Draw the symbol for a beat of silence (𝄽) on the chalkboard or put the stick-on quarter rest on the inside front cover of the Big Book. Have the children sing the song again without tapping as you point to the quarter rest on the beats of silence. Sing the song again as individual children take turns pointing to the quarter rest on the beats of silence. You may wish to have the children sing the song as they make valentines, a valentine box, or Valentine's Day classroom decorations.

I'm   mak-ing   a big red   val-en-tine,   I'm   mak-ing a big red

val-en-tine,   I'm   mak-ing   a big red   val-en-tine,   It's

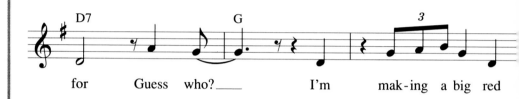

for   Guess   who?____   I'm   mak-ing   a big red

val-en-tine,   I'm   mak-ing a big red   val-en-tine,   I'm

EXTENSION

NOTEWORTHY

beat
beat of silence
Use with pages 155, 157.

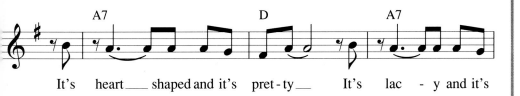

mak-ing a big red val-en-tine, Just for you!

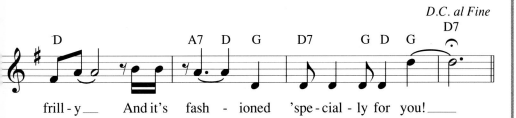

It's heart___ shaped and it's pret-ty___ It's lac - y and it's

frill-y___ And it's fash - ioned 'spe-cial-ly for you!___

SONGBOOK

"America"

TEACHING THE SONG

Have the children listen to the song. Discuss what the song is about (our country, the United States of America). Listen for words in the song that describe our country (*my country, sweet land of liberty,* and so on). Discuss the meanings of any unfamiliar words. Discuss how to show respect for our country as they sing the song (standing straight, singing with accuracy, paying attention). Sing the song several times and identify the high and low parts in the song. Have them try to use their singing voices accurately on the higher pitches.

America

Piano Accompaniment on page PA 118

Music by Henry Carey
Words by Samuel F. Smith

My coun-try 'tis of thee, Sweet land of lib-er-ty, Of thee I sing. Land where my fa-thers died, Land of the Pil-grim's pride, From ev-'ry__ moun-tain-side Let__ free-dom ring.

EXTENSION

NOTEWORTHY

focus on singing voices
patriotic song
Use with pages 155, 157.

Ah! Les Jolis Papillons

CD 6

Piano Accompaniment on page PA 119

St. Pierre and Miquelon
Folk Song

Ah! les   jo-lis pa-pil - lons, Comme ils   vol-ent, comme il   vol'.

Ah! les   jo-lis pa-pil - lons, Comme ils   vol-ent tous en   rond!

SONGBOOK

"Ah! Les Jolis Papillons"

TEACHING THE SONG

Have the children listen to the song and notice that it is sung in a language other than English (French). The title "Ah! Les Jolis Papillons" means "Oh! The Pretty Butterflies." The words mean:
"Oh! The pretty butterflies,
How they fly, how they fly.
Oh! The pretty butterflies,
How they circle in the sky!"
Echo-say the words, two measures at a time. Then echo-sing the song, keeping the steady beat. Sing the song.

EXTENSION

PRONUNCIATION

Ah! les jolis   papillons,
ä   lā   zho-lē′ pä-pē-yoN′

Comme ils volent, comme ils vol′.
kom   ēl vol′ ə   kom   ēl vol

Ah! le jolis   papillons,
ä   lā   zho-lē′ pä-pē-yoN′

Comme ils volent tous en   rond!
kom   ēl vol′ ə tōōs oN roN

(You may wish to use the Recorded Lesson for the children to practice the French words.)

MORE MUSIC TEACHING IDEAS

1. As the children sing "Ah! Les Jolis Papillons," have one child play E and B on the strong beat using a pitched instrument.
2. Add an introduction and coda to the song by playing the rhythm of the last two measures of the song on B G♯ F♯ F♯ E, using a pitched instrument such as resonator bells.

NOTEWORTHY

French language
steady beat
strong beat in $\frac{2}{4}$
quarter notes and eighth notes
Use with pages 183, 189, 215, 217, 219, 223.

SONGBOOK

"Baby Beluga"

TEACHING THE SONG

Have the children listen to the song and determine what the song is about (a little white whale called a *beluga*). Identify the words that repeat in every verse (*baby beluga, oh, baby beluga*). Listen to the song again, singing along with these repeated words. Discuss the information about belugas in the song (they live deep in the sea; they swim; they are white; they have parents; they dive and splash; they can squirt water from their spouts; they can sing). Learn all the words by repeating them several times. Then have the children move around the room like whales, using graceful, fluid movements.

Key: F   Starting Pitch: A   Scale Tones: *so, ti, do re mi fa fi so la*

Baby Beluga

Piano Accompaniment on page PA 120

Words and music by Raffi and D. Pike

E X T E N S I O N

NOTEWORTHY

repeated words
same and different
whales
creative movement
Use with pages 119, 172.

CURRICULUM CONNECTION: SCIENCE

Belugas—are small, white whales that measure 10 to 15 feet long. Most belugas live in the Arctic. Whales must come up to the surface of the water to breathe. They do this through blowholes on the tops of their heads. When a whale exhales, it produces a cloud, called a *blow* or *spout*, that consists mostly of water vapor. (For more information on whales, see page 119.)

Ba - by be - lu - ga.

Oh, ba - by be - lu - ga.

Is the wa - ter warm? Is your ma - ma home with
Sing your lit - tle song; Sing for all your friends. We
With to - mor - row's sun, ano - 'ther day's be - gun, You'll

you so hap - py?
like to hear you.
soon be wak - ing.

Coda

go._____ You're just a lit - tle white whale on the go.

SONGBOOK

"The Bus"

TEACHING THE SONG

Have the children pretend to be riding a bus. Have them sit in two rows with an aisle down the middle and "bounce" in their seats on the steady beat. Then choose one child to be the driver. This child leads the movements that accompany the song, for example, stand up and sit down, move hand round and round, blow the horn, move hands like windshield wipers, wave to the passengers. Do each movement with the appropriate verse. Add new verses to the song based on the children's experiences riding on a bus, or things they imagine might occur on a bus. Think of movements to go with these new verses.

CD 6

The Bus

Piano Accompaniment on page PA 122

Play Song

1. The peo - ple on the bus go up and down,
2. The wheels__ on the bus go 'round and 'round,

up and down, up and down,
'round and 'round, 'round and 'round,

The peo - ple on the bus go up and down
The wheels__ on the bus go 'round and 'round

All through the town.
All through the town.

3. The horn on the bus goes "Toot! toot! toot!"

4. The wiper on the bus goes "Swish! swish! swish!"

5. The driver on the bus says, "Let them on!"

E X T E N S I O N

NOTEWORTHY

dramatization
steady beat
making up verses
Use with pages 43, 49, 51, 53, 85, 133, 149, 161, 189, 201, 215, 217.

Clap Your Hands

Piano Accompaniment on page PA 124   *American Folk Song*

With energy

Verse

Clap,   clap,   clap   your   hands,

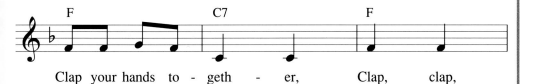

Clap   your   hands   to - geth - er,   Clap,   clap,

clap   your   hands,   Clap   your   hands   to - geth   -   er.

Refrain *(Instrumental only)*

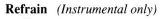

E X T E N S I O N

SONGBOOK

"Clap Your Hands"

TEACHING THE SONG

Have the children clap as they listen to the first section of the song. (If children have difficulty clapping the steady beat, have them hold one hand out and tap it with the other hand. The children may have more success producing a musical sound by clapping with the dominant hand only.) Have the children each find a different way to keep the beat during the refrain, for example, patting knees. When they repeat the first section, the children resume clapping together. Have the children create new verses by substituting different movements for *clap your hands,* for example, *nod your head.*

NOTEWORTHY

steady beat
two sections
creative movement
hearing ♩ and ♫
Use with pages 5, 9, 108, 195, 211.

SONGBOOK

"Down at the Station"

TEACHING THE SONG

Have the children listen, imitating you as you dramatize the song with simple hand movements. Have them listen again, doing the movements and singing along as they are able. Then have the children sing *Chug! Chug! Woo! Woo!* and decide if *Woo! Woo!* is higher or lower than *Chug! Chug!* (higher). Have them sing *Off we go* and decide if the melody moves higher or lower (lower). Form a line and have the children sing the song as they move like a train around the room, sliding their feet to the beat. The first child in line is the engineer and pretends to blow the whistle on *Woo! Woo!*

Down at the Station

Piano Accompaniment on page PA 126   *Traditional*

Down at the sta - tion, ear - ly in the morn - ing,

See the lit - tle puf - fer bil - lies all in a row.

See the en - gine driv - er pull the lit - tle han - dle.

Chug! Chug! Woo! Woo! Off we go.

E X T E N S I O N

NOTEWORTHY

beat
higher and lower
Use with pages 49, 51, 53, 177, 181.

Key: G   Starting Pitch: D   Scale Tones: *so, la, ti, do re mi fa*   10A
                                                                                   CD 6

Epo i tai tai e

Piano Accompaniment on page PA 127   *Maori Folk Song*

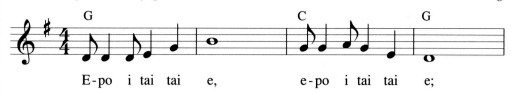

E-po i tai tai   e,   e-po i tai tai   e;

E - po   i tai   tai   e-po   i tu - ki tu - ki,

E - po   i tu - ki tu - ki   e.

SONGBOOK

"Epo i tai tai e"

TEACHING THE SONG

Have the children pat the beat as they listen to the song. Have them listen again, imitating you as you alternately pat the first two beats and tap one index finger with the other for the next two beats. Have them sing the song as they are able, continuing to imitate your movements. This time lightly tap one finger with the other while holding both hands overhead each time the words *tuki tuki* occur in the song. Later, if the children are able, you may wish to have them switch from tapping two fingers together to crossing their arms and tapping both upper arms with their hands. This pattern can be done with rhythm sticks or bamboo sticks, patting the floor instead of legs. The words of the song mean "This is a strong man. This strong man fights like a bull."

EXTENSION

PRONUNCIATION

Epo i tai tai e,
e' pō ē tī tī e

epo   i tai tai e;
e' pō ē tī tī e

Epo i tai tai epo i tuki   tuki,
e' pō ē tī tī e' pō ē tōō' kē tōō' kē

Epo i tuki   tuki   e.
e' pō ē tōō' kē tōō' kē e

CURRICULUM CONNECTION: SOCIAL STUDIES

Maoris (mă' ō-rēz)—were the original inhabitants of New Zealand. They belong to the Polynesian race. Long before the European settlers came to New Zealand the Maoris had established villages and developed a well-organized society. They fished and hunted, and later became farmers and skilled wood carvers. During World War II many Maoris moved from the villages into the cities because of the educational and job opportunities there. Although most Maoris speak English, many continue to speak the traditional Maori language at special social gatherings.

NOTEWORTHY

beat
Use with pages 41, 47, 108, 181, 219, 223.

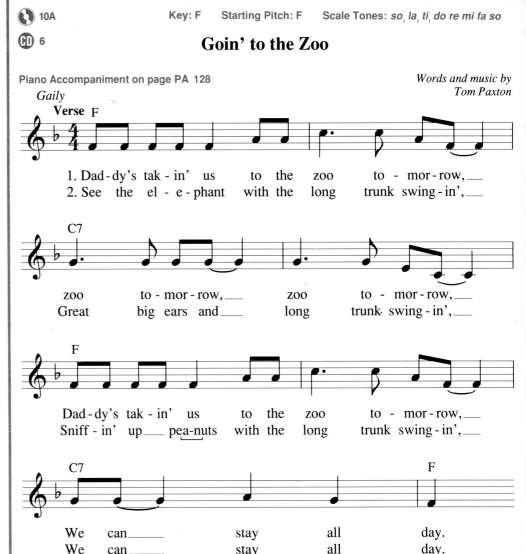
SONGBOOK

"Goin' to the Zoo"

TEACHING THE SONG

Have the children listen to the song and dramatize the movements of the animals mentioned. (You may wish to guide the children by dramatizing the song with them.) Have them listen again, singing along as they are able. Encourage them to notice that the song is in two sections, and that the second section is always the same. Tell them that the second section is called the *refrain*. Have them find the words in the refrain that are sung three times (*zoo, you, too*). Discover that these are rhyming words. Have them think of other words that rhyme with these words (*do, goo, moo,* and so on). Choose one instrument, such as a triangle, and take turns playing on the rhyming words as they sing the song again. Use multiple instruments if they are available. Any children who are not playing instruments can pat the strong beat throughout the song.

Goin' to the Zoo

Piano Accompaniment on page PA 128

Words and music by
Tom Paxton

Gaily

Verse

1. Dad-dy's tak-in' us to the zoo to-mor-row,___
2. See the el-e-phant with the long trunk swing-in',___

zoo to-mor-row,___ zoo to-mor-row,___
Great big ears and___ long trunk swing-in',___

Dad-dy's tak-in' us to the zoo to-mor-row,___
Sniff-in' up___ pea-nuts with the long trunk swing-in',___

We can___ stay all day.
We can___ stay all day.

EXTENSION

NOTEWORTHY

AB or verse-and-refrain form
strong beat in $\frac{4}{4}$ meter
rhyming words
dramatizing a song
Use with pages 117, 127, 181.

Refrain

We're go - in' to the zoo, zoo, zoo.

How a - bout you, you, you?

You can come too, too, too.

We're go - in' to the zoo, zoo, zoo.

3. See all the monkeys scritch, scritch, scratchin',
   Jumpin' round scritch, scritch, scratchin',
   Hangin' by their long tails scritch, scritch, scratchin',
   We can stay all day.

4. Big black bear all huff, a-puffin',
   Coat's too heavy, he's a-puffin',
   Don't get too near the huff, a-puffin',
   You can't stay all day.

5. Seals in the pool all honk, honk, honkin',
   Catchin' fish and honk, honk, honkin',
   Little seals honk, honk, honk-honkin',
   We can stay all day.

6. We stayed all day, and I'm gettin' sleepy,
   Gettin' sleepy, gettin' sleepy,
   Home already and I'm sleep, sleep, sleepy,
   We have stayed all day.

SONGBOOK

"Happy Birthday"

TEACHING THE SONG

Have the children sing this song any day someone in the class has a birthday. Insert the name of the child whose birthday it is in the appropriate place. After singing the song, you may wish to have the birthday child and two friends play three different unpitched instruments as the class sings the song again. The first child plays on the words *happy birthday*, the second child plays on *you*, and the birthday child plays on his or her name. Other occasions, such as Visitors' Day, can be substituted for the word *birthday*.

Happy Birthday

Piano Accompaniment on page PA 130

*Words and music by
Mildred and Patty Hill*

Hap - py Birth - day to you, Hap - py Birth - day to you,

Hap - py Birth - day dear_____ Hap - py Birth - day to you.

E X T E N S I O N

NOTEWORTHY

birthday song
playing classroom instruments
Use with pages 215, 217.

Hokey Pokey

Piano Accompaniment on page PA 130

American Singing Game

With a swing

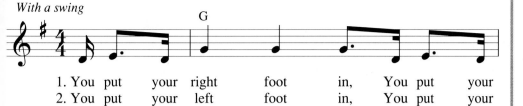

1. You put your right foot in, You put your
2. You put your left foot in, You put your

right foot out, You put your right foot in and you
left foot out, You put your left foot in and you

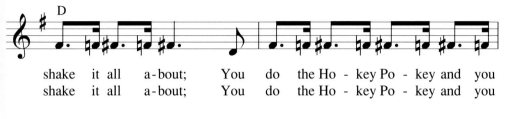

shake it all a-bout; You do the Ho - key Po - key and you
shake it all a-bout; You do the Ho - key Po - key and you

turn your-self a-round. That's what it's all a - bout!
turn your-self a-round. That's what it's all a - bout!

3. You put your right arm in . . .

4. You put your left arm in . . .

5. You put your whole self in . . .

EXTENSION

SONGBOOK

"Hokey Pokey"

TEACHING THE SONG

Form a circle. Listen to the song, and have the children imitate you as you move according to the words in each verse. On the words *you do the Hokey Pokey and you turn yourself around,* turn around in place, moving hips and hands from side to side on the beat. Clap the strong beats with ***that's*** *what it's* **all a-bout.**

NOTEWORTHY
beat
body parts
Use with pages 11, 15, 19, 23, 25.

"Jig Jog, Jig Jog"

TEACHING THE SONG

Have the children pat the beat as they listen to the song. Have them echo-sing the song. Identify the rhyming words or syllables (*pony* and *bony, ride* and *-side*). Have them listen again and identify the part that sounds different (the third phrase). Then have the children sing the entire song. Have some children move like ponies using a high-stepping jog, while others take turns playing the beat on rhythm sticks or temple blocks. (A similar effect can be achieved by alternating tapping inverted disposable cups or large lids on the floor or a table.) Have the children discover where in the song they are singing just two pitches, *mi* and *so* (most of the pitches in measures 1-3, 5-7, and 13-15).

Key: C   Starting Pitch: E   Scale Tones: *do re mi fa so la do¹*

Jig Jog, Jig Jog

Piano Accompaniment on page PA 132   *Anonymous*

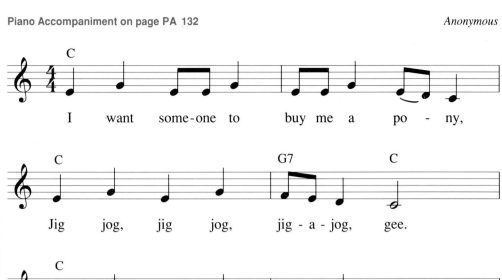

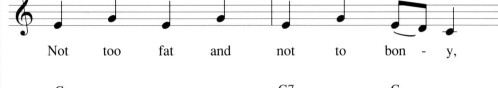

EXTENSION

NOTEWORTHY

mi and *so*
beat
same and different phrases
dramatizing a song
Use with pages 29, 35, 43, 83, 97, 113, 175, 185.

For I want to go for a ride

All a - round the coun - try side,

With a Jig jog, jig jog, jig jog, jig jog,

jig jog, jig - a - jog, gee.

SONGBOOK

"Little Spotted Puppy"

TEACHING THE SONG

Have the children listen to the song and notice where they hear barks. Listen to the song again, barking at those places. Dramatize the last half of each verse, as the words suggest. Then have the children echo-say the words of the first eight measures, two measures at a time. Have them sing the entire song as they are able. Sing the song without the barks, and notice that the barks occur on beats of silence in the melody. Draw two quarter rests (𝄽 𝄽) on the chalkboard or put two quarter rest stick-ons in the middle two doghouses on the top of Chart 37 (page 137). Have the children sing the song again as you point to the rests on the appropriate beats. Sing the entire song, including the barks, with the dramatization.

Piano Accompaniment on page PA 134

Words and music by
Lynn Freeman Olson

1. When a lit - tle spot - ted pup - py,
2. Oh, it real - ly made me hap - py

Just as nois - y as could be,
When I heard that he could stay!

Came to vis - it us in our house,
Now I help with all his groom - ing,

I could tell that he liked me.
And I feed him ev - 'ry day.

E X T E N S I O N

NOTEWORTHY

same and different phrases
beats of silence
dramatizing a song
Use with pages 29, 35, 43, 127, 137, 139, 172.

'Cause he wig-gled his ears, and he wag-gled his tail,
So, he wig-gles his ears, and he wag-gles his tail,

And he barked, and he barked!
And he barks, and he barks!

'Cause he wig-gled his ears, and he wag-gled his tail,
So, he wig-gles his ears, and he wag-gles his tail,

And he barked, and he barked!
And he barks, and he barks!

SONGBOOK

"Little Red Caboose"

TEACHING THE SONG

Have the children listen to the song. Then have them practice making the train whistle sound (*woo-woo-woo!*) as they pretend to pull the chord that blows the whistle. Have the children practice saying the words. Then have them listen to the song again, singing along as they are able. Have the children discover that the first two measures of the song use just two pitches, *so* and *mi*. When the children know the song well, play this movement game. Choose two children to pretend to be an engine and a caboose. As the class sings the song, the engine and the caboose move around the room, sliding their feet to the beat. At the end of the song they select one child to be a railroad car. That child stands between the engine and the caboose and moves with them as the class sings the song again. Continue the game until all the children are part of the train. When the children can sing the song without help from you or the recording, have them increase the tempo as they sing and play the game.

CD 6

Little Red Caboose

Piano Accompaniment on page PA 136   *Traditional*

Lit - tle red ca - boose,   lit - tle red ca - boose,

Lit - tle red ca - boose be - hind the train, ___ the train. ___

Smoke-stack on his back,   go - ing down the track.

Lit - tle red ca - boose be - hind the train.   (Woo - woo - woo!)

EXTENSION

NOTEWORTHY

beat
tempo
mi and *so*
dramatizing a song
Use with pages 5, 9, 133, 149, 161, 177, 181, 189, 207.

CURRICULUM CONNECTION: SOCIAL STUDIES

The Caboose—usually the last car on a freight train, is traditionally colored red. The caboose serves as an office for the conductor, living quarters for the train crew, and sometimes carries passengers. The smokestack mentioned in the song is the chimney for the train crew's stove.

Key: D   Starting Pitch: D   Scale Tones: *do re mi fa so la ti*   🔊 10B   💿 6

Los Pollitos

Piano Accompaniment on page PA 137   *Ecuadorian Children's Song*

Los po - lli - tos   di - cen,   "pí - o, pí - o,   pí - o,"

cuan - do tien - en ham - bre,   cuan - do tien - en frí - o.

SONGBOOK

"Los Pollitos"

TEACHING THE SONG

Have the children pat the beat or pretend to scratch the ground like chickens as they listen to the song. Notice that the song is sung in a language other than English (Spanish). The title "Los Pollitos" means "The Little Chickens." The words mean "Little chickens say peep, peep, peep when they are hungry, when they are cold." Have the children listen again and count the number of beats in the song (sixteen). Have them take turns making vertical marks in a line for each beat on the chalkboard. Then have the children sing the song, pointing the beat. Have them echo-say the rhythm with you, two measures at a time. Discover if the rhythm of each two-measure segment is the same or different (the same). Play the rhythm pattern ♫ ♫ ♩ ♩ on classroom instruments. Decide if the melody of the first two measures moves upward or downward (upward). Have the children take turns playing this pattern on resonator bells (D E F♯ G A A).

Echo-sing the song with the children, two measures at a time. When the children can sing the song well, have them take turns accompanying the song with a D and A bordun on the beat as other children play any two pitches in D pentatonic (D E F♯ A B) on each quarter note in the melody. Have three children pretend to be the cold and hungry chickens as the class sings the song. Then have the children improvise a scene showing what they think happened to the chickens.

EXTENSION

PRONUNCIATION

Los pollitos   dicen
lōs pō-yē′ tos dē′ sen

"Pío, pío,   pío,"
pē′ ō pē′ ō pē′ ō

cuando   tienen   hambre,
kwän′ dō tyen′ en äm′ brā

cuando   tienen   frío.
kwän′ dō tyen′ en frē′ ō

(You may wish to use the Recorded Lesson for the children to practice the Spanish words.)

NOTEWORTHY

beat
higher and lower
hearing ♩ and ♫
Use with pages 29, 35, 195, 211, 215, 217, 219, 223.

SONGBOOK

"Marching Round the Levee"

TEACHING THE SONG

Have the children sit in a large circle with plenty of space in between each child. Listen to the song, patting the beat. Then have them stand and step the beat in place as they listen to the song again. Choose one child to move as suggested by the words of the song, for example,

verse 1—march around the outside of the circle

verse 2—march in and out of the spaces between each child while moving around the circle

verse 3—continue marching in and out of the spaces; stop and face a partner at the end of the verse

verse 4—kneel before the partner, improvising a way to keep the beat; the partner kneels and imitates the movement

verse 5—march around the outside of the circle with the partner

The child chosen as the partner starts the game again. Continue the game to give others a turn.

Marching Round the Levee

Piano Accompaniment on page PA 138

Traditional

1. We're march - ing round the lev - ee,
2. Go in and out the win - dow,
3. Go forth and face your part - ner,
4. I kneel be - fore my part - ner,
5. And now I'll take my part - ner,

We're march - ing round the lev - ee,
Go in and out the win - dow,
Go forth and face your part - ner,
I kneel be - fore my part - ner,
And now I'll take my part - ner,

We're march - ing round the lev - ee,
Go in and out the win - dow,
Go forth and face your part - ner,
I kneel be - fore my part - ner,
And now I'll take my part - ner,

As we have done be - fore.
As we have done be - fore.
As we have done be - fore.
As I have done be - fore.
As I have done be - fore.

EXTENSION

NOTEWORTHY

steady beat
circle game
dramatization of text
sequence of multiple verses
Use with pages 15, 133.

My Head and My Shoulders

Piano Accompaniment on page PA 139   *Zulu Singing Game*

My   head   and   my   shoul - ders,

My   chest   and   my   mid - dle,

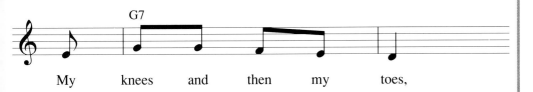

My   knees   and   then   my   toes,

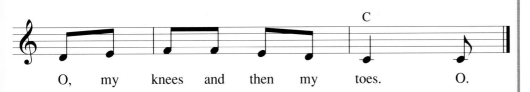

O,   my   knees   and   then   my   toes.   O.

SONGBOOK

"My Head and My Shoulders"

TEACHING THE SONG

Have the children pat the beat as they listen to the song. Then have them listen again, touching the appropriate body part as it is mentioned in the song. Have them discover that they are only moving on the strong beat. Echo-say the words with you as they mirror your movements. Sing the song, doing the movements. Then sing the song, tapping the rhythm of the words.

E X T E N S I O N

MORE MUSIC TEACHING IDEAS

You may wish to teach the children the Zulu words to "My Head and My Shoulders":
I khanda, mahlombe sifuba, nokhalo, madolo, namazwane, madolo, namazwane.

PRONUNCIATION

I khanda, mahlombe
ē kä' ndä mä-lō' mbā

sifuba,   nokhalo,
sē-fōō' bä nō-kä' lō

madolo,   namazwane,
mä-dō' lō nä-mä-zwä' nā

madolo,   namazwane.
mä-dō' lō nä-mä-zwä' nā

CURRICULUM CONNECTION:
SOCIAL STUDIES

Zulu (zōō' lōō)—one of the main Bantu-speaking peoples of Africa. Most Zulus live in the province of Natal in the Republic of South Africa. Zulus were originally farmers and cattle-herders, and lived in well-organized villages under a powerful ruler. Today many Zulus live in cities.

NOTEWORTHY

beat
strong beat in ²⁄₄ meter
rhythm of words
singing ♩ and ♫
Use with pages 9, 11, 15, 23, 25, 95, 97, 193, 205, 209, 223.

SONGBOOK

"Old Dan Tucker"

TEACHING THE SONG

Have the children listen to the song. Then have them echo-say the words with you, two measures at a time. Discuss the humor and the absurd statements in the song, such as *had a toothache in his heel,* and so on. Tell the children that this was a very popular song in Abraham Lincoln's time, and was one of his favorite songs. If possible, have the children echo-sing the song, two measures at a time. Then have them listen again, patting beats one and three during the refrain, and singing along as they are able. When they know the song well, have them stand in a circle, sing the verse, and walk on beats one and three during the refrain.

Old Dan Tucker

Piano Accompaniment on page PA 140

Words and music by
Dan Emmett

1. Old Dan Tuck-er was a fine old man,
2. Come to town the oth - er night.
3. Old Dan Tuck-er and I fell out

He washed his face in the fry - ing pan,
I heard the noise and saw the fight.
and what do you think it was all a - bout?

He combed his hair with a wag - on wheel,
The watch - man he was run - nin' 'round,
He bor - rowed my old set - tin' hen,

And had a tooth - ache in this heel;
Said "Old Dan Tuck-er's come to town."
And did - n't bring her back a - gain.

E X T E N S I O N

NOTEWORTHY

beat
AB form
Use with pages 123, 155, 157, 161, 163, 193, 205, 209.

Refrain

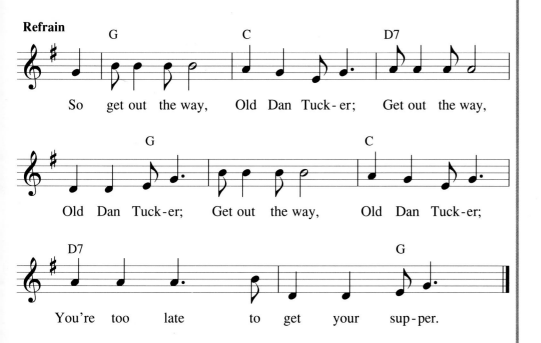

So   get out the way,   Old Dan Tuck - er;   Get out   the way,

Old   Dan Tuck - er;   Get out   the way,   Old   Dan Tuck - er;

You're   too   late   to   get   your   sup - per.

SONGBOOK

"Peanut Butter"

TEACHING THE SONG

Have the children listen to the song, imitating you as you pat the steady beat. Stop patting and whisper the word *jelly* whenever it occurs in the song. Have the children think of different movements to do on the steady beat for each verse, for example, pretend to dig up peanuts and then rotate palms together for verse 1, pretend to pick grapes and then step and twist on the balls of their feet for verse 2, pretend to spread a slice of bread with peanut butter and eat it for verse 3. Sing the song, doing the movements. Have the children identify the different kinds of voices they used with this song (singing, speaking, and whispering).

Peanut Butter

Piano Accompaniment on page PA 142

Camp Song

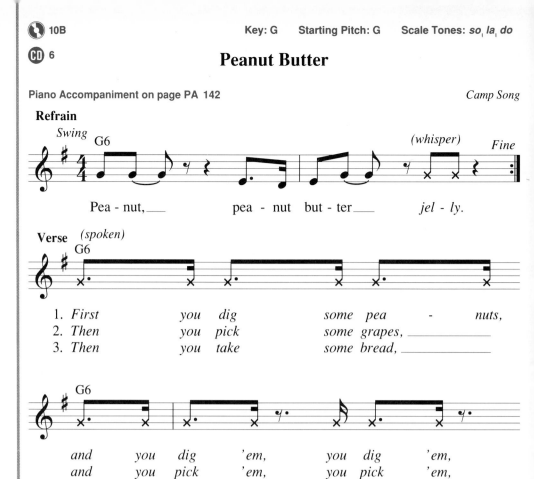

Refrain

Pea - nut,___ pea - nut but - ter___ jel - ly.

Verse *(spoken)*

1. First   you   dig   some pea -   nuts,
2. Then   you   pick   some grapes,_____
3. Then   you   take   some bread,_____

and   you   dig   'em,   you   dig   'em,
and   you   pick   'em,   you   pick   'em,
and   you   spread   it,   you   spread   it,

E X T E N S I O N

NOTEWORTHY

using singing, speaking, whispering voices
dramatization of text
Use with pages 145, 161, 169, 201.

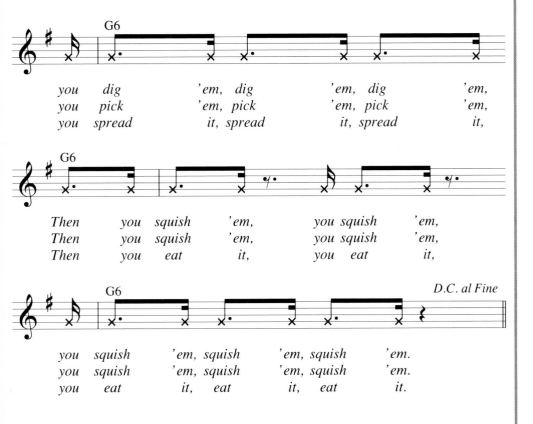

G6

you dig 'em, dig 'em, dig 'em,
you pick 'em, pick 'em, pick 'em,
you spread it, spread it, spread it,

G6

Then you squish 'em, you squish 'em,
Then you squish 'em, you squish 'em,
Then you eat it, you eat it,

D.C. al Fine

G6

you squish 'em, squish 'em, squish 'em.
you squish 'em, squish 'em, squish 'em.
you eat it, eat it, eat it.

SONGBOOK

"Que Bonito Es"

TEACHING THE SONG

Have the children listen to the song. Notice that the song is sung in a language other than English (Spanish). The title "Que Bonito Es" means "How wonderful it is." The words mean:

"Listen, listen.
How wonderful it is.
I sing, I read two languages well.
All of you tell me I will triumph.
How wonderful to be bilingual.
How wonderful to be bilingual."

Discuss the meaning of the words. Practice pronouncing the Spanish words. Have the children listen to the song several times. Echo-sing the song with you, four measures at a time. After they know the song, have the children compare the first four measures with the second four measures and discover whether the second part is higher or lower than the first (higher). Have the children compare similar four-measure segments in the song and find where they are different. (Measures 1-4 and measures 9-12 begin the same, but end differently. Measures 13-16 and measures 17-20 begin differently but end the same.) Have the children accompany the song, playing the beat on maracas or other appropriate instruments.

Que Bonito Es

Piano Accompaniment on page PA 144

Words and music by
Belle San Miguel-Ortiz

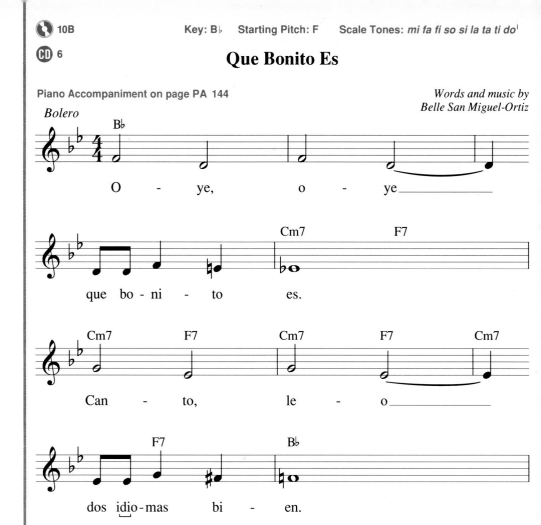

O - ye, o - ye_____

que bo-ni - to es.

Can - to, le - o_____

dos idio-mas bi - en.

Dí - gan - me to - dos,_____

E X T E N S I O N

NOTEWORTHY
beat
same and different
higher and lower
Use with pages 108, 161, 163, 175, 185.

PRONUNCIATION

Oye, oye, que bonito es.
o' ye o' ye ke bo-nē' tō es

Canto, leo dos idiomas bien.
kän' tō le' ō dos ēd' ē-o-mäs bē-yen'

Díganme todos,
dē' gän-me to' dos

Yo triunfaré.
yo trē-ōōn-fä' re

Alser bilingüe que bonito es.
äl-ser' bē-lin' gwe ke bo-nē' tō es

Alser bilingüe que bonito es.
äl-ser' bē-lin' gwe ke bo-nē' tō es

(You may wish to use the Recorded Lesson for the children to practice the Spanish words.)

yo tri - un - fa - ré.

Al - ser bi - lin - güe

que bo - ni - to es.

Al - ser bi - lin - güe

que bo - ni - to es.

SONGBOOK

"Step in Time"

TEACHING THE SONG

Have the children listen to the song, doing the movements mentioned in each verse on the beat. As they become familiar with the song, sing along as they are able.

CD 6

Step in Time

Piano Accompaniment on page PA 146

Words and music by
Richard M. and Robert B. Sherman

1. Kick your knees up, step in time!
2. Spin a - bout and step in time!

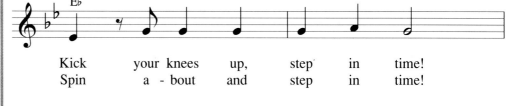

Kick your knees up, step in time!
Spin a - bout and step in time!

Nev - er need a rea - son, nev - er need a rhyme,

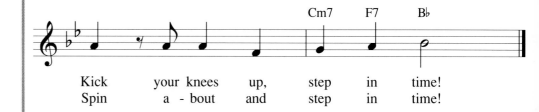

Kick your knees up, step in time!
Spin a - bout and step in time!

3. Link your elbows, step in time! . . .

4. 'Round the circle, step in time! . . .

5. Fly like a birdie, step in time! . . .

6. Step in time, step in time! . . .

EXTENSION

NOTEWORTHY

beat
Use with pages 33, 87, 90, 123, 181, 205, 209.

Uncle Jessie

Piano Accompaniment on page PA 148

New words and new music adaptation by
Bessie Jones

Ad lib

Verse

Now, here comes Un-cle Jes-sie, Com-ing through the field

With his horse and bug-gy, And I know just how he feels.

Refrain

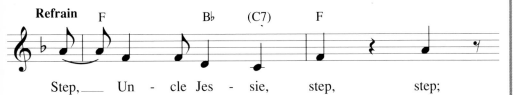

Step,___ Un - cle Jes - sie, step, step;

Step,___ Un - cle Jes - sie, step, step,

Walk,___ Un - cle Jes - sie, walk, walk;

Walk,___ Un - cle Jes - sie, walk.

EXTENSION

ADDITIONAL VERSES

2. Now, if you want a sweetheart,
   I'll tell you what to do,
   Just take some salt and pepper
   And sprinkle it in your shoe.
   (Refrain)

3. Now, if you want Uncle Jessie
   To do what you want him to do,
   You take some garlic and onion
   And put it in his shoe.
   (Refrain)

SONGBOOK

"Uncle Jessie"

TEACHING THE SONG

Have the children listen to the song. Notice that the beat is more definite in the refrain. Listen again, doing the movements described in the refrain. Then have the children form a circle. Choose one child to be Uncle Jessie. As the children sing, Uncle Jessie moves around the circle, walking slowly during the verse and stepping in rhythm during the refrain. The other children tap or pat the strong beat during the refrain. At the end of the refrain, the child in the circle nearest to Uncle Jessie becomes the new Uncle Jessie, and the game continues.

NOTEWORTHY

beat
strong beat in $\frac{4}{4}$ meter
verse-and-refrain form
dramatizing a song
Use with pages 69, 123, 131, 145, 172, 193, 205, 207, 209.

ABA form music that has three parts, or sections. The first section is followed by a different section, which is followed by a repeat of the first section.

accompaniment a musical background for the melody.

bar line a line that divides notes on a staff into sets.

beat the basic unit of time in music.

brass family instruments including trumpet, trombone, French horn, and tuba.

coda a short ending section.

contrast a thing that is very different from something else.

dynamics the loudness or softness of sound.

eighth notes (♪♪).

form the order of sections in music.

forte loud.

half note (♩).

measure a set of notes between two bar lines.

melody the tune; a series of pitches moving upward, downward, or staying the same.

note a symbol of musical sound.

ostinato a repeated melodic or rhythmic pattern.

percussion family instruments such as the drum, wood block, tambourine, and xylophone that are struck, shaken, or scraped to produce a sound.

phrase a short section of music that is a musical thought.

piano soft.

pitch the highness or lowness of a sound.

quarter note (♩).

quarter rest (𝄽).

refrain the recurring section of a song that always has the same words.

rest a symbol for silence in music.

rhythm the organization of musical sounds with regard to their duration.

rhythm pattern an organized group of long and short sounds.

section a part of the whole.

staff the lines and spaces on which music is written.

string family instruments such as violin, viola, cello, string bass, and harp that are sounded by plucking, or drawing a bow across strings.

strong beat the first beat after each bar line.

style the way in which the elements of music are combined to give a piece of music its unique characteristics.

tempo the speed of the beat.

texture the thickness or thinness of musical sound formed when different pitches are played or sung together.

theme the melody on which a composition is based.

tone color the sound that is special to each voice or instrument.

verse words and music that make up the body of a song, and that may alternate with a refrain.

woodwind family instruments including piccolo, flute, oboe, clarinet, and bassoon.

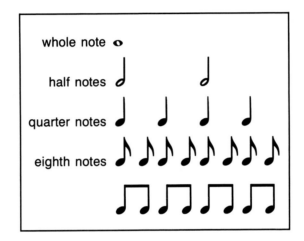

RESOURCE GUIDE TO *MUSIC AND YOU*

PHILOSOPHY OF THE SERIES

The distinctive character of *Music and You* has been achieved by integrating varied approaches and modes of learning into a carefully sequenced curriculum. The approach used in the *Music and You* series is a synthesis of the Kodály, Orff Schulwerk, and Dalcroze approaches, as well as other proven practices and learning theories. All concepts and skills are presented in an easy-to-use, *sequential* format. The articles in the pages that follow describe the varied approaches and special areas emphasized in *Music and You*.

CONTENTS

Organization and Sequencing of the Series	page **293**
The Kodály Approach	page **294**
The Orff Approach	page **295**
The Dalcroze Approach	page **296**
Movement	page **296**
Cooperative Learning	page **297**
Vocal Development	page **298**
The Listening Program	page **299**
Special Learners	page **299**
Songs in Sign Language	page **300**
Keyboard	page **300**

ORGANIZATION AND SEQUENCING OF THE SERIES

The *Music and You* program is carefully structured to ensure continuous growth in musical skills and understanding. Beginning in Grade 1, early units of each book review previously presented concepts. A survey of the content from the early to the later units reveals a logical, step-by-step development of understandings and skills.

The **Scope and Sequence** chart on pages xiv–xv of each Teacher's Edition shows the overall plan for the grade level. This chart shows the objectives according to eight specific elements of music and summarizes what is taught and measured in each unit. Each of the eight units contains either six or ten lessons, depending on the natural division of the school calendar. Half of the lessons are designated as **Core.** These Core lessons constitute a minimum program that covers all the material to be measured in the unit and that can be taught in one half-hour class per week.

The Learning Process in Music and You

The sequence of learning that is built into each grade level of *Music and You* may be shown in this way:

1. EXPERIENCE/PREPARE
2. IDENTIFY/LABEL
3. PRACTICE
4. CREATE
5. EVALUATE
6. MAINTAIN

This process incorporates the key stages outlined in both the Kodály and Orff approaches to music education, as well as in general taxonomies of learning. Creativity is an integral part of each stage of learning. At the experiential level, creativity is exploratory. After a concept is labeled and practiced, the creative tasks are more directed and specific in nature.

Successful learning takes place when there is continual emphasis on *lesson-by-lesson* development of skills and understanding. The **Unit Overview** chart, which precedes each unit, outlines this progress. The chart shows the unit's overall objectives, including the measurable objectives, which are evaluated at the end of the unit, as well as the specific skills and concepts taught in each lesson.

The **lesson plans** in *Music and You* are carefully structured to support the learning sequence. Each lesson plan includes the following:

- *Focus* (generally one musical element)

- *Objectives* (clearly stated in behavioral terms)

- *Setting the Stage* (a motivating activity and often a review of previously learned material)

- *Teaching the Lesson* (a step-by-step, logical presentation from the known to the unknown)

- *Reinforcing the Lesson* (a review and/or preview that relates the lesson focus to other material)

- *Appraisals* (observable behaviors for measuring student achievement)

Additional material provided in the **Extension** section at the bottom of most pages may include More Music Teaching Ideas, as well as background information, supporting materials, curriculum connections, higher-level thinking activities, alternate Songbook selections, and suggestions for students with special needs and talents.

Review and Evaluation pages at the end of each unit summarize the unit's content and offer both an informal check for understanding and a formal assessment of conceptual learning. Many Review lessons organize material and concepts from Core lessons into a short program that may be presented at school assemblies or for parents. The formal written Evaluations are provided on the Teacher's Copying Masters and are also recorded.

The Songbook Section

The final section in each book provides additional songs that may supplement or be substituted for songs in the units. The **Songbook** section includes songs to reinforce the reading sequence, as well as additional patriotic, holiday, and fun songs. Each song is presented with a short lesson. A summary of the specific musical content that may be reinforced by using each song is provided under the heading *Noteworthy*.

Grades 5 and 6 include an additional section entitled **More Choral Music,** which provides several choral selections, most with warm-up and reading exercises. This section helps in guiding students to develop their singing and choral reading skills properly as they learn the selections.

Visual Arts, Related Arts, and Musicals

Music and You incorporates both fine art and movement throughout the series, to help students experience concepts visually, aurally, and kinesthetically. These connections strengthen conceptual learning and can be especially helpful for students with different learning styles.

Music and You combines art with music in a truly functional way, so that art activities are directly related to the music concepts being presented. A wide range of paintings, drawings, and sculpture by recognized masters is presented for visual experiences, all related to the music concepts being developed.

Performance components in *Music and You* reinforce conceptual learning and continue the learning process through the production of programs. The special **Related Arts** sections at each grade level relate the music of heritage classics to the visual and performing arts, and include suggestions for staging.

Musicals provide additional performing experiences. These original scores and scripts, written especially for *Music and You,* are in a variety of styles and reinforce musical learning at every grade level. They include practical suggestions for costumes, scenery, and staging.

The connection of performance components with conceptual learning in *Music and You* gives students the enjoyment and satisfaction of staging a program while reinforcing concepts and skills that are integral to the music curriculum. This uninterrupted sequence of learning leads students to become the best possible performers, listeners, and creators of music that they can be.

THE KODÁLY APPROACH

The Kodály approach emphasizes the teaching of music literacy skills through the use of folk and composed music of the highest quality. It is based on the philosophy of the Hungarian composer, musicologist, and educator Zoltán Kodály (1882–1967), who believed that music belongs to everyone—that the ability to read and write music is the right of every person. Kodály stressed that music education should begin with the very young, that it must be centered on singing, and that children should first learn their "musical mother tongue," the folk songs of their cultural heritage, before exploring music of other cultures. This strong awareness of cultural identity, he believed, provides the best means for understanding music.

The Kodály approach develops musicianship through the sequential teaching of all concepts. It employs a logical teaching sequence that progresses from the known to the unknown, one step at a time. The learning sequence starts with basic rhythm concepts, simple melodic patterns (beginning with *so-mi*), and basic coordination skills, and progresses gradually to conscious knowledge of pentatonic and other commonly used scales. To build solid learning, the teacher guides the students to experience concepts in many different ways, leading them to conscious awareness of the names and symbols for the concepts, and then to discover and come to deeper understanding on their own as they practice and create, using the concepts they have learned.

Kodály recommended a vocal approach that develops ear training by using the natural, playful manner of childhood. Ear training is achieved through the use of relative solmization, a movable *do* system in which pitch syllable names indicate relationships among pitches in a key, rather than absolute pitch. This system, often supported by the use of hand signs, provides excellent training for in-tune singing.

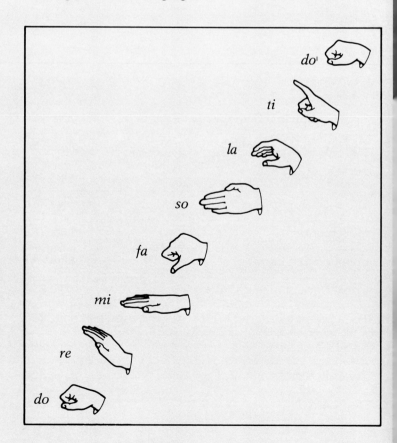

The Kodály approach requires constant attention to expressivity in all musical activities. Teachers learn to monitor the moods and feelings of their students and to vary activities to keep the sound vital and in tune. Some of the strategies used by Kodály educators to help students achieve good vocal development and musicianship include choosing songs with appropriate vocal ranges, modulating to different keys, and using expressive movement and inner-hearing games.

The lesson plans in *Music and You* present basic musical concepts in sequence, providing structure for a Kodály-based, totally sequenced curriculum. The songs were specially chosen for their musical quality and appeal, as well as for their specific rhythmic and melodic content. The large number of pentatonic songs and quality American folk music in *Music and You* will provide teachers using the Kodály approach with a wealth of material from which to choose.

The Teacher's Editions provide the scale tones of every song, as well as a **Rhythmic and Melodic Analysis of Songs** at the end of each book for use in locating songs with specific patterns. The **Reading Songs** that appear at the beginning of the Songbook section in Grades 1–6, in addition to those in the units, may be used to reinforce appropriate music reading skills for each grade level. In addition, the *Music Reading Charts* and accompanying *Teacher's Manuals*, available for Grades 1 and 2, are designed to develop beginning music reading skills in the areas of pitch and rhythm. The Charts introduce, teach, and provide practice in reading skills in a sequenced manner.

THE ORFF APPROACH

The Orff approach is a philosophy of musical development that builds understanding of concepts and skills through active involvement in speech, movement, singing, playing instruments, and drama. Developed by German composer Carl Orff (1895–1982), the approach emphasizes creativity and is based on the instinctive learning behavior of children.

The materials used are primarily folk and composed music of high quality. Much of the music comes from the students' own culture and is an extension of their childhood musical repertoire of chants, rhymes, and other musical experiences. From this music, students isolate basic melodic and rhythmic "building blocks." Once identified and internalized, these building blocks provide students with a musical vocabulary with which they can build their own creations.

One of the goals of the Orff approach is for the music class to be characterized by a spirit of cooperation and joy. Students should enjoy heightened concentration, sharp perception, increased aesthetic awareness and coordination, and a high level of motivation.

Each musical concept is developed sequentially. Students first experience the concept aurally and physically, in imitation of the teacher. Next, the concept is labeled and, through extensive exploration, reinforced. Finally, students develop their own creations, using the concept. Improvisation and movement are used throughout the learning process.

Speech exercises that use familiar rhymes, sayings, and other patterns, often accompanied by body percussion sounds, provide the basis for rhythmic study. These sounds are sometimes transferred to unpitched and pitched instruments. Melodic study, as with the Kodály approach, begins with the descending third, *so-mi* (5–3), and expands into the complete pentatonic and, finally, to the diatonic scales.

Rhythmic and melodic awareness and independence are developed by adding bordurs (accompaniments using the first and fifth steps of the scale), ostinatos (simple repeated patterns), and other accompaniment techniques to melodies. Later, borduns with melodic ornamentation of the first and/or fifth steps of the scale (moving borduns) are used. Harmonic development then proceeds to pedal point and various shifting chord patterns, expanding the tones used in improvisation as the complete major and minor scales and other modes are gradually introduced.

By sixth grade, students will have improvised and composed in free forms, simple song forms, and more complex forms, such as rondos. They will also, ideally, have developed a sense of the creative process from the point of view of a composer.

While not required, Orff instruments provide a variety of timbres and an excellent source of motivation for student aesthetic response. Designed originally by Orff, the instruments are distinctive for their unique suitability for children without compromising musical quality.

Orff instruments include xylophones, metallophones, and glockenspiels, all in various ranges (bass, alto, soprano). The instruments are usually diatonic, with additional F-sharp and B-flat bars that replace the F and B bars when keys other than C major or A minor are used. Timpani, recorders, guitars, other low-pitched stringed instruments, and a wide variety of unpitched percussion instruments are often used. *The Orff instrumentarium*, as this collection is called, is ideal for creative accompaniments for songs, stories, and poems, and for creating opportunities to develop improvisational, compositional, and ensemble playing skills.

Orff teaching strategies and materials are incorporated and carefully sequenced throughout the *Music and You* series. They are in the basic teaching plans, pupil books, and More Music Teaching Ideas and Movement suggestions in the Extension sections. In Grades 3, 4, 5, and 6, additional orchestrations for selected songs can be found in *Orchestrations for Orff Instruments* in the Teacher's Resource Package.

While the Orff approach emphasizes *process*, rather than performance, suggestions for musical presentations that use Orff instruments and the Orff approach can be of great benefit. These are found at every grade level of *Music and You* and provide opportunities for a complete musical experience involving speaking, singing, playing, moving, and creating.

THE DALCROZE APPROACH

Children move instinctively to sound, expressing themselves in movement, gestures, speech, and song. These types of instinctive responses are the basis of the Dalcroze approach to the teaching of music.

Émile Jaques-Dalcroze, a Swiss music educator (1865–1950), incorporated the natural responses of the body into the study of music through movement, which he called *eurhythmics* from the Greek roots *eu* and *rhythmos*, meaning good flow or good movement. He realized that when students are free to express music with large, natural movements, they begin to discover the music within themselves and come to understand many of the concepts we try to teach in music: beat, accent, tempo, direction of melody, phrasing, meter, pattern, rests, and so on.

Although eurhythmics is often considered to be all there is to the Dalcroze approach, it is only part of an approach that carefully integrates ear training, movement, and improvisation. It was Dalcroze's belief that as soon as students become consciously aware of the music, they should be encouraged to express themselves musically through vocal and instrumental improvisation.

The basic tenets of the Dalcroze approach can help teachers in working with students of all ages and ability levels. Many of these strategies have been integrated into the basic lesson plans in *Music and You*.

Children in the primary grades need many experiences of having fun with music by engaging in activities such as "taking a walk with a song" and arriving back at the starting spot on the last note, petting a dog to the beat, and moving in response to pitches going upward, downward, or staying the same. Older students need practice stepping, clapping, and speaking various rhythmic units in opposition to each other, or in canon, so that they may experience the relationships among these patterns. Such activities, along with quick-reaction and conducting exercises, provide students with many joyful, challenging experiences that build confidence, skills, and understanding.

Throughout *Music and You*, students use movement to show understanding of basic musical concepts. Moving to show such concepts as phrase length, differences in the duration of sounds, and tempo changes leads them to develop an inner sense of time, space, and energy. Through the Dalcroze approach, students develop a storehouse of aural and kinesthetic images that can be translated into symbols, i.e., a vocabulary of rhythmic and tonal patterns. This level of awareness eventually prepares them for playing and singing by allowing them to sense the relationship of note values *before* they begin to play, sing, or move.

The Dalcroze approach helps students develop a sharper communication between the ear, eye, body, and mind. Students become actively involved and mentally attentive in listening and responding. Their ears, minds, and bodies are challenged and directed to "follow the music," allowing learning to take place between the student and the music. The teacher can step back and let the music do the teaching!

MOVEMENT

Movement is a child's most natural means of expression. When listening to music, a child's first impulse is to move. The movement becomes a personalized expression of what is heard. Movement activities in *Music and You* are designed to help students extend the expressive qualities of music through movement.

It is important for each young child to develop a vocabulary of movement that includes both fundamental *locomotor* movements (such as walking, running, jumping, hopping, galloping, skipping, and leaping) and *axial*, or nonlocomotor, movements (such as twisting, bending, swaying, stretching, reaching, swinging, and spiraling in place).

Children need sufficient experiences to build the coordination skills required before being asked to make a specific rhythmic response, such as walking the steady beat. In *Music and You*, the development of movement skills is carefully paced to ensure that students experience the steady beat in a variety of ways, first by patting the beat and then by tapping the beat. Walking to a drum beat or to a recording, for example, is a more advanced skill that should be preceded by many experiences in walking freely, with no predetermined beat.

Free response within a given structure is important in guiding basic movement experiences. Thinking in terms of movement "phrases" or "sentences" gives students a general time reference in which to explore basic movement "building blocks." Combining such sentences into longer sections leads to an understanding of form in both dance and music. When the class has become comfortable with walking and hopping, it is time to suggest variations of each: "walk heavily, lightly, slowly, taking long steps; hop lightly, very fast, as low as you can." These movements can be followed by combinations of walking and hopping.

When rhythmic coordination is sufficiently strengthened, a child can be asked to move in the same way and at the same time as another child. **Patterned dances** for the primary grades include simple singing games in which there are few directions to remember and ample time for each step pattern. A patterned dance that requires skipping should be taught only when the majority of students in the class have the ability to skip. In *Music and You*, learning to skip is a natural progression from walking with "bouncy heels," which leads gradually into letting each foot "bounce off" the ground, producing a skip. Since patterned dances are based primarily on locomotor movements, they can be successfully taught by first practicing the general locomotor skill and then setting

it into a specific pattern. Learning a polka step is easier when it evolves naturally out of galloping and quickly changing direction.

When movement is perceived as an important and positive experience in the early grades, students will be more likely to continue moving in music class in upper elementary and junior high. This is facilitated in *Music and You* by using age-appropriate accompaniments and contemporary movement styles.

Teaching musical concepts through movement is a crucial component of contemporary music programs, for educators have come to realize the close relationship between music and movement and the simplicity of illustrating even complex concepts through body movement.

COOPERATIVE LEARNING

Research shows that cooperative learning is one of the most powerful strategies for instruction available. Cooperative learning activities encourage students to spend more time on task and to rehearse information orally, resulting in *increased achievement*. Emphasis on group work requires students both to explain their point of view and to listen to others, stimulating *cognitive development at advanced levels*. During cooperative learning activities, students *grow in self-esteem* as a result of supporting one another and helping one another to learn for mutual gain. In addition, as students enjoy the process of learning and achieve more, cooperative learning activities *promote liking for school*.

What Is Cooperative Learning?

Five elements must be present for small-group learning to be cooperative:

1. *Positive Interdependence.* Lesson structure ensures that groups sink or swim together. This may be done by division of labor, limiting resources, assigning roles, and giving joint rewards.
2. *Face-to-face Interaction.* Socially acceptable interaction is required to achieve the lesson goal.
3. *Individual Accountability.* The group is responsible for the learning of each individual. Every student's mastery of material is assessed in some way.
4. *Interpersonal and Small-group Skills.* One social-skill-building goal is assigned for the period.

5. *Group Processing.* The teacher and/or group members determine the effectiveness of the group in accomplishing the assigned task.

Other characteristics usually found in cooperative settings are heterogeneous groupings, shared responsibility for group leadership, and observation, analysis, and feedback on group functioning by the teacher.

Music and You provides many opportunities for cooperative learning, both in the lessons and in the Extension sections at the bottom of lesson pages. Cooperative learning may be used for an entire lesson or for only part of the class period. The following are general guidelines to keep in mind when planning cooperative learning lessons:

1. Identify the subject matter and social goals.
2. Identify the appropriate group size, from two to six.
3. Set a time limit for the activity, including your explanation of the task and evaluation time.
4. Determine how to assign students to groups. (This is usually done in random order.)
5. Determine classroom arrangement to permit group members to see and hear each other.
6. Explain the learning task, the social skills expected, time limitations, and criteria for evaluation. Identify a stop signal. Check that students understand instructions.
7. Have the students form groups and work on the task. Observe group interactions, taking notes.
8. At the end of the assigned period, have the students share and evaluate their products and group functioning.

The cooperative learning activities in *Music and You* are organized to introduce sequentially the social skills required for effective group work. Beginning with group-forming skills, the activities guide students as they acquire the skills of basic communication, listening, eye contact, sound-level control, taking turns, sharing limited resources, and defending ideas when they differ from those of others. These skills, developed throughout *Music and You*, will bring added excitement and higher-level learning to the music class, while building lifelong social skills.

VOCAL DEVELOPMENT

Music and You is based on the conviction that children need to be taught the skills of singing through a developmental, sequential approach. This approach promotes good intonation and secure singing. Songs selected for the series are in ranges that promote a tone quality that is free, light, and open. Students are encouraged throughout the program to use the upper register of their voices, known as the "head" voice, and are taught how to sing pitches in the lower register, or "chest" voice, with the same unforced tone quality.

The following are the suggested ranges and tessituras for songs used in Grades K through 6.

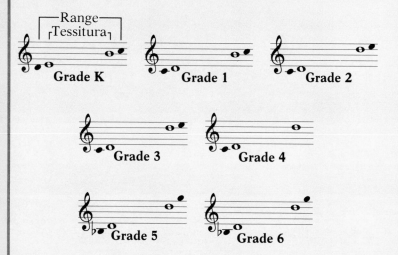

Because of the difference in the rate of development of individual voices, teachers are encouraged to teach a song occasionally in a lower key and gradually raise it as the students' ranges expand.

The following procedures will serve as a guide for teaching students to sing. Suggestions for helping students with each of these steps are provided in the lesson plans of *Music and You*.

The early stages of the sequence outlined below are emphasized more in the early primary grades. It is quite possible, however, that students in the third grade and beyond may need experiences in the initial stages of learning to sing.

1. **Discovering the difference between the speaking and singing voice.** Students who do not realize there is a difference between the speaking voice and the singing voice may "speak" the song instead of singing it. They need to hear and experience the difference between these types of voices.

2. **Exploring the full vocal range.** Students need opportunities for vocal exploration, such as dramatic speech, chants, and sound stories. These promote the use of inflection and provide practice in using their higher ranges.

3. **Discriminating between high and low sounds.** Once the students have had exploratory experiences in high and low sounds, they need to gain control of their voices to produce *specific* higher or lower pitches.

4. **Matching pitch through tone games, echo songs, and call/response songs.** When students have a well-defined concept of high and low, they are better able to match pitch. Simple tone games, such as singing the roll call or answers to specific questions, provide a relaxed atmosphere for students to respond, and also permit assessment of whether they can match the pitch. Simple echo songs or call-and-response songs that use two or three pitches are also good for pitch matching.

5. **Singing in unison with the class.** Students who have difficulty singing songs in tune with others in the class may need help and encouragement to achieve this goal. If a student is singing below pitch, sing the song at his or her pitch level to provide the experience of singing in unison.

In-tune singing is easiest with songs that have simple intervals and a limited range. Place the student with pitch difficulty between two strong in-tune singers and encourage him or her to "listen louder than you sing."

6. **Developing a tonal vocabulary.** If students have difficulty singing new songs in tune, it may be because they do not have well-developed tonal memories. One of the easiest and most effective ways to develop tonal memory is the frequent repetition of familiar folk songs. Experiences with "inner hearing" are also valuable. Have the students sing the first phrase of a song, think the second phrase, sing the third phrase, and so forth. This process forces them to create sound images while retaining the tonality of the song.

7. **Experiencing harmony.** Before introducing harmony experiences, make certain that most of the students are singing unison songs in tune. Introduce harmony through simple ostinatos first. You may wish to add an instrument, such as tone bells or a xylophone, to support the students who are singing the harmony part. Partner songs and descants also provide successful early harmony experiences. Rounds and canons should be introduced after the students have been successful with other types of harmony singing.

8. **Developing vocal techniques.** Young children should be made aware of correct posture and breathing. If the children are sitting on the floor, the teacher should be near the floor as well. Otherwise the children may be forced to look up, impeding the free flow of air and putting tension on the throat. In the upper grades, students are ready for vocalises designed to expand vocal range, improve tone quality and diction, and develop resonance.

THE LISTENING PROGRAM

Listening is of vital importance in the learning process. It may even be said that the ability to listen discerningly precedes all musical learning. Because music is an *aural* art, the development of listening skills is imperative if students are to grow musically.

Many aspects of the music program depend on listening: learning a song or a rhythm pattern by rote, playing instruments in small groups, creating accompaniments, and other performance experiences. While experiences that involve listening as a part of active music making are useful and important, opportunities for the nurturing of "pure" listening skills—of listening for its own sake—are also necessary.

The development of the ability to listen thoughtfully to music requires a systematic presentation of the music without interruption. Students should immediately become actively involved in the music. This strategy fits naturally into the unit design of *Music and You*, for students may be asked to listen for the rhythmic aspects of a selection in one lesson, and for melody, tone color, or other appropriate musical elements in later lessons. Hearing a piece many times is a necessary part of developing discerning listeners and expanding the repertoire of music that students *enjoy* hearing.

The *Music and You* listening experiences include a carefully structured introduction to instrumental tone colors. Beginning at Grade 2, one section of the orchestra is highlighted each year. As students are learning about orchestral instruments, folk instruments from the same family are introduced as well, so that students gain familiarity with a variety of instrumental sounds from all over the world.

Learning to listen to music requires the systematic stretching of the attention span. Listening experiences in *Music and You* begin with short pieces and gradually introduce longer selections as students become accustomed to listening attentively for longer periods. The lessons provide structure for listening, so that students are actively involved in the musical event by making a signal or creative movement response, or by following listening maps that are graphic representations of the sound. Students are asked to "show what they hear" through movement and other signals, such as raising hands. These responses also constitute a valuable part of the evaluation

process. Creative movement permits a higher level of thinking when students are asked to decide *how* to move to show the difference between two sections of music or the shape of a phrase.

The varied **Listening Maps** in *Music and You* range from those that use only pictures to those that show form with geometric shapes, melodic and/or rhythmic notation with patterns to be read, and musical symbols for dynamics and tempo. Some have pictures of featured instruments, and many combine several types of graphics. Many of these maps are on the reproducible Teacher's Copying Masters included in the Teacher's Resource Package for each grade and on the Transparencies provided with each Teacher's Edition.

SPECIAL LEARNERS

Just as no music class is composed of students who all look alike, neither does any class consist of students who all learn alike. The challenge to teachers is to provide music instruction for integrated groups of learners while simultaneously avoiding lower musical expectations for students with different learning rates and styles. This challenge can be met by observing and trying to understand the unique learning abilities of each student.

The focus in *Music and You* is on success for all students. **Special Learners** suggestions appear in the Extension section of many *Music and You* lessons. Often, the same strategy will work for students with a wide variety of special needs. For this reason, most of the Special Learners suggestions are not restricted by labels that identify one particular exceptionality. Many of the suggestions recommend adapting materials or activities to help all students participate successfully in music class.

Students who are mainstreamed into music class are usually categorized as Educable Mentally Handicapped, Learning-disabled, Physically Handicapped, Visually Impaired, or Auditorily Impaired. Each of these categories covers a vast spectrum of abilities and needs; two or more students with the same exceptionality might participate quite differently in musical learning. The variety of musical activities provided in every *Music and You* lesson, combined with the many suggestions for special learners, makes it possible to plan successful music lessons for integrated groups of students.

Suggestions for Special Learners

Listed below are the kinds of learners given special consideration in *Music and You* and some of the recommendations provided for their specific exceptionalities.

Educable Mentally Handicapped. Students described by this label are identified by an intelligence test score below the norm combined with inappropriate adaptive behavior.

Practices such as using a slower rate of presentation, increasing repetition, the inclusion of concrete experiences, and teaching smaller amounts of material at a time are most often suggested for helping mentally handicapped students. Many of these recommendations have been incorporated into the Special Learners suggestions in *Music and You*. These suggestions are intended to serve as guidelines that can be adapted to fit the learning needs of individual students. In addition, the lesson plans are structured to provide repetition of songs and listening selections for all students.

Learning-disabled. The label of learning disability is an "umbrella" term. Students in this category might be poor readers, poor in arithmetic, or poor in writing. The causes of these academic deficits can be a combination of various perceptual problems.

Some learning-disabled students may become confused by text pages that are colorful and highly illustrated. These learners may succeed when notation or graphics are extracted from the page and enlarged.

Physical Handicaps. The suggestions for physically handicapped students in *Music and You* are offered to assist the teacher in designing appropriate alternative activities. Many physically handicapped students may require alternative musical responses when their peers are engaged in creative or structured movement activities.

Auditory Disabilities. Students with auditory disabilities may demonstrate hearing losses ranging from deafness to far lesser degrees of hearing impairment. Special Learners suggestions in *Music and You* that suggest a slower rate of presentation and clarification of materials will assist these students.

Visual Disabilities. The creation of tactile learning aids and manipulatives may be necessary for use with some visually impaired students, while for others the enlargement of notation, graphs, or song texts may be adequate. Many of the Copying Masters at each grade level of *Music and You* will provide a useful source of such materials.

SONGS IN SIGN LANGUAGE

Signing a song adds an expressive dimension to singing that is aesthetically appealing to the eye. Sign language can enhance the performance of a song and, as in choral choreography, can add meaning for the participant as well as for the observer.

Students should understand that the use of sign language in songs is conceptual rather than literal. The objective is to paint a picture of the song by visual means, and therefore it is not necessary to sign every word. The overall meaning of the song is signed.

In conversation, words that do not have specific signs are finger-spelled using the manual alphabet. Finger-spelling, however, is usually avoided in signing songs. If a particular phrase or idea does not lend itself clearly to sign, a combination of sign, gesture, and/or mime may be used.

Signing instructions, including illustrations, may be found in the *Music and You* pupil books, Teacher's Editions, and Copying Masters. Students learn that sign language does not rely solely on the use of the hands.

They discover that facial expressions and body movements are also important in conveying the mood of a song. Positive emotions are expressed with an upward motion. For an upturned "smile," the hands, body, and face move up with a lift. For unhappy emotions, the gestures of the face, body, and hands move downward. When teaching signs to a song, remind students that only part of the meaning is transmitted through the hands; the face and body must tell the rest.

Encourage students to make signs flow from one to the next, and to keep in mind the rhythm of the song and the flow of each phrase. The signing of songs should include very large movements so that the audience can see them easily. When signing a song, the students should always *sing* all of the words, even though they may not sign all of them. For best visual results in performance, the students should wear solid colors contrasting to skin color, so that the hands are highlighted against their clothing.

The signing suggestions in *Music and You* are one approach to learning forms of sign. As students gain familiarity and confidence with signing, they will enjoy creating their own schemes for signing favorite songs.

KEYBOARD

The *Music and You* keyboard strand is sequentially designed to guide student understanding of piano and electronic keyboards, and to reinforce the basic music concepts that form the framework of the program.

In the lower grades, sequenced teaching suggestions reinforce lesson concepts while developing basic keyboard skills. Age-appropriate, hands-on activities allow student exploration of concepts and skills.

By Grades 3 and 4, students are encouraged to play chord roots and full chords, as well as melodic patterns. These experiences begin with one-chord songs and extend to five-chord accompaniments.

Beginning in Grades 3 and 4 and continuing in the upper grades, there is an increased focus on electronic keyboards, providing opportunities for students to create more sophisticated accompaniments while continuing to build understanding of rhythmic, melodic, and expressive elements.

African American Music (See also Ethnomusicology)

Bebey, Francis. *African Music: A People's Art.* Chicago: Chicago Review Press, 1975.

Burgie, Irving. *The Caribbean Song Book: Songs of Puerto Rico, Jamaica, Cuba, Barbados, Dominican Republic, Haiti, Trinidad, Bahamas: Plus Nine Island National Anthems: For Voices in Harmony.* Compiled and arranged. Hollis, N.Y.: Caribe Music Corp., 1977.

Edet, Edna S. *The Griot Sings: Songs from the Black World.* Collected and adapted. New York: Medgar Evers College Press, 1978.

Glass, Paul. *Songs and Stories of Afro-Americans.* New York: Grosset & Dunlap, 1971.

Johnson, James Weldon, and J. R. Johnson, eds. *The Books of American Negro Spirituals.* 2 vols. in 1. Jersey City, N.J.: Da Capo Press, 1977.

Jones, Bessie, and Bess L. Hawes. *Step It Down: Games, Plays, Songs, and Stories from the Afro-American Heritage.* Athens, Ga.: Univ. of Georgia Press, 1987.

Nketia, Joseph H. *The Music of Africa.* New York: W.W. Norton & Co., 1974.

Roberts, John S. *Black Music of Two Worlds.* New York: Riverrun Press, 1985.

Southern, Eileen. *The Music of Black Americans.* 2d ed. New York: W.W. Norton & Co., 1983.

Cooperative Learning

Dishon, Dee, and Pat W. O'Leary. *A Guidebook for Cooperative Learning: A Technique for Creating More Effective Schools.* Holmes Beach, Fla.: Learning Publications, 1984.

Johnson, David W., Roger T. Johnson, and Edythe Johnson Holubec. *Circles of Learning: Cooperation in the Classroom.* Alexandria, Va.: Association for Supervision & Curriculum Development, 1984.

Slavin, Robert E. *Cooperative Learning: Student Teams.* 2d ed. Washington, D.C.: National Education Association, 1987.

Slavin, Robert E., Shlomo Sharan, Spencer Kagan, Rachel H. Lazarowitz, Clark Webb, and Richard Schmuck, eds. *Learning to Cooperate, Cooperating to Learn.* New York: Plenum Publishing Corp., 1984.

Dalcroze (See also Movement)

Abramson, Robert M. *Rhythm Games.* New York: Music & Movement Press, 1973.

Aronoff, Frances W. *Move with the Music: Songs and Activities for Young Children, A Teacher-Parent Preparation Workbook Including Keyboard.* New York: Turning Wheel Press, 1982.

————. *Music and Young Children: Expanded Edition.* New York: Turning Wheel Press, 1979.

Findlay, Elsa. *Rhythm and Movement: Applications of Dalcroze Eurhythmics.* Princeton, N.J.: Birch Tree Group, 1971.

Jaques-Dalcroze, Émile. *Rhythm, Music, and Education.* rev. ed. Translated by Harold F. Rubenstein. London: The Dalcroze Society, 1980.

Early Childhood Music

Andress, Barbara. *Music Experiences in Early Childhood.* New York: Holt, Rinehart & Winston, 1980.

Aronoff, Frances W. *Music and Young Children: Expanded Edition.* New York: Turning Wheel Press, 1979.

Bayless, Kathleen M., and Marjorie E. Ramsey. *Music: A Way of Life for the Young Child.* 3d ed. Columbus, Ohio: Merrill Publishing Co., 1987.

Birkenshaw, Lois. *Music for Fun, Music for Learning: For Regular and Special Classrooms.* 3d ed. Toronto: Holt, Rinehart & Winston of Canada, 1982.

Lawrence, Marjorie. *What? Me Teach Music?* Sherman Oaks, Calif.: Alfred Publishing Co., 1982.

McDonald, Dorothy C., and Gene M. Simons. *Musical Growth and Development: Birth Through Six.* New York: Schirmer Books, 1989.

Nye, Vernice T. *Music for Young Children.* 3d ed. Dubuque, Iowa: William C. Brown Publisher, 1983.

Wood, Donna. *Move, Sing, Listen, Play.* Toronto: Gordon V. Thompson Music, 1982.

Ethnomusicology (See also African American Music)

Anderson, William M. *Teaching Asian Musics in Elementary and Secondary Schools.* rev. ed. Danbury, Conn.: World Music Press, 1986.

Anderson, William M., and Patricia Shehan Campbell. *Multicultural Perspectives in Music Education.* Reston, Va.: Music Educators National Conference, 1989.

George, Luvenia A. *Teaching the Music of Six Different Cultures.* rev. ed. Danbury, Conn.: World Music Press, 1988.

May, Elizabeth, ed. *Musics of Many Cultures: An Introduction.* Berkeley and Los Angeles: Univ. of California Press, 1982.

Kodály

Choksy, Lois. *The Kodály Context.* Englewood Cliffs, N.J.: Prentice-Hall, 1981.

————. *The Kodály Method: Comprehensive Music Education from Infant to Adult.* 2d ed. Englewood Cliffs, N.J.: Prentice-Hall, 1988.

Daniel, Katinka S. *Kodály Approach, Method Book One.* 2d ed. Champaign, Ill.: Mark Foster Music Co., 1979.

————. *Kodály Approach, Method Book Two.* Champaign, Ill.: Mark Foster Music Co., 1986.

————. *Kodály Approach, Method Book Three.* Champaign, Ill.: Mark Foster Music Co., 1987.

————. *Kodály Approach: Method Book Two—Song Collection.* Champaign, Ill.: Mark Foster Music Co., 1982.

Szonyi, Erzsébet. *Musical Reading and Writing.* Translated by Lili Halápy. Revised translation by Geoffrey Russell-Smith. 8 vols. London and New York: Boosey & Hawkes Music Publishers, 1973–79.

————. *Solfège According to the Kodály-Concept.* Keckemet, Hungary: Zoltan Kodály Pedagogical Institute of Music, 1975.

Listening

Bernstein, Leonard. *The Joy of Music.* New York: Simon & Schuster, 1963.

Copland, Aaron. *What to Listen for in Music.* New York: McGraw-Hill Book Co., 1988.

Hoffer, Charles R. *The Understanding of Music.* 5th ed. Belmont, Calif.: Wadsworth Publishing Co., 1985.

Machlis, Joseph. *The Enjoyment of Music.* 4th ed. New York: W.W. Norton & Co., 1977.

Miller, Samuel D. "Listening Maps for Musical Tours." *Music Educators Journal* 73 (October 1986): 28–31.

Movement (See also Dalcroze)

Boorman, Joyce L. *Creative Dance in the First Three Grades.* Toronto: Harcourt Brace Jovanovich, Canada, 1969.

————. *Creative Dance in Grades Four to Six.* Toronto: Harcourt Brace Jovanovich, Canada, 1971.

————. *Dance and Language Experiences with Children.* Toronto: Harcourt Brace Jovanovich, Canada, 1973.

Joyce, Mary. *First Steps in Teaching Creative Dance to Children.* 2d ed. Mountain View, Calif.: Mayfield Publishing Co., 1980.

Staton, Barbara Rustin. *Move into Music.* 4 vols. Morristown, N.J.: Silver Burdett, 1981. (Available through Merrill Staton Enterprises, Alpine, N.J. 07620-1079.)

Weikart, Phyllis. *Teaching Movement and Dance: Intermediate Folk Dance.* Ypsilanti, Mich.: High/Scope Press, 1984.

Orff

Burnett, Millie M., and Patti S. Wiggins. *Today's Creative Children: Sing, Play and Move.* Dubuque, Iowa: Kendall/Hunt Publishing Co., 1983.

Frazee, Jane, and Kent Kreuter. *Discovering ORFF: A Curriculum for Music Teachers.* Valley Forge, Pa.: European American Music Distributors Corp., 1987.

Keetman, Gunild. *Elementaria, First Acquaintance with Orff-Schulwerk.* Valley Forge, Pa.: European American Music Distributors Corp., 1974.

Keller, Wilhelm. *Introduction to Music for Children.* Translated by Susan Kennedy. Valley Forge, Pa.: European American Music Distributors Corp., 1974.

Nash, Grace C., Geraldine W. Jones, Barbara A. Potter, and Patsy S. Smith. *Do It My Way: The Child's Way of Learning.* Sherman Oaks, Calif.: Alfred Publishing Co., 1977.

Orff, Carl, and Gunild Keetman. *Music for Children.* English version adapted from Orff-Schulwerk by Margaret Murray. 5 vols. London: Schott & Co., 1958–66.

————. *Music for Children.* Canadian (North American) version adapted from Orff-Schulwerk by Doreen Hall and Arnold Walter. 5 vols. London: Schott & Co., 1956.

Regner, Hermann, ed. *Music for Children.* Vol. 2, *Orff-Schulwerk.* Valley Forge, Pa.: European American Music Distributors Corp., 1977.

Shamrock, Mary. "Orff Schulwerk: An Integrated Foundation." *Music Educators Journal* 72 (February 1986): 51–55.

Signing

Gadling, Donna C., Pastor Daniel H. Pokorny, and Dr. Lottie L. Riekehof. *Lift Up Your Hands: Inspirational and Patriotic Songs in the Language of Signs.* Washington, D.C.: National Grange, 1975.

Humphries, Tom, Carol Padden, and Terrence J. O'Rourke. *A Basic Course in American Sign Language.* 18th ed. Silver Spring, Md.: T.J. Publishers, 1980.

Kannapell, Barbara M., and Lillian B. Hamilton. *Songs in Signed English.* Washington, D.C.: Gallaudet College Press, 1973.

Riekehof, Lottie L. *The Joy of Signing.* 2d ed. Springfield, Mo.: Gospel Publishing House, 1987.

Sternberg, Martin. *American Sign Language.* New York: Harper & Row Publishers, 1987.

Weaks, Donna Gadling. *Lift Up Your Hands.* Vol. 2, *Favorite Songs with Sign Language Interpretation.* Washington, D.C.: National Grange, 1980.

Special Learners

Alvin, Juliette. *Music for the Handicapped Child.* 2d ed. London and New York: Oxford University Press, 1976.

Atterbury, Betty W. *Mainstreaming Exceptional Learners in Music.* Englewood Cliffs, N.J.: Prentice–Hall, 1990.

————. "The Perplexing Issues of Mainstreaming." *Bulletin of the Council for Research in Music Education* 94 (1987): 17–27.

————. "Success in the Mainstream of General Music." *Music Educators Journal* 72 (March 1986): 34–36.

Beer, Alice S., Natalie L. Bellows, and Anna Mae D. Frederick. "Providing for Different Rates of Music Learning." *Music Educators Journal* 68 (April 1982): 40–43.

Bitcon, Carol Hampton. *Alike and Different: The Clinical and Educational Use of Orff-Schulwerk.* Santa Ana, Calif.: Rosha Press, 1976.

Darrow, Alice-Ann. "Music for the Deaf." *Music Educators Journal* 71 (February 1985): 33–35.

Graham, Richard M., and Alice S. Beer. *Teaching Music to the Exceptional Child: A Handbook for Mainstreaming.* Englewood Cliffs, N.J.: Prentice-Hall, 1980.

Herlein, Doris G. "Music Reading for the Sightless—Braille Notation." *Music Educators Journal* 62 (September 1975): 42–45.

Lam, Rita C., and Cecilia Wang. "Integrating Blind and Sighted Through Music." *Music Educators Journal* 68 (April 1982): 44–45.

Nocera, Sona D. *Reaching the Special Learner Through Music.* Morristown, N.J.: Silver Burdett, 1979.

Robbins, Carol, and Clive Robbins. *Music for the Hearing Impaired and Other Special Groups: A Resource Manual and Curriculum Guide.* St. Louis, Mo.: MMB Music, 1980.

Vocal Development/Choral Music

Bartle, Jean Ashworth. *Lifeline for Children's Choir Directors.* Toronto: Gordon V. Thompson Music, 1988.

Diercks, Louis H. "A Guide to Improving the Diction and Tone Quality of the Choir." *The Choral Journal* 15 (October 1974): 9–10.

Heffernan, Charles W. *Choral Music: Technique and Artistry.* Englewood Cliffs, N.J.: Prentice-Hall, 1982

Marshall, Madeleine. *The Singer's Manual of English Diction.* New York: G. Schirmer, 1953.

May, William V., and Craig Tolin. *Pronunciation Guide for Choral Literature.* Reston, Va.: Music Educators National Conference, 1987.

Rao, Doreen. *Choral Music Experience: Education Through Artistry.* Vol. 1, *Artistry in Music Education;* Vol. 2, *The Artist in Every Child;* Vol. 5, *The Young Singing Voice.* New York: Boosey & Hawkes, 1987–.

Swears, Linda. *Teaching the Elementary School Chorus.* Englewood Cliffs, N.J.: Prentice-Hall, 1984.

AB. *See* Form

ABA. *See* Form

Accompaniment. *See* Texture

Action Songs
Bow, Wow, Wow! 201, 215
Bus, The, 266
Charlie Over the Ocean, 224
Clap Your Hands, 267
Clickety Clack, 184–185
Columbus Sailed with Three Ships, 44 - 45
Comanche Hand Game Song, 56
Draw a Bucket of Water, 200, 203
Farmer in the Dell, The, 62-63
Giant's Shoes, The (poem), 21
Hanukah Is Here, 88
Hello Song, 6–7
Hokey Pokey, 273
I Am a Person, 10–11
I'll Just Be Myself, 38
Jack Be Nimble (poem), 90
Let's Make a Jack-o'-Lantern, 43
London Bridge, 121
Lobby Loo, 130
Marching Round the Levee, 280
Must Be Santa, 254–255
My Dreydl, 248
My Head and My Shoulders, 281
My Little Puppy, 136
My Place, 178
My Thumbs Are Starting to Wiggle, 11
One Potato, Two Potato (chant), 208
Peanut Butter, 284–285
Put Your Finger in the Air, 58
Rig-a-Jig-Jig, 181
Step in Time, 288
Teddy Bear, 106
Ten Little Fingers, 22–23
Thanksgiving Feast (poem), 76–77
Three Little Muffins (chant), 69
Welcome Back to School, 104
When the Flag Goes By, 151
Where Is Thumbkin? 22

Animal Songs
Ah! Les Jolis Papillons, 263
Baby Beluga, 264–265
Bow, Wow, Wow! 201
Butterfly, 183
Ducklings, The, 187
Five Fat Turkeys, 246
Friendly Beasts, The, 250–251
Goin' to the Zoo, 270–271
Hey Diddle Diddle, 61
Hurry, Little Pony, 82
I Heard a Bird Sing (poem), 91
Jig Jog, Jig Jog, 274–275

Learning (story), 176–177
Little Ducky Duddle, 192
Little Spotted Puppy, 276–277
Los Pollitos, 279
Marks: "Rudolph, the Red-Nosed Reindeer" (optional listening), 91
Merry Christmas (poem), 91
Monkey See, Monkey Do, 243
My Little Puppy, 136
Oh, Where Has My Little Dog Gone? 15
Old Gray Cat, The, 27
Old MacDonald, 175
One, Two, Three, Four, Five, 205
Peddler's Song, The, 242
Peter Cottontail, 188
Robin Redbreast (poem), 212
Secret of the Polar Bear, The (poem), 116
Secret Song, The (poem), 166
Square Dance, 126–127
Teddy Bear, 106
Whales Off Wales, The (poem), 118–119
Willoughby Wallaby Woo, 24

Artists. *See* Fine Art Reproductions

Beat. *See also* Duration/Rhythm: divided beat; steady beat; strong beat; Reading Notation
creative activities for, 108, 116, 131

Bells. *See* Instruments, Playing

Biographies
Bizet, Georges, 4
Chopin, Frédéric, 148
Copland, Aaron, 222
Darin, Bobby, 132
Dvořák, Antonín, 23
Fauré, Gabriel, 30
Goldman, Edwin Franco, 163
Haydn, Franz Joseph, 158
Haydn, Michael, 153
Herbert, Victor, 87
Humperdinck, Engelbert, 100
McDonald, Harl, 122
Mozart, Wolfgang Amadeus, 117
Prokofiev, Sergei, 30
Ravel, Maurice, 219
Schafer, R. Murray, 144
Schumann, Robert, 185
Tchaikovsky, Peter Ilyich, 168
Thomson, Virgil, 148
Vivaldi, Antonio, 171
Wilder, Alec, 153
Williams, John, 51

Body Percussion. *See also* Creative Activities, body percussion; Texture

Chants. *See* Poetry/Chants

Classroom Instruments. *See* Instruments, Identifying

Classroom Management/Extra Help
attention, focusing, 1
instruments, practicing, 46
instruments, preparing to play, 110
left and right, identifying, 21
listening, guidelines for, 31
movement, guidelines for, 5, 31
participation, encouraging individual, 69
performance, reinforcing, 61
repeated tones, experiencing, 186
same and different, distinguishing, 162
sounds, guidelines for exploring, 40
sound sources, alternate, 81, 177
words, mouthing for practice, 159

Composers. *See* Biographies

Cooperative Learning. *See also* Groups, Working in
composing with visual aids, 166
dramatizing a song, 38
game, playing a, 34
instruments, identifying classroom, 156
instruments, identifying orchestral, 220
instruments, playing pitched, 64, 92, 96
long and short sounds, 44
melodic direction, 186, 213
pitches, high and low, 147
rhythms, creating, 139
same and different, 170
song, performing a, 120
songs, moving to, 123
steady beat, moving to, 112
tone color, 209

Country Life
Farmer in the Dell, The, 63
Los Pollitos, 279
Old MacDonald, 175
Scarecrow Has a Patch, The (poem), 49

Creative Activities
art/construction, 10, 17, 21, 38, 44–45, 49, 65, 73, 99, 111, 141, 153, 166, 187
body percussion, 24, 140, 175, 190, 192, 199, 201, 267
concept or element, moving to show
  beat, 108, 116, 131
  dynamics, 19, 31
  form, 185, 196, 225
  high/low, 119, 147–148, 167–168, 216
  long/short, 40–41, 54, 225, 244
  melodic direction, 48, 64–66, 115, 132–133, 186, 192, 217

no beat, 105, 119
same/different, 158, 166, 185, 196,
    225
tempo, 4–5, 9, 19, 25, 31, 49, 64–65,
    118, 130, 133, 166, 206-207, 225
instruments, making, 74, 80, 177, 199
instruments, playing
    accompaniments, improvising, 28, 57,
        70, 88, 137
    dynamics, improvising, 57
    melodies, improvising, 64, 72, 84, 174,
        186, 217
    question/answer, improvising, 183
    sound effects, 28, 40, 74, 105, 110, 133,
        137, 166, 217
music, dramatizing
    animal characterization, 27, 35, 66,
        137–138, 153, 160, 175, 187, 222, 225,
        246, 270, 276, 279
    classroom games, 8, 34, 38, 43, 86,
        153, 160, 166, 184, 266, 276, 278
    leader/group, 27, 35, 160, 246, 266,
        268, 289
    movement, 19, 38, 43, 86, 90, 123, 184,
        225, 284
    nature, 175
poems, dramatizing
    characterization, 76, 166–167
    movement, 74, 105
    question/answer, 166
speaking or singing
    concept or element, showing, 195,
        201, 211, 218
    vocal effects, 17, 26, 74, 77, 144–145,
        175, 278
stories, dramatizing
    acting/dialogue, 102
    Christmas, 98, 253
    movement, 49, 51, 53
    unit reviews, 36, 54, 78, 98–99,
        140–141, 196-197, 226–227
verses, creating new, 11, 24, 26, 50, 80,
    86, 104, 175, 223

Cumulative Songs
Must Be Santa, 254-255
Old MacDonald, 175
One Finger, One Thumb, 109

Curriculum Connections
art
    character masks, constructing, 38
    collages, creating long and short, 44
    costumes, fashioning, 27
    melodic direction, creating patterns
        to show, 65
    pagoda puppets, constructing, 219
    props, left and right shoes as, 21
    scarecrow mascot, creating, 49
    self-expression, drawing wishes, 111

ships, creating paper, 45
snowflakes, creating paper, 146
snowmen, creating paper, 115
thanksgiving, drawing pictures of, 73
wind chimes, making, 74
health
    brushing teeth, chart for, 32
    safety, playing on frozen bodies of
        water, 105
language arts
    beginning and end, identifying, 27
    creative writing, 48, 229
    languages, different, 172
    patterns, identifying same and
        different, 160
    rhyming words, identifying, 22
    scenes from Hansel and Gretel;
        dramatizing, 102
    self-expression, describing song, 57
literature
    "Laideronette, Empress of the
        Pagodas," background of, 219
    Raggedy Ann and Raggedy Andy,
        background of, 228
math
    geometric shapes, using instruments
        to identify, 113
    shape book, creating, 13
    time telling, 86
reading
    names, recognizing, 88
science
    animal families, similarities and
        differences in, 187
    bears, 116
    belugas, 264
    brass, 152
    bubbles, experimenting with, 129
    garden, creating and caring for
        windowsill, 215
    larks, 176
    monkeys, 238
    whales, 119
    wind, experiencing and charting, 74
social studies
    caboose, description of, 278
    King, Dr. Martin Luther, Jr.,
        biography of, 256
    Kwanzaa, description of, 93
    letters, mailing, 154
    Maoris, background of, 269
    respect for self and others, 13
    self-concept, 10
    spirituals, 145
    Zulus, background of, 281

Dance. See Movement

Different. See Same/Different

Divided Beat. See Duration/Rhythm

Dramatizations/Pantomimes. See also
    Creative Activities; Groups,
    Working in
After My Bath (poem), 131
Baby Beluga, 264–265
Bear Hunt (story), 28-29
Bizet: "Soap Bubbles" from Children's
    Games (listening), 130
Bizet: "The Top" from Children's Games
    (listening), 4, 19
Brush Your Teeth, 32-33
Bubble Bath, The (poem), 129
Bus, The, 266
Butterfly, 182–183
Chopin: Prelude in C♯ Minor, Opus 28,
    No. 10 (listening), 148
Clickety Clack, 184–185
Copland: The Cat and the Mouse
    (listening), 222, 225
Down, Down, 64–65
Down at the Station, 268
Ducklings, The, 187
El Nacimiento, 253
Farmer in the Dell, The, 62–63
Friendly Beasts, The, 250–251
Goin' to the Zoo, 270–271
Hats (musical), 236–243
Hey Diddle Diddle, 61, 66
Humperdinck: Hansel and Gretel
    (listening), 100–103
Hush, Little Baby, 14
Icy (poem), 105
I'll Just Be Myself, 38
In the Toy Shop, 86
Jack Be Nimble (poem), 90
Jack-o'-Lantern, 244
Jig Jog, Jig Jog, 274–275
Learning (story), 176–177
Little Blue Truck, 12–13
Little Ducky Duddle, 192
Little Red Caboose, 278
Little Spotted Puppy, 276–277
Mail Myself to You, 154
Moving Upward and Downward
    (lesson), 48
My Little Puppy, 136–138
My Oak Tree, 214
Old Gray Cat, The, 27, 35
Peanut Butter, 284–285
Pumpkin Stew, 42–43
Raggedy Ann and Raggedy Andy Visit
    Amazing Amazo (musical), 228–235
Ravel: "Laideronette, Empress of the
    Pagodas" from Mother Goose Suite
    (listening), 225
Review and Evaluation
    Unit 1, 36
    Unit 2, 54

Unit 3, 78
Unit 4, 98–99
Unit 5, 140
Unit 6, 164
Unit 7, 196
Unit 8, 226
Safety Song, 8
Santa's Visit, 98–99
Secret Song, The (poem), 166
Silverstein: "Boa Constrictor"
    (listening), 221, 225
Stars (poem), 110
Tchaikovsky: "The Lark Song" from
    Scenes of Youth (listening), 176
Thomson: Acadian Songs and Dances
    (fourth movement) (listening), 160
Three Little Muffins (chant), 69, 76
Uncle Jessie, 289
Vivaldi: "Spring" from The Four
    Seasons (listening), 175
Where Is Thumbkin? 34
Wide Awake (poem), 31
Wilder: "Effie Goes Folk Dancing" from
    Suite No. 1 for Tuba and Piano
    (listening), 153
Wilder: "Effie Joins the Carnival" from
    Suite No. 1 for Tuba and Piano
    (listening), 153
Williams: "E.T.'s Halloween" from E.T.,
    The Extraterrestrial (listening), 51, 53
Wind, The (poem),74

Duration/Rhythm. *See also* Recorded
    Lessons
divided beat
    Clickety Clack, 195
    Cobbler, Cobbler, Mend My Shoe, 194
    Ducklings, The, 194
    Little Ducky Duddle, 210
eighth note, 175, 211
long and short, 40, 44, 80, 180–181,185
no beat
    Icy (poem), 105
    Sounds of Humpback Whales
        (listening), 119
    Wind, The, 74
quarter note, 114, 120, 125, 136–140,
    162, 175, 211
quarter rest, 18, 114, 117, 124–125,
    128–129, 134, 136–140, 157, 163, 175,
    260, 276
rhythmic ostinatos, 116, 118, 128, 140,
    156–157, 163, 193, 195, 201, 211, 224
rhythmic patterns, 116, 126, 128,
    132–134, 137, 139, 193, 195, 204–205,
    211, 279
steady beat
    Ah! Les Jolis Papillons, 263
    Alphabet Song, 112
    Autumn Leaves, 245
    Baa, Baa, Black Sheep, 122

Bounce High, Bounce Low, 204,
    206–207
Bus, The, 266
Clap Your Hands, 267
Copland: The Cat and the Mouse
    (listening), 222
Down at the Station, 268
Epo i tai tai e, 269
Farmer in the Dell, The, 70, 157
Five Fat Turkeys, 246
George Washington, 162
Going on a Picnic, 223
Go Tell It on the Mountain, 252
Hanukah Is Here, 88–89
He Had a Dream, 256
Hello Song, 7, 24
Herbert: "March of the Toys" from
    Babes in Toyland (listening), 87
Hey Diddle Diddle, 61, 78
Holiday Song, 249
Indian Lullaby, 57, 74
In the Toy Shop, 86
Jack Be Nimble (poem), 90
Jig Jog, Jig Jog, 274
Kum Ba Yah, 93, 98
Let Us All Be Thankful, 247
Little Blue Truck, 68
Little Ducky Duddle, 193–194, 208
Little Red Caboose, 278
London Bridge, 120–122
Looby Loo, 130, 132
Los Pollitos, 279
Marching Round the Levee, 280
Mitten Song, 124
Mozart: "Sleigh Ride" from German
    Dances K. 605 (listening), 117
Muffin Man, 76
Music of the World a-Turnin', 18-19
My Dreydl, 248
My Head and My Shoulders, 281
My Little Puppy, 138
My Oak Tree, 216
Old Dan Tucker, 282
One, Two, Three, Four, Five, 210
One, Two, Tie My Shoe, 71, 76
Peanut Butter, 284
Play Me a Song, 84
Pumpkin Stew, 42, 53
Put Your Finger in the Air, 60
Quaker, Quaker, 172
Same and Different (chant), 170
Santa's Coming, 98
Scarecrow Has a Patch, The (poem),
    49
See-saw, Margery Daw, 189, 194
Sing a Little Song, 2, 6
Take a Bite of Music, 41–42
Teddy Bear, 106, 137
Thanksgiving Feast (poem), 77
Thank You, 73, 77
This Little Light of Mine, 80, 86

Three Little Muffins, 76
Twinkle, Twinkle, Little Star, 120, 122
Zion's Children, 145
strong beat
    Ah! Les Jolis Papillons, 263
    Best of Friends, The, 259
    Bounce High, Bounce Low, 204, 209
    Bow, Wow, Wow! 202
    Draw a Bucket of Water, 203
    Goin' to the Zoo, 270
    Hokey Pokey, 273
    Jack-o'-Lantern, 244
    Japanese Folk Song: Sakura
        (listening), 209
    Little Ducky Duddle, 193, 208
    Lullaby, 238–239
    My Oak Tree, 214, 216
    One Potato, Two Potato (chant), 208,
        217
    Uncle Jessie, 289

Dynamics. *See also* Reading Notation
creative activities for, 19, 31
dramatic effect of changing, 27, 29, 59,
    91, 146
listening for, 17, 19–23, 26–29, 30–32,
    56–58, 87, 143, 145, 163, 171, 218–219
loud or soft, classifying, 17–18
movements to demonstrate, 17, 19, 23,
    26, 29, 57
pictorial representation, 17
playing instruments with, 28, 31, 57, 59,
    86, 193, 209, 245
singing or speaking with, 16, 21, 44, 57,
    77, 84, 91, 143–144, 158, 200, 245, 284
sound sources, drawing loud and soft,
    17

Evaluation. *See* Review and Evaluation

Extra Help. *See* Classroom
    Management/Extra Help

Family
Draw a Bucket of Water, 200
Farmer in the Dell, The, 63
Friendly Beasts, The, 250–251
Going on a Picnic, 223
Hush, Little Baby, 14
Indian Lullaby, 56
Learning (story), 176–177
Lullabye, 158–160
My Oak Tree, 214
Uncle Jessie, 289

Fine Art Reproductions
———— : An Empress of Ch'ien Lung,
    218
O'Kelley: Thanksgiving, 72

Finger Plays
Put Your Finger in the Air, 58
Ten Little Fingers, 22–23
Three Little Muffins (chant), 69
Where Is Thumbkin? 22

Folk Music
African
   Che Che Koolay, 217
   Kum Ba Yah, 93
   My Head and My Shoulders, 281
African American
   Charlie Over the Ocean, 224
   Draw a Bucket of Water, 200
   Go Tell It on the Mountain, 252
   This Little Light of Mine, 80
   Zion's Children, 145
American. *See also* African American;
      American Indian
   Angel Band, The, 81
   Bounce High, Bounce Low, 204
   Bow, Wow, Wow! 201
   Clap Your Hands, 267
   Cobbler, Cobbler, Mend My Shoe,
      194
   Down at the Station, 268
   Farmer in the Dell, The, 63
   Five Fat Turkeys, 246
   Hokey, Pokey, 273
   Hush, Little Baby, 14
   Lemonade, 173
   Marching Round the Levee, 280
   Never Sleep Late Anymore, 135
   Old Gray Cat, The, 27
   Old MacDonald, 175
   One, Two, Three, Four, Five, 205
   One, Two, Tie My Shoe, 70
   Quaker, Quaker, 172
   See-saw, Margery Daw, 189
   Teddy Bear, 106
   Walk to School, 4
American Indian
   Comanche Hand Game Song, 56
   Indian Lullaby, 56
Ecuadoran
   Los Pollitos, 279
English
   Friendly Beasts, The, 250–251
   Holiday Song, 249
   London Bridge, 121
   Looby Loo, 130
   Muffin Man, 67
   Rig-a-Jig-Jig, 181
   We Wish You a Merry Christmas, 85
Flemish
   Safety Song, 8
French
   Ah! Les Jolis Papillons, 263
   Twinkle, Twinkle, Little Star
      (melody), 111
   Where Is Thumbkin? 22

German
   Ducklings, The, 187
   Jack-o'-Lantern, 244
   Let Us All Be Thankful (melody), 247
   Oh, Where Has My Little Dog Gone?
      (melody), 15
New Zealand
   Epo i tai tai e, 269
Portuguese
   Indo Eu, 169
Puerto Rican
   El Nacimiento, 253
Spanish
   Hurry, Little Pony, 82
Traditional
   Apples and Bananas, 190
   Hello Song, 6
   Hello, There! 142
   Little Ducky Duddle, 192
   Little Red Caboose, 278
   Monkey See, Monkey Do, 243
   My Thumbs Are Starting to Wiggle,
      11
   One Finger, One Thumb, 109

Foreign Language Songs
Comanche
   Comanche Hand Game Song, 56
French
   Ah! Les Jolis Papillons, 263
Ghanaian
   Che Che Koolay, 217
Japanese
   Japanese Folk Song: Sakura
      (listening), 209
Maori
   Epo i tai tai e, 269
Spanish
   El Nacimiento, 253
   Hurry, Little Pony, 82
   Los Pollitos, 279
   Que Bonito Es, 286–287

Form. *See also* Reading Notation;
      Recorded Lessons
AB
   Bratton and Kennedy: "The Teddy
      Bears' Picnic" (A and B sections)
      (listening), 137–138
   Clickety Clack, 184
   Hurry, Little Pony, 82–83
   Jack Be Nimble (poem), 81, 90, 98
   Rig-a-Jig-Jig, 181, 196
   Welcome Back to School, 104, 140
ABA
   Schumann: "The Wild Horseman"
      from *Album for the Young*
      (listening), 185
creative activities for, 185, 196, 210,
   215, 225
ending (coda), 96, 156, 263

interlude, 78, 96, 116, 122, 145, 156
introduction, 65, 70, 96, 156
moving to show, 123, 189
phrases
   Butterfly, 183–184, 196
   moving to show, 179, 183–185, 192
   Old MacDonald, 175
   Thank You, 72
pictorial representation of, 122, 171
   same/different, 48, 122, 171
rondo, 171
same/different
   Butterfly, 184, 196
   George Washington, 162
   Jig, Jog, Jig Jog, 274
   McDonald: *Children's Symphony*
      (first movement) (listening), 122
   Muffin Man, 68
   Same and Different (recorded lesson),
      170
   Schumann: "The Wild Horseman"
      from *Album for the Young*
      (listening), 185
   Twinkle, Twinkle, Little Star, 120
   Vivaldi: "Spring" from *The Four
      Seasons* (listening), 171, 175, 196
   Zion's Children, 161
verse and refrain, 20
whole and part, 10, 11, 24, 42

Four-Tone Songs
do re mi so (1 2 3 5)
   Ah! Les Jolis Papillons, 263
la₁ do re mi (6₁ 1 2 3)
   Indian Lullaby, 56
so₁ do re mi (5₁ 1 2 3)
   George Washington, 156

Friends/Neighbors
Best of Friends, The, 259
Hello, There! 142
Hello Song, 6
Holiday Song, 249
I Am a Person, 10
I'd Like to Teach the World to Sing,
   96–97
Love Is the Magic Word, 229
Mail Myself to You, 154
Music of the World a-Turnin', 18–19
Quaker, Quaker, 172
Walk to School, 4
Welcome Back to School, 104

Fun/Nonsense Songs
Apples and Bananas, 190
Bubble Bath, The (poem), 129
Clap Your Hands, 267
Draw a Bucket of Water, 200
Farmer in the Dell, The, 63
Frosty the Snow Man, 117
Giant's Shoes, The (poem), 21

Hello Song, 6
Hey Diddle Diddle, 61
Hokey Pokey, 273
I'll Just Be Myself, 38
I'll Race You Down the Mountain, 207
Jack Be Nimble (poem), 81
Little Blue Truck, 12
London Bridge, 121
Looby Loo, 130
Mail Myself to You, 154
Merry-Go-Round (listening), 216
My Dreydl, 248
My Head and My Shoulders, 281
My Legs and I (poem), 25
My Thumbs Are Starting to Wiggle, 11
Old Dan Tucker, 282–283
One Finger, One Thumb, 109
One, Two, Tie My Shoe, 70
Ourchestra (poem), 199
Peanut Butter, 284–285
Popping Corn, 125
Put Your Finger in the Air, 58
Rig-a-Jig-Jig, 181
Scarecrow Has a Patch, The (poem), 49
Secret of the Polar Bear, The (poem), 116
See-saw, Margery Daw, 189
Sing a Little Song, 2
Snow Man, The 115
Square Dance, 126–127
Staton and Staton: "Merry-Go-Round" (listening), 216–217
Step in Time, 288
Take a Bite of Music, 41
Three Little Muffins (chant), 69
Uncle Jessie, 289
Welcome Back to School, 104
Whales Off Wales, The (poem), 118–119
Where Is Thumbkin? 22
Willoughby Wallaby Woo, 24

Game Songs
Charlie Over the Ocean, 224
Columbus Sailed With Three Ships, 44–45
Comanche Hand Game Song, 56
Draw a Bucket of Water, 200, 203
Farmer in the Dell, The, 62–63, 70
Hello, There, 142
Little Red Caboose, 278
London Bridge, 121
Mail Myself to You, 154–155
Marching Round the Levee, 280
Muffin Man, 67-68
Quaker, Quaker, 172, 174
Rig-a-Jig-Jig, 181
Thanksgiving Feast (poem), 76–77
Uncle Jessie, 289
Where Is Thumbkin? 22

Group Songs. *See* Solo/Group Songs

Groups, Working In. *See also*
Cooperative Learning
Cat and the Mouse, The, dramatizing, 222, 225
concept or element, moving to show
form, 123, 185
high/low, 92, 153
instrumentation, 87, 153
phrase, 179, 183-185, 192
same/different, 184–185
strong beat, 202, 209
tempo, 206
following a leader, 8, 44, 72
games, 56, 203, 209
musical elements, sharing ideas about, 217
music, creating, 217
performing a song, 83, 115, 138, 140
questions and answers, playing
instruments for, 183
speaking in rhythm, 116, 194

Health/Safety
After My Bath (poem), 131
Before the Bath (poem), 128
Brush Your Teeth, 32–33
Bubble Bath, The (poem), 129
Safety Song, 8

Historical Figures
Columbus, Christopher, 44–45
King, Martin Luther, Jr., 256–257
Washington, George, 156

Holiday/Special Day Songs
birthdays
Happy Birthday, 272
Columbus Day
Columbus Sailed with Three Ships, 44-45
December holidays
El Nacimiento, 253
Friendly Beasts, The, 250–251
Go Tell It on the Mountain, 252
Hanukah Is Here, 88
Holiday Song, 249
Hurry, Little Pony, 82
Jingle Bells, 95
Marks: "Rudolph, the Red-Nosed Reindeer" (optional listening), 91
Merry Christmas (poem), 91
Must Be Santa, 254–255
My Dredl, 248
Santa's Coming, 92
We Wish You a Merry Christmas, 85
Easter
Peter Cottontail, 188
Halloween

Black and Gold, 47
Jack-o'-Lantern, 244
Let's Make a Jack-o'-Lantern, 43
Pumpkin Stew, 42
Martin Luther King Day
He Had a Dream, 256–257
Thanksgiving
Five Fat Turkeys, 246
Let Us All Be Thankful, 247
Thanksgiving (poem), 77
Thanksgiving Feast (poem), 76
Thank You, 73
Valentine's Day
Best of Friends, The, 259
I Made a Valentine, 258
Mail Myself to You, 154
My Valentine, 260–261
Washington's Birthday
George Washington, 156

Instruments, Identifying. *See also* Tone
Color
classroom
Farmer in the Dell, The (drum, rhythm sticks, tambourine, triangle), 70
Hey Diddle Diddle (drum, rhythm sticks, tambourine, triangle), 66
instrument identification game (selection of pitched and unpitched), 112–113, 156
Jingle Bells (Chart 26; drum, jingle bells, wood block), 94
Kum Ba Yah (drum), 93
Mozart: "Sleigh Ride" from *German Dances* K. 605 (listening, bells), 117
Never Sleep Late Anymore (triangle, xylophone), 134,140
Prokofiev: "March" from *Summer Day* Suite (listening; drum, rhythm sticks, tambourine, triangle), 59
Put Your Finger on the Sticks (drum, rhythm sticks, tambourine, triangle), 58
Santa's Coming (jingle bells), 92
Teddy Bear (bells, drum, glockenspiel, rhythm sticks, tambourine, triangle, wood block), 112
Thanksgiving (poem; drum, rhythm sticks, tambourine), 72
Thank You (triangle), 73
Twinkle, Twinkle, Little Star (bells), 111
Welcome Back to School (wood block, xylophone), 110
orchestral
Haydn: Concerto for Trumpet and Orchestra (listening, trumpet), 152

Here Comes the Band (poem; flute, trombone, trumpet, tuba), 162
Japanese Folk Song: Sakura (listening; flute, trumpet, violin), 209
McDonald: *Children's Symphony* (first movement) (listening, orchestral families), 123
orchestral instruments (flute, timpani, trumpet, violin), 198, 220
Ourchestra (poem; cymbals, drum, horn), 199
Slow, Medium, and Fast (recorded lesson; flute, timpani, trumpet, violin), 206
Sounds of the Flute, Piccolo, and Violin (listening; flute, piccolo, violin), 197
Sounds of the Trumpet, Flute, Violin, and Timpani (listening; flute, timpani, trumpet, violin), 226
Spring Is Here (flute), 169
Tchaikovsky: "The Lark Song" from *Scenes of Youth* (listening; flute, piccolo, violin), 168, 176, 196
Tempo and Tone Color (recorded lesson; flute, timpani, trumpet, violin), 220
Vivaldi: "Spring" from *The Four Seasons* (listening, violin), 171
What Instruments Do You Hear? (recorded lesson; flute, timpani, trumpet, violin), 198
Wilder: "Effie Joins the Carnival" and "Effie Goes Folk Dancing" from Suite No. 1 for Tuba and Piano (listening, tuba), 153

Instruments, Illustrations of
bass drum, 123
bassoon, 123
cello, 123
clarinet, 123
cymbal, 46, 123
flute, 123, 168, 198
glockenspiel, 83
hand drum, 57, 72, 83, 94
jingle bells, 83, 94
oboe, 123
piccolo, 168
rhythm sticks, 57, 72
snare drum, 123
tambourine, 57, 72
timpani, 123, 198
triangle, 57, 72, 134
trumpet, 123, 152, 198
tuba, 153
viola, 123
violin, 123, 168, 198
wood block, 46, 83, 94
xylophone, 83, 134, 213

Instruments, Making, 74, 80, 177, 199

Instruments, Playing. *See also* Dynamics
bells
Ah! Les Jolis Papillons, 263
Bow, Wow, Wow! 201
Bubble Bath, The (poem), 133
Che Che Koolay, 217
Down, Down, 65
Hanukah Is Here, 88
Hurry, Little Pony, 85
In the Toy Shop, 96
Learning (story), 177
Los Pollitos, 279
Mail Myself to You, 154
Merry-Go-Round, 216
My Oak Tree, 214, 217, 226
Never Sleep Late Anymore, 135, 139, 141
One Potato, Two Potato (poem), 217
Play Me a Song, 84, 88
Popping Corn, 125
Pumpkin Stew, 50, 53
Robin Redbreast (poem), 213
Secret Song, The (poem), 167
See-saw, Margery Daw, 189
Snow Man, The, 118
Spring Walk, A (story) 197
Stars (poem), 111
Teddy Bear, 160
Upward and Downward (recorded lesson), 183
When the Flag Goes By, 151
creative activities for
accompaniments, improvising, 28, 57, 70, 88, 137
dynamics, improvising, 57
melodies, improvising, 64, 72, 84, 174, 217
patterns, upward and downward, 186, 213
question/answer, improvising, 183, 210
sound effects, 28, 40, 74, 105, 110, 133 137, 166, 217
keyboard, general
beat, 211
hands, left and right, 20
patterns, up and down, 186, 213
pitch, high and low, 64, 92
sounds and symbols, high and low, 147
sounds, long and short, 40
tempo, 4
walking fingers, 180
keyboard, song-based
Ah! Les Jolis Papillons, 263
Bow, Wow, Wow! 201
Che Che Koolay, 217
Icy (poem), 105

Learning (story), 177
Los Pollitos, 279
Merry-Go-Round, 216
My Oak Tree, 214, 217, 226
Never Sleep Late Anymore, 135, 139, 141
One Potato, Two Potato (poem), 217
Play Me a Song, 88
Popping Corn, 125
Pumpkin Stew, 50, 53
Robin Redbreast (poem), 213
Secret Song, The (poem), 167
See-saw, Margery Daw, 189
Stars (poem), 110
Upward and Downward (recorded lesson), 183
Orff instruments
Ah! Les Jolis Papillons, 263
Bounce High, Bounce Low (bordun), 204
Bow, Wow, Wow! 201
Bubble Bath, The (poem),133
Che Che Koolay, 217
Columbus Sailed with Three Ships, 44
Cynthia in the Snow (poem), 146
Down, Down, 65
Hanukah Is Here, 88
Hey Diddle Diddle, 61
Hurry, Little Pony, 83, 85, 98
Icy (poem), 105
Learning (story), 177
Los Pollitos (bordun), 279
Mail Myself to You, 154
Monkey See, Monkey Do, 243
Never Sleep Late Anymore, 135
One, Two, Three, Four, Five, 210
Play Me a Song, 84, 88
Pumpkin Stew, 48
Pumpkin Stew (bordun), 53
Quaker, Quaker, 172, 174
Santa's Coming, 93
Secret Song, The (poem) 167
Spring Walk, A (story), 196
Stars (poem), 111
Staton and Staton: "Merry-Go-Round" (listening), 217
Whales Off Wales, The (poem), 119
percussion, indefinite pitch
Angel Band, The, 81
Autumn Leaves, 245
Black and Gold, 47
Bow, Wow, Wow! 201–203, 215
Cynthia in the Snow (poem), 146
Epo i tai tai e, 269
Farmer in the Dell, The, 70
George Washington, 156
Goin' to the Zoo, 270
Goldman: *Children's March* (listening), 163
Go Tell It on the Mountain, 252
Hanukah Is Here, 88

Happy Birthday, 274
Hats for Sale! 237
He Had a Dream, 256
Herbert: "March of the Toys" from *Babes in Toyland* (listening), 87
Hey Diddle Diddle, 66
Holiday Song, 249
Hurry, Little Pony, 83, 85, 98
Icy (poem), 105
I Heard a Bird Sing (poem), 91
I'll Just Be Myself, 52
Indian Lullaby, 57, 74
In the Toy Shop, 86, 96
Jack Be Nimble (poem), 81
Jack-o'-Lantern, 244
Japanese Folk Song: "Sakura" (listening), 209
Jig Jog, Jig Jog, 274
Jingle Bells (Chart 26), 94–96, 99
Kum Ba Yah, 93, 98
Learning (story), 177
Let's Make a Jack-o'-Lantern, 46, 50, 54
Let Us All Be Thankful, 247
Little Ducky Duddle, 193–194, 208
London Bridge, 121
Marks: "Rudolph the Red-Nosed Reindeer" (optional listening), 91
Merry Christmas (poem), 91
Mitten Song, 124
Never Sleep Anymore, 135, 139, 140
No Hats in Sight (chant), 241
Old MacDonald, 176
One Potato, Two Potato (chant), 208
One, Two, Three, Four, Five, 210
One, Two, Tie My Shoe, 76
Play Me a Song, 88
Popping Corn, 125, 128
Prokofiev: "March" from *Summer Day* Suite (listening), 59
Pumpkin Stew, 50
Que Bonito Es, 286
Sakura, 209
Santa's Coming, 93, 98
Scarecrow's Problem, The (story), 54
Secret of the Polar Bear, The (poem), 118
Secret Song, The (poem), 167
Spring Walk, A (story), 196
Stars (poem), 110
Staton and Staton: "Merry-Go-Round" (listening), 217
Teddy Bear, 116
This Little Light of Mine, 80, 86, 99
Twinkle, Twinkle, Little Star, 120
Welcome Back to School, 112
Whales Off Wales, The (poem), 119
When the Flag Goes By, 163
Zion's Children, 163

Keyboard. *See* Instruments, Playing

Listening Maps
Butterfly, The, 182
Copland: *The Cat and the Mouse*, 222
Herbert: "March of the Toys" from *Babes in Toyland*, 87
McDonald: *Children's Symphony* (first movement), 122
Thomson: *Acadian Songs and Dances* (fourth movement), 148
Vivaldi: "Spring" from *The Four Seasons*, 171
Williams: "E.T.'s Halloween" from *E.T., The Extraterrestrial*, 51

Listening Selections
by composer
 Backer, Davis, Cook, and Greenaway: "I'd Like to Teach the World to Sing," 97
 Bizet: "Soap Bubbles" from *Children's Games*, 130, 133
 Bizet: "The Top" from *Children's Games*, 4–5, 19
 Bratton and Kennedy: "The Teddy Bears' Picnic," 137–138, 140
 Chopin: Prelude in C♯ Minor, Opus 28, No. 10, 148
 Copland: *The Cat and the Mouse*, 222, 225
 Darin: "Splish Splash," 133
 Dvořák: *Slavonic Dance* No. 7, 23
 Fauré: "Berceuse" from *Dolly* Suite, 30–31
 Goldman: *Children's March*, 163
 Haydn, Franz Joseph: "Echo" from Divertimento in E♭, Hob II.39, 159
 Haydn, Michael: Concerto for Trumpet and Orchestra, 152
 Herbert: "March of the Toys," from *Babes in Toyland*, 87, 90
 Humperdinck: "Brother, Come and Dance with Me," from *Hansel and Gretel*, 101
 Humperdinck: "The Dew Fairy" from *Hansel and Gretel*, 103
 Humperdinck: "Hocus Pocus" from *Hansel and Gretel*, 103
 Humperdinck: "The Little Sandman" from *Hansel and Gretel*, 102
 Humperdinck: "Nibble, Nibble, Mousekin" from *Hansel and Gretel*, 103
 Humperdinck: "Now That We Are Free at Last" from *Hansel and Gretel*, 103
 Humperdinck: "Prayer" from *Hansel and Gretel*, 102

 Humperdinck: "Prelude" from *Hansel and Gretel*, 101
 Humperdinck: "Susie, Little Susie" from *Hansel and Gretel*, 101
 Humperdinck: "There Stands a Little Man" from *Hansel and Gretel*, 102
 Humperdinck: "Tra-la-la-la" from *Hansel and Gretel*, 103
 Japanese Folk Song: "Sakura," 209, 219
 Marks: "Rudolph, the Red-Nosed Reindeer" (optional listening), 91
 McDonald: *Children's Symphony* (first movement), 122–123
 Mozart: "Sleigh Ride" from *German Dances* K. 605, 117
 Nelson and Rollins: "Frosty the Snow Man," 117
 Prokofiev: "March" from *Summer Day* Suite, 30–31, 59
 Ravel: "Laideronette, Empress of the Pagodas" from *Mother Goose Suite*, 219, 225
 Schafer: *Miniwanka, or The Moments of Water*, 144, 147
 Schumann: "The Wild Horseman" from *Album for the Young*, Book I, 185
 Silverstein: "Boa Constrictor," 221, 225
 Staton, Barbara: "Walk on Down the Road," 157
 Staton, Barbara and Staton, Merrill: "Merry-Go-Round," 216, 224
 Tchaikovsky: "The Lark Song" from *Scenes of Youth*, 168, 176–177, 179, 186, 196
 Thomson: *Acadian Songs and Dances* (fourth movement), 149, 160
 Vivaldi: "Spring" from *The Four Seasons*, 171, 175, 196
 Wilder: "Effie Goes Folk Dancing" from Suite No. 1 for Tuba and Piano, 153
 Wilder: "Effie Joins the Carnival" from Suite No. 1 for Tuba and Piano, 153
 Williams: "E.T.'s Halloween" from *E.T., The Extraterrestrial*, 51, 53
other
 Sounds of Humpback Whales, 119
 Sounds of the Flute, Piccolo, and Violin, 196
 Sounds of the Trumpet, Flute, Violin, and Timpani, 226
by title
 Acadian Songs and Dances (fourth movement) by Virgil Thomson, 149, 160

"Berceuse" from *Dolly* Suite by Gabriel Fauré, 30–31

"Boa Constrictor" by Shel Silverstein, 221, 225

"Brother, Come and Dance with Me" from *Hansel and Gretel* by Engelbert Humperdinck, 101

Cat and the Mouse, The by Aaron Copland, 222, 225

Children's March by Edwin Franko Goldman, 163

Children's Symphony (first movement) by Harl McDonald, 122–123

Concerto for Trumpet and Orchestra (second movement) by Michael Haydn, 152

"Dew Fairy, The" from *Hansel and Gretel* by Engelbert Humperdinck, 103

"Echo" from Divertimento in E♭, Hob II:39 by Franz Joseph Haydn, 158

"Effie Goes Folk Dancing," from Suite No. 1 for Tuba and Piano by Alec Wilder, 153

"Effie Joins the Carnival," from Suite No. 1 for Tuba and Piano by Alec Wilder, 153

"E.T.'s Halloween" from *E.T., The Extraterrestrial* by John Williams, 51, 53

"Frosty the Snow Man" by Steve Nelson and Jack Rollins, 117

"Hocus Pocus" from *Hansel and Gretel* by Engelbert Humperdinck, 103

"I'd Like to Teach the World to Sing" by Bill Backer, Billy Davis, Roger Cook, and Roger Greenaway, 97

"Laideronette, Empress of the Pagodas" from *Mother Goose Suite* by Maurice Ravel, 219, 225

"Lark Song, The" from *Scenes of Youth* by Peter Ilyich Tchaikovsky, 168, 176–177, 179, 186, 196

"Little Sandman, The" from *Hansel and Gretel* by Engelbert Humperdinck, 102

"March" from *Summer Day* Suite by Sergei Prokofiev, 30–31, 59

"March of the Toys" from *Babes in Toyland* by Victor Herbert, 87, 90

"Merry-Go-Round" by Barbara Staton and Merrill Staton, 216, 224

Miniwanka, or The Moments of Water, by R. Murray Schafer, 144, 147

"Nibble, Nibble, Mousekin" from *Hansel and Gretel* by Engelbert Humperdinck, 103

"Now That We Are Free at Last" from *Hansel and Gretel* by Engelbert Humperdinck, 103

"Prayer" from *Hansel and Gretel* by Engelbert Humperdinck, 102

"Prelude" from *Hansel and Gretel* by Engelbert Humperdinck, 101

Prelude in C♯ Minor, Opus 28, No. 10 by Frédéric Chopin, 148

"Rudolph, the Red-Nosed Reindeer" by Johnny Marks (optional listening), 91

"Sakura" (Japanese Folk Song), 209, 219

Slavonic Dance No. 7 by Antonín Dvořák, 23

"Sleigh Ride" from *German Dances* K. 605 by Wolfgang Amadeus Mozart, 117

"Soap Bubbles" from *Children's Games* by Georges Bizet, 130, 133

Sounds of Humpback Whales, 119

Sounds of the Flute, Piccolo, and Violin, 196

Sounds of the Trumpet, Flute, Violin, and Timpani, 227

"Splish Splash" by Bobby Darin, 133

"Spring" from *The Four Seasons* (first movement) by Antonio Vivaldi, 171, 175, 196

"Susie, Little Susie" from *Hansel and Gretel* by Engelbert Humperdinck, 103

"Teddy Bears' Picnic, The" by John W. Bratton and Jimmy Kennedy, 137–138, 140

"There Stands a Little Man" from *Hansel and Gretel* by Engelbert Humperdinck, 102

"Top, The" from *Children's Games* by Georges Bizet, 4–5, 19

"Tra-la-la-la" from *Hansel and Gretel* by Engelbert Humperdinck, 103

"Walk on Down the Road" by Barbara Staton, 157

"Wild Horseman, The" from *Album for the Young,* Book I by Robert Schumann, 185

Lullabies

Fauré: "Berceuse" from *Dolly* Suite (listening), 30–31

Hush, Little Baby, 14

Indian Lullaby, 56

Lullabye, 158–160

Lullaby from *Hats,* 238–239

Melodic Direction. *See* Pitch

Melody. *See* Pitch; Texture

Minor/Modal Songs

Autumn Leaves, 245

Black and Gold, 47

Ducklings, The, 187

El Nacimiento, 253

Hanukah Is Here, 88

Indian Lullaby, 56

Little Blue Truck (mixolydian), 12

Movement

creative

Baby Beluga, 264–265

Bizet: "The Top" from *Children's Games* (listening), 4, 19

Chopin: Prelude in C♯ Minor, Opus 28, No. 10 (listening), 148

Clap Your Hands, 267

Columbus Sailed with Three Ships, 44–45

Cynthia in the Snow (poem), 146

Dvořák: *Slavonic Dance* No. 7 (listening), 23

Fauré: "Berceuse" from *Dolly* Suite (listening), 31

Friendly Beasts, The, 250–251

Hanukah Is Here, 88

I Can Get from Here to There (poem), 179

Icy (poem), 105

I'll Race You Down the Mountain, 207

My Dreydl, 248

My Legs and I (poem), 25

One Finger, One Thumb, 109

Popping Corn, 125, 128

Prokofiev: "March" from *Summer Day* Suite (listening), 31

Schafer: *Miniwanka, or The Moments of Water* (listening), 147

Secret of the Polar Bear, The (poem), 116

Staton and Staton: "Merry-Go-Round" (optional listening), 216–217

Tchaikovsky: "The Lark Song" from *Scenes of Youth* (listening), 168, 177, 179

Whales Off Wales, The (poem), 119

and dynamics, demonstrating, 17, 19, 23, 26, 29, 57

and melodic direction, demonstrating, 154, 182, 184, 223–224, 247

and pitch, demonstrating, 49, 64–67, 85, 92, 117–119, 132, 147, 165, 216

guidelines for, for extra help, 5, 31

patterned

Bow, Wow, Wow! (circle dance), 215

Hokey Pokey (circle dance), 273

Humperdinck: "Brother, Come and Dance with Me" from *Hansel and Gretel* (listening), 101

Looby Loo (circle dance), 130

Square Dance, 126–127

Musicals

Hats
Hats for Sale! 237
Lullaby, 238–239
Monkey See, Monkey Do, 243
No Hats in Sight (chant), 241
Peddler's Song, The, 242
Raggedy Ann and Raggedy Andy Visit Amazing Amazo
Anyone Can Make a Mistake, 234–235
I Am Amazo, 231
Love Is the Magic Word, 229
Mixity Maxity Klippity Klack, 233

Musicians. *See* Composers

Music Reading. *See* Notation

Nature/Seasons/Out-of-Doors
Autumn Leaves, 245
Baby Beluga, 264–265
Charlie Over the Ocean, 224
Cynthia in the Snow (poem), 146
Down, Down, 65
Frosty the Snow Man, 117
Going on a Picnic, 223
Icy (poem), 105
I Heard a Bird Sing (poem), 91
I'll Race You Down the Mountain, 207
It Fell in the City (poem), 114
Jingle Bells, 95
Merry Christmas (poem), 91
Mitten Song, 108
My Oak Tree, 214
Rain (poem), 144
Secret Song, The (poem), 166
Sing a Little Song, 2
Snow Man, The, 115
Spring Is Here, 169
Stars (poem), 110
Twinkle, Twinkle, Little Star, 111
Wind, The (poem), 75

Neighbors. *See* Friends/Neighbors

Nonsense Songs. *See* Fun/Nonsense Songs

Notation. *See* Reading Notation

Orchestral Instruments. *See* Instruments, Identifying

Orff Instruments. *See* Instruments, Playing

Ostinatos. *See also* Duration/Rhythm, rhythmic ostinatos
After My Bath (poem), 131
Before the Bath (poem), 128, 132

Bow, Wow, Wow! 201
Charlie Over the Ocean, 224
George Washington, 156
Little Ducky Duddle, 193, 195, 211
Mail Myself to You, 157
My Little Puppy, 140
Popping Corn, 125–126, 134
Secret of the Polar Bear, The (poem), 118
Square Dance, 126
When the Flag Goes By, 163

Out-of-Doors. *See* Nature/Seasons/Out-of-Doors

Pantomimes. *See* Dramatizations/Pantomimes

Patriotic Songs
America, 262
George Washington, 156
When the Flag Goes By, 151

Pentatonic Songs
do re mi so la (1 2 3 5 6)
Bow, Wow, Wow! 201
My Place, 178
Teddy Bear, 106
do re mi so la do' (1 2 3 5 6 1')
When the Flag Goes By, 151
so, do re mi so la (5, 1 2 3 5 6)
Columbus Sailed with Three Ships, 44-45
Farmer in the Dell, The, 63
so, la, do mi so la (5, 6, 1 3 5 6)
Brush Your Teeth, 32–33
so, la, do re mi (5, 6, 1 2 3)
Charlie Over the Ocean, 224
Draw a Bucket of Water, 200
Go Tell It on the Mountain, 252
He Had a Dream, 256–257
Never Sleep Late Anymore, 135
Old Dan Tucker, 282–283
Old MacDonald, 175
This Little Light of Mine, 80
so, la, do re mi so (5, 6, 1 2 3 5)
Angel Band, The, 81
Going on a Picnic, 223
Music of the World a-Turnin', 18–19
so, la, do re mi so la (5, 6, 1 2 3 5 6)
Zion's Children, 145

Percussion. *See* Instruments, Playing

Performance, For
musicals
Hats, 236–243
Raggedy Ann and Raggedy Andy Visit Amazing Amazo, 228–235

Phrases. *See* Form; Reading Notation

Pitch. *See also* Four-Tone Songs; Minor/Modal Songs; Pentatonic Songs; Recorded Lessons; Three-Tone Songs; Two-Tone Songs
high/low
playing, 64, 84, 92, 118, 133, 147, 161, 180
relationship to instrument size, 48, 64, 151, 153
sound patterns, 51, 64–67, 84, 160, 168, 186, 216
sounds, identifying with movements, 49, 64–67, 85, 92, 117–119, 132, 147, 154, 165, 217
visual recognition, 65, 84, 92, 147, 156, 161, 216
voice, using, 49, 52–53, 84
improvising in pentatonic, 133, 177, 279
major key, accompanying in, 118
melodic direction
creative activities for, 48, 64–66, 115, 132–133, 182, 197, 216
games with movement, 154, 182, 184, 196, 223-224, 227, 247
identifying, 186–189, 196, 212, 214–215, 224, 247–248, 279
playing, 183, 186, 197, 213-214, 216–217, 223–224, 279
question/answer, 183, 197, 210
same/different, 184, 187, 196
mi so (3 5), 161, 173, 274, 278

Poetry/Chants
After My Bath, 131
Before the Bath, 128
Bubble Bath, The, 129
Cynthia in the Snow, 146
Ears Hear, 16
Eight Balloons, 225
Giant's Shoes, The, 21
Here Comes the Band, 162
I Can Get from Here to There, 179
Icy, 105
I Heard a Bird Sing, 91
It Fell in the City, 114
Jack Be Nimble, 81
Japanese Folk Song: "Sakura" (listening), 209
Merry Christmas, 91
My Legs and I, 25
No Hats in Sight (chant), 249
One Potato, Two Potato (chant), 208
Ourchestra, 199
Rain, 144
Robin Redbreast, 212
Same and Different, 170
Scarecrow Has a Patch, The, 49
Secret of the Polar Bear, The, 116

Secret Song, The, 166
Singing Time, 1
Stars, 110
Thanksgiving, 77
Thanksgiving Feast, 76
Whales Off Wales, The, 118–119
Wide Awake, 31
Wind, The, 75

Reading Notation
pictorial representations
 beat, 67, 70, 74, 89, 106, 108, 112, 120, 124
 division of beat, 180–181, 195, 210–211
 dynamics, 17
 eighth notes (♫), 195, 210–211
 form (rondo), 171, 175
 high and low, 49, 84, 92, 147, 161, 187, 194, 213, 216
 long and short, 40, 44
 numbers, 71, 76
 order, 5, 8, 11, 221
 part and whole, 10–11
 phrases, 90
 quarter note (♩), 89, 108, 112, 124–125, 128–129, 134, 139–140, 193–194, 210, 252
 quarter rest (𝄽), 124–125, 128–129, 134, 139–140, 260
 same/different, 172, 174
 silent beat, 124, 128, 134, 140, 193–194, 210, 260
 song, 149–151, 154–157, 160, 163, 214, 225
 steady beat, 21
 story, 51, 53, 100, 102–103
 strong beat, 191, 202–203, 208–209, 226
 tempo, 1C, 4, 30, 206
 texture (melody alone), 42, 48, 50, 53
 texture (melody with accompaniment), 50
 words, 3, 6, 16, 38, 50, 60, 66, 71, 76, 214
rhythm
 patterns using ♩, 120, 124
 patterns using ♩, 𝄽, 138, 141, 156–157, 163, 276
 patterns using 𝄽, 136–137, 276

Recorded Lessons
duration/rhythm
 Echoes and Answers, 175
 Learning to Skip, 157
 Notation for a Silent Beat, 137
 Pointing the Beat with "Hey Diddle Diddle," 61
 Rhythms of Locomotor Movements, 180
 Short and Long Sounds, 40

foreign language pronunciation
 for "Ah! Les Jolis Papillons," 263
 for "El Nacimiento," 253
 for "Hurry, Little Pony," 82
 for "Los Pollitos," 279
 for "Que Bonito Es," 286
form
 Learning "Music of the World a-Turnin'," 18
 Listening for Themes in *Acadian Songs and Dances,* 160
pitch
 High and Low Sound Patterns, 92
 Listening for Higher and Lower, 148
 Melodic Direction in "Looby Loo," 132
 Moving Upward and Downward, 49
 Upward and Downward, 183
 Upward and Downward in "Merry-Go-Round," 216
tempo
 Listening for Fast and Slow, 12
 Slow, Medium, and Fast, 207
 Tempo and Tone Color, 220
texture
 Melody Alone or with Accompaniment, 51
tone color
 Tempo and Tone Color, 220
 What Instrument Do You Hear?, 198

Related Arts Lesson
Hansel and Gretel, 100–103

Review and Evaluation
Unit 1, 36–37
Unit 2, 54–55
Unit 3, 78–79
Unit 4, 98–99
Unit 5, 140–141
Unit 6, 164–165
Unit 7, 196–197
Unit 8, 226–227

Rhythm. *See* Duration/Rhythm; Reading Notation

Same/Different
Butterfly, 184, 196
George Washington, 162
Jig Jog, Jig Jog, 274
moving to show, 184–185
McDonald: *Children's Symphony* (first movement) (listening), 122
Muffin Man, 68
Same and Different (poem), 170
Schumann: "The Wild Horseman" from *Album for the Young,* Book I (listening), 185
Twinkle, Twinkle, Little Star, 120

Vivaldi: "Spring" from *The Four Seasons* (listening), 171, 175, 196

Seasons. *See* Nature/Seasons/Out-of-Doors

Solo/Group Songs
Charlie Over the Ocean (echo), 224
Che Che Koolay (echo), 217–219
Clickety Clack, 184–185
Columbus Sailed with Three Ships (echo), 44–45
Going on a Picnic, 223
Hello, There! (echo), 142
Lemonade, 173
Lullabye (echo), 158–160
No Hats in Sight (chant), 241
One, Two, Three, Four, Five, 205
Peddler's Song, The, 242
Sing a Little Song (echo), 2
Where is Thumbkin? 22

Special Day Songs. *See* Holiday/Special Day Songs

Special Learners
distinguishing color, 8
game, preparations for, 203
instruments, playing, 94
left and right, 213
melodic direction, 188
movement, problems with, 71, 130, 179
movement to show tempo, 14, 130
movement to contrasting sounds, 179
movement, visual aids for, 183
pitch, visual and tactile aids, 52
strong beat, moving to, 202
style, visual aids for, 30

Steady Beat. *See* Duration/Rhythm

Stories
Bear Hunt, 28–29
creative activities for, 49, 99
Learning, 176–177

Strong Beat. *See* Duration/Rhythm

Style
band, 163
baroque, 171
carol, 85
chamber, 153, 158
classical, 117, 152, 158
film music, 51, 149
folk
 African, 93, 217, 281
 American, 4, 14, 27, 81, 106, 120, 135, 172, 267, 273

Ecuadoran, 279
English, 67, 85, 130, 181, 249–251
Flemish, 8, 22
French, 22, 263
German, 244
Japanese, 209
Maori, 269
Portuguese, 169
Puerto Rican, 253
Spanish, 82
impressionist, 219
march, 163
opera, 100–103
operetta, 87
orchestral
  baroque (Italian), 171
  classical (Austrian), 117, 152
  impressionist, 219
  romantic (Bohemian), 23
  romantic (French), 4, 30, 130
  romantic (Russian), 168
  twentieth century (American), 51,
    122, 149
  twentieth century (Russian), 30
pop, 133
post-romantic, 100
romantic
  Bohemian, 23
  French, 4, 30, 130
  German, 185
  Polish, 148
  Russian, 168
twentieth century
  American, 51, 122, 149, 153, 163,
    221–222
  Canadian, 144
  Russian, 30
vocal
  choral, 144, 209
  folk (African), 93, 217, 281
  folk (African American), 80, 145, 200,
    252, 289
  folk (American), 4, 14, 27, 81, 106, 120,
    135, 172, 267, 273
  folk (American Indian), 56
  folk (Ecuadoran), 279
  folk (English), 67, 85, 130, 181,
    249–251
  folk (Flemish), 8, 22
  folk (French), 22, 263
  folk (German), 244
  folk (Japanese), 209
  folk (Maori), 269
  folk (Portuguese), 169
  folk (Puerto Rican), 253
  folk (Spanish), 82

pop, 133
twentieth century (American), 221
twentieth century (Canadian), 144

Tempo. *See also* Reading Notation;
  Recorded Lessons
changing, 25, 130, 221, 278
contrasting, 1C, 14–15, 31, 80
creative activities for, 4–5, 9, 19, 25, 31,
  49, 64–65, 118, 130, 133, 166, 206–207,
  225
fast, 1C, 14–15, 80
identifying
  changing, 25, 34, 130
  by listening, 9, 14–15, 25, 49, 220–223
  by moving, 4, 25, 34, 49, 166, 206–207
  from pictures, 30
  of poem, 25, 68–69, 166
  by singing, 9, 12, 25, 34
listening for, 4, 9, 14–15, 25, 49, 220–223
moving to show
  changing, 25, 30, 32, 43, 130, 146
  steady, 206
  various, 4, 9, 49
singing in
  changing, 25, 34
  steady, 6, 86, 88
  various, 9, 12, 68–69
slow, 1C, 14–15
using various
  by moving, 4, 9, 49
  by playing instruments, 4, 163
  by singing, 9, 12, 68–69

Texture. *See also* Reading Notation;
  Recorded Lessons
accompaniment
  comparing, 96
  dynamics, playing with, 57, 59
  identifying, 42, 51, 163, 218
  pitched and unpitched instruments,
    playing, 86, 88, 135, 138, 204
  pitched instruments, playing, 44, 53,
    61, 172, 201, 279
  unpitched instruments, playing, 46,
    50, 54, 57, 59, 137, 163, 193
body percussion
  form, 11, 104, 140
  with poetry, 21
  same/different, 116, 133
  steady beat, 3, 43, 46, 66, 70, 72, 85, 87
  strong beat, 202
melody
  identifying, 43, 51, 54
  same/different, 42, 50, 96, 120, 163,
    218

Three-Tone Songs
mi so la (3 5 6)
  Bounce High, Bounce Low, 204
  Monkey See, Monkey Do, 243
  One, Two, Three, Four, Five, 205
  See-saw, Margery Daw, 189
so₁ do mi (5₁ 1 3)
  Hurry, Little Pony, 82
so₁ la₁ do (5₁ 6₁ 1)
  Peanut Butter, 284–285

Tone Color. *See also* Instruments,
  Identifying; Recorded Lessons
band, 162
bells, 111, 117
body percussion, 199–200
cymbals, 40, 46, 166
drum, 23, 70, 93, 166, 176
environmental sounds, 16–18, 36, 40,
  177, 199
finger cymbals, 166
flute, 176, 198, 209, 220
glockenspiel, 105
guiro, 176
harpsichord, 209
jingle bells, 80–81, 92
orchestra, 4, 31, 117, 122
Orff Instruments, 133
piccolo, 176
rhythm sticks, 70, 176
sand blocks, 166
tambourine, 70
timpani, 198, 220
triangle, 70, 73, 80, 93, 105, 110, 166
trumpet, 152, 198, 209, 220
tuba, 153
violin, 176, 198, 209, 220
voices, 1, 17, 24, 28, 71, 96, 142–146,
  158–159, 209
wood block, 40, 46, 80–81, 110, 113
xylophone, 110, 113

Transportation/Travel Songs
Bus, The, 266
Clickety Clack, 184–185
Columbus Sailed with Three Ships,
  44–45
Down at the Station, 268

Vocal Development
large intervals, 184
pitch accuracy, 70, 143, 223
vocal quality, 1C, 111
voice range, 52

This rhythmic and melodic analysis provides the teacher with a listing of songs for teaching specific rhythms or pitches. Songs that use only the rhythms or pitches under the heading are labeled "entire." Specific measure numbers are indicated in parentheses when the rhythms or pitches apply to part of a song. The letter "a" indicates that the anacrusis to the measure is included.

The headings of the rhythmic analysis are listed by duration, from shortest to longest. The melodic analysis is organized alphabetically.

Rhythmic Analysis

♫, ♩

Ah! Les Jolis Papillons $\frac{2}{4}$ (entire), 263
Angel Band, The $\frac{2}{4}$ (a1-4), 81
Bounce High, Bounce Low $\frac{2}{4}$ (entire), 204
Clap Your Hands $\frac{2}{4}$ (entire), 267
Cobbler, Cobbler, Mend My Shoe $\frac{2}{4}$ (entire), 194
Comanche Hand Game Song (entire), 56
Ducklings, The $\frac{2}{4}$ (1-2, 5-6, 9-10, 13-14), 187
Five Fat Turkeys $\frac{2}{4}$ (1-2, 5-6, 9-11, 13-14), 246
Hello Song $\frac{4}{4}$ (13-15), 6
Hurry, Little Pony $\frac{2}{4}$ (1-2, 5-6), 82
I'll Just Be Myself $\frac{4}{4}$ (1, 3, 5), 38
Indo Eu $\frac{2}{4}$ (entire), 169
In the Toy Shop $\frac{4}{4}$ (9-11, 13-15), 86
Jack-o'-Lantern $\frac{3}{4}$ (a1-2, a5-6), 244
Jig Jog, Jig Jog $\frac{4}{4}$ (1-3, 5-7, 11-15), 274-275
Jingle Bells $\frac{2}{4}$ (1-2, 7-8), 95
Lemonade $\frac{2}{4}$ (entire), 173
Let Us All Be Thankful $\frac{4}{4}$ (1-3), 247
Little Ducky Duddle $\frac{2}{4}$ (5-8, 13-16), 192
Little Red Caboose $\frac{4}{4}$ (7-8), 278
Little Spotted Puppy $\frac{4}{4}$ (a9-10, a13-14), 276-277
Los Pollitos $\frac{2}{4}$ (entire), 279
My Head and My Shoulders $\frac{2}{4}$ (1-7), 281
Old Dan Tucker $\frac{4}{4}$ (1-2, 3-4, 5-6), 282-283
Old MacDonald $\frac{2}{4}$ (1-3, 5-7, 13-15), 175
One, Two, Three, Four, Five $\frac{2}{4}$ (1-8), 205
One, Two, Tie My Shoe $\frac{2}{4}$ (1-8, 10), 70

Put Your Finger in the Air $\frac{4}{4}$ (a1, a3, a5, a7), 58
Quaker, Quaker $\frac{2}{4}$ (entire), 172
Sing a Little Song $\frac{4}{4}$ (a1-2, a5-6, 12-13), 2
Spring Is Here $\frac{2}{4}$ (entire), 169
Ten Little Fingers $\frac{2}{4}$ (a1-3, 5-7), 22
Walk to School $\frac{2}{4}$ (entire), 4
Where Is Thumbkin? $\frac{4}{4}$ (5-6), 22

♫, ♩, 𝄽

Autumn Leaves $\frac{4}{4}$ (entire), 245
Bow, Wow, Wow! $\frac{2}{4}$ (entire), 201
Clickety Clack $\frac{4}{4}$ (7, 11), 184-185
Hanukah Is Here $\frac{4}{4}$ (entire), 88
Hats for Sale! $\frac{4}{4}$ (1-4), 237
Hurry, Little Pony $\frac{2}{4}$ (1-8), 82
Little Blue Truck $\frac{4}{4}$ (2, 4, 6), 12
Little Spotted Puppy $\frac{4}{4}$ (a1-3, a5-7, a9-16), 276-277
Must Be Santa $\frac{4}{4}$ (1-10), 254-255
No Hats in Sight $\frac{4}{4}$ (1, 3-11), 241
Peddler's Song, The $\frac{4}{4}$ (1-6, 8), 242
Play Me a Song $\frac{2}{4}$ (entire), 84
Pumpkin Stew $\frac{4}{4}$ (entire), 42
Square Dance $\frac{4}{4}$ (1-4, 6-10), 126-127
We Wish You a Merry Christmas $\frac{3}{4}$ (entire), 85

♩

Down at the Station $\frac{2}{4}$ (13-14), 268
Hello Song $\frac{4}{4}$ (1, 5), 6
In the Toy Shop $\frac{4}{4}$ (9-10, 13-14), 86
Let's Make a Jack-o'-Lantern $\frac{4}{4}$ (2, 4), 43
Merry-Go-Round $\frac{3}{4}$ (1-6, 9-14, 17-19, 21-22), 216-217
Snow Man, The (9), 115
Thank You $\frac{4}{4}$ (1, 3, 5, 7), 73
Twinkle, Twinkle, Little Star $\frac{4}{4}$ (1, 3, 5, 7, 9, 11), 111
Where Is Thumbkin? $\frac{4}{4}$ (1-2), 22
Zion's Children $\frac{4}{4}$ (a1, a5), 145

♩, 𝄽

Apples and Bananas $\frac{4}{4}$ (2, 6), 190
Hats For Sale! $\frac{4}{4}$ (11-12), 237
I Am a Person $\frac{4}{4}$ (4, 8), 10
Monkey See, Monkey Do $\frac{4}{4}$ (entire), 243
Music of the World a-Turnin' $\frac{4}{4}$ (9, 11, 14), 18-19
Must Be Santa $\frac{4}{4}$ (2, 4, 6, 8-10), 254-255
My Little Puppy $\frac{4}{4}$ (8-11), 136

Popping Corn $\frac{4}{4}$ (1-3, 5-7), 125
Three Little Muffins $\frac{2}{4}$ (18-19), 69
Welcome Back to School $\frac{4}{4}$ (9-12), 104

Melodic Analysis

mi so (3 5)

Clickety Clack (3), 184-185
Cobbler, Cobbler, Mend My Shoe (entire), 194
Columbus Sailed with Three Ships (a9-13), 44-45
Comanche Hand Game Song (entire), 56
Hats for Sale! (1, 3, 7), 237
Hello Song (9, 11), 6
Hello, There (a1-2, a7-10), 142
Hey Diddle Diddle (entire), 61
I Made a Valentine (3-4, 7-8), 258
Jig Jog, Jig Jog (1, 3, 5, 7, 13-14), 274-275
Lemonade (entire), 173
Little Red Caboose (1-2), 278
Love Is the Magic Word (a8-10), 229
Merry-Go-Round (1-3, 17-19), 216-217
My Dreydl (a5-6), 248
One, Two, Tie My Shoe (entire), 70
Quaker, Quaker (entire), 172
Que Bonito Es (1-2, 9-10), 286-287
See-saw, Margery Daw (1-2, 5-6), 189
Spring Is Here (entire), 169
Teddy Bear (1, 3, 5, 7), 106

mi so la (3 5 6)

Anyone Can Make a Mistake (1-2, 4-6), 234-235
Bounce High, Bounce Low (entire), 204
Bow, Wow, Wow! (3-6), 201
Columbus Sailed with Three Ships (a9-17), 44-45
Friendly Beasts, The (a5-8), 250-251
Merry-Go-Round (1-6, 15-22), 216-217
Monkey See, Monkey Do (entire), 243
My Place (1-4), 178
One, Two, Three, Four, Five (1-8), 205
Peddler's Song, The (5-6), 242
Pumpkin Stew (1-2, 4), 42
Rig-a-Jig-Jig (a1-2, 4-6), 181
Rudolph, the Red-Nosed Reindeer (15-16), 91
See-saw, Margery Daw (entire), 189
Step in Time (1-2), 288
Teddy Bear (1-3, 5-7), 106

TEACHER'S NOTES

TEACHER'S NOTES

TEACHER'S NOTES

TEACHER'S NOTES

ACKNOWLEDGMENTS

Grateful acknowledgment is given to the following authors and publishers. In the case of songs and poems for which acknowledgment is not given, we have earnestly endeavored to find the original source and to procure permission for their use, but without success. Extensive research failed to locate the author and/or copyright holder.

Abingdon Press for *Thanksgiving* from CHERRY STONES! GARDEN SWINGS! by Ivy O. Eastwick. Copyright © 1962 by Abingdon Press. Used by permission.

Karen Abramson-Mazur for the musical *Hats*. Copyright © 1988 by Karen Abramson-Mazur.

Addison-Wesley Publishing Company for *Ears Hear* from OODLES OF NOODLES by Lucia and James Hymes, © 1964, Addison-Wesley Publishing Co., Reading, Massachusetts. Reprinted with permission.

Alfred Publishing Company for *Clickety Clack* by Martha and Hap Palmer from HAP PALMER FAVORITES, 1981. Reprinted courtesy of the publisher. For *When the Flag Goes By* and *George Washington* by Lynn Freeman Olson from IT'S TIME FOR MUSIC, Copyright © 1985 by Alfred Publishing Co., Inc. Used by Permission of the Publisher.

Birch Tree Group Ltd. for *Happy Birthday to You*, by Mildred J. and Patty S. Hill. Copyright © 1935 Birch Tree Group Ltd. Copyright renewed 1962. All rights reserved. Used by permission. For *The Snow Man* by Lillian Willse Brown, from BIRCHARD MUSIC SERIES, KINDERGARTEN. Copyright © 1959 Birch Tree Group Ltd. Copyright renewed 1987. Used by permission.

Board of Jewish Education for *My Dreydl* by S.E. Goldfarb and S.S. Grossman from SONGS WE SING by Harry Coopersmith, United Synagogue of America. Reprinted by permission of the Board of Jewish Education of Greater New York.

Chappell/Intersong Music Group—U.S.A. for the words to *Frosty the Snow Man* by Steve Nelson & Jack Rollins. Copyright © 1950 by Hill & Range Songs, Inc. Copyright renewed and assigned to CHAPPELL & CO. International Copyright Secured. ALL RIGHTS RESERVED. Used by permission. For the words to *Peter Cottontail* by Steve Nelson & Jack Rollins. Copyright © 1950 by Hill & Range Songs, Inc. Copyright renewed and assigned to CHAPPELL & CO. International Copyright Secured. ALL RIGHTS RESERVED. Used by permission.

Cherry Lane Music Publishing Co., Inc. for *Goin' to the Zoo* by Tom Paxton. Copyright © 1961, 1969 Cherry Lane Music Publishing Company, Inc. All Rights Reserved. Used by Permission.

Suzanne Clayton for *Hanukah Is Here* from KEEPING UP WITH ORFF-SCHULWERK, vol. 2. Copyright © 1974 Suzanne Clayton.

William Cole for *Here Comes the Band* from POEMS CHILDREN WILL SIT STILL FOR, compiled by Regniers, Moore and White. Copyright © 1962 William Cole.

Columbia Pictures Publications for *Butterfly, Popping Corn, Little Spotted Puppy, I Made a Valentine*, and *Going on a Picnic* by Lynn Freeman Olson from SONGS FOR OUR SMALL WORLD by Lynn Freeman Olson and Georgia Garlid. Copyright © 1968 by SCHMITT MUSIC CENTER, A Division of BELWIN-MILLS PUBLISHING CORPORATION. All Rights Reserved. Used by Permission. For *Never Sleep Late Anymore* by George Winston & Robert Kersey. Copyright © 1972 BELWIN-MILLS PUBLISHING CORPORATION. All Rights Reserved. Used by Permission.

Curtis Brown, Ltd. for *The Whales Off Wales* by X.J. Kennedy from ONE WINTER NIGHT IN AUGUST. Copyright © 1975 by X.J. Kennedy. Reprinted by permission of Curtis Brown, Ltd.

Randy DeLelles for *Jack Be Nimble, Welcome Back to School*, and *Pumpkin Stew*.

Denver Woman's Press Club for *The Giant's Shoes* from THE CHILD AND THINGS by Edwina Fallis. Used by permission.

Doubleday for *Singing Time* by Rose Fyleman, from THE FAIRY GREEN. Copyright © 1923 by George H. Doran Company. Reprinted by permission of Doubleday, a division of Bantam, Doubleday, Dell Publishing Group, Inc.

Margaret Dugard for *Columbus Sailed with Three Ships*. Words and music by Margaret C. Dugard (version 1). Copyright © 1981.

E.P. Dutton for *Stars* and *Icy* from STORIES TO BEGIN ON by Rhoda W. Bacmeister. Copyright 1940 by E.P. Dutton, renewed 1968 by Rhoda W. Bacmeister. Reprinted by permission of the publisher, E.P. Dutton, a division of NAL Penguin Inc.

Fairfax County Public Schools for *Little Blue Truck* by Lynn Arizzi, and *I Am a Person* by Judy Henneberger and Gail Cope, from THE KINDER-MUSIC HOUSE, Fairfax County Public Schools. Copyright © 1982. Used by Permission.

Aileen Fisher for *After My Bath*. Reprinted by permission of the author, Aileen Fisher.

Danai Gagné for *My Place* (adaptation).

Harper & Row for *Ourchestra* from WHERE THE SIDEWALK ENDS by Shel Silverstein. Copyright © 1974 by Evil Eye Music, Inc. Reprinted by Harper & Row, Publishers, Inc. For *Merry Christmas* from FEATHERED ONES AND FURRY by Aileen Fisher. (Thomas Y. Crowell) Copyright © 1971 by Aileen Fisher. (text only) Reprinted by permission of Harper & Row, Publishers, Inc. For *The Secret Song* from NIBBLE, NIBBLE by Margaret Wise Brown. Copyright © 1959 by William R. Scott, Inc., renewed 1987 by Roberta Brown Rauch. Reprinted by permission of Harper & Row, Publishers, Inc. For *Cynthia in the Snow* from BRONZEVILLE BOYS AND GIRLS by Gwendolyn Brooks. Copyright © 1956, renewed 1984 by Gwendolyn Brooks. Reprinted by permission of Harper & Row, Publishers, Inc. For *Eight Balloons* from A LIGHT IN THE ATTIC by Shel Silverstein. Copyright © 1981 by Evil Eye Music, Inc. Reprinted by permission of Harper & Row, Publishers, Inc. For *The Mitten Song* from A POCKETFUL OF POEMS by Marie Louise Allen. Originally appeared in A POCKETFUL OF RHYMES by Marie Louise Allen. Copyright 1939 by Harper & Row, Publishers, Inc. Reprinted by permission of Harper & Row, Publishers, Inc.

Henry Holt and Company for *My Legs and I* from IS SOMEWHERE ALWAYS FAR AWAY? by Leland B. Jacobs. Copyright © 1967 by Leland B. Jacobs. Reprinted by permission of Henry Holt and Company, Inc.

Homeland Publishing for *Baby Beluga*, words and music by Raffi and D. Pike. Copyright © 1980 by Homeland Publishing, a division of Troubadour Records Ltd. All Rights Reserved. For *Brush Your Teeth*, traditional, adapted and arranged by Louise Dain and Raffi. Copyright © 1976 by Homeland Publishing, a division of Troubadour Records Ltd. From the Album SINGABLE SONGS FOR THE VERY YOUNG (Raffi).

Adele Hooley for *Let's Make a Jack-o'-Lantern* by Daniel Hooley from MUSIC FOR YOUNG AMERICANS. Reprinted by permission of Adele Hooley.

Carol Huffman for the ostinatos and lesson sequence to *The Secret of the Polar Bear*.

Merle S. Lehmer for *Indian Lullaby* by Dr. Derrick Norman Lehmer. Copyright by Dr. Derrick Norman Lehmer.

Loghaven Music for *I'll Just Be Myself* by Lynn Freeman Olson. Copyright © 1987 Loghaven Music.

Macmillan, Inc. for *I Am Amazo* and *Mixity Maxity Klippity Klack*. Copyright © 1988 Macmillan, Inc. (ASCAP).

Macmillan of Canada for *Willoughby Wallaby Woo* by Larry Miyata and Dennis Lee from ALLIGATOR PIE by Dennis Lee, Copyright © 1974. Reprinted by permission of Macmillan of Canada, a Division of Canada Publishing Corporation.

Ruth Manier for *He Had a Dream* from INSTRUCTOR, 1985. Lyrics, music, and arrangement by Ruth Manier, Library Media Specialist.

Musik Innovations for *The Bubble Bath* by Millie H. Burnett from MELODY, MOVEMENT AND LANGUAGE. Copyright by Millie H. Burnett. Published by Musik Innovations, Pittsburgh, PA 15237.

National Museum of Canada for *Oh! The Pretty Butterflies* (or *Ah! Les Jolis Papillons*), a folk song found in *St. Pierre et Miquelon, Bulletin #182* by Carmen Roy. Copyright by the National Museum of Canada.

Harold Ober Associates for *Down, Down* by Eleanor Farjeon from CHILDREN'S POEMS. Copyright 1926, 1954 by Eleanor Farjeon. Reprinted by permission of Harold Ober Associates Incorporated.

Prentice-Hall, Inc. for *Safety Song* by Margaret Lowery from GROWING WITH MUSIC, Book 1 (words by Margaret Lowery). Copyright © 1971 by Prentice-Hall, Inc., Englewood Cliffs, NJ.

Marian Reiner for *It Fell in the City* by Eve Merriam from BLACKBERRY INK by Eve Merriam. Copyright © 1985 by Eve Merriam. All rights reserved. Used by permission of Marian Reiner for the author. For *Wide Awake* from WIDE AWAKE AND OTHER POEMS by Myra Cohn Livingston. Copyright © 1959 by Myra Cohn Livingston. Used by permission of Marian Reiner for the author. For *Rain* from WHISPERS AND OTHER POEMS by Myra Cohn Livingston. Copyright © 1958 by Myra Cohn Livingston. Used by permission of Marian Reiner for the author.

Carroll A. Rinehart for the music of *Black and Gold*. Used with permission of the composer.

Rockhaven Music for *Merry Go Round, Square Dance*, and *Lullabye* by Merrill Staton and Barbara Staton, Copyright © 1981 Rockhaven Music (ASCAP). For *Love Is the Magic Word, Anyone Can Make a Mistake*, and *Holiday Song* by Barbara Staton, Copyright © 1988 Rockhaven Music (ASCAP). For *Let Us All Be Thankful* by Merrill Staton, Copyright © 1988 Rockhaven Music (ASCAP).

Rosha Press for *Alike and Different* (printed as *Same and Different*) by Carol H. Bitcon. Reprinted by permission of Rosha Press, 18361 Whitney Dr., Santa Ana, CA 92705.

St. Nicholas Music for *Rudolph, the Red-Nosed Reindeer*, lyric and music by Johnny Marks. *Rudolph, the Red-Nosed Reindeer* copyright 1949 St. Nicholas Music Inc., renewed 1977. All Rights Reserved. Used by Permission. This arrangement copyright 1988 St. Nicholas Music Inc.

Belle San Miguel Ortiz for *Que Bonito Es*.

Phillip Savage for *My Valentine* by Edith Savage from THE SPECTRUM OF MUSIC, Grade 1, by Mary Val Marsh, Carroll Rinehart, and Edith Savage, Music Authors. Copyright © 1974 by Edith Savage and reprinted by permission.

Jacque Schrader for *I Can Get From Here to There*. Copyright © 1986 by Jacque Schrader.

Shada Music for *I'd Like to Teach the World to Sing* by Bill Backer, Billy Davis, Roger Cook, and Roger Greenaway. Copyright © Shada Music, Inc. All Rights Reserved. Used by Permission.

Silver, Burdett & Ginn Inc. for *The Bus* from *Singing On Our Way* of OUR SINGING WORLD SERIES. Copyright © 1959, 1957, 1949 by Ginn and Company. Used by permission of Silver, Burdett & Ginn Inc. For *Santa's Coming* by Verna Meade Surer, and for *Mitten Song* (music only) by Sue Hanlin from *The First Grade Book* of OUR SINGING WORLD SERIES, Copyright © 1959, 1957, 1949, by Ginn and Company. Used by permission of Silver, Burdett & Ginn Inc. For *The Best of Friends* by Helen Taylor and *Down, Down* (music only) by Fay Ellis from *The Magic of Music — Kindergarten*, Copyright © 1970, 1965, by Ginn and Company. Used by permission of Silver, Burdett & Ginn Inc. For *Sing a Little Song* by Henry E. Dennis, Jr., from *Silver Burdett Music Centennial Edition: Kindergarten* by Aubin, Crook, Hayden & Walker, Copyright © 1985 by Silver Burdett Company. Used by permission. For *Walk to School*, lyrics by Mary Jaye, from *Making Music Your Own*, Copyright © 1971 Silver Burdett Company. Used by permission.

Sing'n Do Company, Inc. for *My Little Puppy* by Elizabeth Deutsch. Copyright renewed 1982 by Elizabeth Deutsch. Published by The Sing'n Do Co., Inc.

Susan Snyder for *Hurry, Little Pony, Play Me a Song*, and the story *Learning*. Copyright 1988 by Susan Snyder.

Society of Authors Ltd. for *Singing Time* by Ruth Fyleman. Reprinted by permission of The Society of Authors as the literary representative of the Estate of Rose Fyleman.

Beverley T. Steadman for the words to *Black and Gold*. Words used by permission of Beverley T. Steadman.

Wonderland Music Company for *Step in Time*, words and music by Richard M. Sherman and Robert B. Sherman. Copyright © 1963 Wonderland Music Co., Inc. Printed by permission.

PHOTO CREDITS:
CLARA AICH: 5, © Safety Town/Nassau County Police Department, 7, 23, 30, 46T, 50, 57, 72T, 74, 83T & B, 94, 123, 124, 134TL & TR, 143, 165, 168T, 180, 198, 200, 202B, 213, 221. VICTORIA BELLER-SMITH: 59, 66, 164. THE BETTMANN ARCHIVE: 220. BRUCE COLEMAN INC.: © Jen and Des Bartlett, 168B. © HENRY GROSSMAN: 101L & R. KENJ KAWANO: 134B. LGI: © Lynn Goldsmith, 152. THE MEMORY SHOP: 51TL. Courtesy MMB MUSIC: 46B. MITCHELL OF BLOOMINGTON PHOTO: 153. THE METROPOLITAN MUSEUM OF ART: Rogers Fund, 1942. (42.141.10), 218. SUPERSTOCK INTERNATIONAL: The Kobal Collection, © Universal 1982, Spielberg, 51TR & B. THANKSGIVING from FROM THE HILLS OF GEORGIA by Mattie Lou O'Kelley. Copyright © 1983 by Mattie Lou O'Kelley. By permission of Little, Brown and Company in association with the Atlantic Monthly Press, 72. TOM STACK & ASSOCIATES: © John Gerlach, 197.

ILLUSTRATION CREDITS:
Cover Design and Illustration: Heather Coope
Illustrations: Shirley Beckes, Patti Boyd, Cindy Brodie, Olivia Cole, Jerry Dior, Mac Evans, Dennis Hockerman, Sal Murdocca, Hima Pamoedjo, Jan Pyk, Yuri Salzman, Bob Shein, John Wallner.

MUSIC AND YOU

USER'S SURVEY

We would like to hear about your experiences using *Music and You* and your suggestions for future revisions. Once you are familiar with *Music and You*, please take a few minutes to respond to this survey. Then remove the page from the book, fold, staple or tape, and return it to us, using the pre-paid postage stamp on the other side.

A. YOUR BACKGROUND

1. Which of the following best describes you? *(Circle one.)*
   a. classroom teacher
   b. music specialist/teach in a music room
   c. music specialist/travel from room to room
   d. music specialist/travel from school to school
   e. Other *(Explain.)* _____

2. What grades do you teach?

3. How frequently do you teach music (per class, per week)?
   a. less than once   b. once   c. twice   d. more than twice

4. How long is each music class period? _____

5. Which of the following music teaching approaches do you currently use? *(Circle one or more.)*
   a. Kodály   b. Dalcroze
   c. Orff   d. Other *(Explain.)* _____

B. SONG MATERIAL

1. What percentage of each type of song material would you like in a music text? *(Indicate percentages to total 100%.)*
   Folk _____   Composed _____

2-1 In Column 2–1 below, indicate the ideal percentage of each category of song that you would like in a music text? *(Indicate percentages to total 100%.)*

2-2 In Column 2–2 below, circle your rate of satisfaction with the amount of song material from each category in *Music and You:* too few (–), just right (ok), too many (+).

	Column 2–1 (Ideal)	Column 2–2 (Music and You)		
Folk/Traditional	_____	–	ok	+
Foreign Language	_____	–	ok	+
Holiday and Seasonal	_____	–	ok	+
Patriotic	_____	–	ok	+
Popular/Contemporary	_____	–	ok	+
Show Music	_____	–	ok	+
Other	_____	–	ok	+

C. *MUSIC AND YOU*

1. Circle the description that best describes your opinion about the length of lessons in *Music and You.*
   a. too short   b. just right   c. too long

2. Use the chart below to indicate your answers *for each area listed.* Circle your answers for each grade that you teach. (– = *not adequate*, ok = *adequate*, + = *more than adequate*)
   a. appropriateness of the skills and concepts presented
   b. quality of folk song material
   c. quality of composed song material
   d. diversity of song styles
   e. number of rounds, descants, and harmony parts
   f. number of opportunities for students to play instruments
   g. number of opportunities for students to move to music
   h. frequency of evaluation

	K	1	2	3	4	5	6	7	8
a.	– ok +	– ok +	– ok +	– ok +	– ok +	– ok +	– ok +	– ok +	– ok +
b.	– ok +	– ok +	– ok +	– ok +	– ok +	– ok +	– ok +	– ok +	– ok +
c.	– ok +	– ok +	– ok +	– ok +	– ok +	– ok +	– ok +	– ok +	– ok +
d.	– ok +	– ok +	– ok +	– ok +	– ok +	– ok +	– ok +	– ok +	– ok +
e.			– ok +	– ok +	– ok +	– ok +	– ok +	– ok +	– ok +
f.	– ok +	– ok +	– ok +	– ok +	– ok +	– ok +	– ok +	– ok +	– ok +
g.	– ok +	– ok +	– ok +	– ok +	– ok +	– ok +	– ok +	– ok +	– ok +
h.	– ok +	– ok +	– ok +	– ok +	– ok +	– ok +	– ok +	– ok +	– ok +

D. RECORDINGS

1. Do you use CDs or plan to use them in the next five years? *(Circle one.)*   yes   no

2. Use the chart below to indicate your answers for *each aspect* of the *Music and You* recordings listed. Circle your answers for each grade that you teach. (– = *not adequate*, ok = *adequate*, + = *more than adequate*)
   a. overall quality of arrangements
   b. use of student voices as compared to adult voices
   c. use of acoustic instrumentation as compared to electronic

	K	1	2	3	4	5	6	7	8
a.	– ok +	– ok +	– ok +	– ok +	– ok +	– ok +	– ok +	– ok +	– ok +
b.	– ok +	– ok +	– ok +	– ok +	– ok +	– ok +	– ok +	– ok +	– ok +
c.	– ok +	– ok +	– ok +	– ok +	– ok +	– ok +	– ok +	– ok +	– ok +

3. Please explain what you like and/or dislike about the recorded lessons.

2. Please list any specific songs and/or listening selections you would like in your next music series. Include grade levels for each.

E. GENERAL

   1. Are there additional ancillary materials that you would like included in *Music and You?* If so, please describe.

3. Any other comments?

① *Fold down along dashed line*

BUSINESS REPLY MAIL
FIRST CLASS MAIL   PERMIT NO. 348   NEW YORK, NY

POSTAGE PAID BY ADDRESSEE

Macmillan/McGraw-Hill School Publishing Co.
School Music Editorial Department, 4th Floor
866 Third Avenue
New York, NY 10126

**No Postage
Necessary
If Mailed
In The
United States**

② *Fold down along dashed line so mailing and return addresses are visible*

FROM

_____
Name (Optional)

_____
School

Address (City/State/Zip)

Home Telephone (Optional)

Would you like to be contacted regarding reviewing for future music-related materials from Macmillan?
                  yes   no

Thank you for taking the time to complete this questionnaire. Please fill in your name and complete

mailing address above, and we'll be happy to send you a *free gift.* If you have further thoughts about what you would like in a music text, your favorite songs, or other comments about *Music and You,* we would enjoy hearing from you. You can write us at the address listed on this mailer.

STAPLE OR TAPE TO CLOSE